FREEMASONRY AND THE ANCIENT GODS

FREEMASONRY AND THE ANCIENT GODS

BY

J. S. M. WARD, B.A., F.R.ECONS., F.S.S.

WITH AN INTRODUCTION BY

THE HON. SIR JOHN A. COCKBURN,
K.C.M.G., M.D., P.G.D. ENG., P.D.G.M. S.
AUSTRALIA

GYAN

Published by

GYAN

Gyan Publishing House
5, Ansari Road
Daryaganj, New Delhi-110002
Phone: 011-47034999, 9811692060
E-mail: books@gyanbooks.com

Distribution Network
gyanbooks.com
India, USA, Canada, UK, Australia

ISBN: 978-93-6208-239-8 (PB)
First Published, 1921

2nd Impression 2024

Printed at: Gyan Press, Delhi.

FREEMASONRY AND THE ANCIENT GODS
Author: J. S. M. WARD

FREEMASONRY AND THE ANCIENT GODS

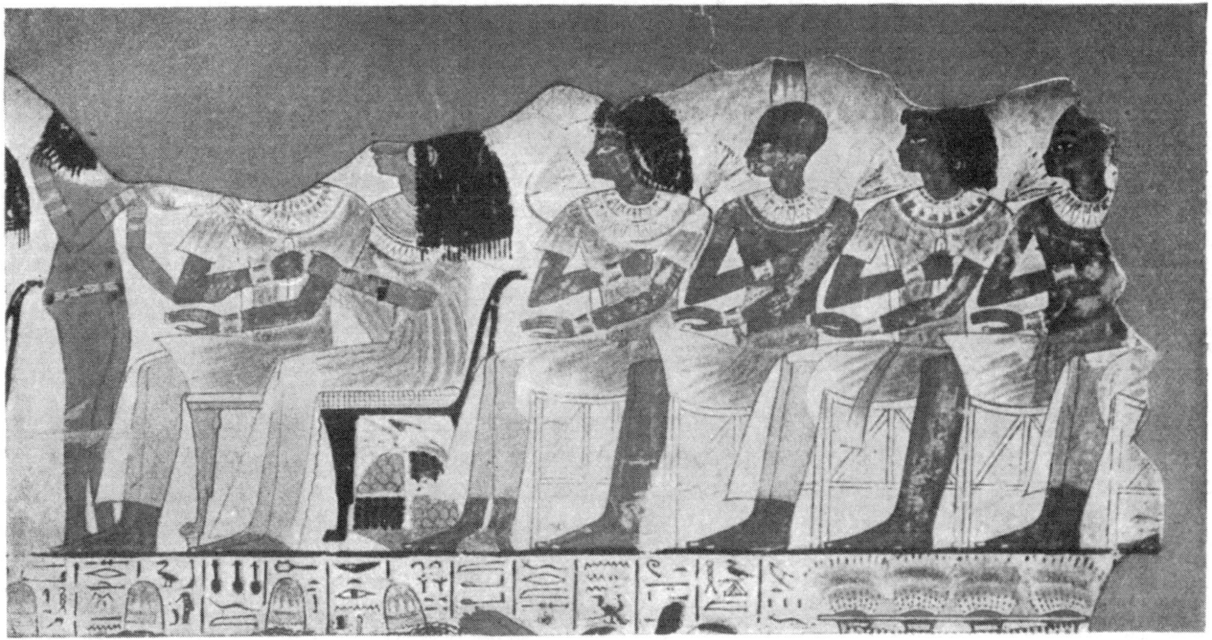

AN EGYPTIAN FEAST

Reception of "New Initiates" in the Underworld. A scene from a tomb of Thebes: original fresco, B.C. 1500 now in the British Museum.

Reproduced by the permission of the Trustees of the British Museum.

Frontispiece]

FREEMASONRY AND THE ANCIENT GODS

BY

J. S. M. WARD, B.A., F.R.Econ.S., F.S.S.

SECRETARY OF THE INDUSTRIES LODGE, NO. 4,100; MASTER MASON; MARK MASTER MASON; ROYAL ARK MARINER; ROYAL ARCH; MOST EXCELLENT MASTER; ROYAL MASTER; SELECT MASTER; SUPER-EXCELLENT MASTER; KNIGHT TEMPLAR; KNIGHT OF MALTA; BRO. OF ST. LAWRENCE; KNIGHT OF CONSTANTINOPLE; KNIGHT OF THE RED CROSS OF BABYLON, 18°; ROYAL ORDER OF SCOTLAND; SECRET MONITOR; RED CROSS OF CONSTANTINE, ETC.

WITH AN INTRODUCTION BY

THE HON. SIR JOHN A. COCKBURN, K.C.M.G., M.D., P.G.D. Eng., P.D.G.M. S. Australia

SIMPKIN, MARSHALL, HAMILTON, KENT & CO. LTD., 4 STATIONERS' HALL COURT : : LONDON, E.C.4

PREFACE

In offering the results of fourteen years of research to my brothers in Freemasonry, I feel it is desirable that I should clearly indicate the line of investigation I have adopted. In my various travels I have found that the brethren are always glad to have suggestions as to the real meaning of our ritual. In the course of my masonic career it has been my privilege " to bear fraternal greeting " to many different Lodges in many different lands, and I have always found the brethren hungry for further suggestive ideas. This book itself is the outcome of a little speech I made at the Cripplegate Lodge No. 1613 last November, when replying to the Visitors' toast. The brief ten minutes I then took up aroused so much interest in the subject that I was pressed to come again and give more, and one well-known brother capped the others by asking me to write a book on the subject; in which case he himself would see that it was published by his firm. Thus encouraged, I have, not without some trepidation, written this work in the hope that others will be led to follow up my investigations. In doing so, no doubt they will disagree with some of my conclusions—even perhaps disprove them—but the sum total of our knowledge cannot fail to be increased.

For years I have worked alone without help or even suggestion from anyone, and it is only in the last few months that I read Bro. Churchward's books on the subject. Before I go further I would like to render homage to him, as, to the best of my knowledge and belief, he is the actual pioneer in this line of research. I do not agree with all his conclusions, just as my successors may disagree with some of mine, but I render here my full recognition of the suggestive value of his work.

He may be right, and I wrong, but I hold that he has concentrated his attention too much on Egypt and not enough on the primitive initiatory ceremonies of savage men, or on Palestine and the Middle East. But I claim him as the pioneer of the new school of masonic research which I hope that my work will call into existence, for which I suggest the name of the Anthropological School in contradistinction to the present Authentic School.

I have little doubt that scattered over the world there are other brothers who, like myself, have been studying Masonry from the anthropological point of view. At present they are inarticulate, or known at most to a few. My greatest desire is to bring them into the open; let them come forward to confirm or contradict my facts and conclusions, and one of my objects will be achieved.

May other brothers, encouraged by what I have written, study the native races among whom they dwell from a new point of view, and look for our signs, our grips and our symbols among them! Have the Terra del Fuegeans any of our signs? I do not know; and to the average anthropologist the fact that at an initiatory rite the members for a moment placed their hands in a peculiar position would mean nothing, but if a Mason were present, and on the look-out for such a sign, he would not fail to recognise our F.C. sign, for example.

After all, we must remember that Freemasonry is still, and always has been, a secret society. In its very essence, written documents are anathema. To this day, our oath proves this, and it is only during the last two hundred years that any deviation from this rule has been winked at. Even now there are Lodges in England whose ritual varies considerably from that in use in London, and in certain cases the sole repository of it is the preceptor and members of the Lodge. Such Lodges absolutely forbid their members to write down one word of it. If this were the original policy of Freemasonry, how can we possibly expect to find documentary evidence for the antiquity of our Order? For all practical purposes, no documents except the ancient charges can be found of a date prior to the foundation of Grand Lodge in 1717. And yet it is not denied by any that Lodges were working previous to that date, and that they accepted men who were not operatives. Further, how can we explain the keenness with which men crowded into the Order in the first half of the eighteenth century, unless it possessed something in the nature of a ritual similar to our present one, which attracted men of a speculative turn of mind?

Yet, despite these self-evident facts, the Authentic School, for all practical purposes, concentrates its research on documentary evidence, and naturally is unable to adduce any real evidence for Masonry, previous to Grand Lodge, save as an operative guild. On the question of the higher degrees, since they could not be operative, the writers of the school usually return the reply that they must have been evolved in the eighteenth century, as our first reference to such-and-such a degree was in, say, 1741.

I venture to maintain that this line of argument is unsound, but before going into the matter it is only just that I should render my tribute to the great work which has been done by the writers of the Authentic School. They have not merely cleared away much rubbish, but they have established a definite school of masonic research based on logical lines, and similar to that of historic research in our universities.

So far as their work goes, they have done it well, and have established a clear record of the later history of Freemasonry, and for this they deserve the gratitude of every Freemason; it is for the new school to delve in another direction. Let the Authentic School still concentrate on documents—there is still enough work to be done to occupy it fully for many years—but let others follow the anthropological line of research, and the sum total of our knowledge will be vastly increased. Above all, it is along this line of research that we may hope to discover the true esoteric meaning of our symbols and ritual.

After all, in Masonry research is only following the same course that it did in secular history. A century and a half ago most educated men knew a fair amount about the written history of the world, but they had never dreamed of Palæolithic man. Had all men steadfastly refused to accept any evidence save written documents, what evidence should we possess even to-day of the existence of our primitive ancestors? But though the archæologist was able to prove his existence by the evidence of his bones and his flint weapons, our real comprehension of our prehistoric ancestors is due to the researches of scientific anthropologists. By studying the customs of primitive man to-day we are able to reconstruct the life of prehistoric man, and so it will be with Freemasonry.

We cannot always expect to find masonic emblems carven in stone, though such *have* been found; but we can trace our signs and symbols—nay, even parts of our present ritual—all round the globe.

When we find the sign of G. and D., as given in Scotland, recognised in Mexico, on the Gold Coast and in Turkey, by men who are not Masons, we are justified in adopting certain theories. When we find that other signs are also in use among widely scattered races, we are justified in claiming that they prove the correctness of our theory.

Briefly, this is the method I have adopted in this work. So far as possible, I have accumulated evidence of the use of our signs and symbols throughout the world; among savages, among the ancient nations and among the peoples of the East, wise in the ancient wisdom. If others can add to the examples, let them do so, for I, for my part, am certain that not one-tenth has been told.

Briefly, the theory I venture to propound is that Freemasonry originated in the primitive initiatory rites of prehistoric man, and from those rites have been built up all the ancient mysteries, and thence all the modern religious systems. It is for this reason that men of all religious beliefs can enter Freemasonry; and, further, the reason we admit no women is that these rites were originally the initiatory rites of men; the women had their own. These for sociological reasons perished, while those of the men survived, and developed into the mysteries.

Thus Freemasonry is the basis of the mysteries, not the mysteries cut down and mutilated. The higher refinements of those mysteries and also of the various creeds which took their place were "for a day," to meet the social or spiritual difficulties of the age; but the basis remained unchanged, and the men who built the temples of the gods had to know their basis so that they might build aright, and not reveal too much to the uninitiated world. It was not, however, essential that they should possess a detailed knowledge of the full mysteries. Therefore it is that to this day, if we look carefully, we can find in our ritual the seed of practically every important dogma of every creed, whether it be the Resurrection or Reincarnation; but so little developed that none need accept them, and so none can take offence. Only, no man can be a Mason unless he believes in God and a future life; for these are the bases of all religions, as ancient as man himself; and these are two of the ancient landmarks of our Order.

One point I find it necessary to emphasise. Throughout the

work I have endeavoured to avoid anything which would tell a cowan what our signs actually are, and this has meant in certain cases refraining from driving home the last nail in an argument, easily as I could have done so. But, nevertheless, this *is* a masonic book, and it should not be treated with less care than a ritual; and I trust that it will only be given to brothers after due proof.

In conclusion I must thank the authors and publishers of the various books from whom I have obtained permission to reproduce illustrations, and from whose texts I have gleaned invaluable information. So far as possible I have acknowledged my indebtedness in the text, and as a further courtesy I have given their books in my bibliography and index. If, nevertheless, I have omitted anyone, I trust he will believe me when I say it is an oversight and far from intentional, for I gladly acknowledge that I, like every other writer, am indebted to those who have gone before.

J. S. M. W.

CONTENTS

PART II

PART III

LIST OF ILLUSTRATIONS

The Author and Publishers desire to express their indebtedness to *The Anthropological Journal, Man, The Bulletin of the Smithsonian Institute*, U.S.A., *The Gods of the Egyptians*, by Dr. Wallis Budge, *Hindu Iconography, Indian Sculpture*, by E. B. Havell, and the Trustees of the British Museum, for reproductions of illustrations in this book.

INTRODUCTION

By the Hon. Sir John A. Cockburn, K.C.M.G., M.D., P.G.D. Eng., P.D.G.M. S. Australia

Masonry is many-sided. It is a gigantic and world-wide organisation for the inculcation of the purest principles of piety and virtue, it dispenses benefactions with a lavish hand, and its educational establishments are second to none. But, admirably as Masonry performs such good works, they do not constitute its distinguishing characteristic. Similar ground is covered by other institutions. Various religious bodies, schemes for social insurances and educational systems undertake each or all of these functions. The code of morality taught by Christianity can hardly be distinguished from that of Masonry. The new commandment of brotherly love is common to both. The difference lies not so much in the precepts as in the manner in which they are conveyed. Other cults communicate their lessons through the medium of spoken or written words. Masonry does so by means of symbols. It may be described as visualised religion. From time immemorial it has been customary to portray moral truths in this manner. The symbols employed for this purpose have usually been taken from architecture as the art most closely allied to religion. Masonry is defined in the ritual as a peculiar system of morality veiled in allegory and illustrated by symbols. It has been found in all ages that emblems and symbols, expressing great truths by a few simple strokes, appeal to the mind more strongly and are better remembered than words; but unless, by means of adequate explanation and understanding, the meaning of the symbols is grasped, and the mind carried along with them, the ceremonies of Masonry lose much of their special quality, and are apt to become as futile as the dry bed of a river through which living water no longer flows. The study of symbolism should therefore always be one of the most important items in masonic literature. Brother Ward's book comes as a welcome and much needed addition to masonic research. The Author is specially qualified for the task he has so well performed. Entering Trinity

Hall, Cambridge, as the winner of an open scholarship, he graduated with honours in the History Tripos. He was initiated in the Isaac Newton Lodge by special dispensation at the early age of twenty, and was no sooner of age than he was exalted in the Euclid Chapter of the Royal Arch. He has taken all the ordinary degrees up to the eighteenth, and is a member of many of the more recondite orders. He therefore brings to bear on the difficult subject of masonic research the mind of a scholar enriched with an ample store of masonic experience.

Brother Ward has travelled extensively. Born in the West Indies, he spent some years in the East Indies. He was secretary of Lodge Rangoon in Burma. His favourite subject is the study of comparative religions. He has had exceptional opportunities for studying on the spot the mysteries and secret societies of the East. These have a close bearing on the subject of masonic research, for in some way, not yet fully explained, modern Masonry has become the repository of the hidden wisdom of the ancients. The arcanum of the sacred and mysterious name of the Deity and the secrets of the Cabbalah are incorporated in its substance. Here and there hints of these appear in the ritual as an outcrop indicating the rich treasures to be obtained by diligent search beneath the surface. Brother Ward, in his travels, was struck by the fact that our masonic signs and tokens are employed as means of recognition between members of secret societies in the Far East. A full description is given of the intricate ceremony of initiation among the Dervishes. The similarity of sentiment and ritual to one of our own ceremonies is remarkable. There is a tradition that Richard I, when in the Holy Land, was initiated into the lower degrees by Saladin. This may be the explanation of some of the similarities between Masonry and the Order of Knights Templars. Many hold the view that, while the Crusades checked the incursion of Eastern races into Europe, the Western world was impregnated with the germs of Eastern thought. Hence are apparently derived some of the devices and customs of chivalry, and, in the opinion of Christopher Wren, the style of architecture known as Gothic. The identity established between several Hindoo caste-marks and masonic symbolism is interesting; as also is a description of the seven degrees in the Hindoo Yogi system. The trinity pervading the cosmogony of India finds its counterpart in our Craft degrees and in the Royal Arch.

Brother Ward correctly points out that, while three represents the Godhead, four is the number of creation and of matter. Their reunion, that is the at-one-ment, and the descent of spirit into matter is signified by folding downwards on to the square the previously upraised flap of the E.A.'s apron. The description of the Mithraic mysteries is suggestive. There is a close resemblance between Christianity and the cult of Mithra. Indeed, some maintain that the organisation and hierarchy of the early Christian Churches were identical with those of Mithra. The parallel is made closer by the statement of some of the Fathers of the Church that our Lord was, like the sun-god Mithra, born in a cave.

Brother Ward reiterates a frequently expressed surprise that the Swastika, one of the most ancient and sacred of symbols, has no place in speculative Masonry, although it still persists in operative Lodges. Operative Masons aver that the omission is due to the fact that Dr. Anderson, who framed the Constitutions of speculative Masonry, never attained the rank of a Master in an operative Lodge, and was therefore ignorant of the nature and meaning of the fourfold square. Brother Ward, without prejudice, sums up the arguments for and against the authority and antiquity of modern operative Masonry. It is unlikely that anyone entering an operative Lodge with open mind could long remain in doubt. The close resemblance, but not copylike identity, between the operative ritual and ancient tradition seems to preclude the idea of modern manufacture. The name by which the Great Architect of Heaven and Earth is revered in operative Masonry is that of a feminine deity, as was the case in the ancient world. The word Geometry, which was regarded by Plato as a divine art, as well as Geology and Geography, is derived from Γη, the Earth Goddess; and both the square and the Swastika, or Gammadion, which is composed of four squares and is sometimes called the Tetragammaton, are signs of earth. So also is the cross, which consists of four right angles opening outwards. It is significant that the golden rule of conduct, typified by these analogous signs, is the key-note alike of Christianity and Masonry, both of which deal with the relationship between man and man, rather than with abstruse questions of dogma. Although the Swastika was originally a sign of earth, it, together with the serpent and other earth emblems, was appropriated to the solar cult when sun-worship and centralisation displaced the worship of earth, and Paganism, which, as the word implies, was the local cult to which the dwellers in villages clung tenaciously. In dealing with Chinese mysteries, Brother Ward refutes the common error that, because the inferior and criminal classes of China belong to secret societies, all secret societies in China are evil. The truth is that many of these institutions inculcate principles identical in their excellence with those of Freemasonry. From the similarity of signs, tokens, and sentiments all over the world, Brother Ward naturally arrives at the conclusion that "Freemasonry did not originate with the building guilds of the Middle Ages, but with the primitive initiatory rites of prehistoric man."

It is not to be expected that, from an origin in the mists which enshroud the far-distant past, a direct line of succession can be traced. If we wished to ascertain the origin of some modern implement, such as a plough, we would not go to an up-to-date manufactory, and, after inspecting a pattern with the most recent improvements, arrive at the conclusion that the name of the maker inscribed thereon was that of the inventor of the plough. The only reasonable course of investigation would be to inquire what sort of implement was used to till the soil in former times. The development of the plough would thus be traced through innumerable successive improvements back to the forked stick which was employed in ancient Egypt to cultivate the fertile lands of the Delta. Similarly, if we would seek the date of the origin of Masonry, we must inquire what was the period at which men first began to teach the principles of morality and justice by means of symbols. We shall thus be led back, through operative Masonry and the medieval guilds, to the Collegia of Rome, past these to the light of tradition from the East, and so on, until we arrive at the invariable practice of primeval man to express his thoughts in pictures and symbols, which long antedated the invention of letters. Brother Ward is of opinion that the link between the ancient mysteries and the medieval guilds is supplied by the Dionysian Artificers and the Comacine Masons. He discusses four possible sources through which Jewish influence entered into Freemasonry, and thinks it probable that all these played a part in the process. He is inclined to the opinion that "perhaps the truest answer as to whence Masonry comes is to be found in the Leylande Locke MS," which, although formerly accepted without question as genuine, is now, on insufficient grounds, denounced as spurious by recent commentators. He does not agree that the Athelstan tradition can be ignored as baseless. The account of the decline of Masonry and its renaissance under Grand Lodge in 1717 concludes Part I of the volume.

Part II deals with the Ancient and Accepted Rite and the so-called higher degrees, and includes a disquisition on the two forms of the cross and the mysterious vesica piscis. Incidentally it may be added that this sign is found carved on the fronts of churches dedicated to the Virgin Mary. Several chapters are devoted to the Order of the Temple, and to the persecutions which ended in its apparent suppression. The Knights of the Temple imbibed from the East the spirit of Gnosticism, which was pre-Christian, although afterwards called a heresy. They appear to have held an esoteric view of Christianity. It was impossible for them to explain their attitude to the orthodox. Even if they had succeeded they would not have escaped the direst penalties; for bigots are usually more bitter towards sects that approximate to their views than to rank outsiders. Part II closes with a beautifully poetic description of a sunset in the Far East, when a huge red cross, such as Constantine might have seen, was figured on the sky.

Part III deals with the recent outbreak of iconoclasm which has wrought such havoc in masonic symbolism, and appears to be a manifestation of the scepticism which is undermining many ancient usages and cherished traditions. The working of provincial, colonial, and American Lodges remains more steadfast to originals than most of those of the metropolis. Under the heading of the Grand Ideal, the author sets forth in glowing words how the mighty power of Masonry might be utilised to preserve the peace of the world. He traces the synthetic movement from isolated Lodges up to the foundation of the United Grand Lodge of England, thence to a future alliance between the Grand Lodges of the British Isles, leading on to a Supreme Grand Lodge of the British Empire, with the further prospect of this vast organisation entering into perpetual alliance with a Supreme Grand Lodge of America. He even discerns, as through a glass darkly, the vision splendid of a time when a Grand Lodge of the whole world will fold its healing wings over the now distracted nations. Nor does Brother Ward content himself with merely a winged flight to this high ideal. He makes a flying survey of a practicable path by which an approach to these altitudes may be made. He suggests that a body of masonic missioners might, by visiting Lodges throughout the country, stir up among the brethren an insatiable desire for light, and more light, on our mysteries. As a study centre he advocates the formation of a Society consisting of qualified brethren who would investigate Masonry from the anthropological point of view. From this centre circles for the study of the Mark, Royal Arch, and the higher degrees might widen out. Undoubtedly there is at present a lack of facilities for gaining knowledge in aught but the formal ritual in these higher branches of the masonic tree. In this regard, however, a tribute should be paid to the admirable work performed by Brothers Henry Budd and Van Duzer in giving annual demonstrations of the working of the intermediate degrees of the Ancient and Accepted Rite which, in this country, are slurred over in one evening. In a final chapter Brother Ward, in dealing with the relation of Masonry to the ancient wisdom, traces a substratum of Masonry in all the great religious systems of the world. He even discovers a pre-Christian origin in the so-called Christian degrees. In this connection, it should be remembered that one of the Fathers of the Church declared that what was afterwards called Christianity had always existed, and that Matthew Tindal wrote a tract entitled *Christianity as Old as the Creation; or, the Gospel a Republication of the Religion of Nature*. He also maintained that true religion must be external, universal, simple and perfect, and should teach the performance of duty to God and man, the former consisting in the fulfilment of the latter—in other words, the practice of morality. Emphasis is laid by Brother Ward on the necessity of collecting evidence of the signs and ceremonies of primitive races before they are swept away by the flood of modernism which is rapidly defacing ancient monuments and destroying time-honoured traditions. The Author is evidently a poet as well as an archæologist. Interspersed throughout the volume are graceful and suggestive verses illustrating the various theses of the work.

Brother Ward's book, in addition to the results of much original research, contains an admirable summing up of what is known of the history of Masonry. It will well repay perusal from cover to cover, and should be kept always at hand as a work of reference. No library, and few masonic students, can dispense with the possession of a copy of this valuable exposition of the true meaning of Masonry.

FREEMASONRY AND THE ANCIENT GODS

PART I

CHAPTER I

A SIMILAR SYSTEM EXISTS AMONG THE MOHAMMEDANS

THE author had not long been in India before he discovered that most, if not all, of our craft signs were known to at least some of the Mohammedans. In particular the Pathans and the men from Afghanistan and the north-west provinces unquestionably knew our signs, and yet were not masons in our sense. There are, of course, in India numerous Lodges in which brothers of every caste and creed meet on the level and part on the square, and the writer remembers one in particular in Rangoon where every office was held by a man of a different race and creed, thereby bearing witness to the wonderful and universal nature of Freemasonry. It was not, however, the presence of Mohammedan brothers in our regular Lodges, but the use by uninitiated Mohammedans of our signs, that aroused the writer's interest. One example must suffice. When in Colombo, Ceylon, in 1915, the author noticed two Pathans greeting each other in a little frequented alley. Sign by sign they went right through all the signs used in craft masonry. What words they used he was unable to hear, and, while he believes that the grips were the same, it was not possible to be absolutely certain, except the major one; but of the signs there was not a shadow of doubt. The writer came up to them, and in his best Hindustani (not very good, he admits) inquired in what Lodge they had been initiated. One or two similar questions led to an emphatic denial that they had ever been in "Satan's house," which is the polite Hindustani name for a masonic temple. In fact they were quite emphatic that, though they had heard of our strange rites, they, "being God-fearing men," had never participated in them. Other experiences of my own, and similar ones related to me by my friends, left no doubt in my mind that certain Mohammedans had a complete system very similar to our own. One story, well known in India, was that the Sirdar of the Ameer of Afghanistan came to a Lodge in Northern India when visiting that district, and claimed to be admitted. He submitted himself to being proved and was admitted. Afterwards the members of the Lodge endeavoured to learn more about Afghan masonry, but he was very reticent. When, however, asked what he thought of our English ritual, he replied that it was not nearly as exciting as he had expected, but would give no further information.

Readers of Kipling will recall to mind the story of the Englishmen who discovered a hill tribe whose religion was simply a debased form of Freemasonry, and perhaps they thought it was another example of "poetic licence." Whether this particular story is actually true as written the author has no means of knowing, but that a non-Grand Lodge system of masonry does exist in Afghanistan he feels absolutely sure.

For some years, while piling up evidence that some such system did exist, he was unable to obtain exact details, but he at length learned that the Dervishes had a whole system of initiation, considerable parts of which were practically the same as our own. This was working in many parts of Turkey in its pristine form, and with local variations was in use among numerous Dervish sects through Asia. For precise details he is, however, indebted to W. Bro. Henri M. Leon, M.A., Ph.D., etc., who, in the *Masonic Secretaries' Journal* for September 1918, gives a most interesting description of the system as worked in Turkey. The following is a summary of his account, and for more complete details those interested should turn to the above transactions:

There are thirty-three distinct orders of Dervish, each having its own peculiar ceremonies of initiation, its individual signs of recognition, test and passwords, and its own form of *Zikr*, or worship.

Some of these ceremonies and signs are strangely analogous to those of Freemasonry. The "lion grip" is as familiar to the Mevlevi Dervish as it is to a Master Mason, and the Royal Arch Degree has a marked resemblance to that of the *Kardashlik*, or Brotherhood, of "The Builders of the Kaaba," the supreme degree of the Mevlevi Dervish, the three rulers in this Islamic degree being "Our Lord Abraham," the exalted Ishmael and Isaac. In the degree of Al-Kavi, or "the Covenant," Abraham is again the Sheikh, or W.M., while the initiate personates Ishmael, the Muslim tradition being that it was Ishmael and not Isaac who was offered as a sacrifice.

The erection of the altar of sacrifice of "rough unhewn stones" is also made the occasion of an "ancient charge," that even rough, hard, unhewn and unpolished stones can be made to contribute to the glory of Allah. The Bektashi has a special girdle, which is practically the "apron" of the Order. In this girdle, which generally has a flap covering a small bag called *jilbend*, is a stone called the *pelenk*. It has seven corners, or points, called *terks*, in token of the seven heavens and seven earths which were created by Allah; also the seven seas and the seven planets; for Allah said: "We have created the seven heavens in seven folds, and seven earths in the same form, all out of light."

The secret word of the Bektashi is called the *terjuman*, or interpreter. It is communicated by the Sheikh to the Mureed, or initiate, in a whisper.

At the opening of an assembly of Bektashi Dervish, this word is taken up in groups of three; the eldest man of each triad proceeds to form another triad, where the *soz* (word) is again communicated in like manner, and gradually in this way reaches the Sheikh in a manner similar to that in vogue in the R.A. Before the initiation of a candidate into the Bektashi order he is deprived of nearly all his clothing, and rigid care is taken that he has nothing on his person of a metallic or mineral character. He not only enters the *tekkieh* (room in which the initiation is performed) blindfolded, but also has a cord with a running noose around his neck; this is called the *dehbend* or *taybend* (both words are used). He is brought in by two guides, called the *Rehpehler*, who are each armed with a weapon called the *tebber*.

The Ceremony

The Mureed has to make seven journeys round the *tekkieh*, or place of initiation. When he has completed his first journey, the Sheikh of the Order produces the *pelenk* from his girdle, and, placing a sharp point thereof against the naked left breast of the blindfolded Mureed, exclaims:

(1) "I tie up greediness, and unbind generosity."

This ceremony is repeated at each circumambulation by the candidate, the Sheikh placing a fresh point of the *pelenk* against the candidate's breast on each occasion, and exclaiming as he does so at each respective journey one of the following sentences:

(2) "I tie up anger and wrath, and unbind meekness and humility."

(3) "I tie up avarice and greed, and unbind charity and piety."

(4) "I tie up ignorance, and unbind the fear of God."

(5) "I tie up passion and lust, and unbind purity and the love of God."

(6) "I tie up hunger and thirst, and unbind spiritual contentment."

(7) "I tie up Shaitan and Shaitanism, and unbind divineness and peace."

The candidate takes the vows, kneeling before the *Maidan-Tash*, or stone altar, on which is placed a copy of the Qur'an, which is opened at the Sura 16 *An-Nahl* ("The Bee") at the following ayat, or verse: "Perform thy covenant with God, when thou enterest into a covenant with Him; and violate not thy oath, after the ratification thereof; since thou hast made God a witness over thee," etc.

When kneeling before the Sheikh, to take the oath the knees of the Mureed touch those of the Sheikh. Each holds the other's right hand with a grip known to a M.M.M., thus forming the letter *Alif* ("A")—the first of the Arabic and Turkish alphabets.

Before the oath is administered the Sheikh recites to the candidate the following extract from the 10th ayat (verse) of the 48th Sura, *Al-Fateh* ("The Victory") of the Qur'an: "Those who, on giving thee their hand, swear to thee an oath of fidelity—swearing it to God; the hand of God is placed on their hands. Whoso violates his oath, does so to his own hurt, and he who remains faithful to it, will receive from God a magnificent reward."

Addressing the Mureed, the Sheikh then says: "Before Allah created the world there was chaos, and all was dark. Darkness has not yet departed from thee. What blessing wouldst thou now desire?"

The Mureed replies: "To see the light."

The Sheikh: "Restore this brother to temporal light."

(The candidate's eyes are now uncovered.)

The Sheikh: "God is the Light of heaven and of earth; the similitude of His Light is as a niche in a wall, wherein a lamp is placed, and the lamp enclosed in a case of glass; the glass appears as it were a brilliant shining star," etc.

The Wazir, or Deputy Sheikh, who is seated in the west (the Sheikh being seated in the east, or at any rate in the direction of Mecca), then takes up the parable, and in a long lecture explains the allegory, contained in the Qur'anical passage just recited by the Sheikh, and every particular thereof, with great subtlety; interpreting the *light* therein described, to be the *light* revealed in the eternal and imperishable volume of the Sacred Law (the Qur'an), or God's *enlightening grace* in the heart of man. Sometimes this lecture is extended by the Wazir stating that it was this light which Sidna Musa (Moses) saw in the burning bush; that it was the same light which was a pillar of flame by night and of smoke by day which went before the Israelites in the wilderness; that it was this light which caused Musa to shine as a radiant star when he descended from Mount Sinai bearing the Tables of Stone; that it is the light which shone in the *Torah* (the Pentateuch) and in the *Injil* (Gospel); it was the light which illumined the Mount of Transfiguration, and it was the same light which Sidna Muhammad (Rosul-Allah) saw on Mount Hira, and which still illumines every letter of the Qur'an.

At the close of this lengthy and "ancient charge," the Wazir advances from the west to the east by seven processions of seven paces each, made in a manner which would not be unfamiliar to a mason of one of the higher degrees, and taking the candidate by the hand addresses the Sheikh thus: "I now present this Mureed for some further mark of your favour."

The Sheikh then invests the candidate, first with the *taibend*, or girdle, which is worn around the waist and is made only of white woollen materials. As this is girded upon the Mureed the Sheikh says: "The colour of this *taibend* is *bayaz* (white), emblematical of purity. So long as thou keepest this girdle around thy waist and thyself in unsullied purity, the envious Shaitan shall have no power over thee."

Other garments are then placed on the novitiate, in a manner similar to that in which a Knight Templar is invested.

When investing the Mureed with the *kamberish*, or cord, the Sheikh says: "I now bind up thy *boy artasy* (waist) in the *yaya yolu* (path) of Allah. O, Holy Name, possessed of all knowledge! Whoever knows His name will become the *naib* (or successor) of the Holder of the *Zorlu Syrr*, the Great Secret!"

Then follows an "historical lecture" in which the initiate is told that "the first *Bina* (founder) of our Order was the angel *Jibrail* (Gabriel), who by the command of Allah initiated Abu-Bekr as Sidna Muhammad-rosul-Allah therein."

The Sheikh then delivers a lengthy "mystic" charge in which he informs the initiate, among other things, that man must know himself before he can know Allah. He who has found the science of his own body, the *Ilm-i-Vujud*, knows Allah, for the Holy Prophet Muhammad-al-amin has said: "To know thyself is to know Allah."

"In this is comprised a knowledge of thy own secret, and thy *syrr* is the secret of thy Creator!"

When the *Nida*, or "proclamation," of the due admission of the Mureed into full fellowship is made, a horn called the *luffer* is blown. The *nida* is made five times in all, namely at each point of the compass, and finally in the *merkez*, or centre, of the Tekkieh, or Lodge.

The H.S. of F.C. and the P.S. of a M.M. are both employed in the Bektashi ritual. The explanation of these signs, however, is not the same as that given in Freemasonry.

The Dervishes have a tradition that Richard I initiated Saladin into the Order of Chivalry during one of the short truces which occurred during the third Crusade (this seems to be a fact), and Saladin, not to be outdone in knightly courtesy, initiated Richard into these, the lower degrees of the Dervishes. Richard, in his turn, initiated a number of knights, including several Templars, who, in their turn, brought it to Europe, and in particular to the operative guilds who built their churches. The Dervishes continue that as, however, Saladin did not give Richard their higher degrees, we European Freemasons have only their lower degrees.

As to whether the Dervish higher degrees are really quite distinct from ours, the writer, so far, has not been able to ascertain. It is, however, obvious that while our higher degrees, which deal with the Mystery of the Cross, would naturally approximate towards the Christian story, they, being distinctly anti-Christian, would be likely to develop theirs in a different direction. Similarly they would find it hard to discover much about our own higher degrees.

Be that as it may, that is the tradition of the Mohammedans to explain the existence of their signs, and much of their ritual, in Christian Europe. It is a story worthy of the most careful investigation, and while, as will be seen later, the writer does not accept it as giving the origin of masonry in Europe, yet it may quite well have been a source from which the Templars derived part of their ritual, and our own operatives may have received a fresh infusion of ideas from the Templar source.

It may, however, be definitely accepted that throughout Mohammedan countries men exist who know our signs and learned them from initiation among the Dervishes. This accounts for the knowledge which the African Arabs possess of the S. of G. and D., to which reference will be made later, and the tradition that the Templars were initiated into the Dervish system will be considered further when we come to deal with that interesting and tragic Order. The Senussi also have all our signs.

Before leaving this subject my readers may be interested to see placed on permanent record a story of which a summary appeared in the daily papers in 1918.

A number of New Zealand Freemasons being in Jerusalem soon after its capture were anxious to hold a Lodge on the actual site of King Solomon's Temple. As is well known, this is now occupied by the Mosque of Omar. They therefore approached the Sheikh in charge of the Mosque and explained the object of their visit, and asked if he would sanction such a ceremony. To their astonishment he replied, "Take me to a small room adjacent to the Lodge and prove me." This they did, and being satisfied that he was a mason, asked him to be present at the Lodge and take office. He agreed to take the part of I.G., and so the Lodge was duly formed.

Now, if any of those who were present at this historic meeting should see this account, the writer would ask them this question: Was the Sheikh a Freemason in our sense of the word, or is it possible he belonged to a Dervish Order? On the one hand, we know that before the war there were Freemason Lodges of the Continental type in Turkey. The one at Salonika is considered to have been the source of the Young Turk movement. Then, too, there is an independent Grand Lodge of Egypt quite distinct from the District Grand Lodge which works under the Grand Lodge of England. The Sheikh may have been initiated in either of these, probably he was, and not in the Dervish system. On the other hand, he might belong to both, and in any case he is not likely to be entirely ignorant of the Dervish ritual. Therefore from him most valuable information might be obtained if he chose to speak and in view of the friendly and masonic reception he gave to our New Zealand brothers, he is likely to be more communicative to an English Freemason than was the Sirdar of Afghanistan.

The Druses of Mount Lebanon

In *Ars Quatuor Coronatorum*, vol. iv, pp. 7–19, we find a most interesting account of this little-known people by the Rev. Haskett Smith. He shows that these people, who are now agriculturists, claim to be descended from the Phœnicians and to have helped to build King Solomon's Temple. They believe in one God, and have a system of initiation which appears to have many points in common with Freemasonry.

Women are excluded from the inner degrees, though they are admitted on occasions to certain services in their Khalwehs, or temples.

Boys pass through a ceremony when they are about six years old, and are then known as Jâkels, or unlearned, but they wear no distinguishing dress till they are really initiated into the degree of Akkal, when of full age; then they wear a white turban round a red fez, which distinguishes them from the uninitiated and popular world.

The next degree is that of the Khateebs, or priests, and these are regarded as being "the sacred repositories of the more hidden and mysterious secrets of their faith." Above these there exist a few members of a higher degree who are regarded as prophets and seers, and deal with the higher flights of astrology.

If we can overlook the fact that the Jâkel is not free nor of the full age,[1] we can correlate these degrees with our three craft and the

[1] When it is remembered that in the Middle Ages an apprentice was *bound* for seven years, and was almost certainly a boy when he entered we see that the Druses carry on the tradition in this point more correctly than we do.

R.A. In view of what has already been written about the Dervishes, this appears to be a correct correlation of these degrees. In their sacred book, *Testimonies to the Mysteries of Unity*, the following condition is laid down for a candidate (presumably for the degree of Akkal): He must be " of full age, free from servitude, and sound of mind and body." The passwords are not the same as ours, but the Rev. Haskett Smith relates that some of their grips and certain of their signs are identical, so much so that a Druse once asked him how he knew the signs of the Druses.

There is an outer and inner guard to their temples. The double triangle in this form  is found engraven on their temples, and the seven planets play a considerable part in their faith and ceremonies. The grand principles on which their Order is founded are declared to be Brotherly Love, Relief and Truth.

In general, their Order appears to have many points of similarity with F.M., but complete evidence is lacking until some mason can obtain their permission to be initiated into the Druse degrees. But this seems to be impossible, as the Druses, like the Brahmins and Parsees, will admit no one who is not born into their faith. Perhaps before concluding this note it would be well to point out that the Druses are not orthodox Mohammedans, if they can be called Mohammedans at all, but they derive the present form of their faith from a " heretical " Mohammedan called Hamze towards the close of the tenth century.

The  with and without the point, the pentacle, and the circle are, of course, sacred, or at any rate venerated symbols among all Mohammedans, but I do not propose to stress the point, since their association with King Solomon and King David, who are Mohammedan saints, would fully account for this fact. The foregoing account of the Druses will, however, prove of considerable interest to my readers.

We will now leave this fascinating subject of the Mohammedan East, having established the fact that not only our signs, but even a very similar ritual to our own exists, which is independent of modern Freemasonry. Let us now turn to India, the one place in the world where the ancient wisdom is still a living force, and see what the gods tell us about Freemasonry.

CHAPTER II

FREEMASONRY AND THE ANCIENT GODS OF INDIA

It is in India that we find some of the clearest indications of the meaning of our symbols. There the ancient gods still hold sway, and the ancient wisdom has been handed down from generation to generation by the priestly caste, from times contemporary with ancient Egypt.

Caste Marks

The very first thing that strikes the attentive observer in India is the multiplicity of caste marks borne by the natives. Diversified as these are at first sight, in reality they resolve themselves into quite a few signs, several of which are still in use among Freemasons with exactly the same significance.

The outstanding ones are:

 the sign in the R.A., and with the Hindoos of Trimurti the Trinity in Unity, or Brahma, Vishnu and Shiva in one.

This sign is also found thus   and separated as follows it depicts Brahma 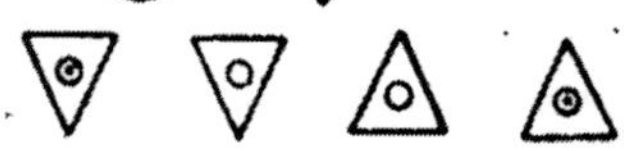 or the Creator; without the circle, thus  it stands for Vishnu the Preserver, and signifies rain which preserves the fruitful earth.

Brethren who have taken the cryptic degrees will thus perceive that their jewel refers to this side of the Godhead. With the point upwards  the equilateral triangle stands for Shiva the Destroyer, and signifies the flame which rises upwards from

BRAHMA THE CREATOR.
Statues of him are rare.

the funeral pyre towards Heaven. This symbol is familiar to us in several degrees, notably the Thirtieth degree.

The position of the Master, the senior and junior wardens in a Scotch Mark Lodge, is brought to mind by this sign of Vishnu 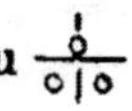 also reminiscent of the tau cross, while this sign  will bring to mind two pillars and is also a caste mark of the Preserver.

In addition to the  the vesica piscis  often with a dot in the centre, is a common caste mark of the followers of Shiva, while His character as the Great Leveller is shown by the use of horizontal lines, e.g. 

The  is the sign of the Sakti sects who worship the female principle of the Deity, and not the male, as, for example, Deva instead of Shiva. It will be noticed it is the Swastika reversed, or Sauwastika. The true Swastika  is not used by the Hindoos as a caste mark, though it is sometimes the emblem of Ganesh,[1] and it is a popular sign with the Jains and Buddhists on their images. It is the sign of life, and is unquestionably now regarded as a solar sign, although originally it may have been stellar, signifying the apparent motion of the stars round the Pole Star. The word Swastika is from swasti, which itself is derived from Su (well) and asti (it is), and therefore means "It is well."

The reversed Swastika is also found as the symbol of Kali the Destroyer, wife of Shiva.

Returning to  or the circle in a triangle, it should be noted that there are practically no followers of Brahma, and hardly a temple or statue in His honour; the only one of which I am aware is that at Pushkar, near Ajmirin, Rajputana. His votaries are therefore comparatively few, and these signs are usually found only on the statue of the god, in a temple dedicated to Shiva or Vishnu.

[1] See Sir George Birdwood in *Report on the Old Records of the India Office* published London, 1891.

The *parm*, or dot, is the mark of the Supreme Being, and with the caste mark of Vishnu | . | or Shiva · indicates that the votary so marked claims for Vishnu or Shiva the prerogatives of the Supreme Godhead, or Brahm the Infinite. Often this dot is placed in the centre of a circle with the meaning of God, the Unknown and Unknowable, Infinite, All-pervading, from whom we all emanate, and to whom we shall ultimately all return; at which point all secrets will be discovered, and from which point, being parts of His Being, we cannot really err, no matter how much we may seem to separate ourselves from Him. The illustration of Shiva opposite p. 14 shows on the forehead of the god this dot, and indicates that the man who made it claimed that Shiva was the nearest personification of the Supreme Being which his mind could comprehend. The ✡ with or without the circle, is strictly the sign of Trimurti, the Three in One, typifying the creative, preservative and destructive natures of the Deity. When Trimurti is depicted, which is seldom, it is as a three-headed man; one head is bearded, as with European mediæval pictures of God the Father, while the heads which represent Vishnu and Shiva are devoid of a beard. The colour of Brahma is "red as blood," of Vishnu "blue as the heavens and sea," and Shiva "white with the ashes of the dead who are ever burned in His honour."

Trimurti is largely an attempt to symbolise the abstract priestly conception of Brahm the Infinite. I have not personally seen any image of Him, but have found illustrations of Him occasionally and understand that a few statues do exist. His sign is pre-eminently the ✡ and He has no other. Occasionally, however, this sign is carved by ignorant craftsmen on a statue of Brahma, which is to be set up in some temple to Shiva or Vishnu, on the grounds that Brahma partakes of the nature of both gods. This He most certainly does not, whereas Trimurti does, and His correct symbol is (✡) with the dot and circle showing Him to be the All-embracing.

The Hindoos in their esoteric teaching not only use this R.A. symbol and give it the same significance as we do, but appear to have similar signs to those used in the complete R.A. ritual.

The following story was told me by a brother who is well known to most London masons, and who had it direct from the principal actors themselves.

THE INNER CHAMBER OF A HINDOO TEMPLE

Three officers of the Indian Army were anxious to enter the inner sanctuary of a temple to Shiva. In India it is often possible for Europeans to gain admission to the outer courts and halls, but the innermost sanctuary is always barred to them, by a guard. In a Shivite temple the symbol there worshipped is usually the Linga, and of no particular interest, but the hall surrounding it is often magnificently carved and adorned.

All three officers were R.A.M., but only two had passed through the ceremony according to the Bristol rite, which includes the three veils. In England the R.A. ritual appears to have been most shamelessly cut about, and no English R.A.M. can be admitted to a R.A. Chapter working under the Scotch or American constitution unless he has at least taken a certain additional degree, and the Irish ritual is even more different from ours than the Scotch.

In America the four veils are still used, and Bristol, by special permission, has also retained their use.

These two companions were, therefore, in possession of the signs and words of this ritual, but the third was not; they were also Past Z.'s. They therefore told their third friend to stand aside, and then approached the Hindoo who was on guard at the inner doorway. Their friend went away so as to be out of sight, and the two officers then advanced to the guard in due form, communicating and receiving in turn the sign and words of the three veils. They, of course, spoke Hindustani perfectly, and told the brother who informed me that the Hindoo Brahmin on guard appeared absolutely astounded on being given these signs, but responded correctly. He then took them within the gate and passed them on to other guards, who checked the passwords and signs; they then were proved in the words, grips and signs of a R.A., two guards taking each man so as to form a triad. They were finally proved as principals of a Chapter, and this being done satisfactorily were admitted to the presence of the sacred shrine itself, where no European had ever penetrated before. The two companions laid particular emphasis on the need for knowledge of the three veils as a preliminary step. I give the facts as they were told me, and have had no opportunity of verifying them; but the man who told me I know for a person of the highest integrity and standing, and he told it to me as he received it from the two men who were "gentlemen and officers of His Majesty's Forces." If any other brother has the opportunity of trying the same test, I hope he will do so, but if so, I should advise him to try it in some big temple such as that at Madura, in Southern India, where he will find priests well instructed in the ancient knowledge, and not in some little village temple where the priests themselves may not be in possession of the higher secrets of the Brahmin system. For my part I am prepared to credit the story, as it fits in so well with (*a*) the use of the ✡ and (*b*) the teaching of the Brahmins among themselves as to the nature of the Supreme Being and the subordinate position of the gods, to which I shall refer more fully in Chapter V.

It is interesting to note that J. F. Newton, in *The Builders*, p. 107, quotes from *Anacalypsis*, by G. Higgins, p. 767, the statement that "Mr. Ellis, by means of his knowledge as a Master Mason, actually passed himself into the sacred part, or adytum, of one of the temples of India." Although in the story quoted above it is the R.A. signs, etc., which obtained admission, the fact that Mr. Ellis found the M.M. signs effective is corroborative evidence. After all, the M.M. degree *is* part of the same system of the mysteries as the R.A., and those acquainted with the higher degree would probably have reached it via the lower. This is certainly the case among the Dervishes, and, as is proved elsewhere, the P.S. of a M.M. is familiar to all worshippers of Shiva.

The only point about the story that puzzles one is that it is stated that the words of the veils were given as well as the signs, but it seems most improbable that the same words would be used by Englishmen at Bristol as by Hindoos in India. Words are the first, as signs are the last, things that are altered in the course of centuries, and often a modern equivalent is given for the old words. Thus, Tat and Tattu were the words used in the Egyptian ritual for the symbols now referred to as B. and J., but it was the same, and so was the meaning. However that may be, such is the story; let us now turn to another point.

HANUMAN, THE SKILFUL CRAFTSMAN.

Hanuman, the skilful craftsman, who built the bridge for Rama the Preserver. He is bringing the food of the tree of life in his left hand with which he preserved the army of Rama.

SHIVA, THE GRAND S.W.

The Grand Senior Warden of the Gods, who shall close our lives. He is holding in his right hand the Lariat of Death, though it looks somewhat like a necklace.

The statues of the gods of India are always depicted in certain symbolic attitudes. This is particularly the case with regard to the arms, which are often multiplied. Attention is drawn to the two gods here depicted. The first is Hanuman, the skilful craftsman who built the bridge for Rama, by means of which He was enabled to cross the straits which divide Southern India from Ceylon, and so to reach that island with His army, and conquer it. It will be noticed that, unlike most of the gods, He has only two arms, and, had the sign used been quite modern, the artist would have been obliged to cover the face of the god with the club ; but when He is not carrying this, the position is often given absolutely correctly, and the writer has frequently seen it so.

Shiva, who carries in His second right hand the cabletow of death, will be referred to at greater length in Chapter III ; as He is the Lord of Death, and therefore of rebirth, it is particularly significant that He should be represented as making the sign He is.

On His forehead He bears the mark of a P. within a C. which signifies that the sculptor considered that Shiva represents the nearest god to the Supreme Being that finite minds can comprehend. The trident in His first right hand indicates that He, " as the Ender of Time," shall end this world " when Time shall be swallowed up into Eternity." " He is white with the ashes of the dead who are ever burned in His honour," whose ashes are scattered over the Ganges to the four cardinal points of heaven, with the scattering sign of the operative M.'s. The cord with a running noose is the symbol of Yama, who is the God of Death, who with it catches the souls of men and draws them forth from their bodies and binds them. It has here been made to look somewhat like a necklace, but is always regarded as the emblem of death when placed in the hands of Shiva. That the S.W. represents Shiva will be shown in the next chapter, but He is also pre-eminently the great M.M., as Hanuman is the great F.C., among the gods.

Hanuman is supposed to be the Son of Vahu, who is the messenger of the gods, but Vahu Himself is seldom found depicted, and never as an image. Hanuman, the Monkey God, is, however, a very popular deity, and His representations are found throughout the length and breadth of India.

The S. . . of a F.C. is likewise to be seen on some of the Assyrian sculptures in the British Museum, of which more anon. It is also, of course, known among the Mohammedans.

Before proceeding further into the connection between India and F.M., it is well to point out that the Hindoos have a complete system of occult and esoteric initiations. The system is generally spoken of as the Yogi system, and an outline of it is given in the following pages. It must be emphasised, however, that promotion is solely by merit, and is not a mere matter of form, and as the secrets include real mystic teaching, and also, it is claimed, occult powers, the candidate cannot proceed to a higher degree until he has really and truly become a master of the one in which he is.

Many of the higher stages are never achieved by the ordinary Brahmins, and the object of the system is to raise the spirituality of the novice by stages till at last he achieves the beatific vision of the Absolute, becomes attuned to It, and is able to become one with It. When this stage has been achieved the work of the soul is finished, and it will no longer be obliged to return to earth in a future incarnation. It will have discovered the genuine secrets on the C., and become one with the Supreme Being. But the path thereto is hard and few there be who find it, and of those who do, still fewer continue unto the end.

This fact is commemorated in the F.C. degree according to the one working, for the candidate is there informed that "as in the previous degree you made yourself acquainted with the principles of moral truth and virtue, you are now *permitted* to extend your researches into the hidden mysteries of Nature and science." Why is he now *permitted*? The reason is that unless a man has obtained a complete knowledge of the moral code, and proved himself to be a man of excellent moral character, it would be dangerous both to himself and to the rest of his fellow men if he were permitted to discover these hidden mysteries. This fact all the old mystery teachers knew, and even if to-day we ignore the claim to occult powers, we yet can realise that if men of low moral character obtain certain of the secrets of Nature and science, this knowledge might well prove a curse to their fellow men.

Those who have lived through the Great War and seen how the discoveries of science have been turned to the vilest uses will recognise also that the Masters of the Wisdom were wise in their generation; and to-day there is a very real danger that with the rapid progress in science man may destroy himself, unless the general moral tone of the human race is considerably raised, so that new discoveries shall not be used for evil purposes.

These facts will make more intelligible the Yogi system as here given, and likewise many obscure passages in our ritual.

The Hindoo System of Initiation

The Hindoo Yogi system is the most complete system of initiation still extant. Unlike most of the ancient systems which have perished, leaving only the dry bones in the shape of fragments of the ritual, the Hindoo system still exists as a living force, and we are able to learn more about its secret teaching than about the actual ceremonies performed.

During my stay in the East I was able to learn a certain amount about the system from certain Brahmin priests, and all that I there learned is borne out by Louis Jacolliot in his *Occult Science of India.* This learned Frenchman was formerly Chief Justice of Chandenagur in French India, and made a most careful study both of the system and of the occult phenomena produced by some of the Yogis. Though at first a sceptic, he was at length driven to recognise that the astounding miracles wrought by the genuine Yogi could only be produced by means other than those known to ordinary Western science, and that vulgar fraud was entirely out of the question. He learned to know and distinguish the tricks of the ordinary charlatan, who abounds in India as in Europe, from the phenomena of Yogi, and deals with both in his book. Those interested in this side of the subject cannot do better than read Willard L. Felts' translation of Louis Jacolliot's book, published by William Rider & Son. Much of what follows is derived from this source.

The subject of occult phenomena lies rather outside the scope of this work, except that it is necessary to point out that the acquisition of occult powers and communication with the Pitris, or Spirits, are two of the objects of research in the lower degrees of Yogi as leading in the higher degrees to union with the Absolute.

" Remember, my son, that there is only one God, the Sovereign Master and Principle of all things, and that the Brahmins should worship Him in secret; but learn also that this is a mystery which should never be revealed to the vulgar—otherwise great harm may befall."

These are the words spoken by the Brahmins upon receiving a candidate for initiation, according to Vrihaspati.

The system is divided into three groups, constituting seven degrees in all. But before taking even the first degree, the candidate passes through a long novitiate which does not end till his marriage. At the age of nine the boy passes through the ceremony of "Upanayana," and he is placed in charge of a "guru," or teacher, who must be at least sixty years old. The Pitris, or Spirits, of the ancestors of the boy are invoked, and he is invested with the Sacred or Triple Cord. He is then allowed for the first time to offer a sacrifice to Fire, and to perform an oblation to the Spirits. All present then say "The child is dead, a man is born." During his course of training he is taught to pronounce the mysterious word formed of the letters A.U.M. in the correct manner, and learns that they stand for the Hindoo Trinity; but its deeper mystical significance is hidden from him till many years later, and he learns only the religion taught to the ordinary villagers, coupled with more elevated moral truths. This stage, which is purely preliminary, continues till his marriage, which takes place when he is about eighteen years old. It is, however, not till his wife has borne him a son that he is allowed to take the first degree proper.

The qualifications are (1) that he has paid the debt of his ancestors by the birth of a son who will perpetuate their race, and (2) that he is deemed worthy of the honour, on the report of his guru.

The degrees are as follows:

1. (*a*) Grihasta, or Master of a House; (*b*) Purohita, or Priest of the popular religion; (*c*) Fakir, or performer of miracles.

2. Sanyassi, or Superior Exorcist.

3. (*a*) Nirvani, or Naked Ascetic and Evocator; (*b*) Yogi, or Contemplative Ascetic; (*c*) Brahmatma, or Grand Master.

These seven degrees are represented in the seven-knotted staff, which is one of the symbols of those who are members of the third group.

The whole system is presided over by a Supreme Council, who elect the Brahmatma, who alone holds the sacred word, which is engraved on a triangle kept in a mysterious box, the key of which is given him on his election.

A brief description of these degrees here follows, but in passing, it should be noted that advancement is only obtained after the most severe physical and mental trials and privations, and the number who are deemed worthy to reach even the sixth degree, or Yogi, are few indeed.

At one time it is stated that there was only one Brahmatma for all India, but to-day almost every important centre has its own Supreme Council and its own Brahmatma, but the actual habitation of this holy man is exceedingly hard to find, at least for a European. The Hindoo priests in Burma (men, be it remembered, who were in a foreign country) recognised a Brahmatma in South India as their Grand Master, but would not tell me where exactly he dwelt. They also stated that he nominated his successor from among his Council, whereas Jacolliot considers the Council elected the successor, but this may merely represent a local variation.

The First Degrees

Initiation: The precise ceremonies are kept a rigid secret, but the discipline and system which follow are given in the *Agruchada-Parikchi*, which is a Hindoo book dealing with the Yogi system, quoted at great length by Jacolliot.

This period of the Brahmin's life covers some ten years, and during it he undergoes a long course of discipline, and is instructed in all ceremonies of prayer, ceremonial cleansing, and the ordinary service of the temple. In addition to ministering to the religious needs of the uninitiated and populous world, he is taught a rigid system of morality, and stress is laid on his devoting part of the day to meditation. He is permitted to perform all the usual functions of a householder, but is distinguished from the uninitiated in that he not only takes part in the temple ceremonies as a priest, but has to spend a considerable portion of his time in invoking and propitiating the spirits and gods. He concludes his day with the following beautiful invocation to Brahm:

Invocation to Brahm (The Infinite God)

"O Brahm! What is this mystery which is repeated every night after the labours of the day are over, and every one has returned from the fields, and the flocks are all in their folds, and the evening repast is ended?

. . . .

"Behold, every one lies down upon his mat and closes his eyes, and the whole body ceases to exist and is abandoned by the Soul in order that it may hold converse with the soul of its ancestors. Watch over it, O Brahm! when forsaking its body, which is asleep, it floats hither and thither upon the waters, or wanders through the immensities of the heavens, or penetrates the dark and mysterious recesses of the valleys and forest of Hymavat.

. . . .

"O Brahm! God all powerful, who commands the storms, the God of Light and Darkness, let my soul not forget, after its wanderings, to return in the morning to animate my body and remind me of Thee."

. . . .

The *Agruchada-Parikchi* then adds this note: "He should stretch himself upon his mat and go to sleep. Beneficent spirits will watch over his repose."

The Second Degree

(Sometimes called the second part of the Degree of Initiation.)

When ten years have passed, the Grihasta has to increase the number of his prayers and fasts, and tends to become more and more a temple priest, though he does not as yet cease to be a "house master."

In this stage or degree he is a Purohita, and ceases to be so much his own master. He spends most of his time in prayer, fasting, and mortification of the body. He eats only once a day after sundown, and his nights are partly devoted to ceremonies of evocation in the temple under the direction of a guru.

All the occult forces are put in operation to modify his physiological organisation and give his powers a special direction.

During this period of his training he is tested through and through, and it is in consequence of the severe trials and strange scenes that he witnesses that the great majority of the Brahmins never pass beyond this second degree.

The mysterious and terrible phenomena which the men of the next or third degree claim that they can produce can only be put into operation by the exercise of a supernatural power, which few are able to master.

Nevertheless, the discipline these members of the first and second degrees have undergone enables them to produce some astounding phenomena, and these prove that their faculties have been developed far beyond anything done by any European. At any rate, they claim to produce these phenomena, a claim which Jacolliot admits appears to be well founded.

These powers are, however, only obtained after a complete submission to a moral code of the most exalted tone, and it is only after they have satisfied their guru on this point that they are permitted to extend their researches into the hidden mysteries of Nature and (occult) science.

As to the members of the third and subsequent degrees, they claim that Time and Space no longer exist for them, and they have command over all terrestrial creatures, and even death itself.

The following invocation to Shiva, which must be performed each morning by men of the second degree, is of considerable interest:

"O Shiva! Thou who destroyest and transformest everything, destroy and transform everything that is impure in me."

Perhaps, however, the most wonderful of all his invocations at this stage of his development, is that to the Goddess Nari, the Eternal Wisdom:

Invocation to Nari

"O illustrious Goddess, I pay homage to Thee! Grant that when I lay aside this perishable envelope I may rise to higher spheres.

"O divine Spouse of Him (Brahm) who moves upon the waters, preserve me, both by day and night. Thou art of a spiritual nature. Thou art the Light of Lights. Thou art not subject to human passions, art eternal and all powerful. Thou art purity itself. Thou art the refuge of man. Thou art our salvation. Thou art *knowledge*. Thou art the essence of the sacred scriptures, and by thy constant fruitfulness the universe is sustained. Thou art the figure of evocation. Thou art prayer. To Thee all sacrifices should be addressed, and Thou art the dispenser of all good.

"All things are in Thy hands—joy, sorrow, fear and hope Thou art present in the three worlds. Thou hast three figures, and that number forms Thy essence, Nari, the Immortal Virgin."

This degree is associated with the element of water.

At midnight, second degree Brahmins, instead of asking Brahm's protection for themselves, evoke the malignant spirits, and say:

"Spirits of darkness, of Heaven, Earth and Hell, come all and listen, and bear these words in mind: 'Protect all travellers and caravans of men who work, who suffer, who pray, or who rest; all those who, in the silent watches of the night, bear the dead corpse to the funeral pyre, and all who travel o'er deserts, forests, or the vast ocean. O Spirits, come and listen. Bear these words in mind, and protect all men.'"

The significance of this is plain. The Brahmin has ceased to seek protection for himself, he now thinks of others; but further still, he no longer prays for protection, but by the powers he has attained is able to protect his less advanced fellow men from the powers of darkness.

At the end of twenty years, the Brahmin makes the decision which henceforth either separates him, not only from the fellowship of the outside world for the rest of his mortal life, but, according to Hindoo belief, decides whether he will end the round of reincarnations for ever.

It is a stern and fateful choice, for should he fail to keep his vow, his fate is believed to be terrible. It means that he must return and start once more on the very lowest rung of material life as a piece of lichen, or some equally humble member of the created universe, and begin once more the slow ascent of the spirit through the lower vegetable and animal kingdoms till, after countless ages of toil, he again reaches man's estate.

Comparatively few dare face this risk, and they are the more disinclined because of the glimpses they have already seen of the full meaning of meddling with the occult unless sufficiently evolved spiritually.

If he decide to go no further, or if his guru refuses to allow him to continue, he becomes (1) a Grihasta. In this case, the only power he is allowed to retain is that of evoking his ancestral spirits. He may, however, be deemed worthy to be (2) a Purohita, or temple priest, in which case he is permitted to exorcise evil spirits. A few, however, are allowed to take a third degree, which must not be thought of as forming a part of the second group, for at most it is merely the completion of the first group, and a preliminary to the second group.

For convenience, we may regard the first three degrees as corresponding roughly to our Craft degrees.

This third degree is that of the Fakir, and his function is to manifest occult power to the multitude by means of exterior phenomena. Marvellous as are some of the miracles these men are said to perform, they are nevertheless rechaining themselves once more to the wheel of reincarnation and, as it were, by exhibiting spiritual pride, stopping their upward spiritual advance.

The Fakir is, however, distinctly higher than the other two degrees, and is allowed to keep in constant communication with the Brahmins of the higher degrees, so as to increase his own magnetic powers. But he is not admitted to the deeper mystical instruction which is given to the higher degree Brahmins in the temples.

The Fourth Degree, or Sanyassi

Only a very few pass beyond this stage and are permitted to undergo the terrible ordeal of the higher initiation, nor do we know precisely of what the ordeal consists, but physical suffering is but the mildest portion of it. We are led to understand that "the powers of darkness" assail the candidate for the fourth degree, or Sanyassi, in a manner often described in the stories of the Buddha. Sometimes these beings take the form of horrible monsters, at others they appear as lovely nymphs, who tempt the candidate to desire evil. At other times, there are scenes of terror, of sufferings undergone by relatives and friends, or of kingly pomp, or of disease and death.

But little authentic information can be obtained. This is the last great trial, the final testing and sifting of the wheat from the chaff, and it is continued for a period of twenty years. Of the powers they obtain, we are informed that they are the Superior Exorcists; that they possess dominion over the viewless spirits of air, and in cases of special emergency, where their religious system is threatened, can, and do, perform marvels; but normally they never display their powers publicly, as they consider that to do so is to chain their souls once more to the Karma of the earth and mortal life.

The Three Final Degrees

5. The Nirvani—Naked Evocators.
6. The Yogi—Contemplative Ascetics.
7. The Brahmatma, or Grand Master.

All these are closely linked together, and may be regarded as external degrees corresponding to the organisation of the Order.

From the point of view of the spiritual development of the individual man, the following stages are recognised which *can* be passed through by every Brahmin who has become a Nirvani, whereas only one man at a time can be Brahmatma of a particular Order, and have charge of the mystic and secret word. There is also a Supreme Council of seventy Brahmins chosen from these degrees, who are "to see that the *Law of the Lotus*, or the occult science, is never revealed to the vulgar," and that unworthy persons are not admitted to the Order.

The spiritual stages corresponding to these degrees are: (1) Salokiam; (2) Samipiam; (3) Sowaroupiam. There is a fourth stage which can, however, only be attained by death, namely, Sayodiyam, or identity.

(1) *Salokiam* signifies *the only tie.* In this stage, the soul strives to go out into the presence of the Deity; it holds converse with its ancestors, and uses its body only to write down the sublime teaching it may have received from the spirits of its ancestors.

(2) *Samipiam* signifies *proximity.* By contemplation, and by disregarding all earthly objects, the knowledge of God becomes familiar. The soul draws nearer to Him and witnesses marvels which are not of this world.

(3) *Sowaroupiam* signifies *resemblance.* In this stage, the soul acquires a perfect resemblance to the Supreme Being, and participates in His attributes. It reads the future, and from it no secrets are hid.

(4) *Sayodiyam* signifies *identity.* This is attained only at death, when the soul becomes finally reunited to the Universal Soul, and is at peace. Its round of reincarnations is ended, and it is one with God, and has reached the C.

It is in these last degrees that the whole mystical teaching of Brahminism is revealed. The major part of the work is, however, by meditation, and the candidate, as it were, initiates himself. The lower members of the Order know little of the lives of their superiors. They are said to live in a state of ecstatic contemplation, depriving themselves of sleep as far as possible, and taking food only once a week. They are never visible within or without the temple, save on the occasion of the great Festival of Fire, held once every five years. On that day they appear at midnight on a stand erected in the centre of the sacred water tank, familiar to all travellers in India near any great temple. They appear like spectres, and the surrounding atmosphere is illuminated by an unearthly light caused by their incantations ; in the midst of this column of light, which appears to reach from earth to Heaven, they appear like demigods and as such are worshipped by the tens of thousands of Hindoos who have assembled to witness the strange spectacle. Unearthly music is heard, and strange unearthly phenomena are seen by the worshippers.

The various degrees are protected by oaths of fidelity, and any breach thereof is punishable by death or some other penalty. Thus "He who has become a Nirvani and shall reveal the superior truths he has been taught to a Sanyassi, shall be put to death," and again, "Whoever has been initiated into the lowest degree and reveals its secrets to any who are not initiated, shall be deprived of his sight, his tongue torn out by the roots, and both hands cut off, that he may neither see, speak nor write the secrets of our Order. He shall further be expelled from his temple, and likewise from his caste."

The Council of the Elders chooses the Brahmatma from among its own Order, and a brief description will be given of this extraordinary being, but first let us add a short account of the fifth and sixth degrees.

The Nirvani is only a Yogi in course of development. He receives most of the instruction given to the latter, but has not yet become master of it. From the ranks of these men are drawn many of those who do the actual work of administration of the Order, but in spiritual development they are still far behind the Yogi.

In former days, both these degrees practised self-mortification amounting actually to a fiendish torture of their bodies, but, probably owing to the teaching of the Buddha, who preached against these excessive austerities, the modern higher degree Brahmins have abandoned these practices in favour of spiritual self-abnegation of the most complete kind. The painful and revolting torments which Hindoo fanatics still inflict on their bodies are now confined to men of the third degree, or the Fakirs, who seem to have taken up this rôle after it had been abandoned by their Superiors.

The modern Yogi maintains that these practices tend to have the same evil effect that the performing of miracles in public brings about, namely produce a form of spiritual pride, and so once more ensnare the soul with earthly trammels.

The Yogi, or sixth degree Brahmins, are those who have reached the highest stage attainable by man on earth. The Brahmatma possesses practically no more spiritual power than they, save only that he alone has the mystic words and is the outward and visible head of the Order. Except for these attributes, he is merely a Yogi of the most advanced type.

To achieve the degree of Yogi, a Brahmin must take an oath of celibacy and "feel the truth that all things are vanity." Above all, he must be animated by "an ardent desire to arrive at perfection."

Usually, this vow of celibacy and poverty is taken at the time he takes the first degree of all, and henceforth he is a wandering ascetic and not a house master, though he may pass through all the ordinary degrees in turn. It is from among such men that the Brahmatma is ultimately chosen.

The Early Career of a Yogi.

When the aspirant has ended his novitiate, instead of getting married, as would a Brahmin who was about to be initiated as a house master, he proceeds to a meeting of those already initiated, and there informs them that he proposes to take the oath of celibacy.

On the day appointed, after a ceremonial purification in water, he arrives at the place of initiation with ten pieces of cloth, four of which he ultimately retains for his own use, while the other six are presented to the officiating Purohitas (or second degree men). He then takes the vows.

The chief guru hands him a bamboo stick having seven joints, some lotus flowers and powdered sandal-wood, at the same time whispering in his ears certain mantras of evocation which are only given to those who, like him, have taken these special vows. This stick is really a wand, and is not intended to be used as a staff; it is similar to the seven-knotted wands of the Cynics.

When the ceremony is finished he departs, taking with him his wand, a calabash for drinking from, and a gazelle's skin to serve as his bed. These are the only articles he may possess.

Henceforth, in addition to the usual ceremonies of a Brahmin, he has to perform certain additional ones, including the following:

He must eat only once, after sundown, and then only as much rice as he can hold in the palm of his hand. He should avoid even looking at women. He must live by alms.

His life should be one long endeavour first, to master his passions, and then to devote himself to meditation, so as to free his soul from his body in order that he may hold converse with the pitris (spirits) in Infinite Space.

If at the age of eighty he is elected to be a Brahmatma, he goes back into life, as it were, marries, and the Brahmins claim that his celibacy has preserved his virile powers so completely, that he is able to have children and live to the age of one hundred.

If, however, he is neither a Brahmatma nor a member of the Supreme Council, all of whom remain in active life till the last, he acts as follows:

He abandons his temple or hermitage, ceases to take part in any religious observances, and retires to some lonely and uninhabited spot to await the coming of death. He no longer receives food, and passes away in the contemplation of the Infinite.

"Having abandoned all his duties," says Manu, "and relinquished the direction of the sacrifices, having wiped away all his faults by the prescribed purifications, curbed all his organs and mastered the Vedas to their full extent, he should refer all ceremonies to others.

"Having abandoned all outward religious observances, he applies his mind solely to the contemplation of the great First Cause. Exempt from every evil desire his soul already stands at the threshold of release, though his earthly envelope still flutters like the flame of an expiring lamp.

"Already his soul has become attuned to the Absolute, and the breaking of the last link with earth will hardly be perceived."

The Seventh Degree, or Brahmatma

The requisite qualifications of this, the highest degree, are (1) that the candidate has taken the vows of chastity ; and (2) that he is a member of the Supreme Council.

It should be remembered that if a Brahmin takes this oath, he must persevere till he achieves union with the Absolute, as otherwise, not having *paid the debt of his ancestors* by producing a son who would continue his line and also perform the proper ceremonies at his funeral, he would have to return in a fresh incarnation at the very beginning of the ladder of life.

All who reached the Supreme Council of seventy members were considered to have ended for ever their transmigrations. It would appear as if some of the members thereof might be former heads of families, but in that case they would probably only be regarded as fifth degree Brahmins or Nirvanis. There is some obscurity on this point, but in practice the bulk of the Council would consist of those who had taken the oath of celibacy, and it was only from their number that the Brahmatma could be chosen.

As soon as elected, however, he had to give proofs of his virility by marrying and producing a son.

A strange ceremony then took place, for the newly born son was placed in a wicker basket and turned adrift on the river.

If he were washed ashore near the temple, he was borne in triumph to that edifice, and by that very fact declared initiated into the Nirvani degree, and from his earliest years was instructed in all the secret teaching of the Order.

If, however, the current carried him down stream, he was rejected as a pariah, and handed over to that caste to raise.

It is interesting to compare this practice with the story of Moses in the Bible. Was he a child of the high priest of an Egyptian temple who thus passed successfully through this ordeal, whereas his brother Aaron failed ? The career of Moses at a later date has many points in it which would lend colour to this theory.

The Brahmatma alone possessed the secret word. This word, which was more sacred even than the letters " A.U.M.," has never been revealed to those below the degree of Brahmatma. It was engraved on a golden triangle and kept in a sanctuary of the temple of Asgartha, of which the Brahmatma alone had the keys. For this reason he wears on his tiara two crossed keys, upheld by two kneeling Brahmins. This word and triangle are also engraved upon the gem of a ring he wears, and it was set in a golden sun which stood upon the altar at which he alone every morning offered the sacrifice of the Sarvameda, or sacrifice of all the forces of Nature.

At his death his body is burned on a golden tripod, and the ashes scattered over the waters of the Ganges in secret.

His death is never publicly announced. Formerly there was only one Brahmatma, but now almost every temple seems to have its own, but the secrets of the degree are still guarded with the utmost care, and, so far as possible, the same rites are performed.

The sacred keys which give the secret word to the newly elected Brahmatma are only handed to him after he has been installed, and this only takes place at the death of the last holder of the office.

The Sacred Symbol of these Degrees

Jacolliot states that every morning members of the three highest degrees should trace on their foreheads this sign—

Its significance is as follows:

The circle indicates Infinity and, in particular, God the Infinite and Unknown, the study of whom is the object of their researches. The border of triangles signifies that everything in Nature is subject to the laws of the Trinity—

> Brahma—Vishnu—Shiva.
> The Germ—the Womb—the Offspring.
> The Seed—the Earth—the Plant.
> The Father—the Mother—the Child.

The serpent is the symbol of Wisdom and Perseverance. It also points out that the multitude is not to be admitted into the revelation of the higher truths, "which often lead weak minds to insanity and death." The seven-knotted wand represents the seven degrees of the Order and also the various sacred and mysterious sevens, such as the seven celestial cities, seven inferior worlds, etc., but, above all, to the initiated it is intended to remind them of the seven emanations of the Eternal Unity.

According to the Brahmins, the Unrevealed God first acts by means of the initial Trinity, who then reveal Themselves in the world through the Manifested Trinity. Thus—

Zyaus (Brahm, the Unrevealed God):

The immortal Germ of all that exists:

Zyaus, or Brahm, divides Himself into two parts, male and female, Nara and Nari, who produce Varadgi, the Word.

These form the initial Trinity, or, Nara, Nari, Varadgi.

These called the universe out of chaos, but in order to manifest themselves in the universe, become

BRAHMA, VISHNU, SHIVA

in order to create perpetually, to preserve eternally, and to destroy and transmute unceasingly.

The point where the serpent and the wand cross is that point from whence we all emanate and whither we shall all ultimately return.

Thus this symbol gives us not only the circle, but also the cross, and these together give us the C.

Thus this symbol epitomises all the symbols of the masonic system, and co-ordinates them on the C.

VISHNU THE PRESERVER IN THE VESICA PISCIS.

Vishnu the Preserver standing in a truncated vesica piscis. The *Satapatbra-Brahmana* says that when Vishnu rose to a pre-eminent position among the gods they became jealous, and, plotting against him, *cut off his head*. However, they soon became alarmed at his loss, and prayed the Asvins, or divine physicians, to restore him to life, which they did. He is also spoken of as the Sacrifice both in the Vedas and elsewhere, and in this aspect is worshipped as Yajna-Narayana. It will be remembered that our J.W. corresponds with Vishnu, and that H.A.B. likewise held that office. (Note the attendant.)

Let us turn for a moment from studying the Hindoo system to compare what Dante describes in his vision of "The Rose of the Blessed":

> "Beatrice . . . my secret wish divined in and thus began—
>
> 'Here is the Goal, whence Motion on his race
> Starts: Motionless the centre, and the rest
> All moved around. Except the Soul Divine
> Wherein the love, which ruleth o'er its orb,
> Is kindled, and the virtue that it sheds:
> One circle, light and love, enclasping It,
> As this doth clasp the others; and to Him
> Who draws the bound, its limit only known,
> Measured Itself by none, It doth divide
> Motion to all . . .
> The vase, wherein time's roots are plunged, thou seest
> Look elsewhere for the leaves.'"
>
> (*Divine Comedy: Paradise*; canto 27, Cary's translation.)

And the poet goes on to describe how in the "Rose of the Blessed" every soul is distinct and retains its individuality, yet also forms one with God. He describes the Cross in the Rose, and later writes:

> ". . . but, so embolden'd, on
> I pass'd, as I remember, till my view
> Hover'd the brink of dread Infinitude.
> O Grace, unenvying of thy boon! that gavest
> Boldness to fix so earnestly my ken
> On the Everlasting Splendour, that I look'd
> While sight was unconsumed; and in that Depth
> Saw in one volume, clasp'd of love, whate'er
> The Universe unfolds; all properties [i.e. qualities]
> Of substance and of accident, beheld
> Compounded yet one individual sight
> The whole. And of such bond methinks I saw
> The Universal form . . ."
>
> (Ibid., canto 33.)

Finally, he attempts to give us some glimpse of the C. of the C., but admits that no words can describe what he then saw (i.e. the Trinity):

> "In that abyss
> Of radiance, clear and lofty, seem'd methought
> Three orbs of *triple hue*, clipt in one bound;

And, from another, one reflected seem'd,
As rainbow is from rainbow: and the third
Seem'd fire, breath'd equally from both. O speech!
How feeble and how faint art thou to give
Conception birth. Yet this to what I saw
Is less than little. O Eternal Sight!
Sole in Thyself that dwell'st; and of Thyself
Sole understood, past, present, and to come.
Thou smilest, on that circling, which in Thee
Seem'd as reflected splendour, while I mused,
For therein, methought, in its own hue
Beheld *our* image painted: Steadfastly
I therefore pored upon the view. As one
Who, versed in *Geometric* lore, would fain
Measure the circle. . . .

"Here vigour failed the towering fantasy:
But yet the will rolled onward, like a wheel
In even motion, by the love impell'd
That moves the sun in heaven and all the stars."

(Ibid., canto 33.)

Here, my brother, we have one of the best descriptions ever written of the Beatific Vision, and the poet himself confesses that words utterly fail him when he attempts to describe what he saw.

Before leaving it, let us, however, note that Trimurti is likewise of triple hue. Brahma is red, Shiva—white, Vishnu—blue.

Brief Summary of the Philosophical Teaching of the Higher Brahmin Degrees

The following is taken from the book of the Pitris, as rendered by M. Jacolliot, but is much condensed:—

"He is one, and He is two. He is two, but He is three. The one contains two principles, and the union of these two principles produces the third.

"He is one and He is all, and this one contains the husband and the wife, and the love of the husband for the wife and of the wife for the husband produce the third, which is the Son.

"The husband is as ancient as the wife, and the wife is as ancient as the husband, and the son is as ancient as the husband and wife, and the One that contains all three is called

A.
U. M.

"Three in One. This is the meaning of the sublime symbol. It is the image of the Ancient of Days.

. . . .

"The union of the husband and wife continues for ever, and from the transports of their eternal love the son constantly receives life, which he unceasingly drops into Infinity, like so many millions of dewdrops fertilised by the Divine Love.

. . . .

"Every drop is an exact representation of the Great All. An atom of Paramatma, the Universal Soul, and each of these atoms possesses the two principles, male and female, which beget the third.

. . . .

"So everything goes by three, from the Infinite to which everything Descends to the Infinite to which everything Ascends (18°), with a motion similar to that of an endless chain revolving about a wheel."

. . . .

Agasa is Life itself, the Divine Essence. It is the soul. It is the man. The body is only an envelope, an obedient slave. As the seed which germinates bursts its shell and shoots out of the dark ground into the light, so Agasa gradually lays aside the material envelope beneath which its transformation takes place, and purifies itself. Upon leaving the world, it passes through fourteen more advanced regions, and each time leaves behind its former envelope and shines forth in one more pure.

After passing through these fourteen stages, it is absorbed into the Supreme Soul.

It therefore has to pass through one stage on earth and fourteen beyond, making fifteen in all. Brethren will be reminded here of the instances of fifteen occurring in our ritual.

The lowest of these super-terrestrial beings are the Pitris, or spirits of the dead. The highest are Pradjapatis, who are about to be absorbed into the Universal Soul. These are ten in number, and as one passes on, another soul steps into the place of the last.

These ten are:

Maritchi = Eternal Reason.
Atri = Eternal Wisdom.
Angiras = Eternal Intelligence.

These form the first three. The second three are:

Pulastia = Supreme Goodness.
Pulaha = Eternal Power.
Craton = Supreme Majesty.

The third triad are:—

Vasichta = The Agent of Creation.
Pratchetas = The Agent of Preservation.
Brighon = The Agent of Transformation.

They are the direct ministers of the Manifested Trinity.

It will thus be seen that men in time rise to the function of the High Gods.

The last is Narada, who represents the union of all the Pradjapatis in the mind of the self-existing Deity and the never-ending production of the millions of beings by whom the universe is being rejuvenated.

"These qualities of Reason, Wisdom, Intelligence, Goodness, Power, Majesty, Creation, Preservation, Transformation, and Union are being constantly diffused throughout Nature under the supervision of the Superior Spirits, and are the product of the unceasing love of the Divine Husband for His celestial Wife. It is in this way that the great 'I am' maintains His eternal life, which is that of all beings.

"For all things in the universe only exist, move and are transformed, in order that the existence of the Great All may be perpetuated, preserved, and purified."

Therefore "nothing exists outside of His Essence and Substance, and all creatures contain in themselves the principles of Reason, Wisdom, Intelligence, Goodness, Power, Majesty; Creation, Preservation, Transformation; and Union. And are therefore made in the image of the ten Pradjapatis, who are themselves a direct emanation from the Divine Being."

The soul-atom departs from the bosom of the Deity, who thus expends His strength that He may grow again, and that He may live by its return. God thereby acquires a new vital force, purified by all the transformations that each soul-atom has to undergo.

Its return "to God who made it" is the final reward. Such is the secret of the Supreme Being and of the Supreme Soul, the Mother of All Souls, the Divine Mother.

The whole teaching of the system is epitomised in this summary:

"The Great All, which is constantly in motion, and is constantly undergoing change in the visible and invisible universe, is like the tree which perpetuates itself by its seed, and is unceasingly creating the same identical type."

Thus it will be seen that the Hindoo Trinity in Unity not only represents the creative, preservative, and destructive, or transformative, side of the Deity, but also the Father, Mother, and Son.

Thus:

Brahma,	Creator,	Father.
Vishnu,	Preserver,	Mother.
Shiva,	Transformer,	The Son.

Compare these with the Egyptian Trinity:

Osiris,	Creator,	Father.
Isis,	Preserver,	Mother.
Horus,	The Destroyer of Set,	Son.

And again the Christian Trinity:

The Creator,	The Father.
The Holy Ghost,	The Spirit.
The Word,	The Son.

The symbol , well known to brothers of one of the higher degrees (the cross being sometimes disguised under the form of a symbol of the Crucified), is thus designed to remind "those who have eyes to see" that all things emanate from the centre, to which all shall ultimately return. When correctly drawn, with the figure of the Christ crucified, it will be found that His sacred, pierced Heart marks the C. of the C., for the figure is twisted slightly as it hangs on the cross. And the cross itself reminds us that He was crucified on the cross of our passions, that is, on the phallic cross. Finally, let it be remembered that the symbol for the earth among astrologers is ⊕, of Mars, who symbolises the passions, ♁, of Venus, or Divine love ♀, while the Sun, or the Divine spirit, is represented thus, ⊙.

This is not the place to write further on this side of our subject, but a hint thus given will be sufficient for many.

Briefly, then, the Brahmin initiate is taught that man is on the fifteenth circle. That by getting into touch with the spirits on the fourteenth circle he will be able to learn from them how to rise. These spirits themselves are in touch with the thirteenth circle, and these with those above, and so at last with the C. of the C., which is God, who is at the heart of the Rose of the Blessed, described by Dante. If he does not do so, he will return again and again to earth till he obtains sufficient spirituality to make the attempt. By the occult knowledge he obtains through the Brahmin system of seven degrees, he hopes to shorten the process, and even obtain the Beatific Vision and Union with the Absolute at the C.

In ancient Egypt the same philosophy appears to have been taught, for the following words on an inscription found at Thebes relate to the first words addressed to an initiate

"Everything is contained and preserved in One. Everything is transformed by Three.

"The Monad created the Duad.

"The Duad created the Triad.

"The Triad shines through the whole universe."

And the symbol for Ra, who stood for the Supréme Being, is ⊙.

The secret doctrines of the Cabbala, as set forth in the Zohar, likewise correspond closely with those of the Brahmins, even including the ten first emanations from the Supreme Being; but their teaching is too well known to the learned brethren to need more than a passing reference. They, too, had a very similar system of initiation and degrees, and, like the Brahmins, thought that the sacred books had an esoteric meaning which must not be given to the multitude.

Thus we have seen that the system of degrees still worked in India consists of seven :

1. Grihasta, or House Master.
2. Purohita, Priest of the Temple.
3. Fakir, Worker of Public Miracles.

These three correspond roughly to our Craft degrees.

4. Sanyassi, or Meditative Evocators, followed by the third group, who bear the mystic sign of the circle with its internal border of triangles and a serpent and wand crossed, consisting of:

5. Nirvani, Naked Ascetics.

6. Yogi, Contemplative Ascetics.

7. Brahmatma, Grand Master.

From these last three are drawn the Supreme Council, one of whom is chosen as Brahmatma, and alone holds the mysterious triangle with its secret word. This word possibly corresponds with that of the R.A., and this degree appears to agree roughly with what we still work as the R.A., though in England it is shorn of much of the awe, grandeur, and mystery which still surrounds the seventh degree among the Brahmins.

CHAPTER III

SYMBOLIC CONNECTION OF F.M. AND INDIA

THE CREED OF THE BRAHMAN PRIEST OF THE TEMPLE OF KRISHNA, RANGOON

I deem that God exists behind the Gods.
So vast is He that my poor feeble mind
Can never grasp Him wholly—Sahib nods ?
The God you own, O Sahib, is but, I find,
A mighty man, most good and just and wise
No doubt; our Gods I deem indeed exist;
They shadow forth His attributes. Surprise
Perhaps enfolds you, that we priests insist
On this ? but only so can man perceive
In any measure what mankind must know,
I find it not so hard you should conceive
Your Christ to be incarnate God, for lo,
I deem that Krishna oft hath walked the Earth,
And, as your Christ, again proclaimed His birth.

J. S. M. Ward.

There is a marked similarity between the three principal officers in a Craft Lodge and the three principles of the Deity. This is so carefully worked out that it can hardly be accidental.

The three principal officers, the W.M., the S.W., and the J.W., represent Brahma, Shiva, and Vishnu. The W.M.'s work is well known.

In like manner Brahma represents the rising sun. He created all things, gods included, out of Brahm the Infinite. He is the first manifestation of Brahm the Unknown and Unknowable.

The Senior Warden's position and duties also are familiar, and Shiva represents the setting sun. But Shiva has other attributes than those of the setting sun, for He represents the destructive side of the Deity, and in this character is often described as representing the Sun in its mid-day heat; but as His symbol is fire which burneth up all things, His connection with the heat of the mid-day sun is merely an analogy for heat and fire.

Shiva is pre-eminently He who closes the life of every man. He is armed, like Yama, the God of Death, with the running noose of death, with which the souls of men are drawn from their bodies and bound and taken away. But since death to the Hindoo is but the beginning of a new life, at first in the spirit plane, and later again on earth (when the soul returns once more by the road of reincarnation), it naturally follows that Shiva is not only the God of Death, but also of Birth and Rebirth.

Not only does Shiva close the life of each individual man, but He shall one day close the L.·. of the world, when as the "Ender of Time" He shall rise grim and dreadful, and brandishing the trisula, or trident, in His first right hand shall overshadow the earth (see illus. p. 14). Then shall fire devastate all that is, and the earth and sky and sea, yea, even the high heavens and the gods themselves shall be consumed. Then shall He immolate Himself on the last and greatest funeral pyre, and Time shall be swallowed up into the circle of Eternity. And all that is and was and shall be, shall become one with Brahm the Infinite, "who is without beginning of time or end of days."

Thus He represents the S.W. in the G.·. L.·. of the World, which is roofed with the canopy of heaven, and is as long as the world and as broad as the same.

He is called sometimes the Second, sometimes the Third, Person of the Hindoo Trinity, according to the aspect in which His devotee regards Him. When He is regarded as the closer of life and of time He is spoken of as the Third Person; but when he is regarded as the *omega*, of which Brahma is the *alpha*, He is then regarded as the Second Principle of Brahm the Uncreated.

Therefore, Brother S.W., when your final duty is performed to-night, pause for an instant and recall to your mind that side of the Deity which closes the life of every man, and which some day will close the work of this planet when Time shall be no more.

Brahma, then, is represented in our Lodges by the W.M. and Shiva by the S.W., and it is therefore not surprising if Vishnu, the Preserver, is commemorated by the duties of the J.W.

Vishnu represents the preservative nature of the Deity—the balance between birth and death which we call life. He typifies the sun at its meridian, not in its destructive, but in its preservative functions. He calls mankind from labour to refreshment and refreshment to labour, without which life must cease. He sends the refreshing rain which makes the desert blossom. He helps and safeguards man in his journey through life. He is the balance poised between Brahma in the east and Shiva in the west. He, seated in the south, gives us the light which lightens our journey through life. Thus it is that throughout India, when entering any place of worship, you should enter, if possible, in the North, the place of darkness, whence you came, before your birth, pass by the East, which marks the moment when you entered this mortal world, continue by the South, which is the way of life, and quit the building or enclosure by the West, which is the gateway of death.

Thus, even in our Western rituals is whispered, nay, in some is shouted aloud, the lesson of the true nature of the Supreme Being.

But it is not only in the position of the three principal officers that this lesson of the triune nature of God coincides with the higher teaching of the intellectual Hindoos. It is also repeated in the three degrees.

The E.A. reminds us of our entry into life, out of darkness into light. The F.C. instructs us how to preserve both physical and spiritual life, and the M.M. teaches us one valuable lesson more; but it does more than this, for is not Shiva the God of Death, and death leads to a new life?

Wherefore it is that the figure of Shiva is and should be of particular interest to all M.M.'s—He who is "white with the ashes of the dead," and through whom alone we can discover the lost secrets. For through Him we reach the C. and become one with the Infinite, and there at (not with) the C. we learn to comprehend the Supreme Being. This becomes possible, according to Hindoo teaching, when having paid the last debt for every fault we become one with the Infinite God, and need no more to return to the round of reincarnation of life in this world.

Let me quote a conversation I once had with the Brahmin priest of the Temple of Krishna in Dalhousie Street, Rangoon:

J.W.: Will this ceaseless round of incarnation never end? Must you be born to suffer, to die, only to be reborn to suffer, to die for ever and ever? Is there no end, no final peace?

The Priest: Yea, truly there is an end; when I have paid the uttermost pice that I owe, when every fault I ever committed in all my past lives is paid for, then I shall return to God who made me.

J.W.: You said "God who made you." Whom do you mean? Is it Brahma, Krishna, Vishnu, or Shiva?

The Priest: It is none of these, but Brahm the Infinite, God the Unknown and Unknowable; He who is behind all the gods, and from whom gods and men alike emanate.

"You Christians, I know, do not understand us, and wonder why we render homage to the gods. This is my answer. I, being a finite creature, cannot possibly comprehend God, who is Infinite. Therefore God, of His great mercy, condescends to make Himself manifest through His attributes. These we can just comprehend and worship. Thus His creative side He shows forth in Brahma, His preservative in Vishnu, and His destructive in Shiva. Other sides of His being He likewise manifests through these other forms which you see in our temples. And I hold that these gods have a real objective existence every whit as real as our own.

"Consider Vishnu whom I serve. I hold that Vishnu hath manifested Himself nine times in India alone. And first He came in the form of animals—a fish, a boar, a lion—for how shall the Preserver be able to preserve and help unless He comprehends the sufferings and trials of the animal kingdom? In His seventh incarnation He came as Rama to help mankind against the powers of darkness; in the eighth as Krishna to uphold the fighting caste, what you would call the practical side of life, against the pretensions of the hermits, or the meditative life. His ninth incarnation was as Buddha, in order to reform our religion, which was losing touch with man because of the excessive demands made on human nature by many of the Brahmins. And I hold that He shall come once more when, in his tenth incarnation as Kalki, He shall come riding on a white horse with a flaming sword in His hand to bring peace to the whole world.

"I have no quarrel with you Christians when you say that Christ was Incarnate God. For my part I have always thought that He was an incarnation of Vishnu sent to guide you Western folk into the road of peace.

"But I have a very bitter quarrel with them when they say that once and once only did God, the Infinite God, condescend to make Himself manifest to poor struggling man. Nay, I say that at countless times and in countless different countries the Preserver has become incarnate to help men on their way, choosing such conditions and giving them that teaching best suited for their advancement in that condition of social and spiritual development they had at that moment attained.

"Thus I hold that God the Unmanifest manifests Himself forth through the gods, and my poor feeble mind is able dimly to comprehend them where it would fail to comprehend Him, and so by easy steps I am led forward to the Light of Truth."

He ceased, and as I left him I marvelled at those ignorant Europeans who would call such a man "an old idolater."

This, then, is the attitude of the intellectual Brahmin as to the nature of the Deity; and its close similarity with the teaching of F.M. as set forth in the position and function of our principal officers, the work in the three degrees, and still more in the R.A., is, to say the least, most remarkable.

This naturally compels us to consider what is meant by the C. of C., which has probably puzzled a good many brothers, as it certainly did myself. Indeed, it was due to the fact that I could get no coherent and clear explanation of the phrase that I set to work to puzzle it out for myself, and this led me ultimately to the present line of research.

But before doing so, it will be best if I refer in passing to the numbers mentioned in the three degrees, and also the junior officers. No doubt brethren will notice that the number which makes a Lodge perfect is the same as that which constitutes the total of the principal and assistant officers, not including the O.G. or T.

They will also recollect that three represents God, and also the spirit in man, whereas four represents Matter and is the number of creation. Three in geometry is represented by the triangle and four by the square. Our aprons, having the triangle entering the square, symbolise the descent of spirit into matter.

Again, in the first degree we get the number three at a very important point in the ritual. In the next degree three still appears, but we get the number five where formerly we got three. In the third degree we carry forward the five on two occasions, but we get seven at the same stage in our proceedings, where in the former degree we had five. The five and the three of the first and second are multiplied to make the fifteen C.'s who were first dealt with, and the second fifteen who received white gloves, as a mark of their innocence. And the same number, fifteen, results from the addition of the 3 + 5 + 7.

Now the planets were always reckoned as seven, and the seven days of the week named after them, not only in India, but all over the world.

That there is some reference to the planets, now almost completely lost, appears from the phrase "the sun to rule the day, the moon . . ., and the master to rule and govern." Many masters will recollect a moment of uncertainty as to where they should point to the S. The "Operatives" claim herein evidence that they are correct in placing their W.M. in the west to see the rising sun instead of marking its position, but in any case this interpretation does not really explain the difficulty. Others consider the correct view is to point to the south for the sun whence it rules the day, and to the west for the moon at the close of the day, but, if so, what planet does the W.M. represent? Perhaps it is the earth, but, if so, one of the other planets must be outside the door of the L.·. Again, it is possible to claim that one of the Deacons is Mercury, but if so, which one?

It is more probable that there once was a closer analogy between our officers and the planets, but it has long since faded away, but the number has been perpetuated by the derivation therefrom of other mystic sevens, such as the seven cardinal virtues, etc. It appears fairly certain that the number seven first struck the mind of primitive man from the fact that a different planet presided at the opening of each successive day, and these seven planets became the seven original powers, or gods, or attributes of the Deity. Seven would thus become the "sacred number," and the tendency would be to derive other sets of seven, such as the seven heavens of the Mohammedans and Hindoos, with their natural corollary of the seven hells. Thence the seven virtues and seven deadly sins, the seven gods of the Cabari, and so forth.

Hindoo mysticism is full of the sacred number seven, and so indeed is every early religious system in the world. It is a curious fact, not without its special significance, that whereas in the Craft the candidate passes in turn through the hands of seven officers, the number twelve is only once referred to in the whole of the three degrees. If the candidate was for the moment synonymous with the earth, this would be natural, for it is the sun which passes through the twelve houses of the Zodiac rather than the earth. On the other hand, in the R.A. the reference to these twelve signs, though disguised, is perfectly clear. If there is anything in this line of speculation, it is evident that, after having passed through the valley of the shadow, the candidate is no longer of the earth earthy, but shines as the sun, and in that capacity passes round the twelve signs.

Hindooism is permeated with astrological law, and every child has its horoscope cast at birth. All the planets are worshipped by name, and have images representing them, and the Hindoo names for these gods give their names to the days of the week; these names corresponding to the same days of the week as ours do. Thus Sukra is called the regent of the planet Venus, and gives his name to Friday, which is called Sukra-war, the French Vendredi, or Venus's day, just as our name is derived from Freya, who, like Venus, was the Goddess of Love.

If, therefore, masonry is as old as we are led to believe, it would indeed be surprising if there were not some references to the seven planets; but since every religion has enshrined within it some references also, it would not be safe to draw any very definite conclusions from the presence of traces of planetary lore. The most that can be said is that their presence indicates that F.M. is older than the nineteenth century, but as no one denies that it is at least a century older, not much benefit will be derived from following this line further.

The unknown Pantheistic deity hinted at in masonry is a matter of vital importance, both to those who desire to know what F.M. teaches, and also to those who hope by means of hints in our present ritual to rediscover something of our past history.

The idea underlying the C. of a C. is well understood in India. As has already been shown, the point clearly denotes Brahm (not to be confounded with Brahma, the Creator), the Supreme Being, Unknown and Unknowable, Infinite and All-pervading, without Beginning or End. From this First Principle emanates all that is, gods, men and physical matter; to It ultimately all returns. At the C. of This all secrets are to be found, and above all, only on or at this C. can the lost secrets be discovered, and we comprehend the nature of the Deity. By this we mean the comprehending of His nature and being, and not merely a string of His attributes learnt by rote.

No finite mind can comprehend His being, and only when we have left this world and become one with Him can we possibly hope to attain the transcendent knowledge and ability to comprehend that knowledge, and this can only be by becoming one with Him. When this is attained we shall be Infinite, being One with Him, and then will all knowledge be ours. Thus it is that even after our final test we receive only figurative ss. (secrets), for even in the next plane of existence we are still far away from the C. of the C. We have, as it were, just passed through the valley of the shadow, and though death will prove to us that death does not end life, we learn that not even then shall we at once attain to a knowledge of the nature of God, and this is made still clearer in the R.A. A parable of the Beatific Vision is found in almost every religion; and, that vision once obtained, the search is practically ended. This point will be developed further in the next chapter, when we come to consider the R.A., and it is sufficient to show that this idea is indicated in the third degree.

But the secret thus hinted at is only given to those who have passed through the third degree. It is not mentioned before the candidate, but we open the L.·. with a reference to it, proceed on our journey from E. to W., but at the end have to return with substituted secrets, for we never reach the C. What is meant by leaving the E. and directing our path to the W.? Does it not refer to the journey of the soul which, according to Hindoo teaching, comes out from the Supreme Being and journeys further and further away till it becomes a separate and distinct ego, falls into matter, and so reaches the Land of Darkness—this world—having left behind it the bright light of the Divine Sun, God Himself; ultimately it completes its circle of life, or earth lives, and returns to the East, to God from whom it has come? But since each soul is but a part of the Divine whole, it can never entirely be separated from God, and that part of it which truly matters, that which is real and true—the Divine spark—cannot err. All else is delusion and vanity, but that which is the cause of its being is, was, and shall be, Divine; and therefore from the C. of C. no true Masons (who understand this meaning of the P. within a C.)

can err. So, be the journey long or short, back to that C. we must return. This is the true teaching of the Brahmins and the explanation of this phrase in our rituals—at least, so I venture to contend.

But, if so, the Supreme Being here indicated is quite distinct from the Jewish idea of God, which is usually recognised in Western Europe. It is distinctly Pantheistic rather than Monotheistic, and could hardly therefore have originated with the Jews, though they might have taken this original idea and covered it up so far as possible with their own Unitarian doctrines.

Before considering this explanation of the C. of a C. in connection with our legend of H., let us briefly consider the names invoked in the three degrees. In the first it is clearly Brahma, the Creator, the G.A.O.T.U.; in the second it is Vishnu, who defines the limitations of man and created beings, the G.G.O.T.U., who lays down the lines beyond which we may not pass if we would be preserved. But who is He who is invoked in the third degree? Is it Shiva the Destroyer? Surely not, for the god therein invoked is not limited. He is neither the Creator, Preserver nor Destroyer. Is it not rather Brahm, the Most High God, who lies behind all the gods, Unknown and Unknowable, Infinite, All-embracing?

I know many of my brethren will say that these three names are merely different names of the same God. But is this so? Note how significantly each name is changed to suit the particular degree. Is it not that we are apt to look at our F.M. from the ordinary orthodox Christian and Jewish standpoint, and not from the Brahminical? If this view be correct, it is not surprising that the Hindoo carver who carved the statue of Shiva and indicates thereon his connection with the M.M. mystery, should likewise place upon His forehead the symbol of the dot within a circle, showing that he likewise claimed Shiva as the nearest manifestation of the Supreme Being, Brahm, whom he would comprehend.

Thus we see that our legend of H., from one point of view, is the allegory of the journey of the soul from God the Infinite back to the Infinite by the road of life on earth, which means ultimately the valley of the shadow of death; and never while in the flesh shall we finite beings be able to comprehend the Infinite Deity, but the first stage in the upward ascent is reached through the gateway of death. The legend of H. is full of significant teaching and will be dealt with fully later, but it is well to bear in mind that no man can tell another this great secret. Each must discover it for himself. The most that another man can do is to indicate where the secret is to be found, namely at the C. H. could not give the secret, though he knew it; it was one which could not be communicated, for the secret was an experience, and no one who has not experienced the Beatific Vision can understand all that is meant by the phrase, although in the next chapter, which deals with the teaching of the R.A. according to Hindoo analogy, an endeavour will be made briefly to indicate what is meant by the phrase: "The Beatific Vision of Mount Athos."

CHAPTER IV

THE R.A. PROVES THE TRUTH OF THIS CONTENTION

Every brother who is a R.A. Mason will remember the different position in which the three principals are placed in the R.A. to that of the Craft. He will recollect also that even at a later period they are never separated. This is because the threefold nature of the Deity is in this degree blended into Brahm the Infinite. It is no longer Brahma, Vishnu, and Shiva who rule the mortal life, but the Supreme Being Himself. We have passed from mortal life, left far behind us the valley of darkness and death, and after passing through the underworld, or Amenti of the Egyptians, in darkness, we are brought up alive out of the pit, and, passing through the crown of the vault, as it were, are in the presence of the Supreme Being Himself, the source of all light. We learn the sublime truth as a result of our labours, that God is of a triune nature and manifests Himself forth in the three forms of Creator, Preserver, and Destroyer. Like a triangle, each side of His nature is equally important and co-equal, but the complete figure, and not the separate sides, is the triangle. Hence it is that the triangle has from the most ancient times been used to represent God the Infinite.

There are, however, two sets of esoteric teaching: (*a*) Of the nature of God, the Gods, and the Trinity in Unity, and (*b*) The nature of Man—body, soul, and spirit.

We have already seen that the teaching of the intellectual Hindoos corresponds very closely to that of the R.A. on the nature of the Deity, and we shall return to consider this aspect of the question towards the end of the chapter when we deal with the subject of the Beatific Vision, which is that ecstatic spiritual experience whereby alone any mortal can achieve comprehension of God the Infinite, the Source of our being, the Beginning and End, who is Himself without beginning of time or end of days.

After this introduction, let us turn and consider the second line

SYMBOL OF THE SUN.

From a temple in Madras. Also the weapon of the gods. The double triangle within the circle. Compare with our R.A. Jewel.

of esoteric teaching, comparing that in the R.A. with that in the Craft—so far as it deals with the nature of man himself.

In the various religions and philosophies of the world there have been many sub-divisions of the nature of man. The Egyptians declared that he consisted of as many as seven elements, but nevertheless these seven elements can conveniently be resolved into the three into which the average Western mind usually divides a man, viz. body, soul and spirit. Without entering into a long discussion as to the relative merits of the Egyptian and Christian divisions, it is sufficient to point out that the Egyptians agreed with us in recognising the body as one element, their next five divisions being really sub-divisions of the soul, and their seventh roughly corresponding with our spirit.

Regarding, then, the soul as the link between the physical body and the immortal spirit, they graded this soul into five sections, each a little less material than the last. Their terminology, in short, corresponds with that of the modern Theosophist, who speaks of astral body, etheric body, etc.

Let us now take these three main divisions of man and consider them in relation to masonry, only noting in passing that each member of the Hindoo triad had his female counterpart, thus making six divinities, with Brahm the Infinite, who comprehends them all, making the seventh.

The Spirit in man is represented by the C. of the C., which is the Pantheistic conception of the Deity, and from which the spirit itself never can diverge. In the Craft Lodge the W.M. represents this element, the S.W. the soul, and the J.W. the body. Hence the significance of the fact that one and the same person invests the brother in each degree by command of the W.M. The soul must raise itself from its crude and material condition to greater heights of spirituality. It will be encouraged and guided by the spirit, but it is the soul, not the spirit, that needs to progress towards God. Each upward step in mortal life is made by the struggling soul, which drags with it its body, and is guided by the glimmering light in the east, which is the emblem of the spirit, that spirit which, while it is within itself, is yet also in a strange mysterious way always at the C., and one with God the Infinite.

Even when we pass through the valley of death we shall not enter at once into bliss, which means become one with God. The soul will only by stages become sufficiently cleansed from earthly dross to be able to become one with Him. Therefore even after being r . . . we still find that it is the same person who invests us.

But when we have journeyed on far beyond the confines of mortal life there will come a point when we shall comprehend the full meaning of the R.A., when having passed through all the intermediate stages we at last become one with the all-embracing spirit. Therefore it is Z. who invests us and not he who sits in the second place in a Craft Lodge. For only the spirit cleansed from all earthly stain can advance us finally to complete union with that Supreme Spirit of which it is, was, and always shall be a part.

This truth is taught, not only in our own R.A., but in all systems corresponding with it, whether it be called, as among the Dervishes, "The Builders of the Kaaba," or is the highest degree of the Yogis, or the corresponding degree in the system of Mithra.

At that point soul and spirit become one, enriched by all the earthly experience and suffering through which the former has passed, and even the body, or so-called material portion, will similarly be transmuted, and as one and indivisible will become one with Him who is All in All. For there are three in one in the R.A., no longer situated in three different parts of the Lodge, but now united side by side, and prophet, priest, and king are only one of their manifold representations. For, according to Hindoo teaching, Spirit and Matter are as Father and Mother, of which parents the Soul is Son, and in the ancient Egyptian mythos of Osiris it is the Son Horus, or Anubis the Soul, who, on the entreaties of His Mother, Isis, or Matter, raises Osiris, His Father, the Spirit, from the grave of corruption to immortality by the lion grip and in the correct manner.

Yea, the soul of man must be ever striving to ascend; a constant battle against overwhelming odds, but in the end it triumphs to find that all is illusion save God the Infinite. And matter is God, and soul is God, and spirit is God, and, now that the illusion of the ego has vanished, even the despised body has its celestial habitation. As St. Paul saith, it is transformed in a twinkling of an eye. Its form may appear to have changed, but matter, like spirit, is indestructible. Hence we can the more easily understand why the Egyptians endeavoured to preserve their material bodies by embalming, not fully comprehending the meaning of their own esoteric teaching, that since

EGYPTIAN SCULPTURE.

Showing Anubis, the Conductor of the Dead through the Underworld, and a Pharaoh.

matter is indestructible and part of God the Infinite, no particular piece of matter is of the slightest importance, since God is all that is, was, or shall be, whether it be of matter or spirit, whether on earth or elsewhere in the universe. Therefore, when we are made one with Him we shall be one with all matter and all spirit, not losing our personality, but expanding it to infinity.

But to our poor finite mind this knowledge cannot be truly comprehended, and it is only for a moment of time we may obtain a glimpse of the truth before the darkness enfolds us once more.

Thus it will be seen that by imperceptible degrees the R.A. teaching of the nature of man, and its teaching of the nature of God, blend the one into the other, till the two merge completely in the sublime ecstasy of the Beatific Vision.

The Beatific Vision

What, then, is the Beatific Vision of which already I have spoken several times ? It is easier to speak of than explain, indeed to fully explain it is impossible, for it is beyond the capacity of our finite minds to comprehend, and much that we can comprehend is beyond human language. It is an ecstasy ; a state of being ; a spiritual experience. But though comparatively few experience it, there is ample evidence that it *does* exist, and is attained from time to time by those whom the gods love.

There is hardly a religion in the world of any real worth but has references to it, and the supreme object of every system of mysteries and initiation is to obtain this state.

The System of Mithra

While there is some doubt as to the exact number of degrees worked by the " soldiers of Mithra," it seems certain it was either seven or twelve. My own belief is that it was seven, corresponding to the seven divisions of man, the seven stars revolving round the pole star, the seven ages of the world, the seven attributes of the Deity, or the six gods and the Supreme Being.

If the seven-degree system be considered the correct form, the degrees were certainly as follows :

(1) The Lion.
(2) The Soldier (Man).
(3) The Ox.
(4) The Eagle.
(5) The Old Man, or Persian.
(6) The Gryphon.
(7) The Sun.

If we compare the names of the first four degrees with the four beasts representing the four evangelists, we shall perceive that they correspond exactly. Nor will Companion of the R.A. fail to recognise these same symbols.

Every name had a symbolic meaning, and Tertullian (*Against Marcion*, i. 18) says that "the Lions of Mithra are mysteries of an arid and scorched nature."

With the exception of the seventh degree, which corresponded with our R.A., we have little detailed knowledge of the system. We know, however, that each degree had its grips and words, its special and appropriate ceremonies, its legends, trials and final triumph of the candidate.

There was a legend of the death and burial of the Saviour and Mediator of Mankind, the Sun God Mithra, who was buried in a rock tomb and raised to life eternal. We know also that the candidate was threatened with death, and that a man (probably the candidate) appeared to be slain. This was, however, only a feigned death, and the victim, after burial in the rock tomb, was *raised* to life by the lion grip.

It would appear as if, in addition to the representation to or by every candidate of the death of Mithra, that at least once a year, at the Vernal Solstice, there was an imposing ceremony depicting the death of Mithra, which is thus described by Firmicus in *De Errore*, xxiii: "They lay a stone image by night on a bier and liturgically mourn over it, this image representing the dead god."

This symbolical corpse is in the tomb (in a cave), and after a time is withdrawn from its tomb, whereupon the worshippers rejoice; lights are brought in and the priest anoints the *throats* of the worshippers with the words, "Be of good cheer. Ye have been instructed in the mysteries, and shall have salvation from your sorrows."

In short, this ceremony synchronised with the Christian festival of Easter. Do not let it be thought that the followers of Mithra copied the ceremony from the Christians, for there is abundant evidence that this was not so. Even the warmest contemporary partisans of Christianity, such as Tertullian, made no such claim. They admitted that the systems of Mithra were earlier than the birth of Christ, but claimed that they were a mockery inaugurated by the devil to discredit Christ's teaching.

Mithra is rock-born, θεος ἐκ πετρας (God out of the rock), and also born in a cave. In a later version He is stated to have been born of a virgin (Elisæus, the Armenian historian, *d.* 480, cited by Windischmann, s. 61, 62).

It is interesting to note that the following gods are also stated to have been born in caves—Apollo, Demeter, Hercules, Hermes, and Poseidon (cf. Pausanias, iii, 25, etc.). Zeus and Dionysos were both worshipped in caves.

In each degree severe trials were imposed and real austerities demanded of the candidate. Binding oaths were exacted and penalties attached to the obligations.

In each degree there were tests and trials by water, by fire, by cold, by hunger, by thirst, by scourging, branding and by the mock menace of death.

In the second degree we know the candidate received a sword and was proclaimed a soldier of Mithra, and Tertullian tells us with unwilling admiration that the candidate in the second degree was then offered a crown, which he refused, saying "Mithra is my crown" (*De Corona*, c. xv). The candidate went through the various degrees "in order that he should become holy and passionless," and the doctrines taught included that of the expiation of and purification from sin by the aid of Mithra, "Captain of the hosts of Heaven and Saviour of Mankind"; and further, that it was because Mithra had undergone a symbolic sacrifice to secure eternal life for His worshippers that those initiated hoped also for eternal life.

Justin Martyr, in his first *Apologia*, tells us "that bread and a cup of water are placed with certain incantations in the mystic rites of one being initiated 'into the system of Mithra.'" Tertullian confirms this, and adds further information: "He also baptises his worshippers in water and makes them believe that this purifies them of their sins. . . . There Mithra sets his mark on the forehead of his soldiers, he celebrates the oblation of bread, he offers an image of the Resurrection, and presents at once the crown and the sword" (*Præscr.*, c. xl, and *De Bapt.*, c. v); and though the gospel story tells us that Jesus was born in a stable, both Origen and Justin Martyr state that He was born in a cave, and in most modern representations the scene is a cave used as a stable.

It was probably because of this fact that the ceremonies of the

Order were always conducted in caves, and when natural ones could not be found, an artificial one was cut or even built. How widespread was the Order may be judged from the fact that even in that distant part of the Roman Empire known as Britain there are more remains of Mithraic temples than of Roman Christian churches.

The religion of Mithra appealed especially to the army. It is said that, like masonry, no women were admitted to its rites, but among historians there is some uncertainty as to whether there were not side degrees, at any rate, which were open to them. In any case it is certain it was pre-eminently a cult which appealed to men of the best type rather than to women.

Mithraism was a development of the old Persian faith, and we know that Artaxerxes Memnon swore " by the light of Mithra." Mithra was the Sun God, and in the Hindoo Vedas He is spoken of as co-equal with Varuna and invoked as Mitra-Varuna, and in Persia Mitra-Ahura were simply the duad, or creative pair. Gradually, however, Ahura-Mazda became regarded as the Supreme Being (as is written in the Zend-Avesta), and Mithra becomes His vice-regent and captain of the hosts of Heaven in the eternal war against the destroyer Ahriman, who, unlike Shiva in India, became the embodiment of evil.

Mithra gradually developed into the mediator between God and man, and it is in this character that He becomes the most important figure in the latter Mithraic cult. The cult had embodied into it much astrological law, even the statue of the slaying of a bull, so familiar to all visitors to the British Museum, and the less well-known figure of Mithra as a lamb or ram with a cross or sword, probably have a reference to the Zodiacal signs of Taurus and Aries—though they also had other meanings—just as Piscis the fish played its part in early Christian symbolism. These three signs each refer back to the astronomical period of the point of the Equinox, which slowly shifts one house in the Zodiac every twenty-one centuries. As, for example, Christ was born at the time when the Sun at the Vernal Equinox was entering Pisces; at the present moment it is entering Aquarius.

These and other recondite matters lie somewhat outside our subject, and must be omitted, save that we may note that the Taurobolium, or baptism in the blood of a bull, which later became associated with Mithraism, was never really part thereof, but borrowed from the Phrygians.

We fortunately know a little more about the seventh degree than we do of the first six. This was because the degree of the sun was obtained by self-initiation. The candidate had to advance himself to this degree by a ritual of meditation, fragments of which were written down; and what claimed to be the system was shown to the writer some fourteen years ago at Cambridge by a don of King's College. He has recently borrowed a copy of this work, and it proves to be a small book edited by G. R. S. Mead, and published by the Theosophical Society in 1907.

The book states that the ritual was "dug out of the chaos of the great Paris Magical Papyrus 57" (Supplement grec de la Bibliothèque Nationale), and adds that the original text has been "worked over by a school of Egyptian magicians, who inserted most of the now unintelligible words and names [*nomina arcana*], i.e. words of power. These obviously later insertions have been removed, but it must be remembered that such words were used to produce a state of hypnotic trance by their constant repetition."

Those interested in the subject should get the book, which is quite inexpensive, but the following quotation from it will prove of interest:

> ". . . and thou shalt see the doors thrown open and the cosmos of the Gods that is within the doors; so that for joy and rapture of the sight thy Spirit runs to meet it and soars up. Therefore, hold thyself steady, and, gazing steadily into thyself, draw breath from the Divine. When, then, thy Soul shall be restored, say: 'Draw nigh, O Lord!' Upon this utterance His rays shall be turned on thee, and thou shalt be in the midst of them."

The ritual ends with this fine prayer, called "The Tenth Utterance":

> "Hail, Lord, Thou Master of the Water! Hail, Founder of the Earth! Hail, Prince of Breath! O Lord, being born again, I pass away in being made great, and having been made great, I die.
>
> "Being born from out the state of birth and death that giveth birth to (mortal) lives, I now, set free, pass to the state transcend-

ing birth, as Thou hast stablished it, according as Thou hast ordained and made the Mystery."

Briefly, the degree of the sun was a system which aimed at producing the Beatific Vision of the Absolute.—that state of ecstasy whereby the adept raises himself above all earthly bounds and becomes united for a moment of time with the Supreme Being. This experience, which has been described by Dante in his "Rose of the Blessed," is a spiritual experience which no human tongue can really describe. But once this state has been achieved, even if the adept returns to ordinary everyday life, all things seem changed. Earth no longer has power over him. He knows how small are human griefs and joys, how transitory all that he sees. A supreme calm has taken possession of his soul, and he is at peace. He has comprehended all that there is, was, and shall be, for he has become one with the Source of All.

In modern Europe the only place where this vision is still sought by a long course of meditation is among the monks of Mount Athos, near Salonika, hence the name by which it is usually known in the West—the Beatific Vision of Mount Athos. Even there few achieve it, but it is interesting to note that part of the *modus operandi* is to fix the eyes on the centre, or *solar plexus*, and repeat over and over again certain invocations to the Deity. This supreme truth may be epitomised as follows: God is everything, and everything exists only because it is part of God. From Him all things come, and to Him all things return; Man, by a life of austerities, prayers and meditations, can raise himself out of his mortal envelope through the seven heavens, and finally become one with God. When this has been accomplished peace, founded on knowledge and comprehension, is achieved, and the soul's journey is ended. It has recovered the lost secrets, and has found them at the C. of the C. This doctrine was taught by the ancient Cabbalists among the Jews, by the ancient Egyptians, by the followers of Mithra. It is still taught in all its pristine grandeur to the highest initiates among the Brahmins, and is the sublime doctrine of the Buddhists. It is the secret of the Builders of the Kaaba among the Mohammedan Dervishes. St. Paul hints at it in his epistles when he tells us he was *exalted* into the third heaven, and saw things not lawful to be uttered; and it is still remembered in the H.R.A. of Freemasonry.

Thus, having passed through the valley of the shadow, we journey on, still seeking through the vaults of the underworld, till at last our purified spirit becomes one with the Supreme Being. There at last we are able to comprehend fully His nature and our oneness with Him, which while in our finite bodies we can only dimly realise, no matter how plainly we endeavour to conceive it in our ceremony of the R.A.

CHAPTER V

BRIEF SUMMARY OF HINDOO AND OTHER EASTERN DOCTRINES TRACEABLE IN FREEMASONRY

The three pillars which we call Wisdom, Strength, and Beauty are also found in the Hindoo temples, where they are usually adorned with human heads. As with us, they are placed in the E.S.W., and represent the Trinity. Churchward also maintains that they are to be found in the Druid temples, and shows a picture of three monoliths supporting a fourth at Louth. The Mayas in Mexico and the Incas in South America also, according to the same authority, had these three pillars in E.S.W.

Churchward's view apparently is that they were originally the altars of the Three in One. In this he may be correct, though it is somewhat difficult to see how one can exactly correlate beauty with the Destroyer, or strength with Him, either. For it must be noted that Churchward considers that the Junior Warden represents Shiva and the Senior Warden Vishnu. I cannot agree with this view, which, to my mind, is entirely contrary to the Hindoo conception of those deities. Shiva is called "the Ender of Time." It is He who shall end this world or close this World Lodge. He corresponds in countless ways with the duties of the S.W., whereas Vishnu is the Preserver, who calls us from labour to refreshment and refreshment to labour. He is the balance between birth and death, and as J.W. is rightly placed in the south. He presides over the fruitful earth and sends the rain which causes the ear of corn to flourish. Hence the ear of corn near a fall of water which used to be carved on the J.W.'s chair, and still should be.

Shiva destroys the day; He transforms life into death. He it is that closes our life, even as the S.W. closes the Lodge when the sun has set, after having seen that every brother has had his due. I have, however, given sufficient reasons in my earlier chapters to show that here I must disagree with Churchward, and on the contrary maintain that Shiva is represented by our S.W.

The two pillars, so familiar to all brothers, are found all over the world, and, strange to say, though their names are different in the various languages, yet the meanings of these words are the same. Thus among the ancient Egyptians they were Tat and Tattu, and their separate and conjoined significance was precisely the same as with us. They are depicted in *The Book of the Dead*, notably in the Papyrus of Ani in the British Museum, as well as on other papyri, and were worn as charms, being made of pottery, etc. These charms were constantly buried with the dead. It seems probable that Churchward is correct when he contends that they referred originally to the North and South Pole stars as seen from the Equator. The Australian blacks set up these two pillars, which they call Nurtunga (N.) and Warringa (S.), at the initiation of a boy into manhood, and they set them up north and south. As they are among the earlier races of the world, and totemistic in their general belief, unlike the later Egyptians, who were solar, we are driven to the conclusion that the Arunta must have come from the equatorial regions, where they could see both Pole Stars, and entered Australia ages ago, and there ceased to develop.

I am inclined to agree with Churchward that these two columns do represent the Pole Stars, and are therefore signs brought forward from the stellar cult, which preceded the solar and lunar cults. In many religions we find a reference to the two pillars which adorn the entrance of both earthly and heavenly temples. It is also possible that they are intended to remind us of the twin pillars upon which man stands, and had in primitive and more outspoken times a reference to the physical pillars between which we enter material life out of darkness into light. Since the first degree is intended to teach us how we enter the world, without wealth, there may be more in this suggestion than meets the eye. If so, it would carry us back to pre-patriarchal times when the "First Mother" was the most important ancestor.

While considering the two pillars, it will be as well to point out that the Jewish Cabbalists had a peculiar system of interpreting the Hebrew Scriptures, and in particular the names therein. By this an inner meaning could be traced which the initiated alone comprehended. Thus the instructed could say "*Being fortified* by the practice of every moral virtue, we are now *will prepared* to face the last trial that awaits us."

Brethren will also be interested to know that the Chinese Society of Heaven and Earth, whieh is described more fully later, has a chop, or badge, which, though printed on paper, is very similar in shape to the jewel of the Mark degree, and among other Chinese characters written upon it is the word "Keh," which means "a pillar," and has the further meaning of "to establish firmly." These two pillars are carried on into Christian times, and are accurately carved at the entrance to several mediæval churches by the Comacine masons.

We may briefly summarise the evidence so far as follows: The Dervishes in Turkey, and the Mohammedans generally, not only have practically all our Craft and R.A. signs, but ceremonies in many ways similar to our own. In addition, they undoubtedly have the lion grip. The Hindoos have a complete system of seven degrees, which convey an esoteric teaching similar to our own, use similar signs, and when we can find out anything about their ceremonies, as in the highest degree—which bears a striking similarity to R.A.—these also appear similar. Among the Chinese it will be found later that masonic phrases have been used with a symbolic significance, and the working tools also are used to apply a moral meaning. Again, the Druses of Mount Lebanon, now entirely an agricultural people, use the implements used in architecture to teach their secret doctrines. They too have a secret organisation exceedingly hard to enter, and claim to be the descendants of the men who actually built the temple of King Solomon.

Before going further, I should like incidentally to answer a cavil I have heard raised by some critical Companions of the R.A., who declare that arches and vaults were unknown ages after the date of the actual building of the first temple.[1] This is not really correct. Recently, in Palestine several vaults which were unquestionably built long before the temple have been discovered. One at Megiddo and another at Samaria are illustrated in *Archæology in the Holy Land*, by P. S. P. Handevik, and others have also been discovered in Mexico. It is true that the examples quoted

[1] The platform which contained the foundations of K.S.'s temple was arched and the arches survive to this day.

are built of overlapping stones, and not on the true principle of the arch, but they are true vaults for all that, and no doubt the true arch evolved from them; but these vaults *are* vaults, and would fit into the story quite as well as if they were built on the principle of what we now regard as the true arch. Incidentally, the key-stone of such an arch would be exactly similar to one which was used for the "Headstone of the Corner."

The actual Eastern and Hindoo doctrines taught in the Craft are the nature of the Deity—that He is pantheistic rather than monotheistic, but emphatically One; that He is the C of the C.; that we shall find the lost secret there because the same Deity is also *within* ourselves, and in some incomprehensible way is never separated from the great I Am; that He manifests Himself to us in His creative, preservative, and destructive sides; and that this is shown by the W.M. as Brahma in the E., by the S.W. as Shiva in the W., and the J. W. as Vishnu in the S. That the triune nature of man is also symbolised by these three officers, the W.M. representing the Divine spirit, the S.W. the soul, which on earth is the means by which man can progress, and the J.W. the body. Maimed though the body be, distraught though the soul be, it is only when the Divine spark quits the body that man's life on this plane is ended. Therefore it is but natural that only the Divine element in us can raise to life eternal. Yet though that Divine spark may prevent annihilation at physical death, it is still the soul which enables us to progress till at length, having passed through the vaults of the underworld (even as *The Book of the Dead* in ancient Egypt tells how the deceased passes through the underworld, Amenti), we at last become united with the Supreme Being and find the lost secrets at the C. of all. Then the God in Man is united with the God of All, and we are invested by Him with the glory of the Godhead. Henceforth the personal ego is no longer needed and, like the worn-out body, is discarded, and we are at one with Him who was what He is and is what He was, and both shall be what He was and what He is from everlasting unto everlasting—which is the teaching of the highest Brahmins in India to-day.

Light is the key which opens the door to our mysteries, and it is the same Light which "shines in every letter of the Koran," and is the Light of Mithra, who is the Light of Ahura-Mazda. It is the same Light from which Moses shaded his eyes when it appeared to him in the bush, and the sign of a R.A. is still made by an Arunta native of Australia when he returns from the final degree through which he passes in the mysterious ceremonies peculiar to that primitive people. It is that Light of which it is written in our Scriptures that "The Light shineth in the Darkness and the Darkness comprehended it not."

But there is one more symbol which must be mentioned here. It is not the Gavel or Hammer, in itself one of the earliest symbols of God, and yet showing forth also the tau cross, nor yet the vesica piscis; these will be dealt with later. It is the Serpent. Those brethren who have taken a certain "higher degree" will remember its presence on their collars, but in every Craft Lodge it is present as the buckle which joins the straps of our aprons. Moreover, in every degree in which we wear an apron after we have become full members we shall find it so used, unless, of course, the masonic furnisher has deviated from the old traditions. But note that the E.A. and F.C. aprons have it not. This is significant. Until we have reached the third degree we have *not* the wisdom of the Serpent. The badge of the first degree denotes innocence; in the second, education has developed our reason; but wisdom is only obtained in the third degree. When we have achieved worldly possessions we find, as Solomon knew, that without wisdom they were of no avail. And the true wisdom is from "Beyond." For the Wisdom of the Serpent is not the low cunning of man, unregenerate; it is the Divine Wisdom of God, and has always so been regarded by the mystic in all ages.

Until a man has been fortified by the principles of moral truth and virtue, and prepared by the education of his intellectual faculties, he is unable to comprehend the Divine wisdom, but the first two alone will not suffice of themselves. This secret is also taught by the Hindoo system of initiation, for it is only the third group of the degrees, the fifth, sixth and seventh, who are entitled to the mark of a circle made of triangles, crossed by a serpent and the seven knotted staff, as already mentioned in Chapter II, page 29. The serpent has at all times and among many different people symbolised the Divine wisdom, and among the deepest thinkers and greatest mystics it has been identified with the second or preservative side of the Deity. In its form of Nehushtan, or the Serpent on the Cross raised by Moses in

THE SACRED COBRA.

Sacred cobra from Buddhist temple in Colombo, Ceylon.
Symbol of the Eternal Wisdom.

the Wilderness, it has been regarded by our Christian teachers as a prototype of Christ. Yet it has also been identified with the Holy Ghost, hence the phrase, "Be ye wise as serpents, but as harmless as doves," etc. The dove is, in Christian symbolism, used to indicate the Holy Ghost, and so this phrase takes on a new significance. But when the serpent is depicted as holding its tail in its mouth, it becomes the emblem of the Ancient of Days, the Almighty. In this aspect it is God the Father, the Creator, but as the circle it further represents Brahm the Incomprehensible, the All-embracing. Thus in itself it is "Trimurti," the Three in One, and it is also the One Incomprehensible, the *Alpha* and *Omega*, the Beginning and End. But it is as the emblem of the Preserver, or the Son, that it is best known. Thus it is shown in Hindoo temples shading Vishnu from the rays of the sun while He sleeps; and the same idea was carried forward into Buddhism, for Buddha is similarly depicted shaded by the five-headed cobra. See photo opposite and that opposite page 258.

As the emblem of the Preserver, it is the link and the balance between birth and death, and its use as the link which joins the bands of our aprons and holds them in place is therefore significant. But though so markedly associated in India with Vishnu, it is sacred also to Brahma and to Shiva, again showing forth the Oneness of the Trinity.

With regard to the serpent as the symbol of evil, I do not propose to say much, as it is somewhat outside our province, since the serpent in our Lodges is emphatically not there as the enemy of man. Students of the Bible will do well, however, to bear in mind that the opening chapters of Genesis are undoubtedly not an historical statement, but a mystical and allegorical story. Even the translation of the Hebrew has been challenged, by men better qualified than myself. Thus the serpent, they claim, should be described as "The Shining One," and the woman Eve, who was formed from the rib of the man, is the psychic body developed out of the spiritual body. The Garden of Eden, these contend, was never on this physical plane, but in the stages of life before matter is reached, and the whole of these chapters is an allegorical account of the descent of the spirit into matter so that it might acquire experience. In this drama the serpent is the "Holy Wisdom" which urges the trembling soul to descend on to the physical plane, and there work out its fate, and finally return to God, after obtaining "the knowledge of good and evil." This view corresponds fairly closely with the Brahmin teaching of the *descent* and *ascent* of the Divine spark in man.

If these be so, we can perceive that once the key to the allegory was lost, the serpent would cease to be divine and become the Tempter, the Evil One. In a similar way, Sut or Set, who at first was at least coequal with Osiris and quite as good, became in time to be regarded as evil, because he represented darkness. There, too, we find the serpent as the symbol of evil, although all the while the winged serpents were the symbols of royalty, and becomes associated with it.

Even among our rough Norse forefathers, the Midgard Snake was, with Surt (the God of Chaos and Fire), the enemy of the gods. But there is a deeper and more complex meaning in this dual character of the serpent which can only be mentioned in passing. Evil is but the opposite of good, and is as necessary for the training of man as good. Hence the Tempter likewise serves God and enables us by bitter experience to learn the needful lessons, and so, when our long journey is ended, we shall find that evil is an illusion and "The Enemy of Mankind" was really its greatest friend, and is in truth the Wisdom of God manifesting itself forth in a strange but necessary disguise.

But lest I should befog some of the brethren, I will leave this thorny subject, only emphasising the point that the serpent on our aprons symbolises the Divine wisdom in all its manifestations, and in itself shows forth His Trinity in Unity. Finally, I would draw the attention of the R.A.M. to the fourth banner, or eagle, which formerly represented the Zodiacal sign of the scorpion or serpent. In later days, this was replaced by the eagle, which has become associated with St. John, and lest its connection with the serpent should be forgotten, that saint is usually depicted with a chalice in which is a serpent. And the Gospel of St. John, of what does it speak if not of the Divine wisdom of the Word and of the mystical side of the Christ's teaching, in contra-distinction to the Synoptic gospels? It is for this reason that the eagle is so often depicted carrying a serpent, as is particularly noticeable in the ancient carvings in Mexico; but of the reasons which led to the substitution of the eagle for the serpent, this is not the place to speak. Nevertheless, mention of Mexico makes it incumbent on me to point out that the serpent played its part in the old Maya religion in that country, just as it does in India or in masonry to-day.

From what has been written above, it will be evident that considerable light is thrown on the meaning of our symbols in masonry by the teaching of the East.

CHAPTER VI

THE LOST SIGN IN MASONRY AND THE "OPERATIVE" MASONS

Swastika.

With the Sun.

Suwastika.

Against the Sun.

Freemasons who have made a study of ancient signs and symbols must often have wondered how it is that among all the ancient signs and symbols which we have retained, that most venerable sign of all, the Swastika, is not to be found.

Now the "Operative" masons still use it in their ritual, and before going further into the matter, it may be as well to summarise briefly and without prejudice, the claims of the "Operative Lodges" and the attitude of some of the most learned members of the Craft to those claims.

The Operatives' Story

There exists both in London and in the provinces a number of Lodges which claim to be the survivors of the Ancient Operative Masons. To-day their members are ceasing to be truly Operative, and tending more and more to be Speculative also; but at first sight their ritual, which consists of seven degrees and seven degrees only, of which more anon, appears to be more primitive and operative than our own. Their story is that the old mediæval masons' guilds after the Reformation declined in importance, since the work of building churches and monasteries had ceased. The old spiritual influence which had inspired their members had also gone, as they not only had less work to do, but what work they had was almost entirely secular in nature, being the erection of houses, particularly country mansions for the new nobility who had been enriched out of the plunder of the religious houses.

The guilds therefore sadly degenerated, and by the time of Inigo Jones had deteriorated into little better than social clubs.

That great architect, Inigo Jones, went to Italy, where he studied Renaissance architecture at its source and came in touch with the Latin guilds, which were still flourishing. On his return to England, he set to work to reorganise and revivify the Southern Guild Lodges, but the good work was brought to a standstill by the Civil War.

After the Great Fire of London, that city required rebuilding, and the number of churches, and in particular the great cathedral church of St. Paul's, not only supplied any amount of employment for masons, but also restored for a time the religious impetus to the Order.

A new Lodge was created at Portsmouth, which in 1673 granted a "journey warrant" to a Lodge of the fourth degree (erectors), when Christopher Wren (who, they say, was made an Arch Guild initiate in 1649) began to clear the ground and prepare the material for the rebuilding of St. Paul's.

In 1675 Grand Master Strong laid the first corner-stone, and Dr. Henry Compton was appointed chaplain and continued to hold daily services on the site till 1710. In this he is stated to have followed the tradition that a similar procedure was followed at the building of K.S. Temple when J., the A.H.P., held daily services on the site thereof. Wren, they declare, is mentioned as an Arch Guild mason in 1674, in 1685 and in 1698. In 1697 this same Lodge sent a daughter Lodge to build Chatsworth, where it is claimed that it still survives, but in a greatly reduced state.

It may be as well here to break off the narrative by explaining that the Operatives say that the Order was divided into two great divisions, namely *Square masons*, who wrought only square stonework, and *Arch masons*, who wrought curvilinear work.

The six lower degrees of each system were practically identical, save that whereas in the *Square Lodges* only straight lines and straight tools, such as a straight twenty-four-inch rule, were employed, in the Arch everything was curved. Thus these latter employed a rope measure which could be curved. The altar in the centre of the Lodge was circular and not square, and the brethren sat in circles.

The seventh degree, however, was held by the same men in both, and whereas a F.C. of a *Square Lodge* might not touch curved work, and vice versa, the Grand Master Masons (three in number) formed the seventh degree, and could do either.

It will be remembered by all masonic students that it was long doubted, and even denied, that Wren was a Freemason, but M. W. Bro. B. Tuckett, Master of the Quatuor Coronati Lodge, in his address at his installation in the autumn of 1919, has shown that if as yet we cannot say for certain that he was a Freemason, we cannot prove that he was not, and that it is antecedently probable that he was.

To resume the Operatives' story: In 1710 Dr. Jas. Anderson became the chaplain in succession to Dr. Compton at a time when it appeared probable that the Guild might be disbanded. To avert this Anderson determined to lay greater stress on the speculative side of the work. Accordingly, in December 1716 he proposed that non-operatives should be admitted on payment of a fee of £5 5*s*. Seven were so admitted, and these were George Payne, Johnson, Stuart (a lawyer), J. T. Desaguliers, D.C.L., F.R.S., Anthony Sayer, John, second Duke of Montague, and Entick (a gentleman).

It should be noted that of these Anthony Sayer was the first Grand Master of the Grand Lodge founded in 1717. George Payne became Grand Master in 1718, and John Theophilus Desaguliers in 1719. John, Duke of Montague, was elected Grand Master in 1721.

There is, therefore, no denying that these men were Speculative masons any more than there is of denying that Anderson also had a prominent part in organising (or reviving) Grand Lodge in 1717, whatever may be thought of the rest of the story. There still, however, remain three of these Speculative masons, and the Operative version is that Stuart was a lawyer, Johnson the doctor who was required to examine initiates in their system, while Entick was father of the later and more famous Entick

To resume their narrative, Anderson, not content with this, altered the time of meeting at the Goose and Gridiron from twelve noon to seven o'clock in the evening, and adopted a special password to distinguish the Operatives from his new Speculative masons. These innovations caused bitter complaints from the old Operative members, who appealed to the Grand Master Masons,

Strong and Wren, who supported them, and Anderson's Speculatives were struck off the rolls.

But Anderson was not defeated so easily, and in the end brought about the formation of Grand Lodge in the interests of the Speculatives. As, however, he had not been through all the higher degrees, he ignored them or, at most, rehashed up fragments of the ritual of these into his system. In the main, he eliminated anything that appeared to him and his supporters to be merely operative in its interest, and hence the disappearance from its proper place of the Mark degree.

Our present third degree, and the foundation of many of our other higher degrees, they also declare were taken from their great Annual Drama, wherein was portrayed the building of K.S. Temple from the laying of the foundation stones to the setting up of the capstone, and even beyond, for the temple thus erected was destroyed, and on the ground being searched at a later date, certain lost plans and secrets were rediscovered.

The Operatives aver that outside London the change came more gradually, and there was no definite breach between the real masons and the non-professionals. In 1724 Francis Drake was initiated at York. As late as 1724, however, one, Scourfield, was declared to have been irregularly initiated.

By 1725 the Speculatives at York had ceased to attend the regular meetings of the Operatives, who met on Saturdays at noon, and instead were holding their own separate meetings on Fridays, in the evening. The old York ritual, therefore, retained much more Operative work in it than did that of the London rite, and it spread among the Operative Lodges in the northern counties. Many of these subsequently joined in Grand Lodge, which was working in London, and so reintroduced a certain amount of genuine old Operative ritual.

Meanwhile in the south, about 1724, many of the old Operatives became disgusted with the alterations introduced by Anderson, and began to hold separate meetings on their own. These were declared irregular Lodges by the Grand Lodge.

In these Operative or irregular Lodges they reintroduced or restored much of the matter which had been omitted by Anderson, in particular the two Mark degrees—M. Man and M. Master, the bases of the Red Cross and Arch, the trial of the three wretches, etc. It was from among this body of irregular Lodges that Lawrence Dermott organised in 1751 his "Grand Lodge of Ancient York Masons."

Briefly, this is the story as told from the point of view of the Operatives of the formation of Grand Lodge. If genuine, it is of the greatest interest as throwing much light on that period of conflict, and explains much of the hostility to the formation of Grand Lodge which we know existed, but which it is not always easy to explain.

But, even if this story is correct, are the present surviving Operative Lodges real survivors, or have their rituals been "faked" by Grant, Stretton, and others during the closing years of the nineteenth century? For, bluntly, that is the contention of some of their opponents.

The author does not feel bound to throw his vote on either side, but prefers to leave the question absolutely open, in the hope that others may have their interest aroused sufficiently to probe the matter to the very bottom.

If these Operative Lodges, or even the bulk of their ritual, are genuine, then they can undoubtedly supply a vast mass of information with regard to our own system; but if the ritual is merely a rehash of our own system plus matter copied from some of the so-called "revelations of Freemasonry" which appeared in the eighteenth century, they are positively mischievous, as they are liable to lead earnest investigators on to the wrong track.

It is perfectly obvious that any well-read masonic student with a knowledge of the symbolism and mysticism of the East could to-day vamp up a very fine "masonic degree," full of interest and of speculative value; but it would be that and nothing more, and, far from casting light on the meaning of our own ritual, might even mislead us. If we were led to believe it was the mother instead of the child of our system, it certainly would mislead us.

These then are the views of some of the most learned of our masonic students who have investigated the claims of these present Operative Lodges:

"We have investigated the claims of the Operatives carefully and fully, and their leaders have failed to produce any evidence whatever that this ritual is old. Even if Operative Lodges distinct from Freemasonry as we know it do exist, unless they have a genuine old ritual they are no different from any other city guild or modern trade union.

"We are prepared to consider other evidence than copies of the ritual, which may quite possibly have never been written down, but transmitted orally. We cannot, however, believe that no minutes, warrants or letters survive which could be produced in support of their contention, were that contention justified.

"What has happened to the journey warrant granted by the Portsmouth Lodge to the Lodge which built St. Paul's, or to one which was sent by the Lodge at St. Paul's to Chatsworth? You contend that this has survived up to the present moment, and that a similar one has survived at Bradon. Then show us the minute books! Surely you must have kept them, or any old accounts. Have you no charges, no old copies of your Constitutions which will bear out your story?

"Bluntly, we have challenged you to produce real evidence that we can handle, but you have not. Against your claim stand this fact—that until quite recently no one had ever heard of you. Freemasonry has been a living force for over two centuries. There exists a mass of documents proving its existence. We have evidence of the existence of numerous spurious bodies and imitations of Freemasonry which attacked us, but none of you or your ancestors.

"Remember, we are not talking of the Middle Ages, when documents would be rare, and age and time might easily have destroyed what once existed. Even so, we have documents showing that masonic Lodges existed. They give us little light on the ritual employed, but they prove the existence of masonic Lodges from which we are descended, but you have not even this. For two centuries you claim to have existed side by side with us, yet not a document can you produce. Even taking the last century, since 1818, surely here at least you have a few letters, a book of minutes! Nothing, absolutely nothing has been produced to support your contentions! Till you do so, we are justified in holding that you are not even genuine masons, but a clandestine body working a spurious ritual."

The Operatives' answer is that they were not allowed to write down anything, since it is contrary to their oath, and that we have deviated from the ancient landmarks in doing so. Therefore every document we produce to show the history of our Order, as well as every ritual, however guarded, is proof that we have so deviated, and justifies their attitude to, and separation from, us.

So here we will leave the controversy, only adding that we should like the matter to be definitely decided once for all, for the present position of uncertainty is most unsatisfactory. If these Lodges are not old, it is doubtful if Speculative masons ought to visit them, for they are not working under a charter from any recognised masonic body. If they are old, then we ought to receive them with open arms and study their system carefully; moreover, we ought to go further and come to some definite working agreement, just as has been done with all other masonic bodies inside the British Isles.

The system consists of seven degrees:

1st degree. Apprentices who are not free, but supposed to be bound for seven years.

2nd degree. F.C. who furnished the stones ready for

8rd degree. Super-Fellow, Fitter and Marker. This is somewhat similar to our Mark Man.

4th degree. Super-Fellow, Setter and Erector. Corresponds to our Mark Master. These were the skilled men who actually built the T.

5th degree. Superintendent. There is no degree quite corresponding with this, but they formed the officers of the Lodges, and our installation and investiture of officers is similar to part of the degree.

6th degree. Past Masters or Harodim. These were the real rulers of the Lodges. The degree itself has no resemblance to our eighteenth degree, or Rose Croix. It is a curious and interesting symbolical degree, based on the crucifixion of a man on a St. Andrew's Cross, as the foundation for a building true to the C. It corresponds to the well-known and ancient mystical idea of the cosmic Christ crucified in the heavens. Naturally, however, I should not feel justified in giving away the secrets of the Operatives, although I am not one, and have taken no oath to preserve their secrets.

I do feel, however, that no harm can result from the above lines, and if one could be convinced that the Operative ritual was genuine and old, this degree would be deserving of the most careful study.

7th degree. Grand Master Mason. There can be but three of these, corresponding with K.S., K.H., and H.A. It has many analogies to our own R.A., but not to our legend. Their reverence for the triangle, etc., is striking, and their word, though not precisely the same, is very similar in its manner of communication and meaning.

It will be noticed that they have not, in these seven degrees, anything corresponding to our M.M. Their contention is that this and most of our *legendary* lore in our other degrees, including even that of the Mark, are all taken from their Annual Drama, at which occasion the Third Grand Master Mason carries out the whole duties of his great Namesake. Nevertheless, the competition of the Speculatives, who worked this as a third degree, was so strong that they felt obliged, under protest, to work a very similar side degree, which they attached to the F.C., and called it the casual degree of a M.M.; but it conferred no special privilege in Lodge, and the old Fitter and Marker still remained the third degree.

Before returning to our main theme, the Swastika, it is only just to mention that if the antiquity of the Operative system were established, it would throw much light on certain variations and customs, which are found in our own Lodges and also on the Continent. Thus the Operatives give the sign of G. and D. to an apprentice, and tell him he must always answer it. Now in Germany, I understand they do the same, though the full explanation is only given in the third degree. In both cases it is not the English form, but one which, in addition to its name and place of use, is found all over the world and always with the same meaning, even among native tribes on the west coast of Africa, who have never heard of masonry as we understand it. Now the three Grand Master Masons each have a square one arm longer than the other, and when they open in the seventh degree, a fourth square lies on the V.S.L. With their three squares and this as a fourth, they proceed to form the Swastika, but further than this, the letter "G" in the c. of the b. is usually represented in Operative Lodges by the Greek *gamma* Γ which is itself a square. Thus this square has a very sacred meaning to them. I am inclined to think for various reasons that they are correct in their contention that originally our "G" was represented by the square ┌, and, of course, four squares when put together will make (a) a geometrical square □, which represents matter and the earth, while (b) the Swastika 卐 represents to-day the sun, among other things, and, above all, life, or the Divine spirit which is the cause of life. As even in our own Lodges there still exists a silent witness to the influence of the Swastika, in our modern Lodges we will proceed to consider the matter carefully, for unquestionably this sign is one of the most important ones throughout the world, and one of the oldest. As we shall see later, it can be found traced on pebbles worked by prehistoric man, on ancient monuments in the East, on the garments of Red Indians in the West, on mediæval brasses in Europe, in Africa, and even in Australasia.

CHAPTER VII

THE LETTER "G"

In our Lodges the Swastika is still remembered, but its presence is disguised. In this section we will consider it in relation to the letter "G," and in the next part we shall consider how it is connected with the practice of proceeding from the N. to the E. and S.

The Operatives declare that in a Square Lodge all symbols should be composed of straight lines. By a Square Lodge they mean one composed of Operatives working on square work as distinct from Arch Lodges, whose members work on arches and other round work.

They declare, therefore, that the "G" should be represented by the Greek *gamma*, or Γ, which is the same shape as Operative square. It should be noted that the Operative square has one arm shorter than the other, and therefore it is the exact shape of the Greek capital *gamma*. Therefore Γ represents "G," which has the same double significance as with us, but also carries a third meaning, namely God the Grand G, who applies the square of His Law to the whole created universe, and is Himself the Law. Thus we get from this one symbol the so-called Buddhist doctrine of the Divine Law, which in their system replaces a personal deity. But it is also synchronised with the Jewish conception of God the Just Judge, who is also the Creator of the universe.

But the Swastika is formed of four *gammas*, or squares, 卐. The Operatives in opening a Lodge in the seventh degree take the squares which form the jewels of the three principals and place them on the V.S.L., and with the fourth square, which is placed thereon, form the 卐.

At this point it is well to draw attention to the fact that the Operatives possess two kinds of squares. The  is the symbol of their sixth and seventh-degree masons, while the square of the second degree is the Ashlar square gauge, shaped thus, . Brethren will know that this square forms part of the cipher used in masonry, the other part being derived from the St. Andrew's Cross, , which is used by the Operatives in their Past Master's degree, or Harodin. It is also remembered in the drinking sign used on one of our own higher degrees. By placing the letters of the alphabet in the square in a certain way, a cipher is obtained. Thus if this were the correct form, which it is not,

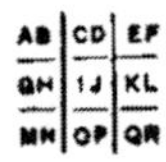

the word "mason" would appear thus: . It will be noted that the second letter of each couple of letters is indicated by placing a dot in the sign thus, A = ; but B = .

The Swastika is found all over the world. As already shown, it is found in India, in almost every creed. Among the Hindoos, among the Jains and Buddhists. The backward hill tribes of Burma use it as a decoration on their woven cloths, and not only it, but also the  and the  (See *Burmese Textiles*, by L. E. Start, published by Bankfield Museum, Halifax.)

In China and Japan it is also on pottery, on embroidery, in pictures and in countless other forms of art. The Red Indians of America also have it woven into their garments, and we find it in ancient remains throughout the whole world. Thus it is to be seen on a Roman Mosaic paving at Brading, in the Isle of Wight, in Assyria, and Babylon and ancient Egypt. Even in prehistoric days it was a venerated sign, and can be seen carved or painted on stone walls found in prehistoric sites in Europe. To the followers of Odin it was a sacred symbol, as it is still to the Australian blacks.

Perhaps, however, the most peculiar fact about it is that it is the only cross found depicted on mediæval Eucharistic vestments, and is to be seen on numerous mediæval brasses of priests in Mass vestments found in our parish churches in England at the present day.

Why is it that no other cross save this one is ever depicted on the vestments of a Christian priest?

How is it that this same, non-Christian, cross is found among the people of Ashanti on the west coast of Africa, among the Pueblo and Santa Crux Indians in America, in China, Australia, and among the followers of Thor and Odin? What does it really represent? Perhaps we shall obtain our clearest indication if we consider the problem why we pass round by the E.

Briefly, we perambulate with the sun, and the same system is followed in many other places where the religion is a development of the solar myth.

When the writer was in Burma he visited the Shwe Dagon Pagoda, Rangoon, in the company of a Burmese gentleman. On reaching the top of the long flight of steps which lead to the pagoda platform, he turned the wrong way, i.e. east instead of west, but the Burman promptly asked him to go round the other way. He explained that it was "not the thing," and when pressed for a further explanation, added it was unlucky. The reason was, of course, that to do so would be to go "Widdershins," or contrary to the sun. The living should never go contrary to the sun; only a corpse or a ghost may do so. The way of the sun is the way of life, the contrary route is that of death. Man comes out of the North, the place of darkness, the land of the unborn, and enters life in the East at birth. He journeys through life in the light of the sun, and quits this world through the Western Gateway of Death. Thus the soldiers' phrase, "Gone West," only repeats and brings down into the twentieth century a very old belief. But just as not only the Egyptians, but all solar folk, believed that the sun at the sinking in the west passed underground till it rose again in the east, so, they thought, did the dead man's soul, and so the ghost enters in the west and goes south and east. Both these conceptions are shown in the 卐. In this form it is the Swastika, from Su-asti = "It is well"; but the reversed Swastika is 卍 or Sauwastika, and is the emblem of death and misfortune as a rule.

Why does the M. make an announcement as to the progress of the C. in a particular manner? It is to commemorate the fact that the candidate follows the track of the sun, whose journey across the sky is represented by the revolving cross. Thus four squares brought together thus □ form a square, the emblem of matter, and arranged thus 卐 the sun itself, the emblem of the Divine Spirit, which enters matter and makes it animate.

Churchward believes that this symbol, although now a solar sign, was originally stellar, and then represented the apparent motion of the stars round the Pole Star. He may be quite correct in this contention, but in most places to-day it has been carried forward into the solar cult, and represents the apparent motion of the sun; and it is in this capacity that it is remembered in Freemasonry. Thus, as we square the Lodge, we tread out four ┌'s, which remind us that we are matter; but we do so by the path of the sun, which reminds us that we are also spirit. So, too, we depart from the east to go to the west, to seek for that which was lost. It is after the C. has been F. that we return from the west (Widdershins), as do the ghosts, bringing with us certain S.S. For it must be remembered that we do not in the Craft attain to union with the Absolute, the C. of the C. For though the newly dead could speak with us, they could not tell us that they had seen God, for He is far beyond them. Only after a long journey can they know Him, and then they will be far distant from us. This has been the teaching of every great religion which has striven to tell one what happens after death, whether it be that of ancient Egypt or modern India.

Thus the 卐 is traceable in our own Lodges, and if the Operatives are as old as they claim, they have it even more clearly shown in their ritual.

The Swastika is perhaps more venerated in China than in any other part of the world, but if this were the only "masonic" symbol that survived in the Celestial Empire, it would not be of much value as showing that a similar system to F.M. existed there. This being a solar, and possibly even a stellar, sign can exist quite apart from F.M., but there is plenty of evidence to show that systems very similar to Freemasonry have existed in China for ages. The question of secret societies in China is a very tangled one, and only a brief account can be given here.

China

In China secret societies abound, indeed probably every Chinaman, whatever his station in life, belongs to at least one. It is naturally most difficult for a European to obtain precise details as to the various rituals and systems in vogue, and the information given below is little more than indicative. The writer hopes, however, that other brothers may be led to come forward and add to the sum total of our knowledge. These secret societies range from what we should call Friendly Societies and Trade Guilds to powerful political associations. It seems certain that some of the greatest of these were definitely anti-Manchu, but what is their precise attitude now that the former dynasty has passed away, it is difficult to say. Among these secret societies one of the most famous is the Th'ien, Ti, Hoi'h, that is, "The Brotherhood of Heaven and Earth." It is, however, generally called simply the Hoi'h, and has several times changed its name. In the early part of the eighteenth century, a society known as the Pe-lin-kiao existed. In 1774 its Grand Master, Wang-Lung, raised a rebellion in the north-eastern province of Chang-tong, which was suppressed, and Wang-Lung and many of his supporters were executed. This rising is stated to have caused the death of over a hundred thousand people. But the Pe-lin-kiao, far from being broken, reappeared in 1777, and further fighting occurred. After this it appears to have changed its name, and it is not until 1880 that we find any historic evidence of the survival of the society. It then appears under the name of the Tsing-lien-kiao. Soon after, we find the Th'ien-ti-hoi'h, which was probably the same as the old Pe-lin-kiao, but if not, then the members of this society merged into the Hoi'h in a manner somewhat similar to that in which the Templars are said to have joined Freemasonry.

After about 1830 that Hoi'h stands out as unquestionably the most powerful secret society in China. It has had several aliases, of which the name San-ho-hoi'h is probably the best known. Its chief centre became the provinces in the south, particularly Canton, and it had Lodges as far away as Java and the Indian Archipelago.

In addition, there seem to be numerous "Lodges" which appear to be quite independent of it, and are known under different names, but which in reality are under the supreme authority of the Grand Masters of the Hoi'h.

Now it is not quite clear whether the Hoi'h, which was already existing in the reign of Kia-King, 1799–1820, was at that time distinct from the Pe-lin-kiao of the northern provinces, or was only the same body under a different name. It seems probable, however, that these two societies were really the same, but organised into two grand Lodges in a manner similar to the Grand Lodge of Scotland and England of the present day, and that they subsequently united into one Grand Lodge; but there is no evidence of any opposition between the two Grand Lodges such as existed in England between the Ancients and Modern. There is little doubt that the northern Lodge was severely persecuted by the authorities at Pekin, who were not so successful in the south, and probably this led the Pe-lin-kiao to merge its separate identity into the Hoi'h about 1830.

The principles of the two societies were undoubtedly identical, and their ritual and oaths appear to have been very similar, allowing for the local variations which we naturally expect to find.

After 1830 the history of this society is that of the Hoi'h. The early history of the latter in South China, as distinct from that of the Pe-lin-kiao in the North, is briefly as follows:

In 1807 the Emperor Kia-King issued an order to his mandarins to suppress the Th'ien, Hauw, Hoi'h, that is "The Family of the Queen of Heaven," the Chinese characters for the name being 天, 后, 會. The mandarins soon replied that the Order had been suppressed, but a new edict followed, again stating that the society still existed, having its headquarters in the southern states, and adding the interesting information that it had Lodges also in the tributary states of the Korea, Cochin-China, and Siam. The mandarins soon replied that they had slain every member of the society, but the society rose Phœnix-like from its ashes under a slightly new name, viz. Th'ien, Ti, Hoi'h, that is "The Brotherhood of Heaven and Earth," or, in Chinese characters, 天, 地, 會. This name signifies in Chinese the three powers of Nature—Heaven, Earth, and the Family, which are the basis of Chinese philosophy and metaphysics.

Edict after edict was issued against this society, which is sometimes known as Hong-kia (or "The Flood Family"), but the Emperors never succeeded in suppressing the Brotherhood, though there are constant records of wholesale execution of complete Lodges.

The Hoi'h has many similarities to Freemasonry, but it is not easy to obtain exact details of the ritual. It appears to be more akin to continental masonry than English, and had unquestionably a revolutionary tendency. How far it was responsible for the ultimate overthrow of the Manchu dynasty it is difficult to say, but the writer believes that it was one of the chief driving forces of the rising. Sinister stories of its doings are on the tongues of many Europeans, but in fairness to the Brotherhood it should be pointed out that they were patriots endeavouring to overthrow an alien tyranny, and most of our information has been obtained from the reports of their political opponents.

If our sole knowledge of Freemasonry were based on the anti-masonic publications which appeared in America at the time of the Morgan incident, or in the books of the Clerical party in France, we should be led to believe that no decent man could possibly be a mason, and the same appears to be true of the Hoi'h. We may admit that the Chinese Brothers interpret their oath absolutely literally, and yet recognise that, except when dealing with a traitor, they are quite decent members of Society.

The Grand Principles on which the Order is Founded.

Brotherly love, relief, and truth are the three grand principles of the Order. The Brethren are exhorted to remember that all are equal, and that justness and uprightness of life and action are expected of them under the penalty of their obligations. They must help a Brother in distress, respect the chastity of a Brother's wife, preserve a Brother's secrets, and obey the commands of the W.M.

Organisation of the Order. There is a Supreme Grand Master, a Senior and a Junior Grand Warden, to whom the various Lodges render obedience. Each "private Lodge" in its turn has a similar triad.

The Chinese names of these dignitaries are *Koh*, i.e. the Elder (W.M.), *Hong* (S.W.), and *Thi* (J.W.), which are translated as the younger Brothers. In Malacca, the titles are *Tai-koh*, i.e. Eldest Brother, *Ji-koh*, second Brother, *San-koh*, or third Brother. There are also a treasurer and other subordinate officers, and there are entrance fees and subscriptions to cover working expenses, etc.

The Oath. The initiate kneels before an altar on which is an image. On his right and left kneel the two Wardens, each of whom holds a drawn sword over his head, so that he kneels in a triangle. The *Koh*, or W.M., dictates the oath at length, which the initiate repeats after him, the Brethren standing to order, usually at the sign of F. Some of the most important clauses, with their specific penalties, are as follows, and the clauses number *thirty-three*, or in some Lodges thirty-six in all.

"If a Brother comes to my house and I have *conjee* (thick rice-water), I will give him *conjee*; if I have rice, I will give him rice to eat. I will treat him according to my circumstances. If I do not, may I perish by a great ulcer."

"If I do not take care of my mother, may the Brethren give me thirty-six strokes of the bamboo."

"If a Brother is poor and I do not help him, may I die on the road."

"If I do not give food to a Brother who needs it, may I be devoured by a tiger."

"If a Brother die and I am earnestly invited to the funeral, and do not go, may I lie unburied at the bottom of the sea."

"If I love wine overmuch, and am not obedient to the *Koh* (W.M.), may the Brethren strike off the rim of my ear."

"If I sell opium and the *Koh* discover it, let him strike off both my ears."

"Brethren should work together in harmony and not quarrel; if I do, may I be punished by the Brethren with ninety-six strokes."

"If I commit adultery with a Brother's wife, let the Brethren run me through with a sword."

"If I fail to assist a poor Brother in distress, may I die an orphan's death."

"If I even mention the thirty-six oaths of the Brotherhood, let them chastise me with 216 strokes."

The most binding clause is, "I swear that I shall know neither father nor mother, brother nor sister, nor wife nor child, but the Brotherhood only. Where it leads or pursues, there I shall follow or pursue, and its foes shall be my foes."

The oath is ratified in one of the following ways, but it is probable that these are not really alternatives, but rather two methods used during two separate degrees.

The first method is:

The initiate is handed a knife and a chalice filled with arrack. He then cuts his finger and allows three drops to fall into the cup. The three principals do the same, and having thus mingled the blood and spirit, each drinks a portion, all standing.

The second method is:

The newly O.B. Brother strikes off the head of a white cock saying, "As sure as a white (pure) soul dwells in this white cock, so surely shall a white soul dwell in me; and as surely as I have ventured to strike off the head of the white cock with the white soul, so surely *shall I lose my head* if I prove untrue; and just as surely as this cock has lost its head, so shall all who are untrue to the Hoi'h, or who are its persecutors."

The Ancient Charges. These are sometimes given in open Lodge, and sometimes a book of rules containing them is kept by the *Koh* and read at each meeting.

The following is a brief summary of these charges:

The members are admonished not to divulge the secrets of the society. They are to be just, upright and honest men; to earn their own living by industry and labour, and not to beg from others. They should, however, lend to the poor, support the sick, and take care of a Brother's house in his absence. They are to receive and entertain a strange Brother hospitably, not to despise a Brother because he is poor, nor to chatter about his poverty to others, but rather to assist him to the best of their ability, to give alms, and above all, assist to bury a poor Brother if necessary.

Further, if a Brother learns that any evil threatens a Brother, he must warn him thereof, and help him escape.

The members have their signs, grips and words, but these are naturally very jealously guarded. One sign is, on entering a house, to take hold of one's queue with the right hand, and twist it from left to right. The lifting of an umbrella or any article with three fingers is another casual sign.

The grip is usually made with three fingers, and the number three is woven into a variety of apparently trivial remarks. The sign of F. is also constantly used to intimate that a Chinaman is a Brother.

One test question is, "Do you come from the East?" or the question may be "Whence come you?" and the answer either "From the East," or from "*Koy-hay*" (from the Brother's family). Each Brother carries a "chop" or seal, which is printed on a piece of silk or calico. The original is kept by the *Koh* or W.M. These appear to vary in shape and inscription, and a detailed translation would take up too much space; but readers who are interested will find full details about this, and additional information about the society, in *The Cross and the Dragon*, by J. Keeson, who is, however, perhaps inclined to be somewhat biased about the society.

One or two points about the seal described there will be of especial interest to our readers. The seal is in a pentagon, and has sixty-two Chinese characters arranged on it. The pentagon contains an octagon, with a second octagon within it, and inside this is a square, and in the square an oblong 2 × 1, and the whole effect is very reminiscent of the jewel of the Mark degree. (See page 86.)

It is partly astrological in its meaning, and among the signs are the names of the planets and the word *Keh*, which means a pillar, with the further meaning of "to establish firmly."

Before concluding this section, the writer would like to give his testimony as to the honourable character of many Brothers of these Chinese secret societies. While in Rangoon he came to know quite a number of important Chinese, men of unquestioned integrity and uprightness of character. They were particularly noteworthy for their honesty and for their generosity to the poor and distressed, not only to their own people, but to men of all races and creeds. Quite a number of these men were members of the Chinese secret societies; and if a tree is known by its fruit, then the Lodges they honoured by their presence could not be the evil places some ignorant folks will pretend.

The truth of the matter is that some Europeans, having met with the machinations of some groups of Chinese criminals, have jumped to the conclusion that some thieves' societies (which exist also among Europeans in the West) were the same as the Hoi'h and similar bodies, and therefore cried from the housetops that all secret societies in China were evil, and all Chinese belonged to the secret societies, therefore all Chinese were evil. That no statement could be more absurd, even those who talk like this would be prepared to admit. Nor is this the only evidence in favour of the belief that a system akin to Freemasonry has existed from time immemorial (see illustration, p. 142). In the Chinese classics we find numerous "masonic phrases"; in the *Book of History*, B.C. 1200, we find this sentence, "Ye officers of the Government, apply the *compasses*."

In *The Great Learning*, written B.C. 500, we find, "A man should abstain from doing unto others what he would not they should do unto him, and this is called the principle *of acting on the square*."[1]

In Mencius (the disciple of Confucius) it is written "that men should *apply the square and compasses morally* to their lives, and the *level and marking line* besides, if they would walk in the straight and even path of wisdom, and keep themselves within the bounds of honour and virtue."

Again, in the sixth book of his philosophy we find: "*A Master Mason* in teaching his apprentices makes use of the *compasses and square*. We who are engaged in the pursuit of Wisdom must also make use of the compass and square."[2]

Chaloner Alabaster, in *Ars quat. cor.*, vol. ii, 121–24, gives a most interesting account of how in the earliest historic records of China there was a society who taught its system of faith in an allegorical form, illustrated by masonic tools. There was also a symbolic temple erected in the desert and the officers of the society wore distinguishing symbolic jewels and *leather aprons*.

It would appear, therefore, as if in China, as in the Mohammedan

[1] *Freemasonry in China*, by G. Giles; also Gould's *History of Masonry*.

[2] *Chinese Classics*, by Legge, 1229-45.

East, the present secret societies have behind them ancestors hoary with age, and that these Grand Originals may well have been closely related to those from which our own system has descended. If there were a body of masons existing in the Near East *previous* to the building of King Solomon's Temple, who assisted at its building, and later spread all over Europe, why should not some of its members have wandered across Asia into China at the very dawn of her history? In a later part of this work, the writer will endeavour to show that such a body, known as the "Dionysian Artificers," did exist, who were masons, and had not only signs and tokens, but also a mystery similar to our own.

The author has no information as to whether similar secret societies exist in Japan, but if they do, they would not create further proof of his theory, since Japan avowedly obtained nearly all her early civilisation from China; and therefore if she had any similar secret societies, they might naturally be ascribed to the same source.

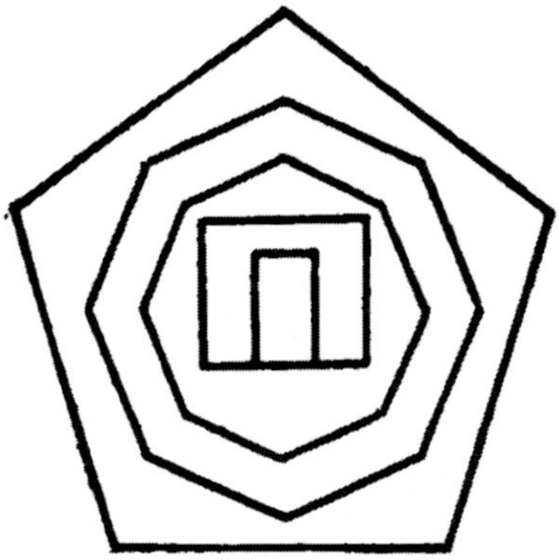

"CHOP" OF A LODGE OF HOI'H.

CHAPTER VIII

THE MARK DEGREE

THE Mark degree appears to be an old degree of the Operatives. Even in its present form its operative side is emphasised, and it shows distinct evidence of being originally two degrees, namely Mark Man and Mark Master. The so-called Operative Lodges work it as two degrees denominated (*a*) the Fitter and Marker, and (*b*) the Setter and Erector. Their working of these two degrees is very similar to our own ritual, save that the legend is not given, but is included as an incident in the Annual Drama.

This Mark degree, though often spoken of in England as a higher or side degree, should more properly be regarded as part of the Craft system. It may perhaps be regarded as the completion of the second degree, or F.C., just as the R.A. is the completion of the M.M. In Scotland, its close connection with the Craft is clearly recognised, but in England, owing to a variety of causes, chief among which was the hostility between the old Operatives and the Grand Lodge of the Speculatives in the eighteenth century, it failed to obtain the recognition of the United Grand Lodge in 1818 as did the R.A.

It has therefore been driven to organise itself on independent lines, and now, with its own Grand Lodge and own Grand Mark Masons' Hall, it is unlikely that it would be possible to restore the direct connection with the Craft. Its rulers in the nineteenth century also adopted a wise policy with regard to the other side degrees, and extended the hand of friendship to many of them, so that its strength has been greatly increased till it now stands out as the leading higher degree authority, with the possible exception of the Supreme Council of the Ancient and Accepted Rite. All devotees of the higher degrees must feel the utmost gratitude for the way in which the Rulers of the Mark have helped the other degrees which now rally round its banner, such as the

Cryptic, the Templar Order, and the Allied Degrees. Indeed, it may almost be regarded as the head of the so-called "York Rite," although its Rulers would be the first to repudiate such an idea. The name of the "York Rite," although not technically correct, *is* a convenient name for a whole group of degrees, and will be used in this work, but its definition will be relegated to a later chapter.

Nevertheless, I consider that strictly the Mark is a Craft degree, and should be carefully distinguished from the degrees of the Cross, which are best represented in England by the degrees worked by the Supreme Council. Nevertheless, there are Cross degrees which are not under the Supreme Council, and to which reference will be made later.

Reverting to the Mark degree itself, I should like to emphasise the fact that there is no justification for those who claim that the Mark is obviously of later date than the Craft degrees. Even as it stands to-day, it bears all the traces of as great antiquity as our F.C. or E.A. Its very operative character is an argument in its favour; but this operative character perhaps in part accounts for the fact that fewer masons take it than are exalted R.A.M's. Its speculative teaching is not so profound as the R.A., but I venture to think that no degree in masonry *is* so profound as the R.A., and it is hardly fair to compare the two. The Mark is not only a very dramatic degree when *properly* worked, but has many interesting points which are apt to be overlooked by those who do not look carefully into the matter.

Take such a simple point as the grips. These are most significant, especially when compared with that employed by the Dervishes when making their candidate take the O.B.

Its penalties are also of curious interest, being found among the Hindoo Brahmins and the Chinese. It is, however, what they are not, rather than what they are, which must strike the careful observer, particularly after the three penalties of the Craft degrees.

The jewel is also peculiarly interesting, and the curious right conferred by the Mark must not be overlooked.

In Australia, among most of the primitive tribes, each man has a peculiar and sacred object, which is given to him at one of his initiations. It is known as his Churinga, and once he has received it, he guards it with the utmost care. Most of these are made of wood, but in a few cases there seems to be evidence that they are made of stone. On them is a Mark, or series of Marks, or a new name engraved, which no man knoweth save he whose Churinga it is. If he hands his Churinga to another native, the latter, when restoring it, must make him a present.

Sometimes it would appear as if the other borrows a man's Churinga for some magical purpose, but at others it appears as if the native pledges it to a man as a bond or pledge.

Always this Churinga is regarded as a very sacred thing and peculiar to its owner, and often the natives deposit them in some sacred spot for greater security.

It appears as if in this primitive and now little understood custom of the Churinga we have the prototype of the pledge by a M.M.M.

The Lewis is also a matter deserving of more attention than it usually receives. The various types of metal Lewises are usually varieties of the Tau, and some of them remind us at once of the triple Tau of the R.A. This fact alone shows how the cross interpenetrates our Craft degrees as well as those degrees more strictly connected with the cross, and how difficult it is to separate our system into two watertight departments.

Bearing in mind this inner significance of the Lewis as showing the cross, we appreciate the esoteric meaning of the Lewis grip, by which those who had to ascend from the water of the Great Sea were assisted up the steep bank to the "promised land." It is by the cross of suffering we are advanced to the promised land, there to receive the white stone from the Bestower of all good gifts. And further, this grip is only extended to those who, after working their time on Mount L., bring the fruit of their labours over the Great Deep to the Shore of the Promised Land.

Then let us note that this is a △ degree, and the peculiar significance of the "fire" will become manifest. But there is no double triangle, no explanation of the nature of the Deity, only that silent witness that God is a Trinity; but of the nature of that Trinity nothing is said. There is no mention of the 0, but the point is remembered. My brothers, there is far more significance in our "fire" than most realise. In all the important side degrees we find a different kind of "fire," and each has its appropriate exoteric and esoteric meaning.

Take our Craft fire. Its exoteric meaning is plain. At the banquet, as in the Lodge, we will guard our secrets under the penalty of our O.B. In the Mark, its meaning is deeper and holier. When we drink to a brother's health, is it not to call down a blessing from the, as yet undefined, Trinity in Unity? We seal our love with the Mark M.'s sign of approval, but in the name of the G.O.O.T.U.

Finally, what is that which was r? Is it not ourselves? We are the stone which we fashion, each one of us, for the Temple of God—and of Humanity. Though the unseeing world may think us of little account, yet He knoweth best, and perhaps the humblest and lowliest in the sight of the world is the one whom He will use to be the H.S. of the C.

Again, I would venture to direct the attention of my readers to the "chop" of the Chinese Society of Heaven and Earth. Does not its shape and the arrangement of the characters on it bear a striking resemblance to our Mark jewel?

This "chop," like our own Mark, is of the greatest practical use, but it has its peculiar symbolic meaning. Our jewel has disguised its pentagon, but in the Chinese "chop" it is shown clearly.

But inside it is the square=matter. Five steps and four make nine. Four right angles make a square, and five steps as if ascending . . .=a pentagon. This square is omitted in our jewel, and our circle of letters is replaced in the "chop" by an octagon. Operative Lodges will note this latter point with interest. The parallelogram—of special significance in the degree of St. Lawrence (another old Operative degree)—is also shown, which is of considerable interest, as the Mark and the St. Lawrence degrees have always been regarded as the most operative of all our present speculative degrees; and several of the duties of a St. Lawrence mason are very similar to those imposed on one member of the Chinese Society of Heaven and Earth to another, particularly those relating to helping him and supplying him with necessities.

I have dealt at special length with the symbolic meaning of certain parts of this degree, as I know many brothers who look for the symbolic meaning of our degrees have been disappointed in the Mark, and not realised where to seek for its inner meaning. Perhaps I ought to make one point clear: This degree deals mainly with man on the physical plane. It teaches the lesson that we should so shape our lives here as to fit ourselves to form a part of the Divine Temple where God Himself dwells. Thus five steps=our five senses, which are represented by the five sides of the pentagon or keystone when not arched. Four steps represent the square or matter, which here means our body. Thus we must discipline our body and five senses, and polish and shape ourselves not so much for our own personal benefit, as that we may be serviceable material for the Supreme Being in the building of His Everlasting Temple. Finally, lest we should forget that we are not only matter, we get the number nine. For five and four make nine, which is three times three, the number which stands for God and man—God in His Trinity in Unity, man who is composed of Body, Soul and Spirit. And since the eternal element in man is God, we obtain a glimpse—faint and fleeting, no doubt, but yet a glimpse—of that great and sublime Truth taught us in the R.A., that the God in man is never entirely separated from the C. of the C., and that God is Matter as well as Spirit, and, therefore, in that mystical sense our body, like all other matter, is also part of God.

Thus we see why the Mark is associated with the F.C. and not with the third degree. From the Operative and practical point of view it was most necessary that a F.C. should be able to mark his work, and take the credit or blame for it, according to whether it was good or bad. But our old Operative brethren, not content merely to work a degree for a practical purpose, symbolised everything they touched, and used the humblest tools to teach the highest spiritual truths. Even their marks which we find carven on the stones they built into their churches are often cabalistic or symbolic. Hundreds of these have been noted and copied down by masonic students, and numbers are thus preserved in the volumes of the *Quatuor Coronati.*

Therefore it is not surprising that this particularly Operative degree should be full of speculative meaning, and from this point of view, also, it is right that it should be associated with the F.C. The F.C. degree teaches us to educate and train our faculties for the service of God and our fellow men, and, above all, to improve our intellects and increase our knowledge. The Mark degree shows us why—so that we may fit ourselves to be utilised as God wills.

I have been careful to avoid disclosing any of our secrets

to those who are not M.M.M., but if what I have written has interested them, although much must be unintelligible to those who have not taken this degree, I would urge them to take an early opportunity to repair their loss. Among a certain section of the Craft there has been a tendency to speak contemptuously of the advanced degrees, and even of the Mark. These brothers, it will usually be found, have *not taken* these degrees, and so are not qualified to speak. I have met many such, and the effect of their attitude led me to believe that all the higher degrees were eighteenth fakes, with little historic or symbolic value. Since I have taken the various higher degrees, I have found in practically every case they were entirely wrong. All the degrees are of interest, and many are certainly very old, far older than most of their members would venture to claim. If you are a keen mason, my reader, do not be content to be guided by those who cannot know. Investigate for yourself, and I think you will not be disappointed.

CHAPTER IX

MASONIC SIGNS AND GRIPS THE WORLD OVER

Brief Summary of their Existence in Asia

Signs and symbols, and grips and tokens, corresponding more or less closely to those used by us are known the world over, and used by men who have never been initiated into any Lodge we should recognise as masonic.

Moreover, these signs have a similar meaning to that which they possess among us. Thus the sign G. and D. is known in Asia, Africa, Central America, and in the Pacific Islands with exactly the same meaning, but it is always the sign as given in Scotland, so far as I can trace, and not that in use in England, nor yet the alternative form used in some parts of the continent.

We will here proceed to consider each continent in turn, and briefly summarise the evidence of this in the case of each, without attempting to be exhaustive.

Considering Asia from this standpoint, we found that it can roughly be divided into three great areas, excluding Asiatic Russia, though, as a considerable part of this contains large numbers of Mohammedans, it naturally follows that among these our signs are also probably known.

These areas are (1) the Mohammedan East; (2) India; (3) China.

(1) The Mohammedan East. This division includes all the former Turkish Empire, Persia and Afghanistan, and its influence penetrates India, and even reaches Malaya and China. The first three countries, however, represent the real heart of the Mohammedan world. The Dervishes have a system which has already been described—as for example, the two I saw proving each other in a back street in Colombo; and from what has been already written, we have seen that Craft, Mark and Arch signs or grips are found throughout the Mohammedan East. Burton, it may be mentioned, states that he was "an Arabian Mason."

(2) India. In this great and populous area, where the ancient

gods are still loved and venerated, we find ample evidence of the antiquity and continued use of our signs.

I have been unable to find our first degree sign, though this by no means proves that it does not exist. The sign of F.C. is pre-eminently associated with the Preserver, and particularly Hanuman, the Monkey God, the faithful attendant of Vishnu in His incarnation as Rama, when as the skilful craftsman Hanuman built the bridge for Rama to cross the Straits in order to conquer Lanka, the old name for Ceylon.

The P.S. of the third degree is associated with Shiva,[1] the prototype of our S.W., who in His capacity of "The Ender of Time" shall close this Lodge when time shall be swallowed up into eternity. Thus we see the association with the Preserver and Destroyer respectively, and this fact possibly explains why I have been unable to find our first degree sign; for if it were associated with Brahma, the fact that His cult has practically disappeared from modern India, and His statues seldom seen, would explain my difficulty in tracing our first degree sign.

With regard to the R.A., the Hindoo use of the triangle, of the double triangle, and of the C. of a C., are strong indications, even if we had not accounts of experiences of R.A.M's., such as that related at length in Chapter II, which is corroborated by similar stories which were common property in India. In addition, it may be well to remind the brethren of the details given in the chapter on the seventh degree of the Brahmins or the Brahmatma, with the mysterious triangle in its chest or ark. But, indeed, the chief purpose of Chapters II to III will have been missed if the brethren have not realised that the real meaning of our whole system, up to the R.A., only becomes intelligible when compared with the teaching of the Hindoos; and as this side of the question was given at great length, it will not be necessary to lay further stress on the matter. Perhaps, however, I should add that the sign of F. is in common use, and that there is a legend that Krishna was slain by "the three wretches" who presided over the three winter months in a way very similar to that related in our own legend.[2]

We can pass over Burma and Malaya and the Dutch East

[1] Also found in Java bas-belief.

[2] Practically all our R.C., R.O.S., and K.T. signs are found among them.

A MALAY DRUM.

Drum used in certain ceremonies in Malaya. Compare little man with illustration on page 106.

(From *Man.*)

Indies, as these have our signs, but appear to derive them from the Mohammedans, Hindoos, or Chinese, as the case may be.

(8) CHINA. This great country has always been famous for the number of its secret societies and the fact that almost every Chinaman belongs to at least one.

The account given in Chapter VII will have shown the brethren that the use of our building tools conveys a symbolic and moral teaching, and is as old as the twelfth century B.C., while certain parts of the ritual of the Society of Heaven and Earth are reminiscent of F.M. With the exception, however, of the sign of F., and another casual sign[1] used in one of our side degrees, I have not been able to prove that the Chinese use our signs with the same meaning that we do, but I suspect this is because I have neither been to China myself, nor met any keen mason who has, and been on the look-out for such evidence. In view of some of the penalties of the Society of Heaven and Earth, it is extremely unlikely that the first degree sign is not employed, to quote but one example. Again, these societies certainly have their secret grips, but their exact nature I have been unable to discover. I would earnestly ask any brother who is living in China and should see this work to endeavour to discover what other signs and grips are in use among the members of the secret societies there, and if he does not wish to write anything on the subject himself, to let me know.

Turning to ancient times, we find, on ancient Assyrian monuments, numerous examples of the S. of F.C., and statues in this characteristic attitude are to be seen in the British Museum. Indeed, it may be well to draw the attention of my readers to the fact that the S. of F.C. is one of the most persistent and widespread of all our signs, and I have traced it in the hieroglyphics of Easter Island in the heart of the Pacific, where it is closely associated with G. and D., and likewise in the ancient manuscripts of the Aztecs and Mayas in Central America. It is, of course, the easiest sign to detect when considering a statue, in this respect unlike the P.S. of a M.M., which can easily be missed by F.M. unless he is particularly on the look-out for it. This latter is also to be found on Assyrian and Babylonian carvings.

In considering such apparent masonic signs, we must bear in

[1] R.C. and R.O.S. signs are also found.

mind that as certain signs are still in common use to denote certain feelings, it is possible to read too much into the position of the arms of a statue. But this danger becomes considerably less when the actual sign is given by a living man, with the obvious intention of conveying a definite meaning.

Thus, taking the S. G. and D., a procession of priestesses might appear to be making this sign, when all that was in the sculptor's mind was to convey the general impression of joy or grief without any reference to a secret cult. Take, on the other side, an example such as that found on a Mexican temple at Uxmal. Here, again, you have a carving made by the ancient Mayas. It is made by a skeleton with a skull for head, and sawn in two, so that only that part of the body which comes above the solar plexus (c) is depicted; lest you should make any error, the sculptor has carefully carved a pair of crossed bones (thigh-bones) near to the skuii.

Such a group of correlating details leads one to consider that this has a definite connection with our sign of G. and D., and our M.M. penalty, even if no other evidence were available.

Thus it will be seen that throughout the East certain signs and tokens are in use among people who are not masons in our sense of the word.

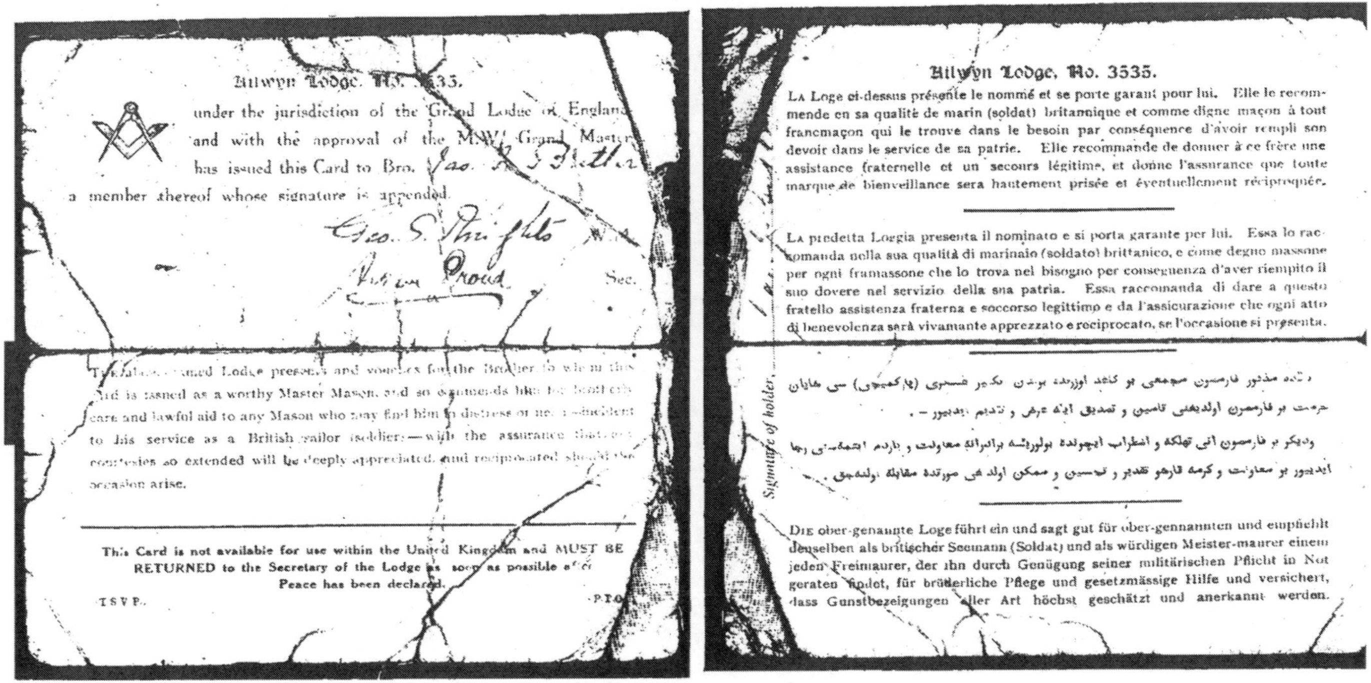

Kilwyn Lodge. No. 3535.

under the jurisdiction of the Grand Lodge of England and with the approval of the M.W. Grand Master has issued this Card to Bro. a member thereof whose signature is appended.

W.M.

Sec.

The above-named Lodge presents and vouches for the Brother to whom this Card is issued as a worthy Master Mason, and so commends him for brotherly care and lawful aid to any Mason who may find him in distress or need incident to his service as a British sailor (soldier)—with the assurance that any courtesies so extended will be deeply appreciated and reciprocated should the occasion arise.

This Card is not available for use within the United Kingdom and MUST BE RETURNED to the Secretary of the Lodge as soon as possible after Peace has been declared.

T.S.V.P. P.T.O.

Kilwyn Lodge, No. 3535.

La Loge ci-dessus présente le nommé et se porte garant pour lui. Elle le recommende en sa qualité de marin (soldat) britannique et comme digne maçon à tout francmaçon qui le trouve dans le besoin par conséquence d'avoir rempli son devoir dans le service de sa patrie. Elle recommande de donner à ce frère une assistance fraternelle et un secours légitime, et donne l'assurance que toute marque de bienveillance sera hautement prisée et éventuellement réciproquée.

La predetta Loggia presenta il nominato e si porta garante per lui. Essa lo raccomanda nella sua qualità di marinaio (soldato) brittanico, e come degno massone per ogni framassone che lo trova nel bisogno per conseguenza d'aver riempito il suo dovere nel servizio della sua patria. Essa raccomanda di dare a questo fratello assistenza fraterna e soccorso legittimo e da l'assicurazione che ogni atto di benevolenza sarà vivamante apprezzato e reciprocato, se l'occasione si presenta.

Signature of holder.

Die ober-genannte Loge führt ein und sagt gut für ober-gennannten und empfiehlt denselben als britischer Seemann (Soldat) und als würdigen Meister-maurer einem jeden Freimaurer, der ihn durch Genügung seiner militärischen Pflicht in Not geraten findet, für brüderliche Pflege und gesetzmässige Hilfe und versichert, dass Gunstbezeigungen aller Art höchst geschätzt und anerkannt werden.

BOTH SIDES OF A CARD GIVEN TO A BRITISH SOLDIER BY HIS LODGE BEFORE GOING TO THE WAR.

Reverse in four different languages, French, Italian, Turkish, German, as well as English.

CHAPTER X

OUR SIGNS AND GRIPS IN AFRICA

THIS chapter may be conveniently divided into two main divisions, the first being ancient Egypt, the other modern savage Africa.

Egypt has exercised a tremendous fascination on many of the brotherhood. In the eighteenth century a tendency grew up of tracing back all our mysteries to Egypt, and even to-day there are masonic students who are apt to fall under its glamour and see Egyptian influence where it does not exist. As a natural result, others have felt the reaction and rushed rather to the opposite extreme, refusing to admit any connection direct or indirect between the ancient mysteries of Egypt and our own system.

Therefore it comes about that any writer who endeavours to adopt a moderate attitude is in danger of being attacked by both parties. I trust, however, that those who feel so inclined will prefer to take the other course, and instead of attacking me for drawing their attention to points of union between the two systems, will rather express their thankfulness that I have avoided ascribing everything in Freemasonry to Egypt—and, of course, vice versa.

The first point of interest is, naturally, the legend of Osiris, and here it may be as well to emphasise the fact that the differences are quite as important as the points in which the two legends are similar. The legend of Osiris is a solar myth, at any rate in its developed form, and there are other similar myths which show certain points in common. Thus the death of Mithra, of Baldur, and of Adonis, being all legends of the Sun which fades before winter and which dies each night, only to rise again, give all these stories a certain similarity.

The story of Osiris is probably well known to all my readers, but the main points may be summarised as follows :

Set, the God of Darkness, plotted the death of his brother, Osiris, by beguiling Him into entering a large coffer or chest, and as soon as He was in it, fastened it down and flung Him, still in it, into the Nile.

Isis, the wife and sister of Osiris, on learning of the murder, set forth to seek for the body. The chest was carried out to sea as far as Byblos in Syria [1] (which was the town of Adonis), where it lodged against a small tamarisk tree, a plant like the acacia.

The tamarisk at once grew round it, and became a great tree. The king of that country cut it down and used it as a column in his palace, but was unaware that hidden within it was the coffer.

But Isis, led by a vision, came to Byblos and obtained the column from the king, and there exist pictures of her weeping over a broken column, while Horus pours ambrosia over her.

She took the body back to Egypt, but Set found it and tore it to pieces, fourteen or fifteen in all, and scattered these throughout Egypt, fearing that if it remained whole, it might come to life again.

But love triumphed over evil, for Isis again set out on her search, and gradually recovered the pieces and gave the body decent burial. Meanwhile, his son, Horus, attacked and fought Set, and, after a fierce struggle, slew him.

Then he went to raise his father, and after Isis and Nephthys had failed, Anubis [2] in the correct manner raised him with the lion grip. Henceforward, Osiris, having triumphed over the grave, reigns as King of the so-called dead, bearing the Ank cross as his sceptre, and, as Judge of the dead, he is seated on the square.

This use of the square as the emblem of the upright judge is one of the clearest pieces of evidence we possess, yet I have heard brothers laugh at Churchward's references to it. Yet the square in the throne is unmistakable. It is not only Osiris, but all the gods who judge the dead whom we find so depicted. Take, for example, the scene from the papyrus of Ani in the British Museum, where Ani and his wife are entering the hall of Judgment. Here the twelve judges are all seated on thrones

[1] Budge contends, however, that this Byblos was in the Delta of the Nile.

[2] A son of Osiris and Isis.

KRISHNA STEPPING ON THE SERPENT OF EVIL.

Krishna, the eighth incarnation of Vishnu, stepping on the Serpent of Evil. Durga or Kali the Destroyer is also depicted doing the same on the demon Mahishaswa.

This demon was the arch-enemy of the gods, and had driven them even out of heaven, and they were only saved by Durga. One Hindoo explanation is that Mahishaswa typifies *Ignorance*.

on which the square is carefully picked out in a distinct colour, which differs from the remainder of the throne. Or again, look in the same papyrus and you will find Osiris and Maat, when acting as judges, are placed on squares. The God, Nefer-Hetep, a type of Horus I, is also seated on the square, but it would be tedious to continue piling up examples. On the other side, Ptah-Seker-Ausan is shown in a reproduction in Dr. Wallis Budge's book, *The Gods of the Egyptians*, seated on a throne which is *not* a square, since He is not acting as a judge. Moreover, I would like to point out that Newton in *The Builders* also accepts the fact as proved.

Before proceeding further, it may be well to add a few more names of similar solar myths. In India, we find Krishna, who corresponds to Osiris, and was an incarnation of Vishnu the Preserver (who correlates, be it remembered, with the body), was slain by the rulers of the three winter months. Vishnu himself was slain by the other Gods and restored to life.

Among the Greeks, the legend of the death of Dionysos was the central theme of the Mysteries of Eleusis. The Druids had a similar story,[1] and so had the Cabiri, who, on the island of Samothrace, told in their Mysteries how Atys, the Sun, was slain by his brothers, the Seasons, and restored to life at the Vernal Equinox. In the *Æneid*, by Virgil, the hero accidentally plucks up a shrub which is beside him as he rests on the side of a hill, and discovers the body of the murdered Polydorus.

Churchward, in his *Arcana of Freemasonry*, declares that several of the incidents and phrases known to us can be explained by reference to *The Book of the Dead*, including the following:

	Chapter.
The Desire for Light	VIII
The First Penal Sign	XC
Heart Torn out by Fingers	XXVII & XXVIII
Body Burnt to Ashes	LXXXVI
The Giving of Bread to the Hungry	CXXV
Left Foot First	The Papyrus of Nesu-Amsu

Let us slightly expand the last reference. We learn that Horus,

[1] In a Druidical temple at Iona is a contemporary sculptured slab showing two figures greeting each other in a significant manner and with the lion grip.

in his fight with Apepi, the great Serpent of Evil, first placed his left foot on the serpent before slaying it. Thus we are taught to start by trampling underfoot the evil forces in the world, and particularly those in our own nature. In India Krishna does the same (see illustration facing p. 98).

It should also be noted that the Egyptians would admit only "freemen" to their mysteries, and in consequence slaves were specifically barred.

The first P.S. was not the only masonic sign in use among the Egyptians. Thus the H.S. of a F.C. is shown both in statues and papyrus. The Leyden Papyrus of Nu shows S. of F.C. being used.

The lion grip was used to raise Osiris, and in chapter lxiv of *The Book of the Dead* there is a rubric which will prove of interest to R.A.M's., which Churchward translates as follows:

"This scroll of papyri was found in the city of Khemennu upon a block of iron of the south, which had been inlaid with letters of real lapis lazuli under the foot of the God during the reign of His Majesty the King of the North and South, Men-Kau-Ra triumphant, by the Royal Son, Heru-Ra-Ta-f triumphant. He found it when he was journeying about to make an inspection of the temples." He who recited this chapter had to be arrayed in white and hold a sceptre in his hand, and the chapter begins with the words "I am Yesterday, To-day, and To-morrow" (The *alpha* and *omega*, etc.).

In chapters xvii and xviii of the ritual are many incidents and phrases strongly reminiscent of our own eighteenth degree. Here the candidate or soul passing through Amenti had a veil of darkness over his head, and had to pass through difficulties, darkness and danger, till he was presented to the Circle of Princes, when the veil was removed by Thoth (R), and he was given a place in the Circle of Princes. Before being received into the Circle of Princes and partaking of food with them, the "soul" has to pass through the Valley of the Shadow of Death, and to ascend seven steps.

Plutarch tells us that the Egyptian priests had a ceremony in which they walked seven times round a circle seeking Osiris and burning incense, but they did not find Osiris, but Horus, the son, instead.

The two pillars which occur in *The Book of the Dead* are called Tat and Tattu, and the separate significations were "In strength"

ANUBIS MINISTERING TO OSIRIS ON HIS BIER.

100]

At the head kneels Nephthys and at the feet Isis.

and "To establish," and their conjoint meaning, "To establish firmly."

Newton in *The Builders* relates the following interesting discovery:

The "Cleopatra's Needle" given by the Khedive Ishmail to the United States in 1872, and now in Central Park, New York, had a number of masonic emblems and implements buried in its foundations at Alexandria. These were discovered when it was taken down in 1879 to be brought to America.

The emblems included (1) a rough Ashlar cube; (2) a polished and perfect Ashlar cube (both in pure white limestone); (3) the square cut in syenite; (4) an iron trowel; (5) a lead plummet; (6) the arc of a circle; (7) the serpent symbols of wisdom; (8) a stone bearing the master's mark; (9) a stone trestle board; (10) a hieroglyphic, meaning "temple." These symbols were so arranged as to show that they had a symbolic meaning, and were seen by the Grand Lodge of New York, and pronounced to be unmistakably masonic and similar in shape to those in present use in the masonic Lodges in the U.S.A.

This obelisk was originally one of a pair set up in front of the temple of the Sun God at Heliopolis, probably in 1500 B.C. It was removed to Alexandria and re-erected there in 22 B.C. by a Roman architect named Pontius. Whether the emblems found in 1879 were originally in the foundation at Heliopolis, and were replaced in their old position when it was re-erected by Pontius, or were placed there for the first time, we know not; but they cannot be later than 22 B.C. at least, and show that at that date these masonic emblems were used in Egypt to convey a symbolic meaning.

Horus Bentutet was the first artificer in metals, and his name was a p.w. in the Egyptian system, but without going further we may certainly admit (1) that the Egyptians had a complete system of symbolic teaching, which was divided into degrees, and which taught the nature of the One Incomprehensible Deity behind the forms of the gods, and of life beyond the grave; and (2) that many parts of their ritual and their signs and symbols were similar to those still in use among us. We may even go so far as to admit that their ritual does explain some of the difficult passages in our own.

The Egyptian system seems to have consisted of two series of mysteries—the Greater and the Lesser. The former had ten degrees, and taught the mystery of the cross and the vesica piscis, or life beyond the grave; while the lesser had seven degrees, and dealt with the nature of the Deity. These divisions are only approximate, and indicate roughly the nature of the teaching of each series, for naturally both sets of teaching are traceable in each, as they are to-day in our own Craft and higher degrees. The greater mysteries had, moreover, a deeper mystical teaching than had the lesser, and only those who had proved themselves to be worthy of the honour were admitted into them. We have ample evidence that these systems existed from the writings of the ancients, among whom must be mentioned Plutarch and Apuleius, who were both initiates. Their oath of silence forbade them to tell us much that we would like to know, but they are nevertheless our best authorities. The greatest witness to the ancient Egyptian mysteries is, however, *The Book of the Dead*, which appears to serve a twofold purpose: (1) an account of what befalls the soul after death, and (2) as a ritual of the mysteries themselves for use by the priests and the initiates in the secret ceremonies held in the temple, which must be distinguished from the ordinary festivals and temple services open to the uninitiated and popular world. Even to the initiate only the exoteric meaning was explained at first, the esoteric meaning being given only to those who proved themselves worthy. One of the best indications that an initiate was deserving of further light was if he himself, by meditation, discovered the inner meaning, at least in part, of the ceremony through which he had passed. This rule still holds good to-day in modern Freemasonry. The exoteric meaning is the only one given. Indeed, often much of this is omitted, the more the pity. We are so busy "making masons" that we seldom have time to teach our newly made brethren what masonry means. Even the lectures are hardly ever given, and these contain a mine of exoteric information, particularly the legends. The tracing boards are a summary of these three lectures, which are divided into fifteen sections, and are supposed to be given in open Lodge in the form of a dialogue between Master and S.W. The questions asked of the candidate in passing and raising are tests of his knowledge of these lectures, and are really an oral examination on them; while the question, put by the W.M. after he has answered, which is now meaningless, had a real significance when the candidate and brethren had been present at one of these lectures. Our present system of " cramming " a candidate with question and answer, which he learns like a parrot, has reduced what was once a real test to an empty form. The pity of it. Yet men were never more hungry for real knowledge of the meaning of our system than they are to-day; but, if we desire to discover the esoteric teaching of our wonderful ritual, we must begin by knowing its exoteric meaning.

Lodges of research are all very well; they gratify the wishes of the masonic student, but they do not touch the bulk of the rank and file, who are apt to become weary of seeing the same ceremonies repeated year after year with no indication of their real meaning. Why cannot the good old custom be revived, and once or twice a year, at least, the ancient lectures gone through? If this were done, I firmly believe many who now drop out of active masonry would remain in it, and become keen students of the meaning of our symbolism.

Nevertheless, brethren must not expect that it would be possible, under the most perfect circumstances, to teach in every case the esoteric meaning of our system. Hints and suggestions can be given by the careful student to the beginner, but much of what is most valuable cannot be fully explained verbally. We must discover them ourselves, for there exists no language into which to put them. That is why our ancient brethren used symbols instead of words. Some of our teaching as to the nature of the Deity is beyond words, and there are other parts of our system of which this is equally true. Moreover, there is a danger which must be guarded against with the utmost care. The instant a man begins to explain these mysteries, there is a risk of his beginning to dogmatise. Being human and finite, we are all fallible, particularly when we endeavour to explain the Infinite. Our truths are at best but partly true, and what appears to be the true meaning of a particular point, may not appear to be correct to another brother. After all, he may be right, and even if we think he is not, who are we to tell him he is wrong? We cannot *know* that we are absolutely right; we can only believe we are. Therefore, those who would teach others must ever strive to keep humble, and say rather, " It seems to me that this is so and so," rather than declare dogmatically that it is so.

Yet, being only human, this is a difficult task, particularly if a dogmatic and ignorant man, who obviously has not studied the matter at all, gets up and flatly contradicts some cherished belief of ours. This may lead to a breach of that brotherly love which should at all times distinguish Freemasons. Therefore, I would ask my readers to forgive me if at any time I appear too dogmatic, and remember that I only say that these things appear to me to be so, and not that they are. For here we see as through a glass darkly, yet I believe that through Freemasonry we shall see more clearly than through other glasses, and so perhaps hasten a little that time which even for the best of us is far distant, when we shall see face to face.

These same reasons for reticence were even stronger in ancient days in Egypt, when a far larger proportion of the population was ignorant and illiterate. Even in India to-day, we find that despite the efforts of the British Government the people are still mainly uneducated, and totally unready for the highest wisdom of the esoteric teaching of the Brahmins. Indeed, it is an open question whether our efforts to hasten their education have not gone too far, and endangered their religious outlook and social system before they were "prepared" for a higher conception.

But I must avoid allowing myself to fall a victim to the lure of ancient Egypt, and I shall therefore close this section by pointing out that the seven lesser mysteries of Egypt correspond with our Craft, Mark, Arch and similar lower degrees, while the ten greater are prototypes of the so-called higher degrees, particularly those worked under the jurisdiction of the Supreme Council thirty-third degree.

For the most part prototypes, if not the actual original forms, of most of our Craft degrees will be found all over the world, whereas the principal areas in which prototypes of the degrees of the cross are to be found are Egypt and ancient America.

Some, perhaps, might explain this as due to the fact that the lower degrees are older than those of the cross, and originally stellar, whereas the cross, at any rate in its present form, is a solar symbol, and its mysteries were worked out by solar folk.[1] I am inclined to think that the cross was quite as much stellar

[1] It has, however, a stellar significance, e.g. the constellation of Cygnus and also the Southern Cross.

as the Craft degrees, and its survival in America and Egypt is due to the fact that no hostility against the Christian ideas of the cross ever arose there, whereas in some other districts, notably the Moslem East, the cross, being regarded as a Christian sign, was, so far as possible, eliminated.

Nevertheless, there are traces of the cross in pagan countries to this day, outside America. Thus the Bantu, before their conversion to Christianity, used the cross in their worship of the spirits. The Australian blacks also possessed it, including the double and treble cross, which may interest members of the Malta degree, also those fortunate ones who have been honoured with the thirty-third degree.

In Central Africa, copper ingots from time immemorial have been made in the form of a cross, but despite these facts, it does seem to be true that the degrees of the cross have only been worked out fully among the American Indians and by the ancient Egyptians. As the cross and vesica piscis will be considered fully at a later point in this work, we will close this summary of Egypt with noting that Bes, one of the earliest and most primitive Egyptian gods, wears the *Templar* cross suspended round his neck (see Dr. Wallis Budge, *The Gods of the Egyptians*, published by Methuen & Co.).

Savage Africa

In modern Africa, among the more primitive tribes there still exist elaborate initiatory rites and curious, often sinister, secret societies.

Among the Nilotic negroes the sign of an E.A. is in common use. Indeed, when one of these tribes has to take an oath, he does it in that manner, and it is the only form of oath he considers binding. Burton, in his travels in Abyssinia, declares he came across a secret society there, whose oaths were more terrible, and where secrets were more closely guarded, than those of the Freemason. He appears to have failed to obtain any details about this society, which may have been, of course, merely one of the Dervish societies whose ritual would be similar to that described in Chapter I; but it may be a descendant via the Copts of some of the ancient Egyptian mysteries, and it is sincerely to be hoped that some brother who goes out there will make it his chief endeavour to discover more about them. Times have changed, even in Abyssinia, since Burton's day, and better luck is probably awaiting the next investigator than that which he had.

The Pigmies have been shown by Churchward to represent the Great Spirit by this sign  which he believes developed into the axe, which is similar to the hammer, and was the sign of the chief or ruler.

It is still used in the same sense to indicate the three rulers in the Lodge. In Portuguese East Africa the lion grip and the eagle's claw are in use among the natives. Nor must mention be omitted of the fact that the usual form of greeting between two modern Egyptians is masonic and includes the lion grip, as has been testified to me by several soldier masons who have been in Egypt during the war. This fact may be explainable as due to the circumstances of their being members of one of the Dervish orders, but more probably it is derived from an indigenous source, and goes back to primitive times, while all the Senussi have a similar system to the Dervishes.

All over the Mohammedan North, as is to be expected, the bulk of our signs are known and recognised by the Bedouins, being no doubt familiar to them from their own Dervish rites; but a different explanation is needed to account for the facts which have been noticed on the west coast of Africa among the pagan and savage tribes.

The S. of G. and D. seems to be common to all the secret societies of the west coast. These societies are very numerous, and range from what appear to be small benefit societies of a perfectly harmless nature up to the Leopard Society and similar sinister and dangerous bodies, some at least of which are inter-tribal in character, and a few nothing more than murder societies, who before the British occupation terrorised the whole area.

Even these bodies had, however, a beneficial side, for we learn that so powerful were they, that if they ordered two tribes who were at war to cease fighting—a right often exercised—their order was obeyed. If it was not, the recalcitrant chief was promptly killed. These societies had (and probably still have) their initiatory rites, their grips, signs and tokens; and among the objects which they regarded as sacred was the triangle.

The Hausas still use the lion grip and the sign of F., each

CIRCUMCISION RITES IN EAST AFRICA.

Boy making the sign that he is ready for the ceremony to begin. During the operation, which is a most painful one, his arms are held in this position by his "guide" (S.D.) lest they should fall to his side.
The second picture is after the sacrifice has been made.

(By kind permission of *Man*.)

repeated three times when greeting an old friend; and it is probable that close investigation would reveal the fact that they had also other signs familiar to us (see note at end of chapter).

These facts may explain to the brethren the following story, which appeared in several papers a few years before the war, and was even deemed worthy of being placed on permanent record in the *Ars. Quat. Cor.*

It runs somewhat as follows:

Two men, both of them masons, were wrecked on the coast of Africa opposite Madagascar. Neither knew the other was a mason, and soon after they landed, they got separated. In his distress one decided to try what an appropriate Scotch sign would do for him among the natives, hardly expecting any success. To his surprise it was recognised, and the obligation acknowledged. They took him up and looked after him, and passed him from tribe to tribe till he reached the Arab slave raiders of Northern Africa. These also recognised the obligation, and passed him safely across the Sahara Desert until they landed him safely in Algiers. Here a French Lodge took him up and passed him on to Marseilles, whence other French masons passed him to Calais, and so across to England.

When he was wrecked he had a few shillings in his pocket, and he had the same sum when he landed in England. His long journey had cost him not one penny, and had been made in an absurdly short time.

Two years later, his companion in misfortune also arrived home, penniless and in rags, and broken in health by the privations he had undergone.

In view of the facts I have already given, the explanation of the marvel is fairly clear. If the blacks of Portuguese East Africa have some of our signs, and we know they have, it is unlikely they would not have the sign used by the sailor.[1] We know the Mohammedan tribes have it, and so the link is complete which connects the savages of the east coast of Africa with the French Freemasons in Algiers.

The following story was told me by a venerable brother I met at a Lodge in Leeds. He even gave me the name of the explorer, but I have omitted it purposely.

[1] In British East Africa they certainly use it, and also a sign used in the — degree.

This explorer was exploring Central Africa, and for certain reasons was asked to allow himself to be made a member of one of the tribes; he therefore submitted to being initiated. At the close of the ceremony, a curious apron made of leaves was placed upon him. Years after, he was initiated into Freemasonry in England, and afterwards told the brethren present how he had been through almost exactly the same ceremony in the heart of Central Africa, even including being invested with an apron, although, as he added, it was certainly made of more perishable material than that with which he had that night been honoured.

Among some of the tribes in South Africa, curious initiatory rites are also in vogue which are strongly reminiscent of our own ceremonies. The candidates are blindfolded, and certain signs and grips are among the secrets communicated. No women are ever admitted to these rites, and this is the universal rule; but many savages have rites for the women also, and just as it is death for a woman to approach a man's Lodge, so it is death for a man to attempt to spy on the women at these times.

The bulk of these rites among the primitive races are for the initiation of a boy into manhood. In the opening ceremonies they tell him whence he came and how he was born. In the next series they teach him how to be a useful member of his tribe, and instruct him in the tribal customs, how to become a good hunter and fighter, and so forth, and finally they tell him how to die, and that death does not end all. It seems probable that the women's rites are on similar lines, but never having met any women who have investigated them, and men, white or black, being absolutely debarred, it naturally follows that I can give no details. It is known, however, that a certain operation somewhat similar to circumcision is generally included; but of the more mystic side, if it exists, nothing is known.

Before closing this section, it is advisable to emphasise the urgent necessity of directing the attention of masonic students to these primitive rites. With the rapid spread of civilisation, and the growing success of the Christian and Moslem missionaries, the natives, year by year, are abandoning their old customs, and soon they will have utterly perished. For the most part, the investigators have not been masons, and would miss these very things we desire to know. What are their secret signs: what do their passwords *mean*: do they have any ritual steps? These are the sort of things which the ordinary anthropologist ignores. He tells us that they knock out a tooth, or they circumcise the boy. He describes the tattoo marks very often. All these things are permanent and outward signs which cannot be kept hidden, but of what the boy is told we know little, of their signs and grips we know still less; and it is only a Freemason who could recognise their great significance. Nevertheless, the facts I have succeeded in gleaning are sufficient to show that in this field there is still the prospect of interesting discoveries.

We must not expect to find an exact replica of our system. Two thousand years of Christianity and Bible teaching have naturally left their mark on every page of our ritual; but it is just in such things as signs that alteration is least likely, and these are the very things of which we find evidence.

These rites cannot be more than prototypes, but if they are, then we have made a most important addition to our masonic knowledge, and the full significance of this will be shown later.

Incidentally, we obtain a definite answer to the question: Why cannot women be admitted in Freemasonry? It is, "our rites being descended from the ancient initiatory rites of a boy into manhood, you never were and never can be admitted. You had your initiatory rites once, your primitive sisters still have them. Go to them, and on the basis of them build up your own system; but do not endeavour to mix the two, which were never intended for both indiscriminately."

Note.—In a photograph in *Travels in West Africa*, by M. H. Kingsley, a number of Bantu natives are shown seated in a circle, and all are making the first S. of an E.A. The ceremony is described as making a magic charm.

CHAPTER XI

AMERICA AND AUSTRALASIA

Both among the ancient and modern Red Indians there is abundant evidence of our signs and symbols. As has already been stated, many of these relate to the higher degrees. On some of the old Maya manuscripts are what are undoubtedly scenes from the prototypes of our higher cross degree and also what appear to be of a higher degree, probably the thirtieth. As, however, I am not yet a member of that degree, and have always made it a rule not to pry into any degree I have not yet taken, I cannot say for certain; but unquestionably the scenes depict a degree subsequent to the eighteenth, and show, among other things, a lariat round the neck of the candidate, he is being taught to make a certain sign and other peculiarities which, coupled with the facts to which I shall allude when we consider the eighteenth degree, leave little doubt in my mind that we have here a sequel to what we now call the Rose Croix. The sign would be quickly recognised by a member of the R.O.S.

On the famous Fenton vase from Guatemala, which is one of the finest relics of the Mayas, there is a scene which is reminiscent of a certain episode in the ninth degree; but it is of the craft degrees that I propose to speak here.

In *Mexican Antiquities*, published by the Bureau of American Ethnology, among the undoubted signs shown are numerous representatives of the H.S. of F.C. The sign of F. is also shown, the drinking sign of a well-known higher degree is also much in evidence, L.S.R.H., R.S.L.H., together with numerous examples of signs known to members of these degrees.

At Uxmal, Mexico, over the portal of an ancient temple is carved the upper half of a skeleton making a significant sign, and, so that there shall be no possibility of mistake, two crossbones are carved above the skull. Among numerous examples

PRE-SPANISH CONQUEST RELICS.

Pictograph on a boulder from West Indies, and also stone charm. Compare with pictures facing pages 106, 114. Note exaggerated navel and position of legs.

(From *Bulletin of Smithsonian Institute, U.S.A.*)

MEXICAN PRESERVER.

Compare this with the skeleton on the vesica piscis. He died, was buried, rose again, and ascended into heaven, where he reigns in that bright morning star (Venus) whose coming heralds the dawn. Note skull and cross under his feet.

THE MEXICAN PRESERVER WITH CORN IN HIS HAIR NEAR TO A STREAM OF WATER.

He was preserved despite the wound in his foot.

(From *Bulletin of Smithsonian Institute, U.S.A.*)

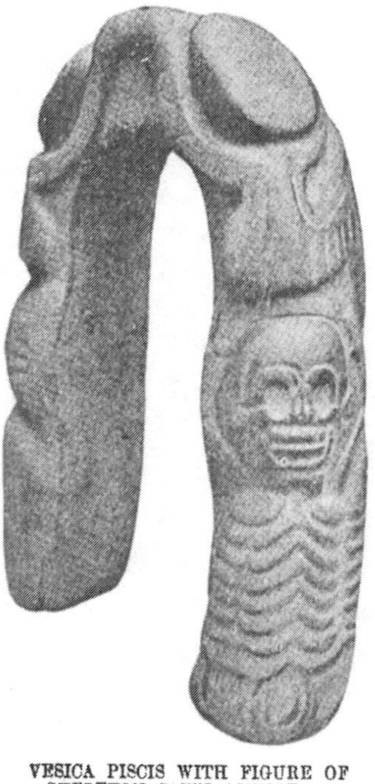

VESICA PISCIS WITH FIGURE OF SKELETON SAWN ASUNDER.

Death is but the beginning of a new life.

MEXICAN PRESERVER, SHOWING WATER AND BLOOD.

(From *Bulletin of Smithsonian Institute, U.S.A.*)

of Maya and also of Inca pottery a number of figures have been discovered wearing what appear to be masonic aprons, and the illustration opposite page 238 is very significant.

Even to-day the Indian population in Central America, untouched by modern Freemasonry, have many signs and actions which remind us of the Lodge. Thus a well-known London Freemason, known by repute at least to almost every masonic student, told me himself that he had been greeted on the major grip by an Indian while out in Central America. I asked him at once if he were sure the man had not been initiated into one of the Spanish Lodges, and his reply was: "I am sure he had not; if he had he would not have done it, as it was before strangers."

The same form of greeting was also used by the North American Indians, who have likewise the s. of F.C. Among certain tribes of the Crow Indians they have all our eighteenth-degree signs, correctly done. Similar signs are shown in certain Egyptian papyri (see Churchward).

As the higher degrees will be considered more fully later, America need not detain us long, but enough has been said to show that our craft signs were used in ancient Mexico. The R.A. ✡ is also found there. It is surrounded by a double circle divided into twelve segments corresponding with the twelve signs of the Zodiac, or the twelve banners of the children of Israel; within the double triangle is another circle.

The triangle, the tau cross, the □, and the pentacle are also found, the last two being used as jewels suspended round the neck of various principal officers, depicted taking part in certain mystic rites. An ear of corn near a fall of water is shown on a Mexican MS., and is named Anauaacatl, and was the symbol of the Preserver, who in the illustration opposite has maize ears in his hair and is wounded near to a stream of water.

Australia

In Australia we find men still existing in the most primitive state. Much has been written about the Australian aborigines, and it is not necessary to repeat it here; it is sufficient to say that they had barely reached the neolithic state of culture, and indeed the inhabitants of Tasmania, now extinct, seem to have been palæolithic. Many of their rites appear to throw light on the more advanced eschatology of the Egyptians; but, ignoring these, we will concentrate on certain points which are of interest to us as Freemasons.

They have a whole series of rites of initiation of a boy into manhood. These take years to work through, and indeed by the time the last is taken the boy has become an old man.

Many of the rites are distinctly painful, including not only circumcision but apparently also subincision; a tooth is knocked out, designs are cut on the body, and other severe tests imposed. The candidate is blindfolded at certain times; his nerves are tested by the weird shrieking of the bull-roarer; he has to fast, to remain in solitary confinement, and in general is led to understand that the information he seeks can only be obtained after trials long and bitter. As with American tribes, he is taught in the first degree whence he came and is "made a man"; in the next stage he learns the history of his tribe, its customs and certain rules of life; he is taught how to become a useful member of society, and the ceremony is associated with two pillars, called Nurtunga (North Pole Star) and Warringa (South Pole Star). The position is therefore the same, but there is no temple behind them, so that their significance is apt to be overlooked.

Parts of their third degree have been photographed and are shown in numerous anthropological papers; but the average F.M. may be excused for not recognising it owing to certain differences; it is mixed up with a certain higher degree.

It is called the Bora, and is a very striking degree even in its somewhat primitive form.

Among the incidents depicted and often photographed by non-masonic anthropologists, is one in which a human figure made out of sand stretched out in the form of a St. Andrew's Cross is seen. On either side stand a row of black men forming an arch, not of steel but of wooden boomerangs. The conductor of the candidate leads the latter through this arch, and the men demand from him a word. He has to pass through dangers and difficulties before he reaches the end of his journey through the valley of the shadow of death.

It is a very severe test of a candidate's fortitude, but there is no going back once the candidate has entered the Lodge. To disclose the secrets of any of these degrees is certain death

PICTOGRAPHIC WRITING FROM EASTER ISLAND.
Figures include those of men, which note. Each line is reversed
(From *Anthropological Journal*.)

to an initiate, and a like fate awaits any woman discovered by the O.G. endeavouring to act the part of a cowan.

But here the influence of the white man is undermining the sanctity of the old customs, and soon they will have passed into the limbo of forgotten things. The more need for a careful and immediate investigation.

I have only been able to identify one distinctly masonic sign, and that is one belonging to the R.A. It is used when returning from the Intichiuma ceremony, which is apparently their highest degree; it is correctly made.

Among their sacred objects is a pyramidical stone, the cross, and the swastika.

Although I have been unable so far to find any of our craft signs among the Australian blacks, in the lonely Easter Island in the far Pacific, evidence exists for at least two of them.

This island has always been a mystery to the modern world, with its strange monolithic statues and terraces.

The original inhabitants appear to have advanced a considerable distance along the road towards civilisation, for they seem to have evolved a rough kind of hieroglyphic writing. An example of this exists in England, and is now in the possession of the British Museum, and a photograph of it appears in pp. 1-3, vol. iv, 1904, of *Man*, published by the Anthropological Institute.

The glyphs consist of pictures of men, animals, etc., and are carved on a piece of wood; the writing has the peculiarity that each alternate line is written upside down, or, in other words, the piece of wood must be reversed after reading each line (see opposite).

Among these glyphs are to be seen human figures making signs. These occur several times. My readers should also study the illustrations of objects from New Guinea opposite p. 114.

Reference has already been made to the Churinga, which has a somewhat similar significance among the Australian blacks to that which the mark has with us, and many of their rites have a distinct resemblance to the ancient Egyptian ceremonies, such, for example, as their ceremony of the hunting and slaying of the great snake.

Before leaving these primitive races it is advisable to point out that I have not attempted to be too exhaustive; my purpose has been mainly to show how certain masonic signs and ceremonies

8

are known and practised the world over among men who know not Masonry as we know it. I have shown some of them in every continent outside Europe. Has this no significance?

Modern Europe, of course, lies outside our province, since the use of our signs among men who are not Masons might merely indicate that they had been copied either intentionally or otherwise. For this reason it is only necessary to mention, in passing, that one of our P.SS. is regularly used in the British Army, and even good Masons failed to recognise it, so accustomed were they to its use, until I pointed it out to them; then, of course, they "could not think why they had not recognised it before." The origin, no doubt, can be traced to the Military Lodges of the eighteenth century.

But in ancient and mediæval Europe there are also traces of our signs and symbols which are deserving of special mention, and these will be considered in the next chapter.

CHAPTER XII

ANCIENT EUROPE

MODERN, and even mediæval Europe is of course in a different category from the other continents. No one denies that Freemasonry has existed in Europe in our modern sense for several centuries, and developed out of the mediæval Guilds. Students may disagree as to how far back our present ritual goes beyond the seventeenth century, but the use of our signs and symbols in the mediæval ages will hardly cause much surprise to the brethren, whereas their use in ancient Mexico is no doubt a revelation to many.

Nevertheless, certain facts about ancient Rome may well be included here. Among the ruins of ancient Pompeii is a building almost perfect, known locally as "The Masonic Temple" (see illustration facing p. 118). It has received this name because of the discovery therein of a peculiar mosaic table which can best be described as a tracing-board. It is made of marble and inlaid with the following symbols. On a ground of grey-green stone is a human skull inlaid in grey, black, and white; above it is a level in coloured wood, the points, however, being made of brass. From the top is suspended a plumb-line; beneath the skull is a six-spoked wheel, on the upper rim of which is a butterfly with red wings edged with yellow, while its eyes are blue. On the left there is an upright spear, from which hang a scarlet and also a purple robe. The upper part of the spear is surrounded by a white braid of diamond pattern.

On the right there is a thorn-stick from which hangs a coarse piece of cloth in grey, brown, and yellow, tied with cord and over it a leather knapsack.

This unique survival is now in the National Museum at Naples, and is fully described by S. R. Forkes in his *Rambles in Naples.*

It is not the author's purpose here to discuss the Roman Collegia further at this point; that will come later. He wishes merely to point to this striking evidence that some at least of our symbols had a peculiar "masonic" significance in ancient Rome.

The level, square and compasses, the cube, the plummet and circle, are all found carved on the sarcophagi of Roman Masons, and if we revert to the "Masonic Temple" at Pompeii, we find that it had two columns at the entrance, while on its walls are depicted interlocking triangles.

The constitution and officers of the Roman Colleges of Architects closely resemble our own lodges; but of that more anon. Sufficient details have already been given about the Order of Mithra, but it may be well to emphasise the fact that the "grip" of Mithra which served to distinguish a soldier of Mithra by night as well as by day was the lion grip, and other "masonic" signs and tokens would have been known to the initiates of that religion. In *Puck of Pook's Hill* Kipling has given us a most fascinating story dealing with this theme, which should be read by every brother. (See fresco opposite.)

About the signs and symbols used by the Druids little is known which will enable us to trace a close similarity between them and Freemasonry. It is quite possible that they did use similar signs in their initiatory rites to those in use among the primitive races; but, except for what is written on p. 99, as no manuscripts survive, we are left in the dark.

We do know that they venerated the triangle, the swastika, and the three rays of light depicted thus \|/, which latter is reminiscent of certain caste marks in India, but this does not take us very far. Fascinating as the theory may be, the evidence is too slender to establish, even tentatively, any direct connection between the ancient Druids and Freemasonry. There are other lines of descent which seem much more probable.

When we come to mediæval times in Europe we naturally find traces of our signs, particularly the S. of P.; but two early examples must suffice for the present.

I am informed by Wor. Bro. T. Argles, Deputy Provincial Grand Master of Cumberland and Westmorland and Past Grand Deacon of England, that in the porch of Peterborough Cathedral there is a carved group of the Trinity, and the "Son" is making the sign of P.

FRESCO FROM POMPEII.

Fresco from the house of the "Tragic Poet," Pompeii. It depicts the preservation of Œdipus. This was probably painted by members of the Roman College of Architects.

(From *Womankind in Western Europe*, by T. Wright.)

Now what does P. represent? Is it a prayer, perseverance, or preservation? It might be any of these, but let us delve deeper. In the East the god Hanuman is always associated with Vishnu the preserver; he, the faithful craftsman who built the bridge for Rama (who is an incarnation of Vishnu) is nearly always depicted in one position. Hanuman it was who preserved the life of the heroes of Rama's army by hastening to the Himalayas and by bringing back the sacred fruit that restored them to health and enabled them to continue the fight against Ravena, the king of the evil powers. He, in this instance, preserved them. The same idea is shown on the fresco at Pompeii.

Consider also this further example also related to me by Wor. Bro. T. Argles.

At Ravello Cathedral, near Sorrento in Italy, there is an old twelfth-century mosaic showing Jonah coming up alive out of the whale's mouth: the body is naked, and you can see it only from the waist upwards, and he too is making the same sign.

Now if ever a man was preserved it was Jonah; but, more than this, ecclesiastics have always regarded him as a prototype of Jesus Christ, for, just as Jonah came up alive after three days in the "whale's belly," so Christ after three days rose from the tomb. Here, then, we see the principle underlying the sculpture of the "Son" at Peterborough, Jonah at Ravello in Italy, and Hanuman in India.

For Jesus, the Second Person of the Trinity, is the Christian conception of the Preserver whom the Hindoos call Vishnu; but in his eighth incarnation they call him Chrishtna, Chrishna, or Krishna, of whose miraculous birth and tragic death, murdered by the three wretches, they tell marvellous tales.

In Freemasonry the same sign has an exoteric, an esoteric, and often an inner esoteric meaning besides, so perhaps in these three possible interpretations of the letter P we obtain a glimpse of these three meanings each in its way correct, and if so we can interpret them all by this sentence: by perseverence in prayer we are preserved. That this is not an overdrawn interpretation we shall see if we turn to the story of Jonah. In the Bible we read that Jonah persevered in prayer to the Almighty for the three days he was in the fish's belly, and in answer to his prayer God preserved him and brought him forth alive.

Leaving the meaning of this symbol, it will suffice if we point out that these two examples, which are by no means unique, serve as a link between ancient and modern days. From ancient Egypt to modern London, from India to Easter Island, we find this sign, while this Byzantine ivory of the sixth century A.D. fills in the gap between the Roman Collegia and the Comacine Masons, who must have made the mosaic at Ravello.

Coincidence, some may whisper. I do not think so; that would be a far greater marvel than descent from a common ancestor, and, after all, is the gap so large? No one denies that the word "duke" is a lineal descendant of the Latin *dux*, and, if so, where is the difficulty, supposing that our signs have descended by regular transmission for 2,000 years? And if we admit the 2,000 years we have admitted everything, for, as we know that the Egyptians used this sign and that they were still a living force in the days of Rome, we can go back another 4,000 years; and whence did they derive it if not from the initiatory rites of their savage ancestors? And from similar savage ancestors the ancient people of Easter Island likewise have obtained it.

It is not necessary to postulate Atlantis; there may have been such a continent, with a high state of civilisation, but we could do without it perfectly well if we are prepared to admit, as a hypothesis, that our modern religions have evolved from the primitive religious beliefs of our savage ancestors. And does anyone deny this?

In that case it is not necessary to assume that the Indian derived from Egypt, or the Mayas from the same spot; they may quite easily each have developed from a common savage stock ages before Egypt itself existed as we know it.

THE MASONIC TEMPLE, POMPEII, WHERE THE SO-CALLED "M.M. TRACING BOARD" WAS FOUND.

BYZANTINE WORK OF THE SIXTH CENTURY FROM THE BRITISH MUSEUM GUIDE-BOOK. AN IVORY BOX SHOWING DANIEL IN THE LIONS' DEN.

(By kind permission of the Trustees of the British Museum.)

CHAPTER XIII

THE ORIGIN OF FREEMASONRY

I VENTURE to contend that I have in the last twelve chapters produced sufficient evidence to justify the theory that Freemasonry is descended from something far older than the building guilds of the Middle Ages. My readers may hesitate to accept the evidence I have produced as conclusive, but at least they should, I think, be prepared to accept it as a working hypothesis. Personally I go much further, but my object will be achieved if I can rouse my brothers to adopt this theory and investigate further along these lines.

Boldly this is my contention, that our present system is derived originally from the primitive initiatory rites of our prehistoric ancestors. I base this contention on the fact that many of our most venerated signs and symbols, grips and tokens, are used to-day by savage races with precisely the same meaning as with us. I cannot agree with those who would contend that it is either a matter of coincidence or else that they are purely natural signs which express simple elementary sentiments. I query this explanation in the case of a sign which would be more natural given by wringing one's hands in front, which is not a masonic sign, or burying one's face in the hands. But let that example pass. Will anyone pretend that the F.C. sign is a "natural" one? To me it seems highly artificial. Unless taught to do so, I cannot conceive of anyone unwittingly showing it correctly. Moreover, put aside the position, would it not be more natural to H. with the other hand? I cannot speak more plainly, but surely my critics will see what I mean. Ancient Egypt, ancient Assyria, the gods in India, the carvings of the ancient inhabitants of Easter Island and Mexico and Rome, all bear witness to the fact that we still to-day make this *unnatural* sign correctly.

The Dervishes in Turkey and the ancient people of Central

America equally bear evidence in a like strain. But it is not on one sign that I base my argument. It is sign after sign, P.SS. included, R.A. signs, R.C. signs. Yes, even the P.S. of the R.O. of S., which is shown on a vase from Chama, Central America, and elsewhere. Again and again we meet with them as we travel from continent to continent. Each alone and solitary might fail to convince, but their culminative evidence is overwhelming. If it is not coincidence that the ancient people of Easter Island in the Pacific had signs such as I have mentioned, what explanation other than the one I suggest is correct ?

My critics will perhaps contend that " the one has been copied from the other." Who copied from which ? Did the ancient Egyptians and Assyrians copy it from us ? Did the Easter Islanders do so ? The Easter Island tablet to which I refer was already unintelligible to the few miserable remnants of the native population when white men came among them and Freemasonry was well established, with its present signs in England long before that date. Neither they nor we could in that case have copied from each other. Obviously ancient Egypt did not copy from us. Well, then, did we copy our signs from some ancient Egyptian papyrus ? You can produce no evidence that we did. Masonry had its secret signs in the days of Ashmole, long before any scientific study had been made of Egyptian antiquities; but my persistent critics refuse thus to be answered. They reply, " You cannot prove that the signs of Freemasonry were the same in Ashmole's day (A.D. 1646). For all you can show, some learned brother in the eighteenth century, seized with enthusiasm, may have seen the sign in a papyrus or on a statue and introduced it." In that case, where did the Easter Islanders obtain it ? They did not see any Egyptian papyrus. And what about the ancient (pre-Spanish conquest) people of Central America, and the Dervishes of Turkey, and the traditional art of India or Pompeii ? Why should all these different races be united in using this artificial sign and associate it with the Preserver, or the Son ? That is the point. The same sign with the same exoteric and the same esoteric meaning.

I have devoted considerable space to the signs indicated, but I could as easily have dealt with the others like the P.S., or lion grip. Ancient Egypt and ancient Mexico, savage West Africa, savage East Africa, Moslem Dervish and Byzantine, alike have and use them in the same way and with the same basic idea as we do. Rose Croix in Egypt, in Mexico, in modern London, in India.

I have refrained from laying any stress on certain well-known masonic symbols; the square and compasses, the ✡, the ▽, the ⊙, the ⊤, and a host of others. These are more likely to have been obtained indirectly than the grips and signs, and, if we had to rely on them alone, the case would be weaker. Therefore I have concentrated mainly on the signs. But let us not ignore them, for when coupled with the signs and tokens they add considerably to the strength of the argument. India, which still has complete the ancient traditions, uses them in such a way as to throw light on parts of our own ritual of which many of us had lost the meaning. Take, for example, the inverted triangle, the sign of Vishnu. How comes this associated with the cryptic degrees? Why do we wear it as the jewel of these degrees? Surely the whole of these degrees turn on the subject of Preservation. The over-zealous friend of K. S. who was spared, the way in which the great secret of the R.A. came to be preserved, and the other degrees, carry on the same idea. Who is the outstanding character of the series? Is it not H. A. B., and is not the J.W. the Preserver? And has it ever struck the brethren that the Preserver and the Son are one, and that both these aspects of that Person of the Trinity are shown forth by H.A.B.? Need I write plainer?

For the humble square and compasses we have already traced a most respectable genealogical table. We have found these workmen's tools invested with a symbolic meaning, twelve centuries before Christ, among the Chinese. We have seen that they were buried at the base of the "Cleopatra's Needle" now re-erected in New York and carved on sarcophagi in Roman days, and with them we find associated the double triangle ✡, the ⊙, and many other signs familiar to us either in the craft or the advanced degrees.

All over the world we find traces of the initiatory rites of a boy into manhood, with their tremendous and primitive oaths of secrecy, their exclusion of women, their secret signs and tokens.

But, alas! their days are numbered; even now they are becoming neglected, and, even when still carried out, the ritual is done in a more and more perfunctory way. The old men die off and the young men, spoilt by a Western civilisation which they cannot yet properly assimilate, have learnt sufficient to despise these old rites and not enough to venerate them. They are "heathenish" customs, and so are condemned, and soon the world will know them no more. Already much has been lost, but, before it is too late altogether, I beg my brother Masons throughout the world to investigate and note down and place on permanent record any signs and tokens common to them and to Freemasonry. But perhaps a brother will reply, "And of what use will that be? Supposing I do find one or two of such signs still used by the older men in the Arunta initiatory rites, where can that fact be placed on permanent record?" I admit the difficulty. In vol. iv, pp. 7-19, of *Ars Quatuor Coronatorum*, is a most interesting account by Brother Hackett Smith. In it he tells us that the Druses used certain of our signs and tokens, but a blank is left, not a letter to indicate which, not even F.C. or the like. Those would have been sufficient, but merely a blank is left. Hackett Smith has passed to the Great Lodge above, and no one to-day can remember what the signs were, so the information is lost. No doubt the reason for the blank is a fear lest some non-Mason would be able to recognise the name of the sign, and, having been among the Druses, be able to use the sign when not entitled to do so. But surely this is straining at a gnat. Suppose he does know the meaning of F.C., he is no nearer recognising that sign when used by a Druse as being Masonic. He is just as likely to think that some different and casual sign is that of the F.C., nor would he find it easy to induce a Druse to show him that sign. Yet, to complete the sentence—straining at a gnat and swallowing a camel—we find in another volume of the *Ars Quatuor Coronatorum* pictures of an eighteenth-century Freemasons' Lodge, where not only are signs actually shown, but part of the ritual as well. Even with that much more practical help, I will boldly say no non-Mason could enter any Lodge where the J.W. did his duty properly.

These things are not sufficient. The way in which non-Masons might discover our secrets is when some easy-going brother gets friendly with a man, asks him if he is a Mason, and takes his word for it without properly testing him, then proceeds to bring him to his Lodge as his guest.

Yes, I admit the difficulty that brethren might collect this information and then find no place where it could be placed on permanent record, and this is one of the reasons why I advocate the formation of a Lodge of Anthropological Research, despite the fact that other Lodges of Research do exist. There is room for all, in my opinion, and the more the better, in reason; but there is especial need for a Lodge of the type I indicate later.

My contention, then, is that Freemasonry derives originally from those primitive rites which first taught a boy whence he came, then prepared him to be a useful member of society, and finally taught him how to die and that death did not end all. On these primitive rites, I consider, man built up the mysteries and the various religious faiths of the ancient world, some of which have survived to the present day, while others have developed into other religions, Christianity included. To this part of my theory I propose to devote the next chapter.

CHAPTER XIV

WHAT THIS PART OF THE BOOK PROVES

SLOWLY, and step by step, we have studied the meaning of our ritual and learned that its signs and symbols are found the world over among people who never heard of Freemasonry as we understand it. More than this, we have found that, by studying the remnants of the primitive rites and the customs and beliefs of the people of India, Mexico, and ancient Egypt, etc., we are able to understand much of our ritual which otherwise is obscure and unintelligible. Do these facts throw any light on the origin and descent of Freemasonry?

I contend that they do, and, in setting out the thesis which now follows, I would emphasise the fact that I base my contention not on any one fact but on the sum total, and, above all, on their cumulative effects. Doubtless many of my readers may hesitate to agree with my theory, but all I ask is that they should consider it in the light of a working hypothesis, and, using it as such, accumulate further data which will enable them to form their own opinion with an open mind without prejudice.

THE THESIS

This, then, is my thesis: I consider that the evidence I have adduced proves that Freemasonry did not originate with the building Guilds of the Middle Ages, but with the primitive initiatory rites of prehistoric man.

In support of this view I quote the evidence already adduced of the signs, grips, and tokens used before the Middle Ages and still in use among primitive races who cannot build as did the mediæval guilds. These signs used on the west and east coasts of Africa, the Lion Grip and Eagle's Claw used on the east coast of Africa, or the R.A. sign used by the Arunta natives of Australia after their final initiation indicate what is meant.

If we turn to ancient races who could build, we find that most of these signs were known to the ancient Assyrians, Egyptians, and the Maya people in Central America, that is to say, long before our mediæval Guilds existed.

We have discovered that similar signs were associated with certain gods in India, and the same signs were associated with the same manifestations of the Deity in Egypt and ancient Mexico.

We are surprised to learn that even those " higher " degrees, such as the eighteenth, which are usually called Christian, had their prototypes in ancient Egypt and Mexico, even the same signs being used, as is proved by their preservation in the ancient manuscripts of those races which have survived to this day. Further that these higher degree signs are associated with the Preserver in India and with Buddha elsewhere. We learn that masonic phrases were used in China many centuries before Christ, and that all our masonic tools, etc., were deposited under an ancient Egyptian " Needle." In Pompeii we find what is practically a masonic tracing-board and a significant fresco, and we are then brought into direct connection with the Comacine masons who are the real link between the ancient mysteries and the mediæval Guilds. Moreover, the Mohammedan East has a complete system so closely similar to our own that the members of their Order could prove themselves in ours; and, in short, in no single continent do we fail to find what we consider are the signs and tokens by which Masons prove themselves to a brother.

But I have written enough on this theme, and, before turning to answer certain objections which I know will be raised, I would like once more to appeal to my brethren the world over to accumulate more evidence before it is too late.

The usual answer given to me when I point out these facts is, " It is coincidence," or, " After all, our signs are perfectly natural signs, and we have merely chosen them and given them a particular meaning." Surely this argument is very, very weak. If they were such " ordinary signs " would it not be easy for men who are not Masons to enter our Lodges? Let it be admitted that in some of the higher degrees some of the signs are natural ones, but others emphatically are not, and it is the latter I have found most widely spread. Moreover, it is just because they are so unnatural that I have been able to " spot them " every time, whereas I have not admitted certain others which might be natural signs though rather similar to those in use in other degrees.

The Lion Grip is, after all, a peculiar grip, so is the M.M.M.

grip used by the Dervishes at the time of taking the oaths; but the cumulative evidence seems to me to eliminate entirely the question of chance or of merely natural signs.

When one sees an ancient Mexican manuscript in which the prototype of the eighteenth degree is depicted; when one sees, as one does, similar scenes enacted and the appropriate signs made at each point, chance seems to be out of the question. In short, some of my opponents appear to be suffering from the same complaint as that with which they charge me—excessive credulity; only, whereas they would charge me with seeing Masonry where it does not exist, I would venture to suggest that they see chance where it *cannot* exist. In short, chance and coincidence are to them what the blessed word "Mesopotamia" was to the old lady—a name by which they designate anything they cannot explain. After all, is it not more antecedently probable that my theory is correct than their theory of coincidence and chance? If they really believe that Hanuman, the faithful attendant of the Preserver, always uses the sign he does by chance they little know the changeless East. The hands of the Hindoo god are practically always placed in a symbolical attitude. If Hanuman were making the M.M. sign then they might argue it was chance, for certainly it would be meaningless, but the sign he makes is the sign he ought to make: He who preserved the hosts of Rama; He, the faithful attendant of Vishnu the Preserver; He, the skilful craftsman, who built the "Bridge of Rama," makes the correct sign. And so, too, does the Dread Destroyer; and do not overlook the significance of the bas-relief in Java. The triangles, the signs, the caste marks, the attributes, correspond exactly; and yet some would say it is coincidence.

But, if it is not coincidence, how did these signs descend from ancient times to the mediæval Guilds? That is the question I shall endeavour to answer in the succeeding pages, and when my brethren have read these pages I would ask them to consider whether my theory is not antecedently more probable than that of chance. Perhaps some may fear to accept such a theory because they think the uninitiated and popular world will laugh at the claim of Freemasonry to be the oldest system in the world. But what does it matter if they do? We are not called upon to discuss Freemasonry with outsiders; nay, we ought not to do so. It is no concern of the cowan what we think, believe, or know.

This, then, is my theory. Man evolved by slow and painful stages to his present high estate. How long it took him no man can estimate. A hundred thousand years is probably far too modest an estimate, for every year the archæologist and the anthropologist push back the dawn of man to an earlier and earlier period. In his earliest condition as a man he was probably a gregarious creature travelling in a pack or herd, and the most logical theory is that he evolved in the same areas as the monkey folk, but descended from their home in the trees and began to roam the savannahs in search of food, and, later, game. He spread north, east, south, and west, and by slow degrees reached every known continent except the Antarctic. In those places where we find him in the most primitive state, such as in Australia and parts of Africa, we find even to-day he has certain strange initiatory rites. So old are they that often he had forgotten their meaning, but until the white man corrupted him and taught him to despise his old customs he continued to perform certain initiatory ceremonies because it had always been done, and it is not in the power of any man or any body of men to alter the ancient rituals. Stripped of all unnecessary verbiage, these rites are the initiatory rites of a boy into manhood, and they teach him roughly (1) whence he came; (2) how to be a useful member of society; (3) and that finally he must die, but that death does not end all. Sometimes these rites go further and teach him (4) what will happen to him after death when he passes to the land of his ancestors, and (5) something at least of what is meant by the Great Spirit, or God, whence he came and to whom he will ultimately return.

As man developed, the simple and misty conceptions of the savage failed to satisfy his spiritual needs, but he did not discard entirely his old rites and symbols, his grips and tokens. Instead of creating a brand-new religion, he built on to the skeleton supplied by the primitive rites more and more ritual and deeper religious truths. In short, out of these primitive rites the various civilised people of ancient times evolved gradually what we now know as the mysteries. It is not necessary to assume, as some do, that all the mysteries were created in Egypt, nor even that they are all the descendants of a hypothetical Atlantis. Such a civilisation may have existed, but we can see that even without it the same phenomena would have occurred.

The two outstanding examples are, of course, Egypt and Mexico. No doubt they have points in common, but we need not—unless we wish to do so—assume that one must have copied their ideas from the other. If each race started with similar primitive initiatory rites their mysteries were bound to have much in common. From the very nature of things they were both dealing with the same problems of Life, Death, and the Hereafter.

The medicine men, who in primitive times had presided at the initiatory rites, naturally became priests. With the innate conservatism of their days, a conservatism which, in fact, is inherent in the whole human race, they retained all that they could of the ancient signs and symbols. These symbols were already holy things. They had been evolved before men had obtained an extensive vocabulary, and they remained because they expressed ideas which even to-day are difficult to translate into words. As the spoken language evolved words were brought in to explain what was meant, but the old idea still retained its power. A pillar still meant strength, and the sign for pillar still meant strength, though in different parts of the world the word used for a pillar naturally varied. Additional meanings were given to the signs. The P.S. still reminded the initiate of the p. of his O., but to this primitive idea was added an esoteric meaning reminding the adept of the three great centres of the occult forces in man.[1] But it was not necessary to explain these second meanings to every initiate, and so by degrees there grew up an exoteric and an esoteric meaning. Often a further and still a further esoteric meaning would evolve, and at the present day there are parts of our ritual which have at least four or five meanings, each within the other, each evolving out of the last, and the innermost of all can only be grasped when the candidate has worked through all the others.

In the days when none but the priestly caste had time to study and learn, there was ample justification for the policy of the priests of not disclosing much of their inner knowledge to all and sundry. Indeed, no other course was possible, but nevertheless it was bound to lead to abuses. The guardians of the hidden things grew more and more personally selfish and gradually closed

[1] The Hindoo legend says that the Brahmins sprang from the head of Brahma, (2) the soldiers from his breast, (3) the peasants from his loins. Only the despised Sudra caste had no occult centre, and sprang from his feet.

all knowledge to the outside world. They encouraged ignorance in the rest of the people so as to enhance their own power and prestige, with the natural result that upright men arose who broke with the priests and went direct to the outside world, and, instead of a steady evolution of religious thought, reformers arose who endeavoured to reform the old religions and often ended by breaking away altogether. Moses was probably one of the priestly caste who did this, but the pages of history are full of the names of these heroes. But every man must build on what has gone before, and so the essential teaching of the mysteries became the dogmas of the new faiths. Thus, from the initiatory rites of the savages evolved the mysteries, and from the mysteries arose the various religions of the world.

We might, if we chose, trace the evolution from pretotemism to totemism, thence to the hero cults, and so by easy stages through stellar and lunar cults to the solar cult, which is the one on which practically all the great religions of to-day are based.

But, from the point of view of modern Freemasonry, it is the solar cult which interests us most, for our own Mythos, in its main essentials, belongs to this order of things. Nevertheless, Freemasonry has embodied in it traces of every cult which has gone before, and the stellar cult is particularly noticeable in the R.A. But, before considering the Mythos in full, we must endeavour to explain how Freemasonry became associated with the mysteries rather than with the popular religions which broke away from them, for, although we shall consider this more fully when we have dealt with the Mythos, yet it seems desirable to indicate how essential it was that the building craft should be bound to the priestly caste by more than ordinary obligations.

As later we shall endeavour to show that more than one stream helped to produce the river of modern Masonry, we shall here concentrate mostly on ancient Egypt, only adding this proviso, that we think that the Dionysian Artificers had more to do with shaping the form in which modern Freemasonry was destined to develop than had Egypt, though that country naturally had a profounder though more indirect influence.

As the mysteries were evolved and the medicine men became priests the latter were no longer content to meet on the tops of high mountains, at the bottoms of deep valleys, or in the depths of the jungle, as had been the case in primitive days. In fact, it was becoming impossible to do so; as man began to settle down and build cities and cultivate the soil it became difficult, if not impossible, to find convenient spots in the open which were sufficiently secluded. In addition, the natural ambition of the priests to build suitable habitations for the gods led to a demand for stately temples. When building these it became necessary to construct them in such a way that the more elaborate ritual of the mysteries could be carried out correctly. But, as the tendency was growing more and more to exclude the bulk of the people from the inner rites, it naturally followed that unless the men who built the temples were bound to secrecy many of the secrets thereof might be divulged. The priests themselves could not do all the work, and, if men ignorant of all that was to take place were left to do the building, the work could not be done correctly. Therefore, the builders were gradually organised into privileged Guilds, and to them were entrusted many, though not all, of the secrets of the mysteries. They became a class apart, not, of course, so learned as the priests, but knowing more than the outside world. It was not necessary, however, to explain everything. Probably they did not see the whole of the ceremonies, and almost certainly they received only the exoteric meaning of the ceremonies through which they passed. Nevertheless, the mere fact that they were so highly privileged gave them a corporate spirit not possessed by any other trade, and they would cherish carefully the signs, grips and tokens now lost to most of the outside world and as much of the ritual as they could remember. Moreover, not only did this simplified system of the mysteries appeal to their religious nature and to their professional pride, but it also gave them a great practical advantage when travelling from place to place. The grips and signs would be used as a secret method of making themselves known to each other, and would be jealously guarded and passed on unchanged even after the mysteries themselves had fallen before the attack of Christianity.

And all the time, far away in the jungle of Central Africa, or hidden on the lonely Easter Island in the midst of the Pacific, were men who also used these same signs and honoured them as holy things, since they had learnt them when they passed through the ceremony of being initiated into manhood. But, of course, neither knew of the other.

CHAPTER XV

THE MYTHOS

THE legend of H. A. is one of the most dramatic stories in existence, and its very simplicity adds rather than detracts from its dramatic force. Yet there is little evidence in support of its historic truth. What evidence we have actually contradicts the chief incident. The Bible tells us that H. A. finished his work, and Josephus relates that he returned to his own country and lived there to a ripe old age. The fact that Josephus should mention that he lived to a ripe old age makes one wonder whether the alternative version of the story was already in existence and known to him. A Rabbinical tradition states that Solomon ordered the slaughter of all those who had assisted at the building of the Temple lest they should afterwards build temples to the false gods; but there is not the slightest evidence in favour of this tradition, and on the contrary everything to render it antecedently improbable.

But the story as we know it bears a striking resemblance to several known solar myths. The Egyptian story of Osiris and Horus, the Norse legend of the murder of Baldur, and the Palestinian myth of the death of Adonis, all tell in a dramatic form the allegory of the sun which dies each day and rises on the next, and, still more, the overthrow of summer by winter and the resurrection of the sun and with it of all life in the spring. Now it will be noted that Adonis was a local deity of the Syrian and Palestinian coast, and, further, it will be remembered that in the Egyptian legend the body of Osiris in its ark or chest was washed ashore at Byblos, the city of Adonis, and lodged in a tamarisk-tree, a shrub similar to the acacia. Here we are able to link the acacia, Adonis and Osiris, Egypt, Phœnicia, and Palestine together.

H. A. was a Phœnician, and this is not without its significance. Further, a large part of the workmen who built the Temple are said to have been Egyptians, and H. K. of T. was of course a Phœnician. Phœnician characters have been found on the foundation stones of the great Temple of K. S., and, though I have not heard that any Egyptian characters were found there, we know that Egyptian workmen were employed. Thus we get a strong Phœnician and a weaker Egyptian blending of two elements. But there is another Biblical character, Adoniram; surely this is no one else than Adonis Hiram. If, then, the origin of our story is derived mainly from the tale of Adonis, we see how it could be connected with H. A. But, further, the name of Adonis is the Greek version of the god's name rather than the Syrian, and if this be so we obtain evidence of the Greek influence and the Dionysian artificers. Finally, we perceive that a mixed body of men drawn from various nations and each with its own national gods might refuse to reverence a local Syrian god like Adonis, but would willingly unite in honouring the name of the great architect and skilled craftsman of the Temple. Very strict Jews who were drawn into the craft at a later date would have bitterly opposed any reference to the Phœnician god Adonis, but would see no reason why they should not commemorate the actions of H. A. the man. As time passed and those who knew H. A. in the flesh passed away, the tendency would be for the masons to associate with his name much of their mystery lore.

It should be carefully noted that H. A. is not a true Jew. He is a Phœnician and the subject of a Phœnician king. Nor is there any evidence that the Jews themselves were builders or skilled at all in masonry. On the contrary, all the evidence goes to show that they were at that time a race of shepherds and small farmers, and Solomon had to import aliens to build his Temple. These would, of course, have their own local faiths, among which the cult of Adonis would naturally be one of the strongest. But the masons excluded women, and in their version there was no room for a woman; so we have no woman of any kind, not even Isis, the loving sister wife. Moreover, it is not an elaborate allegory such as that of Osiris, for, though there is a distinct hint of the doctrine of the Resurrection, it is but a hint and nothing more. In the story of Osiris it is made abundantly plain that Osiris rises from the dead and reigns as King of Heaven, but we are left only with the solitary light in the East, the light of hope that he did rise. It is a simple legend, and, like all that appertains to the craft, it can be accepted by all because it does not dogmatise. In short, the mysteries of many lands were mingled together at the beginning of K. S.'s Temple. No doubt the men who came to build it imbibed some of the Jewish ideas of God. These would appeal to them, for in their mysteries they had learnt, as a great and terrible secret, that all the gods were but forms of the one true God, and at Jerusalem they found themselves building a temple to Him where He could be worshipped openly. This discovery probably explains the vast importance which the Building Guilds henceforth attached to the building of this particular Temple.

But to make the matter clearer, we must ask ourselves what was the organisation which erected the Temple. That it was an elaborate and highly organised body of workmen is plain, not only from masonic legend, but from the account in the Bible itself. The true explanation seems to be that they were the body later known as the Dionysian Artificers.

We know that there were Masonic Guilds in ancient Egypt, and we also know that the laws of the building trade were a jealously guarded secret known only to those who had been initiated.

H. J. Da Costa, in 1820, in a *Sketch for the History of the Dionysian Artificers: a Fragment*, gives most interesting details of this Guild, and Laurie, in his *History of Masonry*, chapter i, draws on Da Costa, who quotes numerous authorities for the existence of this body, who must not be confounded with the play-actors who were later known by the same name. Strabo, in his *Geography*, lib. xiv, 921, wrote of them: "Lebedos was the seat and assembly of the Dionysian Artificers who inhabit Ionia to the Hellespont; there they had annually their solemn meetings and festivals in honour of Bacchus." Robertson, in his *Greece*, tells us they were a secret society having signs and words to distinguish their members, and used emblems taken from the art of building, quoting Eusebius, *de Prep. Evang.* iii, c. 12, in support of these statements. Why Waite should ignore them it is difficult to say, for their existence, which seems to be completely proved, explains many things. They appear to have arrived in Phœnicia and Asia Minor about fifty years before the building of the Temple of K. S., and Strabo traces them through Syria, Persia, and India, and their existence would explain the masonic legends in China to which we have already referred. If they reached India there is no reason why they should not have reached China in small parties, and it would be from them that the strange society who taught their tenets by symbolising architectural tools and wove their legends round a mysterious temple set in a desert would have derived their inspiration.

I fail to see how the evidence of Strabo and Eusebius can be lightly brushed away. On the contrary, they usually carry great weight, and I hold that the Dionysian Artificers are the link which completes the chain of descent connecting modern Freemasonry with the ancient mysteries and the still more ancient initiatory rites. We know that in its original form the legend of Dionysos was very similar to that of Adonis; and if we want further corroborative evidence we have it in that apparently strange statement of Josephus that the architecture of K. S.'s Temple was of the style called Grecian. "What, Grecian architecture in the days of King Solomon!" most people would exclaim, "why, it did not exist until nearly five hundred years later: Josephus was wandering." But was he? After all, was he not trying to explain that it was the prototype of Grecian, as distinct from Egyptian or Assyrian work, built by the men who, when they reached Greece, evolved the style we now regard as Grecian, and that it was not a mere repetition of ancient Eygptian or Assyrian styles?

CHAPTER XVI

WHEN DID THE PURELY JEWISH INFLUENCE ENTER ?

VARIOUS alternatives suggest themselves in answer to the question as to when the purely Jewish influence was grafted on to the craft.

It has been proved conclusively that the Jews were never great builders, neither in the days of K. S. nor later.

The most probable sources are four in number:

(*a*) At the time of K. S.
(*b*) From the Alexandrian Jews.
(*c*) Through the Cabbalists, particularly during the time of the Crusades.
(*d*) In the eighteenth-century Deistic England.

Freemasonry could not have originated among the orthodox Jews of King Solomon's days.

Not only were they not builders, but their conception of God was and still is entirely different from that which underlies the masonic ritual. The Jewish conception of the Deity was that of the Just Dealer. Those who kept their contracts with Him were certain that He would carry out His promises, not merely in the hereafter but in this mortal life. Those who broke their contract with Him would be made to suffer both here and hereafter. He is a personal God, with a very distinct individuality. He is not an all-embracing first cause, but a person—Creator and Judge. Justice is His outstanding characteristic rather than tender fatherly love.

This conception is very far removed from the Hindoo idea of the c. of a c., or of the Creative, Preservative, and Destructive sides of the Deity. This latter conception is pantheistic, whereas the Jewish conception was and still usually is distinctly monotheistic and therefore hostile to the idea of the c. of a c. This monotheistic conception was the one usually set forth in the Bible and was and is the belief of the orthodox Jews, but there was another conception held in secret by many of the more mystical and learned Jews, and the typical representatives of this view were the Alexandrian Jews and the later [illegible]s.

If we study our ritual carefully we shall perceive that the monotheistic idea of God, and in particular the idea of a jealous God, is but little in evidence in the craft working. It is ignored rather than contradicted, but the fact is nevertheless significant.

It is probable, however, that the Dionysian Artificers did import into their ritual certain Jewish elements of the time of K. S. The building of the Temple itself was an important historical event in the world of that day, and the king himself left his impression in the legendary lore of the whole of Syria and the neighbouring countries, but we need not assume that in those days all the details which we now find incorporated in our ritual were included. Careful analysis will show that these have been copied wholesale from the Bible at a much later date.

The next infusion of Jewish ideas probably took place at the opening of the Christian era. By that time the whole known world had passed under the control of Rome, and Alexandria was the intellectual capital of the Empire, overshadowed politically by Rome itself, but, so far as spiritual thought was concerned, far above the Imperial city as a centre of intellectual activity.

Rome might produce far greater poets and writers than Alexandria, but it had never been a centre of [illegible] aspirations, and under the corrupt influence of the Imperial Court it was sinking rapidly to the lowest depths.

In Alexandria, on the other hand, there congregated intellectuals from every country, and this city was the meeting-place of the East and West.

Although situated in Egypt, Alexandria was essentially Greek in its culture, but it had a mystical school in its centre which could not have flourished in the sceptical atmosphere of Athens. The Jews of Alexandria were of a very different type from the orthodox Pharisees of Jerusalem or still more materialistic Sadducees.

Without attempting to go into the matter in detail, it is sufficient to say that they held views similar to those associated with the

Cabbalists of the Middle Ages, and among these was a conception of the Deity which was much nearer Pantheism than Monotheism. They held that there was a secret tradition explaining the true esoteric meaning of the Bible, and that, while the ordinary Jew should only be given the exoteric meaning, they and their followers had the key to the real interpretation of the V.S.L.

At this time the East was already beginning to react on the West, and numerous mysterious religions were arising. Of these, four became famous and fought for the mastery of the Western World. They were (1) the worship of Isis; (2) the Great Mother; (3) Mithraism; and (4) Christianity. All these in their earliest form seem to have been secret societies with their initiatory rites and various ceremonies open only to a limited number who had proved themselves worthy of the honour; but, in addition to these well-known systems, there were many others, and every craft, guild, or collegia had its own little cult and secret teaching.

It is, therefore, exceedingly probable that a further infusion of Jewish ideas took place at this time and influenced the Roman Collegia; but this new Jewish infusion would be distinctly pantheistic rather than monotheistic.

To an Alexandrian Jew the Masonic Collegia, with their traditional connection with the K.S. Temple and a hero who was its chief artificer, would appeal irresistibly, and, with the general trend towards secret societies and systems of initiation, it would be only natural if they endeavoured to enter the order and influence it along the lines of their own speculation.

The third probable source of Jewish influence is the period of the Crusades. At that time the most learned men in Europe were the Arabs and the Jews who lived under the Caliph. We know that these were for the most part Cabbalists who carried on the secret tradition and held similar views to those already ascribed to the Alexandrian Jews. To them may very probably be due the use of Jewish words as pass-words; in particular, the words in the first and second degree, when read backwards according to Cabbalistic rules, give a secret meaning to which reference has already been made.

There are numerous points in our ritual which remind us of the Cabbalists, and not only in the Craft but also in the Mark and Arch. Nor must it be forgotten that by this time the Dervish system of degrees was in full swing, and Mohammedan tradition states that [illegible] was initiated into this [illegible] [illegible] and in his turn gave it to some of his knights, including the Templars. Now the teaching of these Dervish degrees is distinctly mystical, and in many points far removed from the ordinary orthodox Mohammedan beliefs, though so carefully veiled that an orthodox and bigoted Mohammedan, unless very intellectual, would probably not realise the fact.

Now we know that the Templars at first were just an ordinary semi-monastic body, but by the time they were driven out of Palestine they were a secret society with strange initiatory rites and working in an "unholy alliance" apparently with the Old Man of the Mountains. That there was some working agreement between this heterodox Mohammedan leader and the leading Templars seems certain, and subsequent events tend to make us believe that the Templars themselves, though probably innocent of the viler charges made against them, were to a considerable extent tinged with heresy. In other words, they had learnt to think for themselves, and were not content to accept every dogma of the orthodox clergy.

The persistent tradition connecting the Templars with Freemasonry cannot be ignored. Even the Dervishes have it, and to explain the fact that we have a similar system to theirs, say that the Templars gave it to the [illegible]r churches.

I suggest that what happened was that the Christian masonic Guilds, particularly the Comacine Guilds, obtained at this time a fresh infusion of Cabbalistic Jewish ideas which checked the tendency, which must have been strong, to become a purely Christian and orthodox body. That the masons, while deeply religious, were not strictly orthodox, is acknowledged by most antiquaries. The carvings they placed in their churches are only one of the indications—carvings which caricatured the higher clergy.

Their use of the cross and the vesica piscis as the basis of their architecture, both in the details and in their ground-plans and most of their symbolism, points to a considerable leaven of non-orthodoxy, to put it mildly. Incidentally it shows that they were far from being the ignorant men some would contend, but that, on the contrary, some at least were highly educated and intellectual men for the period in which they lived.

I have little doubt personally that a considerable amount of our speculative teaching is traceable to the Cabbalists via the Templars. The Crusaders who divided up the Holy Land into petty feudal States, and still more the Templars, built European castles and churches which must have been erected by men who were members of the Western mediæval Guilds, and almost certainly by men who had derived their knowledge from the Comacines.

These men, on returning to Europe, must have brought back with them the ideas with which they had come in contact in the East. The fact that the Dervishes say that "though Saladin gave Richard I. their lower degrees, he did not give him their higher degrees, and therefore you have not got them," is also most significant. It means that there was no fresh infusion of Jewish and Mohammedan mystical ideas into our high degrees. These, being associated with the cross, were left to develop more and more in line with orthodox Christian views instead of along the lines of the wisdom of the East.

Yet, the cross and the vesica piscis played their part at this date.

The builders brought back into Western Europe a new style, the true Gothic, based on these symbols, and it spread with lightning rapidity; nor must the fact be forgotten that its earliest form, the Early English, is found almost exclusively in these islands instead of on the Continent.

If the builders came back imbued with Gnostic and Cabbalistic symbolism and mysticism, is it surprising that they put these new ideas into practice in England, the realm ruled by Richard I, from whence no doubt many of them had come? The rapidity with which the Gothic style spread throughout Europe is most striking, and can only be explained by the fact that one great society was at work whose members were in constant touch with headquarters and responded quickly to any new inspiration which emanated thence. This society was, I contend, the Comacine Guild of Masons. Before leaving this point let me stress the fact that the new style was not a copy of Arabic architecture; it was European architecture inspired by new symbolic and mystical ideas derived from Syria and Egypt, and, above all, from the Cabbalists, but transmuted into a purely European style by the men who built our churches.

The final collapse of the Crusades and the dissolution of the

Templar Order left the masons the only organised body who possessed the secret tradition of the Cabbalists, and no doubt led to a large number of speculative minds entering their ranks who otherwise would have joined the Templars.

The persecution of the Albigenses and similar avowedly heretical sects compelled those who wished to speculate and refused to accept orthodoxy to enter the only body which would effectively protect them and whose system assured them of secrecy. No doubt among the various alchemists who still wandered up and down Europe or hid themselves in remote corners of the world were many who held similar Cabbalistic views, but for the most part they were lost spirits, and it was only in the Masonic Guilds that men of such beliefs could find others of like learning and would be safe from the ever-present fear of betrayal.

There remains a fourth probable source of Jewish influence which appears to have taken its rise in the eighteenth century. That century was strongly Deistic so far as its intellectual activities were concerned. A natural reaction from the bitter religious struggles of the sixteenth and seventeenth centuries had led many to turn away from the Christian sects. The broadening of men's minds and the spirit of greater religious toleration led many to seek for a common ground of agreement instead of striving to magnify petty differences of religious dogma.

The granting of complete religious toleration to the Jews during the Civil War had enabled that persecuted people to find in England a home of refuge still denied to them on the Continent. They were naturally attracted to a system which drew for its ritual on the story of the building of K. S.'s Temple, and would tend to emphasise the Old Testament side of its ceremonies. In this they would be assisted by the Deistic spirit of the age, and we can probably assign to this period many of the purely Biblical incidents incorporated in our system. The more general knowledge of the Bible which resulted from its translation into the vernacular and the high authority attached to the Written Word would all materially assist in strengthening the Jewish side of our ritual; but it must be noted that this infusion of new ideas would be Biblical and mainly orthodox Judaism and not mystical and Cabbalistic. A degree like that of the Super-Excellent Master in the cryptic degrees, could only have been derived from an orthodox Jewish source, whereas the peculiar attributes of the three principal officers in a Craft Lodge could not have come from the Bible any more than could that of the conception of God revealed in the p. within a c.

These, then, are the four possible sources from which the Jewish element in our ritual could have been derived, and I personally believe that all four have helped to produce the present result; but I think the last two are the chief influences now reflected in our ritual.

CHAPTER XVII

BRIEF SUMMARY OF THE TRUE LINE OF DESCENT OF MODERN FREEMASONRY

(*a*) The ancient initiatory rites and corroboree ceremonies of our prehistoric ancestors are, I venture to contend, the true origin of Freemasonry. The signs which are still found among savage men the world over, which are not merely similar but have the same significance, point to this conclusion.

As I have already devoted so much space to setting forth this portion of my theory, I shall not devote too much space to it here, but content myself with pointing out the persistence of one particular sign — of a F.C.

The Easter Islanders had it, it is found on Assyrian monuments and in Egyptian papyri. It is the characteristic sign of Hanuman in India; it is to be found far away in ancient Mexico, a land cut off entirely from Egypt, and is shown on a manuscript which is unquestionably older than the Spanish conquest of Mexico, though how much older none can say for certain. In Pompeii we find it. The Dervishes in Turkey use it in their ritual, and it is shown on a twelfth-century mosaic of Jonah in Italy. In England we can see it displayed by the Second Person of the Trinity, carved over the doorway of Peterborough Cathedral,[1] and our own masonic tradition states that it took its origin long before the building of K. S.'s Temple, surely therein hinting to us of its great antiquity.

(*b*) On the basis of the early initiatory rites man, as he became more civilised, built up the mysteries. Signs which had been given to all men were now restricted to the priestly caste and those favoured few who were, like them, admitted into the

[1] An illuminated MS. in the Bibliothèque Nationale, Paris, of the thirteenth century carries it down a century later.

OLD CHINESE PAINTING.

Depicting the five Buddhas arranged in a St. Andrew's Cross, the future Buddha at the centre. The signs of the cross and vesica piscis should be noted. Every sign here is of particular symbolic interest.

(Original in Author's Collection.)

mysteries. The signs were still retained as sacred and symbolic, but may not as yet have been used as a test for admission. This took place when the Masonic Guilds arose.

The same signs and initiatory rites were the basis not only of the mysteries of Egypt, but of those of Central America, and we are able to recognise not merely the signs but even scenes from some of the degrees.

This is particularly true of some of the so-called Christian or Cross degrees, which we should least expect to find there, yet Mexico and ancient Egypt are as far apart as it is possible to find any two great civilisations, and China and India also have them. So far as we can judge, no direct intercourse between them ever took place. Perhaps the reason why Maya civilisation never spread throughout America is that no great wandering Masons' Guilds ever arose. It appears probable that the priestly caste kept the building trade entirely in their own hands, and allowed no independent body similar to the Dionysian Artificers to arise.

(*c*) The Dionysian Artificers were a Masonic Guild with secret signs, grips, and words. They were existing in Phoenicia at the time of the building of the Temple; it was they who built it, and, having completed this work, they journeyed in groups or Lodges through Asia and into Europe. They had their special cult associated with Dionysos, a solar cult of Syria, and the union of the god Adonis and the man H. are remembered in our ritual by the name of the successor of H., Adoniram.

These Dionysian Artificers carried forward our grips and signs and also a similar legend to our own, together with a remembrance of the great Temple they had built, to farthest China, and, what more directly concerns us, into Greece. As a result of their advent Greece springs into prominence as a centre of art and architecture, and the style they have developed becomes known as Grecian, so that Josephus at a later date could describe the style of K.S.'s Temple as Grecian, though what he meant no doubt was that it was the prototype of the Grecian style.

From Greece the Dionysian Artificers passed into Italy and became known as Collegia.

(*d*) The Roman Collegia must now be dealt with at some length. Most of the trades had their Collegia, or Guilds, and so powerful did they become that the Emperors on several occasions tried to suppress them by edict. But these edicts could not be effectively enforced: at the time they were issued Orders were exempted which could prove their great *antiquity* and that *they were religious* in character. Most of the condemned Collegia became charitable, religious, or funerary bodies, outwardly at any rate. They held memorial services for a dead brother, marked his tomb with the emblems of his trade, and administered financial relief to his widow and children. On a builder's tomb we find the square, the compasses, and the level, and other trades similarly used their tools as emblems to mark the grave of a brother.

But from the very first the Colleges of Architects appear to have enjoyed special privileges and exemptions, due no doubt to the high prestige they inherited from their descent from the Dionysian Artificers, as well as to the importance of the work they did. They had their own constitutions and regulations in both religious and secular matters, and their whole organisation was a [illegible] [illegible] of a modern Masonic Lodge. "Three make a College" was a rule recognised and endorsed by the Roman law. Each College was presided over by a master (*magister*) and two wardens (*decuriones*). There were a secretary, a treasurer, a chaplain (*sacerdos*), and also probably certain other officers.

The members of the College consisted of three grades corresponding closely to [illegible], [illegible], and [illegible]. They had semi-religious rites of initiation, and, although we possess no precise details, considering the fact that the solar drama was at this time the [illegible] both of [illegible] and the religion of Isis, the popular Roman cults, we feel little doubt as to the type of drama enacted by our ancient brethren, even if we did not know that the predecessors had been followers of the cult of Dionysos who was slain by the Titans.

All the masonic emblems were used by the Collegia; the square, the compasses, the cube, plumb-rule circle, and level are constantly in evidence.

The building of the Collegia unearthed at Pompeii in 1878 has already been described, but we will summarise and repeat the description.

There were two columns in front, and the walls were decorated with [illegible], the constant [illegible]. Upon a pedestal in the room was found a tracing-broad or table of inlaid mosaic. In the centre is a [illegible] with a [illegible] and [illegible] and other symbolic designs, but for further details my readers have only to refer back to the chapter which gives examples of masonic symbols in Europe, nor can we spare time for more than a passing reference to the obviously masonic significance of certain remains found at the Roman Villa at Morton, Isle of Wight, described by J. F. Crease in *Ars Quot. Cor.*, vol. iii, pp. 88-59, as well as to the fresco at Pompeii.

When Christianity was converting the rank and file of ancient Rome it did not fail to attract the members of the various Colleges, among whom were included many of the masonic fraternity.

Strange to say Diocletian, when he set out to destroy Christianity, dealt very leniently with the Collegia of Architects, but, when some of them refused to make a statue of Æsculapius, he fell upon them, and four Master Masons and one apprentice were tortured to death. But henceforth these four became known as the Four Crowned Martyrs, and they are found depicted holding the implements of their trade and are now well known to every masonic student, because a picture of them appears on the cover of every issue of that admirable publication, the *Ars Quatuor Coronatorum*. They became, in short, the patron saints of Masons throughout Europe, no doubt replacing some tutelary gods long since lost, and a poem in their praise is to be found in the oldest written record of the craft, the Regius MS. Their names are said to have been Claudius, Nicistatus, Simphoranus, Castorius, and the humble apprentice Simplicius.

Their bodies ultimately were brought from Rome to Toulouse and placed in a special chapel erected in their honour at St. Sernin.

Any brethren who chance to be visiting Rotterdam will see them depicted in an old fresco at the Church of St. Lawrence, and with them is one who appears to be King Solomon, likewise holding a pair of compasses.

The link that, I contend, joins the mysteries to the Collegia was the Dionysian Artificers; the gap between the Collegia and the mediæval Guilds is filled by the Comacines.

CHAPTER XVIII

THE COMACINES

IN *The Cathedral Builders: the Story of a Great Masonic Guild*, Leader Scott has set out to prove that the Magistri Comacini supply the link between the Roman Collegia and the mediæval Guild. While basing the following on her researches, I would only add that, in endeavouring to make the story a connected whole, I have not hesitated to draw on secular history for certain additional facts where necessary.

On the break-up of the Roman Empire the guild system was destroyed by the barbarian invaders, but a [illegible] which had taken refuge in Comacina, a fortified island in the midst of Lake Como, survived.

This island of refuge, now only a ruin, was never taken by the Lombards, and when the Lombards in due course realised the advantage of order and civilisation, the then King of the Lombards thought the best way to encourage building was to place the control of it in proved and competent hands. He therefore issued an edict that the masons of Italy should henceforth be under the control of the masons of Lake Como. But the kingdom of the Lombard King stretched no farther south than Rome, and so it is that even to-day, north of Rome [illegible]; whereas the powerful bodies south of Rome were secret societies such as those of the charcoal-burners, suppressed by the Austrians in 1820, or the modern Mafia.

The Comacines kept alive the traditions of classical architecture and developed them into the Early Lombard and Romanesque styles. When William, nicknamed the Tanner's Son, was Duke of Normandy, an Italian called Lanfranc was brought over to become Abbot of Bec in Normandy, and to build the abbey he brought with him Italian masons. These men must have been members of the Comacine Guild.

William at the battle of Senlac defeated the English Harold and made himself King of England. He made Lanfranc Abbot of Canterbury. Lanfranc would naturally bring with him the Italian masons who had built his abbey at Bec to build his new cathedrals and churches. All over England churches and castles began to arise, built in the Norman style and, what is still more striking, on the stones of these Norman churches we find what we do not usually find in the case of the few Saxon churches[1] which survived, the masons' marks. Hundreds of these marks have been collected and noted down in the *Ars Quat. Cor.* and elsewhere, and the fact that many have a symbolic meaning is indisputable. These marks are the signs, be it remembered, of a well-organised body. Unless these marks were registered in some Lodge they would be almost useless.

The Comacines journeyed from place to place where work was to be found. When a church or castle was finished they must go elsewhere. There must therefore, even at that date, have been a regular Lodge and a recorder of marks, otherwise any unscrupulous brother could have forged another's mark without risk of detection.

These marks persist at least up to the time of the first ancient charges—that is to say, the opening of the fourteenth century, to which date the Regius MS. appears to belong. Similar marks are found in ancient Roman, Greek, and Hindoo buildings, and in Asia Minor, Jerusalem, and Egypt.

This particular charge collects a mass of legendary lore of all dates and periods, but perhaps its most striking feature is the fact that much of its teaching is of a distinctly speculative nature and would be far above the heads of the ordinary operative, but —and this is the point often missed—this teaching would not be beyond the true Comacines.

Besides these British old charges there are others on similar lines for the German Steinmetzen, and in France the "Corps d'État" and the Companionage.

To return to the Comacines. King Rotharis was the Lombard King who issued the above edict on November 22nd, [illegible] and from the wording it is made abundantly clear that the King was not creating a new body, but confirming the privileges

[1] But a higher degree sign is shown in an Anglo-Saxon MS. from the Cottonian Library in the British Museum.

of an old and well-established fraternity, and that these men were not ordinary workmen, but artists, skilled architects, sculptors, and decorators; in short, the Comacines were a college of architects rather than a trade union of stonemasons.

Now this is a most essential point, for over and over again those who endeavour to prove that the speculative side of Freemasonry is no older than the eighteenth century base their chief arguments on the fact that ordinary ill-educated workmen in the Middle Ages could not have appreciated, much less evolved, the speculative side of Freemasonry. Even the third degree, they argue from this, must be modern, and obviously therefore all the higher degrees also, yet we find the prototype of the eighteenth degree in far-away mediæval Mexico, among people who were certainly not more cultured than the men who designed and built and carved Canterbury or Ely.

Under Charlemagne, and even before him, the Comacines began to migrate across Europe, and they followed the missionaries of the Church. The legends which associate the craft with King Athelstan may be more correct than most have believed,[1] although probably at first these incursions into England were temporary, sporadic, and of comparatively short duration. Nevertheless, Bede in 674, when mentioning that builders were brought from Gaul to build the church at Wearmouth, uses phrases and words found in the edict of King Rothares, and one is almost compelled to believe that he is deliberately quoting them.

Nevertheless, I believe that the final and sustained connection began at the time of the Norman Conquest.

Certain important facts must be borne in mind:

(1) The simultaneous manner in which the styles of architecture were changed throughout Europe, e.g. the change from Romanesque to Early Gothic.

(2) No individual architect can be named for any of the great cathedrals.

Sometimes the name of a great bishop is given, no doubt a piece of flattery; but obviously a busy man like a bishop could not have designed and supervised the amount of detailed work our cathedrals involved.

Moreover, not even the names of the sculptors are known, or the men who painted the frescoes or designed the stained glass

[1] Otherwise how comes a R.C. sign in a Saxon MS.?

windows. The ground-plans of the great abbeys and cathedrals were not merely extraordinarily well worked out, but were in themselves symbolical, [illegible] and [illegible].

It was not till 1355, when the painters of Sienna seceded, as did the German masons later, that the names of individual artists who were anxious to obtain personal glory began to appear.

And all through these dark ages the memory of King Solomon and of his great temple on Mount Moriah was kept alive.

From an inscribed stone dated from A.D. 712 we learn that the Comacine Guild were organised into Magistri and Discipuli under the rule of a Gastaldo, or Grand Master. They called thei[illegible] places [illegible], and Leader Scott gives a very considerable list of these. They had [illegible] and W[illegible] signs, tokens, grips, pass-words, and oaths of secrecy and fidelity. They [illegible] [illegible] and [illegible], and the Four Crowned Martyrs were their patron saints. Among their emblems we find square and compasses, level and plumb-rule, the arch, King Solomon's knot, and above all the lion's paw, also the [illegible] and c[illegible].

They had also their appropriate regalia, and Leader Scott gives illustrations of them in this regalia.

The Guild Masons are quite distinct from the Comacines in certain respects, though closely associated with them in others. The Comacines were all educated men according to their lights, and speculative, as well as architecturally operative. The Comacines were, until they split in the fourteenth century, a universal body, whereas the Guild Masons were local and restricted. The Comacines were older than the Guild Masons, more aristocratic, if we may use the word in its best sense, and inheritors of ancient tradition from the past, not only as to the technical details of architecture but also as to the speculative and mystical side.

No doubt one of the reasons why the credit of the great cathedrals is usually given to some ecclesiastical patron, and not to the Comacine Master Architect, is because the historians were monks and incidentally not particularly efficient as geometricians and mathematicians, as James Dallaway points out. In connection with the last point it is well to bear in mind that during the early [illegible] Ages [illegible]t mathem[illegible], and from them no doubt much of their unorthodox mysticism was derived by the Comacines.

This powerful Guild was no respecter of ecclesiastical pretensions, as Findel has pointed out in his *History of Masonry*, where he has given a long list of bitter caricatures of the clergy carved by them.

To quote but a few examples. In Strassburg a hog and a goat may be seen carrying a sleeping fox as a sacred relic, while a bear carries a cross and a wolf a taper and an ass is reading mass at an altar.

In the cathedral at Brandenburg a fox robed as a priest is preaching to a flock of geese, while in the minster at Berne the Pope is depicted in hell.

If anyone else but a man protected by the powerful Comacine Guild had ventured to go so far no power on earth would have saved him from ecclesiastical fury; yet these insulting sculptures have not even been removed.

If we wish to emphasise the continuity of masonic tradition carried on by the Comacines we need but refer to Wurzburg Cathedral, where B. and J. were placed in the correct position at the porch, although now removed and placed inside the church, or to the altar at Daberan in Mecklenburg, where, in addition, can be seen a carving of the Last Supper in which the Apostles are shown in well-known masonic attitudes.

All through the Middle Ages the Comacines were tending to broaden the [illegible], and [illegible] o[illegible]rch; while always remaining i[illegible], they refused to become narrow and dogmatic.

The Guild Masons were, as already said, a separate body, and the essential part about them which distinguishes them from the Comacines was that a Guild of Masons of this type had jurisdiction in a certain locality only, and, further than that, no member of that Guild could work outside his town. He had a monopoly of the building in his particular city, with one significant exception, namely ecclesiastical buildings.

The Comacine, or true Freemason, could go anywhere, and his speciality was ecclesiastical buildings. When at work in a town he often employed Guild Masons to do the rough work, and when so doing he called the [illegible] "[illegible]." Guild Masons were admitted as [illegible] or [illegible], but only in cases where they displayed unusual ability both as craftsmen and in intellect. If, after trial, the Guild Mason failed to come up to the intellectual standard of the true Freemason he was, according to J. Fort Newton in *The Builders*, sent back to the guild. The inter-play between the Guild Masons and true Freemasons, the lineal descendants of the Comacines, is an interesting study, but we cannot devote much more space to it.

The following summary of the *modus operandi*, taken mainly from Hope's *Essay on Architecture*, will prove illuminating.

A body of Freemasons would appear at a town or spot near the castle of some great lord who desired to build a church or enlarge his castle. They were under the [illegible] from a[illegible]r, who nominated one man out of every ten as a Warden to supervise the other nine. They first erected temporary huts for their own use, and then a central Lodge. Sometimes they stipulated that the townsfolk should provide tiles for the roof of this Lodge and white aprons of a peculiar kind of leather, and gloves to protect their hands from lime and stone.

If required, they called in the assistance of the local Guild Masons to help them with the rough work, but they do not seem to have admitted them to the assembly in the Lodge with which they opened each day's work.

Here they met in secret, none but Freemasons present, and with a Tyler to guard the door against cowan and eavesdropper.

The word "cowan" is probably of Scotch or north-country origin, denoting a dry-dyker (one who b[illegible]) and is therefore not a true mason, although he pretends to do mason's work.

The Guild Mason proper, if he survives at all, probably does so in the so-called "Operative Lodges" to which reference has already been made. No doubt the Guild Masons picked up some of the symbolic and mystical ideas of their more educated Freemason brothers, but it is from the latter rather than from the former that modern Freemasonry is descended, and unquestionably the higher degrees were never known to the ancient Guild Masons, though probably the mark and kindred operative degrees as well as much of the craft ritual became known to them by degrees, and when Freemasonry proper began to collapse at the time of the Reformation many Freemasons may have joined the operatives, just as at an earlier date many T[illegible] took r[illegible].

This point has brought us up to and beyond the ancient charges, and makes this a convenient point at which to end this chapter. We have traced the chain from the ancient primitive initiatory rites through the mysteries by way of the Dionysian Artificers to the Roman Collegia, thence the Comacine Masons have carried us to the ancient charges. Does the chain hold throughout ?

If any brother answer, "It is a pretty theory, but antecedently improbable," I would reply, I consider that, on the contrary, it is antecedently probable ; far more probable than an explanation based on "coincidence or chance."

What many students fail to realise is the persistency with which old beliefs linger on and even keep in the direct succession.

How many who are unacquainted with the fact would believe that in Italy, almost within sound of the bells of St. Peter's, the worship of the ancient gods of Rome still continued at any rate up to the middle of the nineteenth century ? Yet Leyland has proved that the witches and outcasts of the Apennines worshipped the ancient Roman gods, particularly Hecate, and had done so from time immemorial. Further than that, they had developed the cult and evolved a new goddess Aradia, daughter of Hecate, who was their special patron. If that is possible, why is the theory I have submitted impossible or even improbable ?

CHAPTER XIX

THE ANCIENT CHARGES AND WHAT THEY TELL US

THE total number of ancient charges and constitutions is at least seventy-eight, most of which have been discovered since 1860, and all appear to be copies of still earlier documents. These ancient charges have been discussed at considerable detail for nearly three-quarters of a century, and it is not necessary to go over the whole ground again.

In the main, they give us a picture of the craft at a period when it was past its prime, but are nevertheless of the greatest interest; but they must be studied with an understanding eye. The very anachronisms and contradictions they contain are often the most illuminating part of them, and from this point of view perhaps the best for us to consider is the earliest, known as the Regius MS., which is in the King's library, and was not discovered until 1839, when James Halliwell unearthed it. Experts assign it to 1390 or fifteen years later than the first mention of the word Freemason, which occurs in the *History of the Company of Masons of the City of London* in 1375.

The legendary part tells how Euclid recommended the study of Masonry in Egypt. The author rapidly brings us to England in the days of Athelstan, who calls together a great assembly of masons and gives them a charter and lays down certain rules of the craft, fifteen for master masons and fifteen for the craftsmen. These are given at some length, and end with the legend of the Four Crowned Martyrs. The author feels, however, that he has not done justice to the great antiquity of the Order, so he goes back to Noah and the Flood, carries us past the Tower of Babel, gives us further details about the learned clerk Euclid, who is said to have founded the seven sciences, and closes with a series of notes on etiquette.

At first it was taken for granted that these charges referred exclusively to operatives, but closer investigation convinced such eminent Freemasons as [illegible] and [illegible] that there was much which could only be described as speculative and only capable of comprehension by fairly intellectual men.

The second of the ancient charges is the Cooke MS., which belongs to the opening years of the fifteenth century. This is in many ways far more interesting, for it becomes evident that the author had used two earlier MSS., and is endeavouring to harmonise two distinct traditions.

One of these MSS. traces the origin of the [illegible] and the other to the [illegible] In consequence we get some absurd anachronisms, as when he makes Euclid the pupil of Abraham.

The "historical lecture" begins with a sketch of the lives of the [illegible], which relates how [illegible] and [illegible] their [illegible] on [illegible], o[illegible] and the other [illegible] After the Flood one of these was found by [illegible] and the other by [illegible], who each proceeded to teach the knowledge they had derived from them. Others substitute the name of Euclid for that of Hermes. The knowledge of geometry and masonry thus reached Egypt, where the Hebrews learnt it and took it with them to the Holy Land. We next learn that [illegible] [illegible], and gave them wages nearly as they are now. Strange to say, very little is told us about the building of the Temple, though our author adds that "Solomon confirmed the charges that David had given to masons," and that he taught them their usages, differing but slightly from those now in use.

Only a slight allusion is made to the chief artificer of the Temple, and his name is not mentioned except in disguise, but in place of it we obtain a host of pseudonyms such as Aynone, Aymon, Dynon, Amon, Benaim, etc., in the various MSS. The author then rapidly traces the masons into France and England, and then returns to Euclid and brings that part of the tradition up to the time of the entry of the Order into England.

What does this tangled mass of legend indicate? (1) The great antiquity of the Order; (2) that in some way the ancient [illegible] and the b[illegible] both [illegible] to create [illegible]. Hermes, Euclid, and Pythagoras point to the part played by the Dionysian Artificers and later to the influence of the Comacines as preservers of the ancient traditions of early days.

And perhaps the truest answer as to whence Masonry comes

which is found in any of these ancient MSS. is that given in the Layland-Lacke MS. which was in the Bodleian Library. It is believed to be as old as 1486, but this is disputed by some. "Where did it begin?"

It began with the *first* men of the *East*, who were before the first men of the West. "Who brought it to the West?"

The Phœnicians, etc.

"How came it into England?"

Pythagoras, a Grecian, travelled to acquire knowledge in Egypt and Syria, and in every other land where the Phœnicians had planted Freemasonry, and, gaining admission into all lodges of masons, he learned much and returned and dwelt in Magna Græcia. Here he formed a great Lodge at Crotona, and made many masons, some of whom travelled into France, and there made many more, from whence in due time the art passed into England.

"But why," some will ask, "is there no mention of H.A.?" Surely the answer is that, as this was a great masonic secret, the writers were anxious to avoid writing anything to disclose it; but, further, the purpose of these charges was to remind brethren of things they might forget, and to tell the younger men things they might not know. But no mason who had once learned the drama of H.A. would forget it, and if it formed part of their rites all must learn it in due course. After all, the Strassburg builders carved the legend in stone, see *Bulletin of the Supreme Council, Southern Jurisdiction, U.S.A.* (vii. 200). Surely that is sufficient evidence!

What can we make out of these charges? Firstly, I cannot agree that the constantly repeated reference to the great Masonic Assembly held by Athelstan can be ignored because the various accounts are contradictory.

I feel sure that the tradition had some basis in fact, though we may not as yet be able to decide how far it was the epoch-making event that these old MSS. seem to claim. Secondly, I contend that this conflicting legendary history shows that the brotherhood had a tradition—a tradition which I contend is a sound one—that they were descended from a remote period, that they derived ultimately from a blending of Syrian and Egyptian thoughts and organisations, were carried westward via Greece and Rome into France and thence to England, and I believe, if we studied the charges in the light of the theory I have propounded, they might yield still further information.

CHAPTER XX

THE DECLINE OF THE GUILDS

THE disintegration of the great Comacine Guild began in the fourteenth century, as has already been mentioned, the first sign being the [illegible] of the S[illegible].

So far as we can trace the course of subsequent events, the dissolution of the Universal Brotherhood took place slowly. No doubt many influences were at work, one of the most important being the rising tide of nationalism which slowly undermined the international ideals of the World Church represented by the Pope, and the World State symbolised by the Emperor. With the growing national feeling and the concomitant national antipathies which arose, German, French, and English Comacines would lose touch with the original body in Italy. They no doubt became known in England as Freemasons, and it is significant that the first of the ancient charges appeared at the very time when we know that the disintegration of the Comacine Brotherhood must have begun. By the end of the fifteenth century the separation was no doubt complete, and at the same time we begin to perceive that the spirit of the mediæval builders is dead.

On the Continent Gothic work becomes feeble and shallow and soon passes away before the rise of Renaissance architecture. Now, whence came Renaissance architecture? From Italy, the home of the Comacine, and is it surprising if the heart of Masonry was able to send forth a new outburst of building which overthrew the style still employed by schismatic Lodges of the Continent which had broken away from the parent Lodge, and so lost touch with the natural source of their inspiration?

In England we find our insular position and racial characteristics enable our Freemasons here to evolve a new and peculiarly English style, the Perpendicular, which does not grow sterile, but develops into Tudor, and then is abruptly cut short by the so-called Reformation.

Without allowing ourselves to be drawn into ecclesiastical controversy, we can all unite in agreeing that Henry VIII's policy of monastic spoliation dealt the death-blow alike of mediæval Freemasonry and of the Perpendicular style. The work of the operative Freemason was gone. Henceforth, neither monasteries nor churches were built, and when, after an orgy of destruction, men set themselves to reconstruct, they built country houses out of the spoils of the monasteries rather than churches. Moreover, the old continuity was largely broken; a new series of architects arose, scholars who had studied abroad, in France or even Italy; men who went back to the remains of classical architecture for their inspiration rather than developed on the lines of their predecessors. Of course, as one generation runs into another, so the old Freemasons and the new architects blended. Often, no doubt, the latter employed the members of the old school to carry out their modern ideas, and so we see numerous examples showing a blending of detail; but the break is unmistakable and real for all that. The type of building which most closely resembled the old monasteries was the college, whether at Oxford or Cambridge, and here, no doubt, the local tradition enabled the Freemasons to carry on their mediæval ideas more truly than elsewhere; but the Civil War completed the break which the Reformation had begun, and by the time of Wren the days of the old Freemasons were drawing to an end.

Wren's work may be left to the next chapter, and the rest of this devoted to a brief consideration of Freemasonry during this epoch.

It would appear, that when the Reformation ended the steady stream of church work, the Freemasons themselves rapidly declined in importance. There appear to be indications that many fraternised with the Guild Masons, or rough masons, with whom, in the days of their glory, they would not have condescended to associate. Some of the Lodges degenerated into little more than social clubs, while no doubt many were destroyed at the time when so many guilds were plundered by the new nobility in Edward VI's reign. Yet the persistent tradition that they continued to exist cannot be ignored, and even the legend of the raid made on the Freemasons of York by Queen Elizabeth is not without significance. Modern historical students are more than sceptical as to whether it ever occurred, but the fact that such a tradition arose indicates that Lodges of Freemasons were existing right through this period.

Before going further, a last emphatic protest must be made against thinking that Freemasons and guild masons were one and the same. After the able article by L. M. Phillips in the *Contemporary Review* of October, 1918, this point should be considered settled once for all. This accepted, much that was obscure becomes plain.

Most of our present masonic symbols were used with a symbolic and mystical meaning right through this period. Thus the square and compasses, the rule and plumb-line, the two pillars, the perfect ashlar, the point within a circle, the circle between two straight lines, the winding staircase, etc., are found not only on monuments, but on vases and trinkets, and, above all, in the watermarks, used by paper-makers and in the initials of books (see *Lost Languages of Symbolism*, by Bayley; *Architecture of the Renaissance in England*, by J. A. Gotch; *Notes on Some Masonic Symbols*, by W. H. Rylands, *A.Q.C.* vol. viii, 8vo, etc.). It is often assumed that these are evidences of the existence of the Rosicrucians or some other equally elusive fraternity; but, as Whaite has shown, no real proof of the existence of a Rosicrucian Society has ever been adduced, whereas the existence of Freemasonry at this epoch is not really in dispute. A far more logieal view is that even at this date there were men associated with Freemasonry who were essentially speculative, and, as the opportunity for church building grew less and the ferment of the intellectual world grew greater, naturally these active minds would begin to direct their attention to expressing their ideals in literature instead of in architecture.

It is not necessary to go so far as to claim Shakespeare as a Mason because he speaks of "square men," but his use of the phrase shows that it was already used in a symbolic sense, and whence did he derive it? Again, the old brass square found in an old bridge near Limerick and dated 1518, with this motto inscribed thereon—

> "Strive to Live with Love and Care
> Upon the Level, by the Square"
> (See *The Builders*, by Fort Newton),

shows us masonic phraseology and symbolism long before 1717, despite Albert Pike. But the evidence of the masons' marks alone is sufficient to prove that symbolism, often of a very elaborate order, was an essential part of mediæval as of Reformation Freemasonry.

Speculative or " accepted masons " appear to have been *accepted* in comparatively early days, and, though no doubt most were ecclesiastics, there appear to have been others, scholars and rebels against orthodoxy, who found here a haven of refuge. The records of early Freemasonry are exceedingly scanty, but we find in the minutes of the Lodge of Edinburgh in 1600 that a John Boswell, who was not a working mason at all, was a member of the Lodge.

In 1670, in the Lodge of Aberdeen, out of forty-nine members, thirty-nine were " accepted masons," and in no way connected with the building trade.

On May 20, 1641, we learn that Robert Moray, " General Quartermaster of the Armie of Scotland," was initiated at Newcastle by members of the Lodge of Edinburgh who were with the Scottish army which had entered England in arms against King Charles. This is the earliest surviving record of the initiation of a Speculative Freemason in England, but a few years later the famous Elias Ashmole, the great antiquary, was initiated at Warrington, in Lancashire, at 4.30 on October 16th, 1646, as he himself records in his diary.

There was a second initiate, Colonel Henry Mainwaring of Kartichain, Cheshire, also a speculative, and more than that, by looking up the wills of men whom he mentions as present at the Lodge, we find that *all* must have been accepted or speculative masons.

Only once later does he mention Freemasonry, and that is under the date March 1682, when he mentions that he attended a Lodge in London, gives the name of a number of obviously speculative Freemasons, and ends by saying that " Wee all dyned at the Halfe Moone Taverne in Cheapside at a Noble Dinner prepared *at the charge* of the *newly Accepted Masons*."

Again, John Aubrey, who wrote *The Natural History of Wiltshire*, has written on the reverse side of folio 72 of the MS. which is in the Bodleian Library at Oxford, and apparently dated 1686: " This day [May 18, 1681] is a great convention at St. Paul's Church of the fraternity of the free [" free " crossed out and " accepted " substituted by him] Masons; where Sir Christopher Wren is to be adopted a brother, and Sir Henry Goodric of the Ye Tower and divers others." This last quotation introduces matters of controversy, for there is reason to believe that Wren was initiated in 1641, but for the moment we will avoid these quicksands and merely point out that this quotation and the previous ones all show that right through the seventeenth century "gentlemen," who were not in any sense operatives, were coming forward and seeking initiation into Freemasonry. Now, why should they do it? Obviously not so as to associate with Guild Masons, rough operatives of humble birth and little education. This fact alone would dispose of the suggestion that the Freemasons and the Guild Masons were one and the same. But even if the Freemasons were men of a higher status, comparable, in short, with modern architects, why should country gentlemen wish to enter a purely technical society? I contend that it was just because there was a vast amount of symbolic and mystical teaching still carried on in the Lodges.

I would go further, and contend that unless we then possessed the M.M. degree at least, the craft ritual would never have attracted such men. If an antiquary like Ashmole found an old solar myth such as our legend, old signs and symbols with a mystical meaning and hoary with age, we can quite understand why he should join the Order and remain a member of it.

But more than this, why was it that the speculatives crowded in more and more, and gradually deprived the operatives of most of their power, and finally struck out on new lines forming a Grand Lodge in 1717, unless there was in Masonry far more than a technical trade society? Finally, we know that the French Companionage or Sons of Solomon had the legend of the third degree before 1717, but so carefully was it guarded that it was not discovered to have been their secret till 1841 (see *Livre du Compagnonnage*, by Agricol Perdignier, 1841).

Briefly, then, the Reformation deprived the Lodges of their ecclesiastical work—work, be it remembered, which had been carefully withheld from the Guild Masons in favour of the Freemasons.

The rising tide of Renaissance architecture led to the development of a new type of architect who need not have passed through the Lodges to earn a living. The Civil War completed the work of disrupting the building traditions. The Lodges tended to sink into social clubs, and their members, who were educated men, were, in many cases, delighted to admit non-builders who were men of education and social influence, who would sustain the prestige of the Lodges. But it must not be supposed that all the Lodges approved of this policy; on the contrary, there was undoubtedly considerable opposition, particularly when it became evident that the speculatives were likely to obtain control of the organisation. Some Lodges, we know, never would admit non-operatives; thus, as late as April 24th, 1786, two brothers were proposed as members of the Domatic Lodge, No. 177, London, and were refused because they were not operative masons (*History of Lion and Lamb Lodge*, 192, *London*, by Abbott). I contend that it was just because Freemasonry carried forward the traditions, legends, and symbols of the once powerful and erudite Comacines instead of being descended from the humbler Guild Masons, that it was able to attract men to it as speculatives and so survive the day of operative usefulness and develop into a still greater and wider power in the world than ever before.

The truth is, many masonic writers have been so anxious to meet the objections of the sceptics that unwillingly they have given away the outer defences of the Order. Instead of boldly stating that the reason why Freemasonry developed into a Speculative Order was because it was already speculative and full of mystic lore, they have tried to prove that it was originally only an operative guild and its speculative side as being due to the deliberate working up of its ritual from outside sources by Rosicrucians and such like nebulous bodies. If the Rosicrucians ever existed at all, it is far more likely that they were an offshoot of the Comacine Freemasons than that speculative Freemasonry developed from them.

We have now reached the period of the establishment of a Grand Lodge, and can take up the story from the time of Wren and consider it from the point of view of the operatives as well as of the speculatives.

CHAPTER XXI

THE DARKNESS BEFORE THE DAWN

By 1580 the old Gothic builders had practically died out owing to the Reformation, and their Lodges, when they survived at all, became merely social clubs, often consisting chiefly of non-operatives. The reintroduction of the classical style or renaissance architecture was due to many causes, but one of the chief exponents of the new [illegible], who, with the assistance of Lord Herbert, brought o[illegible] from Italy who, op[illegible], rearranged the southern Lodges on the plan of the colleges of Italy. If this tradition be correct it would mean that modern Freemasonry probably derives from the remodelled Lodges at the beginning of the seventeenth century. Now, if this is so, we shall at once perceive that what Inigo Jones really did was to return to the original source of Freemasonry in Italy, or, in other words, the Comacine Lodges.

Long ere this date their seat on the island of Lake Como had been destroyed, but the Lodges which derived from them were no doubt still carrying on an independent existence. It is rather difficult to trace how many Lodges existed in England, but one tradition is that there were eight Guilds, which were apparently arranged as follows :

1 in the City of London.
1 at Westminster. (This Guild is perhaps represented by the present Operative Lodge in London.
1 which apparently served for the Southern Counties.
1 at Bristol.
1 at Chester.
1 at Anglesea.
1 at Lancaster.
1 at York.

There would appear also to be evidence that, at any rate at one time, a Lodge existed at Durham, for the arms thereof are still said to hang in the Guild Hall. Whether these Lodges had jurisdiction over subordinate Lodges or not is a matter of dispute. Yarkar apparently thought they had, but the tradition of the present-day operatives is against this view. What is perfectly clear, however, is that the whole system, despite the attempt of Inigo Jones to rejuvenate and reorganise it, was slowly collapsing, and although we shall be better able to understand the opposition which the Grand Lodge experienced after we have considered the operatives' version of the story, we cannot doubt that, but for the establishment of the Grand Lodge in 1717, Freemasonry would have perished almost entirely. Even the operative Lodges which survived, if they did survive, did so largely because they were galvanised into activity by opposition to the pretensions of Grand Lodge. The Civil War naturally affected the Guilds detrimentally, and it was only after the restoration of the King, and the Fire of London, that they obtained a further lease of life, due to the great demands made on them for rebuilding London. The fact that the Guilds survived accounts for the rapidity with which London was rebuilt, and the enormous number of churches erected.

The position of Christopher Wren is still a matter of dispute. The operative tradition is that unquestionably he was a Freemason, and this tradition I feel cannot be ignored. Further, I fail to see why we should discredit Dr. James Anderson's statement in the *New Book of Constitutions* published in 1738. It is in reality the only record we have, at any rate from our point of view, of the founding of the Grand Lodge of England, and, if we are prepared to accept the other facts and statements which will be given at full length later, I fail to see on what grounds we can disbelieve this emphatic sentence: "And after the rebellion was over—A.D. 1716—the few Lodges at London, finding themselves neglected by Christopher Wren, thought fit to cement under a Grand Master as the centre of union and harmony," etc. The operatives' version runs somewhat as follows. The St. Paul's Guild from which they derived was established at the Portsmouth Quarries in 1673, and it gave a journey warrant to a Lodge of the fourth degree when Christopher Wren (said to have been made an Arch Guild Initiative in 1649) began to clear the ground and prepared the material for rebuilding St. Paul's. In 1675 Grand

Master James Strong laid the first corner-stone. Dr. Henry Compton was appointed Chaplain, and continued daily service on the site until 1710. In 1697 they sent a Guild to Chatsworth to build the big house there, and it is claimed that this Guild still exists. In 1710 Dr. James Anderson became Chaplain in succession to Dr. Compton, at the time when it was probable the Guild might be disbanded. In September 1714 he proposed that non-professionals should be admitted, which was carried by the casting vote of the chairman. Later in the same year there is a record of the admission of seven members who paid £5 5*s*. each. These are Payne, Johnson, Stewart, a lawyer, Desaguliers, Anthony Sayer, John, Second Duke of Montague, and Entick, a gentleman. Of these, Anthony Sayer, Payne, and Desaguliers are well known, as also is Montague. Johnson was the doctor who had (according to the operative rite) to investigate the physical condition of candidates, while Stewart was a lawyer, and Entick father of the later Entick. In the interests of these he appears to have changed the time of the meeting at the Goose and Gridiron from 12 noon to 7 in the evening, and adopted a password to distinguish the operative Freemasons from his non-professionals. Serious complaints were made against this deviation from the traditions of the Order to Wren and Strong, and, as the result, these non-professionals were struck off the rolls. The animosity of the operatives to Anderson is said to have been due to these and similar unconstitutional acts on his part.

In York, on the other hand, there does not seem to have been any real quarrel between the operatives and the non-professionals. There is, however, a record that in 1724 a Brother Scourfield had been initiated irregularly, whatever that may mean; but, at any rate, up to 1724 there appears to have been no difference between the operatives and the non-professionals. In 1725, however, they had separated, the former to meet on Saturdays at noon, and the latter began to meet on Friday evenings. The modern York rite certainly seems to have had more flavour of the operative guild rites than those in use in the south of England. By 1724 the opposition among the operatives had grown so strong at the alterations of Anderson, that it is stated that they began to hold meetings of their own, which the new Grand Lodge called "irregular Lodges." These restored much of the work which had been omitted, such as the Mark, the Basis of the Red Cross of Babylon and of the Arch, the trial of the Three Wretches, etc. And, further, out of these bodies sprang the Grand Lodge which Lawrence Dermott organised in 1751.

Such, briefly, then, is the tradition held by many of the operatives at the present day, and, while I am unable to say definitely that their story is correct, it does, as I pointed out earlier in this book, explain many difficulties which arise when we consider this period. It accounts not only for the opposition to Grand Lodge which certainly seems to have existed, but also explains the origin of many of the side degrees, and also some of the higher degrees. The operative tradition is that Dr. James Anderson was only a lower degree man, and had not the higher degrees; that he brought with him the lower degrees, and what little information he had about the higher he mixed up most terribly. The traditional hostility of the Mother Grand Lodge of 1717 to most of the higher degrees would be explained if they really belonged to the rebel or opposition Lodges, and, since all the latest evidence [1] points to the fact that the so-called higher degrees are quite as old as Grand Lodge, some such explanation is necessary to account for the fact that Grand Lodge not only claims no jurisdiction over them, but even appears to have opposed them.

Before closing this chapter, it is well to point out that there are certain degrees which bear a distinctively operative stamp. In that group I would specifically include the Mark, the Royal Ark Mariner, and the degree of St. Lawrence the Martyr. The latter two would appear to have been developed by men of an operative class rather than speculatives. The tradition of their origin also favours this view, and the obvious utility of these degrees, particularly the Ark and St. Lawrence, for proving that a man is a genuine operative and not one of these "new-fangled speculatives," gives a ready explanation of their popularity.

The fact that St. Lawrence is believed to have originated in Lancashire, a place far away from the Grand Lodge of London, also confirms me in this opinion. In short, I am inclined to think that these last two degrees at any rate were worked up in the eighteenth century by the operative members, with the deliberate purpose of distinguishing themselves from the speculatives, and forming, as it were, a little group of genuine operative masons.

[1] See the Installation Address of the W.M. of the Quatuor Coronati Lodge, 1919.

It is noteworthy that the operative Lodge in London appears to have no trace, either of legend or ritual, out of which these two degrees can be evolved, although the Mark forms an integral portion of their system of seven degrees. On the other hand, we must look to the Comacines and their later representatives the Freemasons, as distinct from the Guild Masons, for the origin of such speculative degrees as the Rose Croix of Heredom, the Royal Order of Scotland, etc. Such degrees as these were probably never imparted, even in the latter days, to Guild Masons. How far the present operative Lodges, if genuine, are descendants of the Guild Masons rather than the Comacines or Freemasons, is probably a moot point. No doubt by the beginning of the seventeenth century the two groups became blended together in such a way that a hard-and-fast line could not be drawn between them. In the main, however, I am inclined to the view that the guild masons are represented, if at all, by the operatives, whereas modern Freemasonry derives from the old Comacine Masons, although no doubt both guild and later Freemason each incorporated parts of the systems properly belonging to the others.

CHAPTER XXII

FORMATION OF GRAND LODGE

In the last chapter we considered a tradition of the formation of Grand Lodge from the operative point of view. Let us now consider it briefly as set forth in our own records. Unfortunately the Minutes of Grand Lodge only commence on June 24th, 1723, and our only history of the events that led up to the formation of Grand Lodge in 1717 is that found in the *New Book of Constitutions* of Dr. James Anderson in 1738. This account is very brief, and it may therefore be quoted in full.

"King George I enter'd London most magnificently on 20 Sept. 1714. And after the Rebellion was over, A.D. 1716, the few Lodges at London finding themselves neglected by Sir Christopher Wren, thought fit to cement under a Grand Master as the Centre of Union and Harmony, viz. the Lodges that met,

"1. At the Goose and Gridiron Ale-house in St. Paul's Church Yard;

"2. At the Crown Ale-house in Parker's Lane, near Drury Lane;

"3. At the Apple-Tree Tavern in Charles-street, Covent Garden;

"4. At the Rummer and Grape Tavern in Channel-Row, Westminster.

"They and some other old Brothers met at the said Apple-Tree, and having put into the chair the oldest Master Mason (now the Master of a Lodge), they constituted themselves a Grand Lodge pro Tempore in Due Form, and forthwith revived the Quarterly Communication of the Officers of Lodges (call'd the GRAND LODGE), resolv'd to hold the Annual Assembly and Feast, and then to chuse a Grand Master from among themselves, till they should have the Honour of a Noble Brother at their Head.

"Accordingly, on St. John Baptist's Day, in the 3rd year of King George I, A.D. 1717, the ASSEMBLY and Feast of the Free and Accepted Masons was held at the foresaid Goose and Gridiron Ale-house.

"Before Dinner, the oldest Master Mason (now the Master of a Lodge), in the Chair, proposed a List of proper Candidates; and the Brethren by a majority of Hands elected Mr. Anthony Sayer, Gentleman, Grand Master of Masons (Mr. Jacob Lamball, Carpenter, Capt. Joseph Elliot, Grand Wardens) who being forthwith invested with the Badges of Office and Power by the said oldest Master, and install'd, was duly congratulated by the Assembly, who paid him the Homage.

"Sayer, Grand Master, commanded the Masters and Wardens of Lodges to meet the Grand Officers every Quarter in Communication, at the Place that he should appoint in the Summons sent by the Tyler."

It is worth noting, in passing, that there is a record in an old book called *Multa Paucis*, which states that six Lodges, and not four, were represented at the meeting. The first point to note in this account of what took place in that year is the assertion that it was a revival of the old quarterly and annual assemblies, and not an innovation. For Anderson states in a note that it should meet quarterly according to ancient uses. A further fact is the careful observation of St. John's Day. St. John in winter and St. John in summer have always apparently been closely associated with Freemasonry, and this is a matter of the utmost significance. If we merely looked at Freemasonry as consisting of a Corporation of Masons, and nothing more than that, we should have expected that St. Thomas, who was a patron saint of architecture, would be their patron saint, and his day the day on which they assembled. But these two St. Johns were Christian substitutes for the ancient midsummer and midwinter festivals associated with the solar cult. In other words, we have here a striking piece of evidence in support of the view that Freemasonry had existed as a co-operative organisation long before Christianity was established. Otherwise there seems no reason why they should have seized on these two sun festivals.

Another point to be realised, in considering this account, is that at first, at any rate, the only idea was an attempt to reorganise the Lodges of London, and, perhaps, its immediate environments, including Westminster.

Grand Lodge, in fact, grew in spite of itself. Once started, it rapidly spread first over England, then throughout the world. No doubt considerable credit is due to the men who organised it and who faced and beat the opposition it aroused. But the real reason for its success was that it supplied something which was badly needed, and as time passed it was obliged to assume powers of which it had probably not originally even dreamt. Another point which perhaps is not sufficiently realised, and which is worth noting, in view of the tradition held in some quarters that the operatives were hostile to the new Grand Lodge, is the fact that, of the four Lodges known to have taken part in it, only one, namely that at the Rummer and Grape Tavern, had a majority of accepted masons among its members, the other three being mainly operative Lodges apparently. Therefore, the members of these Lodges must have been in strong sympathy with the speculative section, or it would never have succeeded at all. At the same time, one cannot ignore the fact that the leading spirits in these earlier years were nearly all accepted masons, and, moreover, members of the Rummer and Grape Lodge. Of all these four Lodges only one has survived, apparently, and that is No. 1, meeting at the Goose and Gridiron; in other words, an operative Lodge. After various changes of name it is now The Lodge of Antiquity No. 2. For further information about this interesting Lodge readers should see *The Grand Lodge of England*, by A. F. Calvert. The men quoted in the last chapter, such as Anderson, Payne, Desaguliers, were all members of this Lodge. Perhaps the explanation of the apparent conflict which here appears between the two versions which I have attempted to outline is the fact that the speculatives, being men of education, were at first heartily supported by their humbler brethren, but after a time their obvious endeavours to develop Freemasonry in the interests of the speculatives aroused opposition from the older operative members, who, nevertheless, having once placed the power in the hands of these able men, were unable to recover control, and were, therefore, obliged either to submit or to go out and form what were afterwards known as Irregular Lodges. The fourth point is this. Why, of all the trade guilds, is it that masonry alone has survived into the twentieth century as an active force? Nay, more than this, why has it developed into the tremendous power it is to-day? If any mediæval craft was overthrown by the Reformation it was certainly that of the builder. The spirit of Gothic architecture was dead, and even the style passed almost into a term of reproach. The occupation of the Master of a Lodge was gone, and his place was taken by an architect who was no longer a man trained in the Lodges as of old, but one trained by means of books and foreign travel. How comes it then that it did not pass as the other Guilds have done, or, at best, develop into a trade union? Surely the only explanation is that it lived because of its symbolic and speculative side, which did not perish when its craftsmanship did. This speculative side attracted to it the best intellects of the eighteenth century, and it was because it had this speculative side, and the other guilds had not, that it drew men in ever-increasing numbers into its fold.

In 1721 the new Grand Master, the Duke of Montague, felt that the old charges were inadequate, and instructed Dr. Anderson to make a digest of them, so as to formulate a better set of regulations for the Lodges. Anderson had probably already suggested the idea to the Grand Master, and a committee of fourteen learned brethren, with the assistance of Anderson, examined the manuscripts and reported, and the book was published in 1723. This work, however, did not contain the account of the organisation of Grand Lodge, which seems to have been added in 1738. Opinions may differ as to whom the chief credit for this is due. Past Grand Master Payne, and Dr. Anderson, were certainly each deserving a considerable share of it. But perhaps the most striking feature of all is the charge in regard to religion. The old charges had read somewhat as follows. The first charge is this: "They should be true to God and Holy Church, and use no error or heresy." The new charge was as follows. "A Mason is obliged by his Tenure, to obey the moral law; and if he rightly understands the Art, he will never be a stupid Atheist nor an irreligious Libertine. But though in ancient times Masons were charged in every country to be of the religion of that country or nation, whatever it was, yet it is now thought more expedient only to oblige them to that religion in which all men agree, leaving their particular Opinions to themselves: that is, to be Good men and True, or Men of Honour and Honesty, by whatever Denomination or Persuasion they may be distinguished; whereby Masonry becomes the Centre of Union and the Means of conciliating true Friendship among persons that must have remained at a perpetual distance."

The effect of this charge was profound: it threw open Freemasonry to all men who were prepared to believe in God and a future life, without in any way tying it to Christianity, and enabled it to become world-wide. When we consider the period in which it was written—a period, be it remembered, torn by the most bitter religious controversy, Roman Catholic against Protestant, Anglican against Dissenter—we shall be astonished at the broad liberality and charity which it breathes, a distinguishing characteristic which has ever since marked Freemasonry. But Grand Lodge did not stay here. As early as 1724 it started the work of charity for which it has become famous. A proposal in that year was made by the Earl of Dalkeith, which was received with the greatest enthusiasm, to raise funds for a general charity for distressed masons. It is certainly a curious coincidence that one of the first to petition for relief was Anthony Sayer, the first Grand Master. With regard to Anderson himself, from a short sketch of his life in *The Gentleman's Magazine* for 1783, we learn that he was a native of Scotland, and for many years Minister of the Scots Presbyterian Church in Swallow Street, Piccadilly. Towards the end of his life he appears to have suffered many misfortunes, and he died in 1739. For those who would like to find out more about this interesting character I would refer them to Gould's *History of Masonry*, vol. iii, or to *The Grand Lodge of England*, by A. F. Calvert. The fund started in 1724 was organised under the control of the Board of Benevolence, and no further words of mine are necessary to remind my readers of the vast amount of useful work this Board has since performed for Freemasonry.

CHAPTER XXIII

THE EARLY HISTORY OF GRAND LODGE

It is not necessary to write in detail the history of the development of Grand Lodge. Indeed, a library has already been built up on this subject. For the convenience of readers a brief summary is given here, and those who desire further information will find ample details in the Library of Grand Lodge itself. Certain facts, however, may be pointed out. Thus, the organisation of Grand Lodge was not accepted without a certain amount of opposition. From the first the Grand Master was given more powers than was ever granted to the President of an ancient assembly. In the old days, apparently, the Wardens as well as the Master were elected, both in the Lodges and in the General Assembly, and a reminiscence of this fact still exists when a new Lodge is formed, for the two Wardens as well as the Master must be elected by the founding brothers. In 1721 we find that twelve Lodges attended in June, sixteen in September, twenty in December, and by 1728 the number had grown to thirty, and all of these were in London. It was not till 1724 that we hear of Provincial Lodges acknowledging its obedience, the first being the Lodge of the Queen's Head, City of Bath.

The first Lodge on foreign soil was founded by the Duke of Wharton in 1728, and it was regularised the following year, by which date Lodges had also been established at the East India Arms, Bengal, and also at Gibraltar.

Meanwhile the old Lodge at York had proclaimed itself a Grand Lodge as early as 1725. In 1729 a Grand Lodge of Ireland was created, and one of Scotland in 1736. These two Lodges were self-constituted by the joining together of existing Lodges, and did not derive from England; but the next Grand Lodge, that of France, in 1736, appears to have derived from England, as did the various

German Lodges which formed the Grand Lodge of the Three World Hemispheres of Berlin in 1744. Gradually Lodges, and subsequently Grand Lodges, were thus built up throughout the world.

It is not always easy to trace the first beginnings of Freemasonry in these overseas areas. Thus in 1680 there came to South Carolina in America a man named John Moore, an Englishman, who in 1703 was Collector at the Port of Philadelphia. In a letter written by him in 1715 he mentions " having spent a few evenings in the festivities of my masonic brethren." Some authorities regard this as the first evidence of Freemasonry in America, but there is an earlier record which seems to indicate that long before the formation of the Grand Lodge of England masonic Lodges existed in the New World. This record is a curious document in the early history of Rhode Island, and runs as follows:

" This year, 1656, wee mett att y House off Mordacai Campanell and after Synagog gave Abram Moses the degree of Maconrie."—See *History of Freemasonry*, by Hugh and Stillson.

On June 5, 1730, Daniel Coxe of New Jersey was appointed Provincial Grand Master in New York of New Jersey and Pennsylvania. He does not appear, however, to have exercised his authority, and three years later, in 1733, Henry Price of Boston was appointed to the same office in New England, and Americans regard him as the father of regular masonry in U.S.A. Benjamin Franklin was a prominent Freemason, being initiated in 1730–31. Thus Freemasonry, by the middle of the century, had spread throughout the world. How far the Lodges consisted of new masons deriving their succession from English masonry, and how far they simply were the nucleus of older bodies of masons who now came into the open is impossible at the present moment to say; but it is highly probable, in the writer's opinion, that masons who already existed now began to come out in the open where heretofore they had remained quiet and, to some extent, a decadent body. The publication of the *Book of Constitutions* in 1723 was a public announcement of Freemasonry, and the challenge, if such it can be called, though probably it was never intended as such, was taken up at once.

Freemasonry has been, and even still is, an object of deep

suspicion to those who are not members of the Order, and no more bitter opponent of it exists than the Roman Catholic Church. It is not desirable to enter into matters of controversy, but in fairness to the fraternity it must be pointed out that from 1723 onwards it has been subject from time to time to unprovoked attacks, nearly always by misinformed people who know nothing about the Order, but draw on their imagination for the facts and arguments they adduce in opposition to it.

The first of these were the Gormogons, a body whom it has been suspected were organised by the Jesuits. The Gormogons served their day and passed. In fact, the year 1738, the year in which Clement XII published his Bull against the Masons, saw the end of the Order.

It is not necessary to go through the various attacks and so-called revelations and persecutions which Freemasonry has been subjected to, except to state that in some countries at least these persecutions were of a very real nature. We have records of men being put to the rack in Spain rather than betray masonic secrets, and numerous records of men being imprisoned for Freemasonry on the Continent.

The most recent attack occurred in a paper which one would hardly credit would take up such a story, namely, *The Morning Post.* The first of a series of such articles appeared on Monday, July 12, 1920.[1] It is not necessary for me to attempt to contradict the rigmarole and rubbish which these articles contain. No doubt most reading masons will have seen them and smiled at them. The thesis of the writer is that the whole of the social unrest of the world, whether it be the Revolution in France or the present Revolution in Russia, can all be traced back to the Freemasons, who themselves are dominated by a Jewish clique. The statements in this paper should be read by all brethren, as they show how the simplest facts can be distorted by an ill-informed and suspicious mind. I would particularly direct the attention of members of the eighteenth degree to No. 3 of this series, which appeared on July 14, 1920, where the whole purpose of that degree is deliberately twisted into an anti-Christian and pro-Jewish ritual by the most barefaced piece of misinterpretation. The source of the informa-

[1] At the same time the Reactionary Government in Hungary has closed the Lodges and seized their property. Be it noted the Bolsheviks had done the same, showing of course that the Lodges were *not* Bolshevik.

tion on which these charges are based appears to be certain attacks by the clerical party in France in the early part of the nineteenth century. Books which even then were absolutely false and misleading, and to-day are hopelessly out of date, are quoted in proof of these charges. The fact that some of the Continental Lodges have got mixed up with politics may be granted, but this in no way proves the contention of the author of these articles, for his thesis is that Freemasonry is a vast international organisation, aiming at the overthrow of the throne and the altar—in other words, Christianity and Civilisation. That an ill-balanced and ignorant cleric in, say, Portugal, might write such rubbish is conceivable, but that a paper of the standing of *The Morning Post* should publish such absurdities is almost incredible. There are nearly three million masons in America and about half a million in the Grand Lodge of England alone. In the much-abused Grand Orient of France there are probably not more than thirty thousand. Anybody who knows English or American Freemasonry can merely laugh at the idea that the Grand Orient of Paris—which has been excommunicated by the other masons since 1876—can possibly control their activities; but, nevertheless, these attacks will enable our brethren to understand the persecutions through which our eighteenth-century ancestors had to pass, and they may well be proud of the many brethren who were prepared to suffer imprisonment and actual torture rather than reveal the secrets of Freemasonry, as actually did happen. The fact that must be borne in mind is that we have promised not to give away these secrets. Logically, it may be argued that no great harm would have been done if these brethren, to save themselves from torture, should have done so: the harm would have been that they would have broken their most sacred oath. We can rejoice, I think, that they were prepared to follow the example of our Founder even into the Valley of the Shadow. Of course, attacks of this sort do harm—to the attackers. The greatest mistake the Roman Church ever made was when she forbad good Roman Catholics from becoming Freemasons. The fact that some of the Continental Lodges are anti-clerical is due almost entirely to the fact that, by preventing Roman Catholics joining Lodges, the Pope left these Lodges to be controlled by men who were already hostile to the Papacy, and, since in many countries on the Continent there is practically no alternative Christian religion to Roman

Catholicism, it meant that these men tended to become anti-Christians. That is the whole secret of the attitude of certain Continental Lodges. At the same time brethren should bear in mind the fact that the very constitution of Freemasonry forbids its use for political purposes and actually debars discussion of religious or political matters in Lodge, and this certainly should include the banquet after the Lodge. Too much caution cannot be adopted in these matters.

A much more serious matter than these attacks, which in the end only strengthen Freemasonry, was an actual split in Freemasonry in England. The Ancient Lodge at York in 1725 assumed the title of "Grand Lodge of All England." It appears never to have extended its authority very far, but in 1761 six of its surviving members revived it, and it continued with varying success until its final collapse in 1791. Its few supporting Lodges were chiefly in Yorkshire. It was never hostile to the Southern Grand Lodge; it was simply independent, and it has left its impression on the ritual of some of these Lodges in the North even to the present day.

Very different was the schism which started in 1753. It is believed that this originated in a group of Irish masons, who, having some quarrel with Grand Lodge, denounced it, stating that it had adopted new plans and departed from the ancient landmarks. They claimed that they reverted to the old forms and were *ancient* masons. They called the other body *Moderns*. It is possible also that there was a certain amount of Jacobite influence in this schism, but, if so, it has never been clearly established. It is noteworthy, however, that the so-called Moderns elected as their Grand Master the Prince of Wales, while the other body elected the Duke of Atholl. The dominating figure, however, was Laurence Dermot, their Secretary, and their success was entirely due to his indefatigable labours. To a certain extent it would appear as if some of the charges made by the Ancients against the Moderns were justified, in short, that Grand Lodge had altered certain parts of the ritual; but probably the charges were exaggerated. The hostility between these bodies was for many years very bitter, and another schism occurred in 1788 to complicate matters. This was led by William Preston. The trouble here seems to have arisen over a quarrel as to whether the Antiquity Lodge, of which Preston was the Master, by inherent right was

OLD EIGHTEENTH-CENTURY APRON.

By Finch, in the author's possession; probably Irish. The scenes relate to the third degree, the capture and trial of the conspirators, the R.A., and also the K.H.S.

entitled to grant itself a dispensation to appear outside Lodge in masonic clothing. It was a small matter, but when Grand Lodge decided against the Master the Lodge withdrew from Grand Lodge and formed an alliance with the old Grand Lodge of "All England" at York, and from them obtained a Constitution for a Grand Lodge of England South of the Trent. By 1789 Preston and his friends saw their mistake, apologised to Grand Lodge, and returned to the fold. Unfortunate as some of this controversy appears to us to-day, it undoubtedly led to great masonic activity on the part of the craft, and much of its development may be traced to the zeal of the various partisans.

Gradually, however, better feelings prevailed and in 1809 Committees were formed to find out the best method of reunion. The reunion was in the nature of a compromise, and traces of this compromise can still be seen in our present organisation. The Grand Lodge of Reconciliation was held on St. John's Day, December 27, 1813. Again we should note the significance of the day. The hall contained delegates from 641 Modern and 359 Ancient Lodges, so mixed as to be indistinguishable one from the other. Both Grand Masters had seats in the East, and the union was happily cemented. One of the most significant features of the compromise was that the "Ancient Masons" insisted that Masonry must erase such distinctive Christian details as had crept into the ritual. One of the unfortunate after-effects was that most of the higher degrees were left, as it were, stranded, and hence Freemasonry in England is still broken up, and the various degrees ruled by different Grand bodies, the craft itself officially taking no notice of anything except the Royal Arch.

The sentence which declares that Freemasonry consists of three degrees and three degrees only, including the Most Holy Royal Arch, is, to say the least, on the face of it, evasive. The Royal Arch is not included in the three degrees—it is quite a distinct degree, and the Chair is also a distinct degree, so that even on that basis we get three craft degrees, the Chair degree making the fourth, the ordinary Royal Arch the fifth, and then the Chair degrees of the Royal Arch. It is not necessary to follow Freemasonry abroad or to enter into controversy over the so-called Morgan outrage in America. It is sufficient to say that, despite opposition and despite calumny, Freemasonry continues to spread, and never with greater speed than to-day; and I contend that the

12

appeal which it makes to men of every colour and creed in every race and in every clime is due to the fact that it is the common basis from which all our religious systems have developed. Its social aspect appeals strongly to some, its noble principles, particularly that of charity, to others; but, above all, the fact that in it men of every religion and creed find what is practically a religion which they can all accept is its greatest asset.

In the pages that have gone before I have endeavoured to trace its descent from the ancient primitive rites of our savage ancestors through the mysteries of the Dionysian Artificers, via the Comacine masons, and the Mediæval masons up to the present day. I have also attempted to show the meaning of some at least of our signs and symbols. Before turning to the higher degrees I would merely emphasise the fact that in our craft alone there is a mass of lore and symbolism which still requires the most careful study.

THE HINDOO TRINITY

He, who created us ages ago,
Sleeps in forgetfulness silent and lone,
Bathed in a radiance, scarlet of glow,
Freed from all trouble, unloved and unknown;
Leaving to Shiva to reap and to sow.

He, the Preserver, whom blessings we owe,
Moves on the Earth mid its travail and pain,
Seeking to lighten its burden and woe,
Grieves at our losses, and joys in our gain.
Blessed be Vishnu, who aids us below.

Dreadful to some are the mountains of snow,
Honoured by Shiva, high raised on His throne;
Loved by the multitude bending full low,
Gracious of countenance, gentle of tone.
Taking our spirits, He frees them from stain,
Speeding us cleansed on our journey again.

J. S. M. Ward.

END OF PART I

QUETZALCOATL POINTING AT THE MYSTIC "NAME" ON AN ALTAR (see p. 250).

(From *Bulletin of Smithsonian Institute.*)

OLD CHURCH SEAL.

Cast from an old church seal showing St. Lawrence the Martyr with his gridiron. (Note the use of the vesica piscis.)

PART II

CHAPTER I

THE SO-CALLED HIGHER DEGREES

What They Are

The additional degrees in Freemasonry are known by various titles, but none of them can be considered entirely satisfactory.

The most usual is "the Higher Degrees," but this is resented by some zealous supporters of the craft, and in its place "the Advanced Degrees" has been suggested. The term "Side Degrees" is also occasionally heard, but its use is dying out. It was a suitable name when there was no regular supreme body controlling a particular degree, as, for example, the "Secret Monitor," before the establishment of its own supreme body.

Briefly, in former days, many degrees were conferred in a somewhat haphazard way. After an ordinary Lodge Meeting two or three brothers would say to another, "Would you like to be made a Secret Monitor?" If the other assented, they took him *aside* and conferred it on him. No doubt in such cases the ritual was fairly simple, and consisted of little more than the grips, tokens, and words.

Among degrees which were probably of this kind, the Secret Monitor, the Royal Ark Mariner, and St. Lawrence the Martyr may be regarded as typical.

But there were certain degrees which could never have been of this nature, of which the Rose Croix is one. The symbolism and ritual is too elaborate, and without that symbolism and ritual they would have no meaning.

We can, therefore, see that among the additional degrees there are two classes at least. I think, however, we can go further and distinguish three groups: (1) those which are really part of the craft system; (2) those which are based on the cross and vesica piscis; (3) side degrees, or degrees of practical utility.

Of course, owing to the somewhat chaotic state into which Freemasonry fell, hard-and-fast distinctions cannot always be drawn accurately.

Taking the third group first, we find the various degrees included in it have one feature in common. Their ritual and symbolism is weak, and their chief object is "mutual help and support." In the case of St. Lawrence and of the Royal Ark, we can see quite clearly that they owe their origin to a feeling among the operatives in the eighteenth century that they must have some means of distinguishing "a real mason" from these "new-fangled speculatives." No doubt they felt themselves being deprived of real fellowship, and would hesitate to ask a "speculative gentleman" to help them in their private difficulties, whereas they would feel less hesitation in asking a genuine operative to do so.

The Secret Monitor appears to have arisen in the U.S.A. about the time of the Civil War. As Masonry grew and its members increased (there are to-day nearly three million masons in the U.S.A.) many no doubt felt that the old spirit of mutual help and personal friendship would die out unless strongly reinforced. The Secret Monitor was the outcome of this feeling. To a London Mason, the same feeling must often have occurred. We meet in Lodge or Chapter three or six times a year, hardly get to know each other, and, unless we meet in a "higher degree," never run across each other elsewhere.

The best feature of the Secret Monitor is that every brother is placed in charge of a Deacon. These Deacons are responsible for so many brethren. It is their duty to write to them at intervals between the meetings, and at meetings to report to the Conclave that they are well. Should any trouble befall a brother, he should apply for help to his Deacon, who is bound to do all he can for him. It is an admirable scheme, but its success depends almost entirely on the conscientiousness of the Deacons. If they are slack, it naturally collapses completely.

I trust I shall not be considered unduly carping if I point out that one of the principal defects of the additional degrees is the fact that the officers, instead of being appointed for merit, are nearly always appointed in rotation, whether suitable or not.

I have been present at an installation when half the officers appointed had not troubled to turn up, or even write that they could not come, and when hardly an officer present knew a sentence of his work. The officers were appointed according to the date of their taking the degrees. So long as they were subscribing members, even if they never attended they were considered to have an absolute claim. The effect on the solemnity of the ritual can be imagined, but if the same system were used in a Secret Monitor Conclave, the whole basis of the system would be destroyed.

With the passing of the operatives, the St. Lawrence and the Royal Ark have nothing to maintain them save the prettiness, or otherwise, of their ritual, and such simple symbolism as it contains.

The Secret Monitor, however, has much to recommend it from the point of view of " mutual aid and support."

In it are two degrees, and attached to it are the seven degrees of the Scarlet Cord. Thus a zealous brother, anxious to collect degrees, can acquire nine under the auspices of the Grand Council of the Secret Monitor, or, if we include the Chair degree, ten in all.

The Royal Ark Mariner is worked in a special Lodge, which is attached to a Mark Lodge in a similar way to that in which a Royal Arch Chapter is attached to a craft Lodge. It is under the control of Grand Mark Lodge.

St. Lawrence is the first of the Allied Degrees, of which more anon.

Group I

DEGREES ASSOCIATED WITH THE CRAFT

We can roughly divide Masonry into non-Christian and Christian Masonry, or, in other words, Masonry which deals with the Nature of God and Masonry which deals with the Cross. As will be shown later, these latter degrees need not in all cases be regarded as essentially Christian, although the rule in England is that none but Christians are admitted, and in one or two cases degrees which are clearly not Christian can only be obtained by those who have taken Christian degrees. For example, this is the case with the Red Cross of Babylon, which can only be taken by those who have already obtained the St. Lawrence the Martyr.

If it were possible, which it is not, the ideal arrangement of these non-Christian degrees would probably be:

Entered Apprentice.
Fellow Craft.
Mark Man and Mark Master.
Master Mason.
Past Master.
Most Excellent Master }
Royal Master. } Cryptic Degrees.
Select Master. }
Super-Excellent Master. }
Royal Arch.
Red Cross of Babylon.
Grand High Priest.

This series would take a candidate historically from the building of the Temple, give him many interesting details of its construction, tell him the great tragedy, explain to him how it was that the secrets came to be hidden, and where. Then tell him why the Temple was destroyed, how it came to be rebuilt, of the discovery of the lost secrets, of the heroism of a certain brother who won the approval of the King of Persia and enabled the Second Temple to be completed.

Finally, it would give a prophetic hint of the new priesthood of the Order of Melchisedec, foreshadowing the New Dispensation.

From the point of view of symbolism, it would keep distinct the teaching of the Nature of God from that relating to the Mystery of the Cross.

But historic events have rendered this impossible in England.

Though we gained much by the Union of 1813, we lost much. One thing seems to be clear, and that is that the Duke of Sussex was a strong Deist, and did his best to eliminate not only any Christian teaching from the craft degrees, in which he was right, but the Christian degrees themselves. The result was that they were allowed to disintegrate, and many nearly perished altogether. That they survived at all is a striking testimony to their real intrinsic value. These degrees therefore had to fend for themselves, strange alliances were made and sovereign bodies formed, often with little regard to any logical arrangement.

We cannot blame those responsible, rather we should render

unstinted praise to those who saved so much from the wreck; but what has been done cannot be undone, and we now find ourselves with a multitude of governing bodies where two or three at the most would have sufficed.

Lest, therefore, some of our readers should be led astray, we shall give a complete list, as far as possible, of all degrees now worked in England, together with their supreme bodies.

Group II

THE DEGREES OF THE CROSS

The Cross degrees are as follow.

The Ancient and Accepted Rite may conveniently be grouped here, because the degree known to most brethren is the eighteenth; but many of the intermediate degrees are not Christian, and I am led to understand that the thirtieth degree cannot be regarded as strictly Christian either.

The Knight Templar, the Mediterranean Pass, and the St. John of Malta, are all conferred under the jurisdiction of Grand Priory.

The Royal Order of Scotland, which has two degrees, the Harodim and the Rosy Cross. The Red Cross of Constantine, Knights of the Holy Sepulchre and of St. John, are conferred under authority from the Grand Imperial Council. Both these groups are in imitation of the Chivalric Orders of the Middle Ages, and there is also the Rosicrucian Society, which has nine grades.

These degrees cover all that can be strictly associated with the Cross, but both St. Laurence and the Knights of Constantinople are distinctly Christian in tone, and, besides these, the Council of the Allied Degrees works the Grand Tyler of King Solomon and a form of the Secret Monitor; but they can in no sense be regarded as Christian. Indeed, these last two degrees are very similar to one of the cryptic degrees, and to the first degree of the Secret Monitor.

All the Additional Degrees

The Mark and Arch

The first degrees which should be taken after the third degree are the Mark and Arch. Some brethren will advise that the

Mark should be taken first, because its symbolism is so closely associated with the craft, while others will claim that the Arch should come first, because it supplies the genuine secrets of a M.M. After taking these two, brethren will be well advised to wait some considerable time till they have learnt at least something of what they mean.

Attached to the Mark is the Royal Ark Mariner, which has already been mentioned as an operative degree. It is associated with the Flood, but beyond this we may not give any hint. It is not associated with the Ark of the Covenant, which belongs to one of the cryptic degrees, nor is it similar to the twenty-first degree of the Ancient and Accepted Rite.

The Cryptic Degrees

Before taking these, a brother must be a Mark and Royal Arch Mason. The degrees are four in number, and usually given one after the other on the same evening. They are Most Excellent Master, Royal Master, Select Master, and Super Excellent Master. These degrees are ruled by the Grand Council of Royal, Select Masters, etc. They are most interesting degrees, and claim to explain certain parts of the Royal Arch which are otherwise obscure.

There is a general belief that the degree of Most Excellent Master is the same as the Scottish degree of Excellent Master. This is not really correct.

In Scotland an English Royal Arch Mason is not admitted until he has gone through the ceremony of passing the Veils, which is usually done by conferring on him the degree of Excellent Master. As I have already pointed out, the passing of the Veils was originally part of the Royal Arch, and is still part of the Ritual at Bristol. There is no doubt it should still be insisted upon, and in most parts of the United States an English Royal Arch Mason is placed in a similar position as in Scotland, i.e. not admitted till he has passed the Veils. The four Veils correspond to the Wardens of the Gates in Amenti, and, until we have passed through the superphysical stages represented by them, we cannot hope to approach God Himself.

I cannot, however, find any evidence that the Scottish Excellent Master is conferred anywhere in England.

Having taken the Cryptic degrees, the brother will be well advised to take the Templar degrees.

The supreme body is Grand Priory, which, like the Grand Council of Royal and Select Masters, has its headquarters at Mark Masons' Hall, Great Queen Street, W.C., whence full particulars can be obtained. The robes worn in England are a tunic and mantle of white, adorned with a Red Cross, a cap, sword-belt, cross-handled sword, black sash, star and jewel.

The Mediterranean pass is now treated as an intermediate step leading to the St. John of Malta. The distinguishing symbol of the latter is a jewel, for, though there is a complete uniform, black mantle with a white cross shaped thus , and a red tunic, it is seldom worn save by officers of the Priory.

The Templar degree is conferred in Preceptories, while the St. John of Malta is given in a Priory.

Strictly, these are orders and not degrees, though the later name is often loosely used.

Speaking roughly, we may say that, while the Templar may be likened to the third degree, the St. John is metaphysical and symbolical like the Royal Arch; but this must not be read as meaning that there is much similarity between these degrees and the M.M. and R.A., for there is not.

None but professing Christians can be admitted to these degrees. As considerable space will be allotted to the Templar and St. John of Malta, we will not devote much more time to them now, except to point out that in America the habit is quite different, and in no way resembles the correct mediæval robes as do the English. It has an apron and a cocked hat, and the St. John of Malta also has an apron with a red cross in the middle. An Irish brother showed me a St. John of Malta apron and told me it had to be worn in the Emerald Isle.

In America, the ritual of St. John of Malta is seldom given in full, as a rule merely the signs and words being communicated after the brother has been made a Knight Templar. In England it is worked in full, and when well done is a most interesting degree; but it requires a large number of officers to carry it out properly.

In consequence it is usually conferred in Grand Priory. This often results in there being far too many candidates, which somewhat detracts from the work, for which reason the author is glad that it was conferred on him in his own priory.

After taking the Templar and St. John, for which the candidate must be a R.A.M., a brother will be well advised to pause again, and after a while take the Rose Croix, for which the qualification is only one year a M.M. As this is a degree of the Ancient and Accepted Rite, we shall discuss this in full later, and we will here omit any further account except to point out that the candidate must be a professing Christian, and that the address of the Supreme Council, thirty-third degree, is at 10, Duke Street, S.W.

The degrees I would advise brethren to take next are those conferred by the Royal Order of Scotland.

As there is a certain amount of misunderstanding as to the qualifications required for these degrees, I will endeavour to explain the exact position.

The Grand Lodge of the Royal Order of Scotland can only be held in Scotland, and its seat is at Edinburgh. In England, the degrees are conferred in Provincial Grand Lodges. There is one at York, another at Windsor covering eleven counties, Metropolitan, which covers London, and several counties adjoining, and a new one is being constituted now in the West of England, and there is one for the counties north of York.

The Grand Lodge itself lays down that for the Harodim, or first degree, a candidate must be a Master Mason, of five years' standing. This rule holds at York and Windsor, but the Metropolitan Provincial Grand Lodge in practice will only admit members of the thirtieth degree of the Ancient and Accepted Rite. This is somewhat analogous to the system in vogue at the Apollo Lodge, Oxford, which admits only members of the University, although there is not even a by-law to that effect; simply everyone knows that only members of the University will be admitted into the Apollo, and those who are not 'Varsity men apply to other Oxford Lodges. Similarly, London masons who are not members of the thirtieth degree of the Ancient and Accepted Rite must go to Windsor if they wish to join the Royal Order of Scotland.

The degrees conferred here are, to my mind, some of the most interesting in Freemasonry. Historic records show that the Royal Order was hard at work in London as far back as 1748, and, even then, there were two Time Immemorial Chapters.

The ritual is in a curious old rhymed verse which bears every sign of great antiquity—and the whole arrangement of the degree confirms one in the belief that, even in its present form, it is exceedingly old.

The Windsor branch meets at the old Guild Hall in that town, and its proper designation is the Provincial Grand Lodge of the Southern Counties of England.

In the ritual, one is reminded of many degrees, e.g. parts of the Red Cross of Babylon, the Arch, the Rose Croix, etc. During a portion of the ceremony the candidate has to go "contrary to the sun," and this is correct, for we have passed beyond the veil before we are eligible for this degree, and the manes always goes from west to east, according to ancient beliefs.

At this point the keen mason will pause, and then according to his personal choice and opportunity, take any of the remaining degrees which follow. He will naturally be anxious to take the thirtieth degree as soon as he can; but, in practice, this is seldom given to anyone who has not been installed as "Most Wise Sovereign" in a Rose Croix Chapter. The remaining three degrees are but sparingly given as a reward for masonic service, and their number is strictly limited.

The degrees he can take are as follows: Knight of the Red Cross of Constantine, after which he is eligible for the Knights of the Holy Sepulchre and of St. John. The Royal Ark Mariner, Secret Monitor, with its pendant of the Scarlet Cord, which, as already stated, has seven degrees, and the Allied degrees. This group has control over a very large number of degrees, but in practice the only six worked are St. Lawrence the Martyr, Knight of Constantinople, Red Cross of Babylon (a most interesting degree and closely associated with the R.A.), the Grand Tyler of King Solomon, or Mason Elect of Twenty-seven, the Secret Monitor and the Grand High Priest. For the last degree, the candidate must have been a Principal in the Royal Arch, otherwise Mark and R.A. are the necessary qualifications. No regalia is worn in these degrees except by the officers, but there is a separate jewel for each degree. The Rosicrucian Society has nine grades, and the qualification for the first, Zelator, is that of being a Master Mason. The object of the Colleges, as they are called, is to study the real meaning of Masonry and the ancient mysteries. Promotion to the various degrees is strictly by merit, and for the higher grades it is usual for a member to qualify by reading a paper on some abstruse subject or render conspicuous service to the Society.

The ceremonies are said to be decidedly interesting and instructive, and all brothers who are anxious to study what masonry really means would be well advised to enter this Society if they can.

There is one other degree which must be mentioned, though little is said about it in ordinary works on Freemasonry. This is the Illustrious Order of Light. It is worked only at Bradford, and requires, I understand, a most elaborately decorated room or series of rooms for the correct performance of its ritual. In practice, admission is usually restricted to those who have taken the fifth grade in the Rosicrucian Society. I gather that the degree takes a long time to carry out, and is based on the Egyptian and Indian mysteries. If properly done, it should therefore be very impressive, but I can find little authentic information as to its origin or history.

At Newcastle, it is stated that the Templar High Priest still exists, but I have never met anyone who claimed to hold this degree, so cannot speak with any certainty. The Grand Council of Knights of the Grand Cross of the Holy Temple of Jerusalem, which has existed at Newcastle from time immemorial, certainly had power to confer it; but, as they entered into a Treaty of Alliance with the Grand Council of the Allied Degrees on January 1st, 1897, it is possible that they might hesitate to carry on the degree, since the Council now only works the six degrees already mentioned.

We have now recorded all the degrees of undoubted authenticity worked in England. In most cases, the governing bodies of these degrees are to be found at Mark Masons' Hall, the most notable exceptions being the Ancient and Accepted Rite and the Royal Order of Scotland.

Several of these degrees, and the Ancient and Accepted Rite, will be dealt with at greater length in succeeding chapters.

With regard to the fees charged, details can usually be obtained from the respective ruling bodies, while, as to the clothing and jewels, any masonic furnishers such as Kenning & Son, or Messrs. Spencer & Co., in Great Queen Street, can supply information.

One hint may, however, be useful. Brethren anxious to take

the eighteenth degree should inquire whether their masonic furnisher has a second-hand set. Very often it will be found that he has, owing to the fact that brothers who have taken the thirtieth degree no longer require the clothing, etc., of the eighteenth degree.

Excluding the intermediate degrees of the Ancient and Accepted Rite, which are not worked, and the various Chair degrees, there are, if we include the seven grades of the Scarlet Cord, at least forty-five degrees actually worked in England. If we included the various Chair degrees, and such degrees as the Mediterranean Pass, the seventeenth degree and twenty-ninth degree, etc., which are passing degrees, we could nearly double the number. It will thus be seen that the earnest student has plenty to study.

CHAPTER II

THE ANCIENT AND ACCEPTED RITE

Fourth Degree to Eighteenth Degree Inclusive

The designation of the several degrees of the Ancient and Accepted Rite:

1. Entered Apprentice. 2. Fellow Craft. 3. Master Mason.	Not worked by Supreme Council for England and Wales.
4. Secret Master. 5. Perfect Master. 6. Intimate Secretary. 7. Provost and Judge. 8. Intendant of the Buildings. 9. Elect of Nine. 10. Elect of Fifteen. 11. Sublime Elect. 12. Grand Master Architect. 13. Royal Arch (of Enoch). 14. Scotch Knight of Perfection.	Composing a Lodge of Perfection.
15. Knight of the Sword or of the East. 16. Prince of Jerusalem.	Composing a Council of Princes of Jerusalem.
17. Knight of the East and West.	
18. Knight of the Pelican and Eagle, and Sovereign Prince Rose Croix of H.R.D.M.	
19. Grand Pontiff.	
20. Venerable Grand Master.	
21. Patriarch Noachite.	
22. Prince of Libanus.	
23. Chief of the Tabernacle.	
24. Prince of the Tabernacle.	

ROSE CROIX REGALIA.

Note (1) The Serpent of Wisdom forming the Circle of Eternity.
(2) The Cross and the Pelican.
(3) Crown of Thorns.
(4) The Mystic Name in the triangle.
(5) The Roses.

REVERSE OF ROSE CROIX REGALIA.

Red crosses on black. Note the reverse of the Jewel with a white cross and an eagle rising towards the sun.

25. Knight of the Brazen Serpent.
26. Prince of Mercy.
27. Commander of the Temple.
28. Knight of the Sun.
29. Knight of St. Andrew.
30. Grand Elected Knight K.H., Knight of the Black and White Eagle.
31. Grand Inspector, Inquisitor Commander.
32. Sublime Prince of the Royal Secret.

33rd and last Degree: Grand Inspector-General.

In England the fourth to the seventeenth degrees are not worked; they are conferred by name only, and the candidate then proceeds to the eighteenth degree.

On the Continent some of these degrees are worked, and in the United States of America it is customary to work through the whole series.

The method adopted there is as follows. A Lodge of permanent officers is formed which works, say, the fourth and fifth degrees; another Lodge of permanent officers works the sixth and seventh, and so on. The candidate witnesses the degrees, takes the oath, and then moves on to a Lodge which works the next set. By this means, it is possible to work the various degrees properly, and at the same time advance any number of candidates. As the custom in America is to make all degrees rather more dramatic, than is done here, it naturally follows that, in practice, what the candidate sees is a drama enacted before his eyes.

In England the Supreme Council has graciously allowed the King Edward VII, Rose Croix Chapter of Instruction, to rehearse two degrees annually at their festival. For example, this year they "acted" the ninth and tenth degrees, and very impressive these degrees were. All members of the eighteenth may attend these festivals, and I cannot too strongly urge them to do so. The Authorities feel that it is not desirable at present to work any more degrees in England; but, recognising the natural desire of members of the eighteenth degrees, to know more about these "intermediate degrees," have agreed to this excellent method of doing so.

A brief summary of these intermediate degrees will no doubt prove of interest, and, without revealing more than we ought, a certain amount can be given. In the *Freemason's Manual*, by How, will be found a summary of each degree, and I have taken this as my guide, amending where he seems to have been led astray by following too closely continental working. I feel that there can be no harm in my doing what How has done; but, of course, neither signs nor words can be given, and even the summary must be brief, lest the outside world should learn too much. Therefore I would once more urge the keen Rose Croix Mason to attend the Annual Festival which is usually held at Mark Masons' Hall, Great Queen Street, in April.

The Fourth Degree, or Secret Master.—In this degree we are mourning for one who was slain just before the completion of the Temple. The degree explains the mystic significance of those things which were contained in the Sanctum Sanctorum, viz. the Altar of Incense, the Golden Candlestick, the Table of Shewbread, and the Ark of the Covenant.

The Master represents Solomon, and there is only one Warden, who represents Adoniram.

The Lodge is hung with black, and lit by eighty-one lights. The badge is white, with black edging; it has a blue flap on which an all-seeing eye is placed. The jewel of the degree is an ivory key suspended from a white collar edged with black. On the key is the letter "Z," which refers to Zadoc, who was High Priest in the time of Solomon.

The candidate is warned by a "voice" not to aspire to anything for which he is unfit, and learns that he must obey the call of "duty inexorable as Fate."

No tools are used in this degree, as work on the Temple had been suspended owing to a certain tragedy.

The lessons of this degree may be summed up in the two words, "Duty" and "Secrecy."

Fifth Degree: Perfect Master.—This degree may be considered as the continuation of the fourth, and, like it, is a tribute of respect to the departed brother.

The Lodge is hung with green, and should have eight columns, four on either side. The Master represents Adoniram, and there is only one Warden, who is called "Inspector," and represents Stolkin.

The Deacon, or "Conductor," as he is called, represents Zabdiel, who was the father of Jashobeam, the first Captain of the Guards

ANCIENT TEMPLE IN MEXICO.

Note lack of windows. It would be in such buildings that the Mexican Mysteries of the Cross would take place.

(From *Bulletin of Smithsonian Institute.*)

(1 Chron. xxvii. 2.). There should be sixteen candles, four at each cardinal point.

The badge is white with a green flap. On the apron is embroidered a square stone on which is the letter J, and the whole is enclosed within three circles. The green flap is to remind the Perfect Master that, being dead to vice, he must arise to virtue.

The jewel is a compass extended to sixty degrees.

The legend is as follows.—At the death of H. A. B., Solomon being anxious to pay a tribute of respect to his friend, ordered Adoniram to build a tomb for his body. The latter in nine days built a superb tomb and an obelisk of black and white marble. The entrance to the former was between two pillars which supported a square stone surrounded by three circles, and on the stone was engraved the letter J. The heart of H. A. B. was enclosed in a golden urn to the side of which was fixed a triangular stone inscribed with the letters J. M. B. with a wreath of acacia round them. This urn was placed on the top of the obelisk.

This summary does not do justice to this degree, which contains many details relating to the discovery of the body, and is full of symbolic teaching.

Sixth Degree: Intimate Secretary.—There are only three officers in this degree: Solomon, Hiram, King of Tyre, and a Captain of the Guard. The first two are the only officers inside the Lodge, which represents the Hall of Audience, and is lighted by twenty-seven lights. The two kings wear royal robes of blue, and the rest of the brethren are called Perfect Masters, not Intimate Secretaries. Their badges are white with a red border, and on the flap is a triangle. There is also a red collar, to which is attached a solid triangle interlaced. The members of the Lodge are called Guards.

The two kings are seated in front of a table, on which are two naked swords, a roll of parchment, and a human skull. They are arguing fiercely when H. of T. sees the candidate, who represents Joabert, peeping round the door, and, rushing forward, drags him into the room.

The legend on which this degree is based is briefly as follows. H. came to S. and complained that he had not treated him fairly in a certain matter. Joabert, knowing the two kings were at variance, was fearful lest Hiram should do Solomon some serious injury. He therefore followed him to the door of the Audience

Hall and listened, ready to rush in and help his master if necessary. Hiram, seeing him, seized him and demanded that S. should put him to death for eavesdropping. In the end, Hiram not only forgave him, but consented to his being made Intimate Secretary. Peace and harmony were restored between the two kings, and the degree made permanent to commemorate the event.

In this degree, for the first time, the candidate is given a sword with which to defend himself should anyone endeavour to extort from him the secrets he now holds.

There is an interesting tracing-board in this degree which is thus explained. "The window in the clouds represents the vault of the Temple, and the letter J which is inscribed therein indicates the Tetragrammaton or Sacred Name of God. The door represents the main entrance from the palace, the tears refer to the repentance of Joabert in King Solomon's chamber, when he lamented his excessive zeal; but they also symbolise the grief of K. S. in the apartment hung with black to which he was wont to retire to weep over the unhappy fate of H. A. B. It was in this same room that the dispute with H. K. of T. arose.

This is a most dramatic degree, and contains also considerable symbolic teaching, as, for example, that the triangle represents the three theological virtues, Faith, Hope, and Charity. Its resemblance to certain other degrees which are worked in England will be recognised by those who have taken them, and also the points in which it differs.

Seventh Degree: Provost and Judge.—There appears to be considerable variation in the working of this degree. Even so simple a matter as the number of lights used varies, one authority giving it as five, How gives it as six, while another authority gives it as twelve. The most important officer is Tito, who is sometimes stated to have been the High Priest at the time of K. S. The purpose of the degree is to invest an officer who shall have charge of the keys of the most sacred parts of the building.

A point which strikes the student as peculiar is the use of the Latin name Tito, and the title of Provost, which is derived from Latin via French.

One version of the degree contains a curious piece of symbolism, namely, two crosses tau-shaped, i.e. T T, which are within a triangle which is within a circle. There are also two roses, one white and the other red, and we are told that "the white rose represents the purity and innocence of H. A. B., and the red his blood." This symbol, however, does not appear in all the various rituals.

The badge is white lined with red, and has a pocket "to hold the keys and plans." The collar is red, to which is suspended a golden key on the wards of which is engraved the letter A.

The hangings of the Lodge are red.

Eighth Degree: Intendant of Buildings.—This degree is sometimes called "The Master in Israel." The principal officers are K. S., the Inspector, who represents Tito, and a Junior Warden, who represents Adoniram. The legend states that the object of its institution was to supply the loss of H. A. B. The badge is white, bordered with green and red; on the centre is a nine-pointed star, and on the flap a triangle, within which is a certain letter. The Lodge is illuminated by three groups of nine lights, or twenty-seven in all.

The most interesting part of this degree is the metaphorical use of the major points in the craft in conjunction with the five orders of architecture, and we are told that "The Intendant of Buildings" must have made the five steps of exactness, penetrated the innermost part of the Temple, and beheld the Great Light containing the three mysterious characters.

To a certain extent there does not appear to be much purpose in this degree. Adoniram was the successor of H. A. B., and there was no other building save the Temple; at any rate, the degree refers to no other, and therefore there does not seem to be much need of this officer.

Ninth Degree: The Knights Elect of Nine.—For the first time the body is called a Chapter instead of a Lodge, and its members are knights.

K. S. is called Most Wise, and H. of T. is Most Puissant. There are a large number of officers, most of whom, however, do nothing save support the two kings in the east. The Chapter-room represents the secret chamber of K. S., and is hung with black flecked with red and white tears, and it is illuminated with nine candles.

The badge is of white satin, on which is painted a severed head and a dagger, while the border is black. The sash is black with nine red roses, and to it is attached a small gilt poniard. Sometimes, instead of a sash, a collar is worn.

In France this is regarded as the fourth degree, for many of the intermediate degrees have been omitted or amalgamated so as to reduce the series in number. This is an important degree, and has a striking legend. Briefly it tells of the pursuit of the three murderers. One is caught hiding in a cave and slain out of hand by Joabert, who is represented by the candidate. This form of the legend is the original one, and is still the one followed in the Northern Jurisdiction of the United States; but, in the Southern, Joabert no longer takes the law into his own hands. To continue the Northern form of the legend, when Joabert returned with his companions to K. S. carrying the severed head and bloodstained dagger, he is upbraided by the king and nearly put to death for taking the law into his own hands. K. S., however, relents, pardons him, and constitutes this degree to mark the event.

In the ritual of the Southern Jurisdiction the king thinks Joabert has slain the miscreant; but, on finding that he has not, but has bound him and brought him prisoner with him, he tells Joabert it is well he has not, for those who slay even a murderer without the sanction of the law after due trial are themselves murderers.

As the criminal symbolises Ignorance, I think the Northern version is better, for Ignorance should be slain by everyone at sight.

The oration which concludes this degree is very fine, and the grip is a peculiarly symbolic and interesting one.

Tenth Degree: The Knights Elect of Fifteen.—This, in a way, is a continuation of the last degree. The remaining criminals are hunted down by the *fifteen* knights, captured in a quarry, and brought to the king for due trial. There are very fine soliloquies by the two culprits, which for poetic feeling are hardly to be equalled anywhere in Masonry.

The moral of these two degrees may be summed up as follows. We must be tolerant of other men's religious views, because all religions have much that is true in them, and we must combat ignorance by education, bigotry by tolerance, and tyranny by teaching true liberty, which does not mean anarchy, but ordered government according to the wishes of the majority.

The hangings of the Chapter in this degree should be similar to those in the ninth degree. The badge is like that worn in the former, save that it has three severed heads placed on the tops of three arches.

Both these degrees are exceedingly interesting and dramatic, and deserve the closest study. While looking at the famous

Fenton vase, an old Maya relic from Guatemala, I was surprised to notice that some of the characters were standing in a position in which the nine knights have to stand during part of the ceremony. The rest of the scene was also reminiscent of the same part of this, the ninth degree. No archæologist disputes the fact that the scene depicted on the vase is symbolic, and probably represents some ritual in the Temple.

A man is seated on a small throne who wears a pentacle, and also the feathered headdress which shows he is a king, while before him kneels another man, who is evidently not so high in rank, as shown by his headdress, and also by the fact that he wears a □ attached to a cord round his neck.

This symbol is generally considered to represent a lodge-room, and indicated that its wearer is a member of what we should call a craft degree.

Behind this kneeling man stand others in the peculiar attitude to which I have referred.

It will thus be seen that, in addition to eighteenth and thirtieth degrees, the Mayas appear to have had the prototypes of some of the other degrees still worked as a part of the Ancient and Accepted Rite.

Eleventh Degree: Sublime Elect.—This degree is sometimes called "Twelve Illustrious Knights." We are informed that K. S. subdivided the workmen into twelve divisions in imitation of the twelve tribes of Israel and appointed the twelve "Sublime Elect" to have charge of them.

These worthy masons had to render to the King a daily account of the work performed by their sections, and receive from him the payment due to them which they afterwards disbursed.

The assembly is called a Grand Chapter; K. S. presides, assisted by a Grand Inspector and a Grand Master of Ceremonies. The room is hung with black, the apron is white with a black border and lining, and on the flap is a red cross. There is a black sash suspended from the right shoulder to the left hip having on it three hearts in flames, and a poniard hanging from it.

To a certain extent, this costume is reminiscent of the Templar costume worn in the U.S.A.

It is stated that this degree is included with the ninth and tenth to form the fourth degree of the French rite. This degree in some form appears in practically every series of higher degrees, and three words belonging to it are stated by How to be similar to those used in the H. R. A.

Twelfth Degree: Grand Master Architect.—This is distinctly operative and scientific in tone. The rules of architecture and the connection of the liberal arts with Masonry, are dwelt upon at some length. The assembly is called a Chapter, and is decorated with red and white hangings, while its ornaments are the columns of the five orders of architecture and a case of mathematical instruments. The jewel is a gold medal, on one side of which, in high relief, are depicted the five orders of architecture, while on the other side is a cube, triangle, and other appropriate devices. This is suspended by a blue ribbon.

The twelfth degree seems to have great possibilities, and it might serve a most useful purpose by instilling into the members of our order sound judgment as to architectural forms. This instinct is by no means so well developed as might be desired, judging by some of the so-called examples of masonic jewellery and furniture which are to be met with in many Lodges.

Considering we are Masons, it is our duty to acquire at least a minimum of architectural knowledge, sufficient to enable us to know at sight the difference between the Early English and Decorated styles and to appreciate what is good and what bad architecture in our modern buildings.

Thirteenth Degree: The Royal Arch of Enoch.—This degree is sometimes known by the name of the Master of the Ninth Arch. It has a certain similarity to our own Royal Arch, but the differences are so great that I should be only misleading my readers if I did not emphasise them. The officers are King Solomon, who is Master; Hiram, King of Tyre, who is attired as a traveller; a Grand Treasurer representing Giblim; a Grand Secretary representing Joabert; and a Grand Inspector Stolkin. These last two characters have already been the heroes of earlier degrees, and should therefore by now be well known to my readers. Enoch was an early Biblical hero, and the book of Enoch, now lost,[1] is quoted by St. Jude, who says, "And Enoch also, the seventh

[1] What was claimed to be an Ethiopic version was found in 1773, and an English translation appeared in 1882, and another in 1893; but, from its contents, it would appear either that the text was very corrupt and filled with magical and astrological formula, or else that it was not the work known of old.

from Adam, prophesied of these, saying, 'Behold the Lord cometh with ten thousand of His saints to execute judgment upon all,'" etc. The tradition is that Enoch, foreseeing that the world would be overwhelmed with some disaster, either through flood or fire, determined to preserve some at least of the knowledge at that time possessed by man. He therefore engraved certain records on two columns, one of brick and the other of stone. These columns were preserved through the Flood, and subsequently discovered, the one by the Jews, and the other by the Egyptians. This legend is undoubtedly very old, as we find it in the mediæval charges. The thirteenth relates the discovery by the Jews of fragments of this column during the building of King Solomon's Temple. The top of a vault or arch is discovered; one of the masons is lowered down and finds certain relics. The thirteenth and fourteenth degrees both deal with this tradition. The badge of the thirteenth degree is white with purple border. The jewel is a triangle having in the centre a representation of two people letting down a third into a vault. This is the only Royal Arch degree on the Continent, but in North America the English Royal Arch, as well as the thirteenth degree, is worked. It will be noted that the period of this degree is that of the first Temple.

Fourteenth Degree: Scotch Knight of Perfection.—This is the last degree relating to the first Temple, and, as already stated, is closely associated with the preceding degree. The apron is white with red flames bordered with blue, and bears the jewel on the flap. The jewel is a pair of compasses extended on an arc of ninety degrees surmounted by a crown, with a sun in the centre. Among the decorations of the Lodge in the United States is a transparency placed behind the chair of the Master, depicting a burning bush, enveloping a triangle, and the letters יהוה in the centre of the fire. In the west is a Pillar of Beauty. The pedestal is formed from the fragments of Enoch's pillar, which, being found in the ruins, were put together for that purpose. On a table is placed bread and wine and a gold ring for the newly admitted brother.

The companions, when seated, form a triangle, and the twenty-four lights are placed, three and five in the west, seven in the north, and nine in the south. The hangings of the Lodge are white, and a brother who had seen this degree worked in America told me it was one of the most beautiful degrees in Freemasonry. The legend informs us that K. S. formed into a Lodge of Perfection certain worthy Masters, and that, whenever this Lodge met, nine Knights of the Ninth Arch (thirteenth degree) tiled the nine arches which led to the Sacred Vault. None were permitted to pass without giving the passwords of the different arches. A number of ancient Masters were jealous of the honours conferred on the members of the thirteenth and fourteenth degrees, and claimed the same honours. This was refused, and K. S. told them that those whom he had advanced to the Degree of Perfection had wrought in the difficult and dangerous work of the ancient ruins, had penetrated into the bowels of the earth, and had brought out treasures to adorn the Temple. He then told the petitioners to go in peace and aspire to perfection by good works. The discontented Masters determined to go to the ancient ruins and search in the bowels of the earth, that they might have an excuse for making a further application to K. S. for the honours they coveted. The next morning they removed the cubicle stone and descended into the cavern with a ladder of ropes by the light of torches; but no sooner had they all reached the bottom than the whole nine arches fell in upon them. K. S. heard of this accident and sent Joabert, Giblim, and Stolkin to make inquiries as to what had happened. On reaching the spot they could find no remains of the arches, nor could they learn that any of those that had descended had escaped. They then carefully examined the spot, but found nothing, save a few fragments of masonry inscribed with hieroglyphics, which Solomon declared were fragments of one of the pillars of Enoch. The tradition also tells us that in later years K. S. degenerated, and set up temples in honour of the false gods, to please his wives. The Perfect Masons were much grieved at this conduct, but, though they kept their faith pure, they were unable to avert the wrath of Jehovah, which ultimately led to the destruction of the Temple. The tradition further affirms that, at a later date, descendants of these Perfect Masons accompanied the Christian princes on their Crusades to the Holy Land. As a reward for their services, they received the privilege of electing their Chief, and their valour called forth the admiration of all the Christian princes of Jerusalem. The latter, believing that their mysterious rites inspired them with courage and virtue, asked to be initiated. The Masons granted their request, and Freemasonry became diffused among the nobility of Europe, and ceased to be entirely operative.

This latter part of the tradition may perhaps be ascribed to the Chevalier Ramsay. This interesting masonic character was born at Ayr in Scotland in 1686, and in early life went to France, where he associated with the French *noblesse.* His French friends despised Masonry on the plea that it originated with operatives, and he therefore endeavoured to maintain that it really derived from the Crusaders. In 1728 he attempted to persuade the Grand Lodge of England to substitute certain knightly degrees for old craft masonry; but, his suggestion not being approved in England, he promulgated it in France with more success.

This, at any rate, is the view held by some brothers; but it is only fair to add that many competent authorities reject it altogether.

The Scotch Knight of Perfection is the last degree which deals with the Temple of K. S., and a Lodge of Perfection claims rule over all degrees from the fourth to the fourteenth inclusive. It is, however, in its turn subject to the Grand Council of Princes of Jerusalem (sixteenth degree). One of the oldest Lodges of Perfection in America was that at Albany, constituted on the 20th December, 1767, and derived its authority from Kingston, in Jamaica.

Fifteenth Degree: Knight of the Sword and of the East.—The fifteenth and sixteenth degrees are under a separate body to the lower degrees, and are controlled by the sixteenth degree Grand Princes of Jerusalem.

In the fifteenth degree the meetings are called councils, and the hangings are water-green. The fourteenth degree is the last that relates to the Temple of K. S. the fifteenth being connected with the second Temple built by Zerubbabel. This degree refers to those valiant masons who, with trowels in their hands and swords by their sides, rebuilt the Holy City and Sanctuary.

The Chamber is illuminated by seventy lights in memory of the seventy years' captivity. The sash is green bordered with a golden fringe, and is worn across the body from the right shoulder to the left hip, and on the front is a picture of a bridge with the letters Y and H. The apron is white lined with red and bordered with green, and has on it emblems of war and its consequences. To it is sometimes attached a dagger.

The tradition related is that Cyrus permitted the Jews to return to their own country and rebuild Jerusalem and the Holy Temple. Under Zerubbabel, a descendant of David and an ancestor of Christ, assembled 42,360 persons, excluding servants and slaves, who numbered an additional 7,337. For the protection of the people on their long march, Zerubbabel armed 7,000 masons and placed them in the van. They experienced no opposition till they reached the banks of the Euphrates, where, however, they found an armed force prepared to dispute the passage of the bridge. In the conflict that ensued the enemy were cut to pieces or drowned in the river. The colours of this degree are in allusion to this incident. The journey to Jerusalem took four months to accomplish, and the work of restoring the Temple was begun within seven days of their arrival. The workmen were divided into two classes; over each a Master and two assistants presided.

The work had scarcely begun when the Samaritans commenced to attack the workmen in order to prevent the completion of the edifice. Nehemiah therefore ordered the masons to work with sword in one hand and trowel in the other, so that they should be ready at all times to defend themselves and their work from the attacks of their enemies.

It was upon the masons who assisted at the construction of the second Temple that Cyrus conferred the title of Knights of the East.

This degree occurs in both French Rites as well as both those worked in the U.S.A.

In the shortened rite worked by the Grand Orient it is the sixth degree. The Council Room should contain the seven-branched candlestick, the brazen sea, the table of shewbread, and the other treasures of the first Temple carried off by the Babylonians, and now restored to the Jews by Cyrus.

The ruler of the Council is called Sovereign, and represents Cyrus, King of Persia. The second officer is the Chancellor, who represents Nehemiah; the Grand Orator is Esdras, the Grand Treasurer Mithridates, and there is also a Grand General. Zerubbabel and two others appear before the king and obtain from him authority to rebuild the Holy City.

Sixteenth Degree: Grand Prince of Jerusalem.—The Assembly is called a Grand Council, and is divided into two apartments. In the first, Darius the King of Persia is seated on his throne in his palace in Babylon. The dais of the throne is blue, but otherwise the hangings are red.

The other apartment is supposed to be in the city of Jerusalem, where Zerubbabel presides, and it is hung with orange. Both rooms are illuminated by five groups of five candles.

The emblematic colour of the degree is yellow, the apron is red-lined and bordered with pink, the flap is yellow, having on it a balance on which are the letters D and Z. The jewel is a gold medal with the same emblem on one side, while on the other is a two-edged sword and five stars.

The degree itself is very similar to that worked in England as the Red Cross of Babylon, but there are certain differences. It is a most interesting and dramatic degree, and contains much symbolic interest.

The first Grand Council of Princes of Jerusalem of whom we have any record was formed at Charleston in 1788, and took over the control of all degrees from the fifteenth to the fourth.

A Prince of Jerusalem has numerous privileges when visiting the lower degrees. Thus, he must be seated on the right of the Master, and has the privilege of addressing the assembly without first asking the permission of the Master.

The officers are designated as follows:

1. Most Equitable Sovereign Prince Master.
2. High Priest.
3. Most Enlightened Senior Warden.
4. Most Enlightened Junior Warden.
5. Valorous Keeper of the Seals and Archives.
6. Valorous Treasurer.
7. Valorous Master of the Ceremonies.
8. Valorous Tyler.

At least five members must be present or the Council cannot be opened.

In America the Council of Princes of Jerusalem performs important administrative functions, and the anti-Masons declare that Morgan was brought before this body and tried.

In England the degree is known only by name, although some of its real importance is shown by the fact that the Lodge of Perfection is closed and a separate Council of Princes of Jerusalem opened before the fifteenth and sixteenth degrees are conferred by name.

Seventeenth Degree: Knight of the East and West.—All degrees, up to the sixteenth inclusive, have dealt with the Old Testament. This degree seems to jump clean away from the series, for it deals with the Book of Revelation, the seven seals there mentioned, and the wrath of the Lamb.

It is claimed that it was organised by the Knights engaged in the Crusades about 1118, or during the same period that the Templars arose. We are told that eleven Knights took the vows of secrecy, friendship, and discretion between the hands of Birinus, Patriarch of Jerusalem.

The presiding officer is Most Equitable Sovereign Prince Master, and the other titles are similar to those used in the sixteenth degree.

The badge is yellow, edged with red, with a two-edged sword as an emblem on it. The jewel is a heptagon of silver, having a gold star at each angle, and in the centre a lamb on a book with seven seals. The reverse has a two-edged sword between the scales of a balance, and the jewel is suspended from a blue ribbon.

The council-chamber should be hung with red, spangled with gold stars. In the east, under a canopy, is placed a throne elevated on seven steps, supported by the figures of four lions and four eagles; between is an angel with six wings. On one side of the throne is displayed a transparency of the sun at high noon, while on the other is one depicting the moon. In the east also are two vases, one containing perfume and the other water.

On the south and north sides are canopies over the seats of the "Ancients," while on the west are two seats under canopies for the Wardens. These seats are elevated on five steps. Twenty-four knights must be present to form a full council.

On a pedestal in the east is a large Bible from which are suspended seven seals. The covering of the floor displays a heptagon within a circle, over the angles of which appear certain letters; in the centre is the figure of a man clothed in white with a golden girdle round his waist; his hand, which is extended, holds seven stars, and he wears a long white beard; his head is surrounded by a nimbus, while from his mouth issues a two-edged sword. Seven candlesticks stand around him bearing the mysterious initials.

The seven stars by which his hand is surmounted are explained as signifying the seven qualities which should distinguish a Freemason, namely, friendship, union, submission, discretion, fidelity, prudence, and temperance. But there is also a higher meaning attached to them derived from passages from the Old Testament, e.g. they represent the seven eyes mentioned by Zechariah, which typify the Divine Providence, and the seven lamps of the Apocalypse, which symbolise the Holy Spirit, whence are derived the seven spiritual gifts of man.

As a candidate for the eighteenth degree must possess the password of the seventeenth degree, the signs and words of this degree are communicated to him. Moreover, a special Grand Lodge of Knights of the East and West is opened and the words and signs given in detail.

From what has been written above it will be seen that this degree is full of symbolism, and most interesting; but it must be confessed that it seems to be in the wrong position, it should succeed the eighteenth degree, not precede it. As the nineteenth degree also deals with the Apocalypse, its present position is difficult to explain. It must be admitted, however, that several of the degrees above the eighteenth appear likewise to be out of their historical order, for the twenty-first goes back to the Tower of Babel and the twenty-fourth to Moses and the Tabernacle, and Moses appears in the twenty-fifth and twenty-sixth also, while the twenty-seventh is Templar.

We have now given a brief summary of the intermediate degrees, and formed, as it were, a bridge between the third and the eighteenth. All of them are of interest, and some of them extremely dramatic. In general interest they are all fully the equal of certain degrees which are worked in full in England. The summaries given have naturally been so cut down as to avoid giving away the secrets of the degrees lest some unauthorised person should endeavour to work them on his own; but this reticence naturally detracts from the interest, and justice cannot be done to them. For which reason we would again urge all Rose Croix Masons to attend the next festival of the King Edward VII Chapter of Improvement, when the eleventh and twelfth degrees will probably be worked. If all goes well, this festival should take place in April 1921.

Eighteenth Degree: Sovereign Prince Rose Croix of Heredom.—As this degree is worked in full and is indeed the mainstay of the Ancient and Accepted Rite, more reticence is necessary in discussing it. Moreover, as any Master Mason of one year's standing is eligible, there is not the same reason for giving information.

For the purpose of uniformity, a few details are appended, and its symbolism will be discussed as fully as is permissible in a later chapter.

The fact that this degree in some form is found in practically every country where masonry flourishes is proof of its considerable antiquity, but I have already adduced evidence in support of my theory that it is traceable back to our prehistoric ancestors. The rite of the Bora among the Australian blacks is a prototype of our degree (see Appendix). In *The Book of the Dead*, in Egypt and among the ancient manuscripts of Central America appear evidence that the prototype of this "High Church Degree" was worked long before Christianity, as we know it, arose.

For the proper working of this degree four rooms are required. In the first, the intermediate degrees are conferred by name. The second should be hung with black, save for a transparency in the east, on which are three crosses. The third room should represent the D . . . H . . . , while the fourth should be brilliantly illuminated and hung with red.

The ceremony is one of the most impressive in Freemasonry, and in England it is restricted to professing Christians, but this rule does not hold in America or on the Continent of Europe.

The symbolic teaching expresses the passage of man through the valley of the shadow of death, accompanied by the masonic virtues of Faith, Hope, and Charity, and his final acceptance into the abode of light, life, and immortality.

The badge is twofold; on one side it is black silk, having in its centre the cross of Calvary, on the other side it is white satin edged with rose-colour. On the apron is embroidered a pelican feeding her young, while on the flap is a triangle within which are certain Hebrew characters.

The collar is similarly two-faced: one side black with red crosses upon it, and on the other rose-pink and richly embroidered. Among the symbols on it, a crown of thorns and a serpent holding its tail in its mouth, emblem of eternity, may be noticed. The jewel is a golden compass extended to an angle of sixty, and surmounted by a celestial crown on one side, a scarlet cross within the compass made of enamel, and beneath it a pelican feeding her young. On the reverse the cross is silver, with a white eagle with wings extended as if rising in the air; on both sides, at the joint of the compasses, a rose.

If a sword is worn the grip and mounts should be gilt and the leather scabbard red, while the sword-belt should be of the same colour.

The M.W.S. is to wear a red enamel Greek cross surmounted by a celestial crown, suspended round the neck by a red ribbon. The Past M.W.S.'s may wear the same cross within a blue garter, on which is enamelled the name of the chapter, surmounted by a celestial crown pendant from the breast.

The last room should have thirty-three lights on the altar, which should be decorated with red roses. The full title conferred on the candidate is Knight of the Pelican and Eagle, and Sovereign Prince Rose Croix of Heredom.

CHAPTER III

THE REMAINING DEGREES OF THE ANCIENT AND ACCEPTED RITE

Nineteenth to Thirty-third Degree Inclusive

Having taken only the eighteenth degree, I have not felt myself at liberty to study the rituals of the degrees above that number, and am therefore unable to do more than briefly summarise what How says about them. I have already pointed out that he has followed in many cases the Continental system rather than the Southern Jurisdiction of the United States, from whence our own Supreme Council thirty-third degree derives its charter. Under these circumstances, I have been unable to check his statements, but give them as a brief summary to complete the picture. I cannot help feeling that we ought to study these intermediate degrees more closely than we do, not to work them, but so as to be able to comprehend some at least of their symbolism and meaning, and their bearing on the degrees which are worked. Thus many of the degrees between the fourth and the eighteenth do throw considerable light on degrees we can actually take in England, and it seems possible that, from some of those which lie between the seventeenth and thirtieth, we may derive inspiration in our researches into the Templar and other chivalric degrees. In view also of the fact that something which appears to approximate to our own thirtieth degree existed among the ancient Mayas, it is possible that we might be able to trace other curious examples if we knew more about these intermediate degrees.

Nineteenth Degree: Grand Pontiff.—This degree, despite its title, confers no administrative powers on its holders. The hangings of the Lodge represent the vault of heaven—celestial blue, spangled with golden stars. All the members are clothed in white and wear blue fillets embroidered with twelve gold stars. The sash is crimson, with gold stars, and to it is suspended the jewel, which is a square having on one side an Alpha and on the reverse an Omega.

The two chief officers are, a Thrice Puissant in the East, who is seated on a throne under a canopy of blue and wears a white satin robe, while the Warden sits in the west and holds a staff of gold.

The object of the degree is the study of the Apocalypse, and particularly those portions which deal with the New Jerusalem (see Rev. xxi. and xxii.).

This degree pairs with the seventeenth, but, unlike it, is placed in a more suitable position, being taken subsequently to the eighteenth degree.

Twentieth Degree: Grand Master ad Vitam.—Its other title is "Grand Master of all the Symbolic Lodges." We are now brought back to the subject of Temple-building, but it is a fourth Temple.

The historical lecture relates the destruction of the Third Temple by Titus in A.D. 70, and tells us that the Christian Freemasons who were in Palestine at that epoch were filled with grief at its loss. They left the Holy Land and determined to erect a Fourth Temple, which could not be destroyed, for it was to be a spiritual edifice. They divided themselves into a number of Lodges, and dispersed throughout Europe.

One group came to Scotland, and established a Lodge at Kilwinning, and there deposited the records of the Order in an abbey they built there. At this point the first historical difficulty arises, for the abbey was not built till about 1140, and the legend does not state where they were during the period between A.D. 70 and A.D. 1140.

When we come to consider the officers of this degree, we are faced by what can only be called a strange anachronism, for the presiding officer, who is called Venerable Grand Master, represents Cyrus Artaxerxes. The younger Cyrus was the younger brother of Artaxerxes, the second King of Persia of that name, and died at the age of twenty-four in 401 B.C. Taylor suggests that the period of Artaxerxes Longimanus, who died 425 B.C., is meant. This period corresponds with Ahasuerus, mentioned in the book

14

of Esther, whose wife was the daughter of Cyrus I. If this is correct, then there is an anachronism of over four hundred years. In any case, the names Cyrus and Artaxerxes belonged to two distinct persons. At the fall of Jerusalem a Parthian prince, Tiridates, was reigning in Persia. The only possible explanation would be if the framers of this degree had discovered a successor to Tiridates with this double name, reigning at about the date of the destruction of the Temple by Titus; but I cannot trace such a one myself.

The Lodge, when perfect, contains nine Grand Masters, who all wear collars of yellow and blue. The jewel is a triangle, on which are engraved the initials of the words of the degree.

Twenty-first Degree: Patriarch Noachite, or Prussian Knights.— This degree is also called "the Very Ancient Order of Noachites," and we suddenly find ourselves transferred to the time of the building of the Tower of Babel. It has practically nothing in common with the Royal Ark Mariner, though sometimes it has been suggested that it has.

The Lodge is supposed to be held in the open, or at any rate open to the moon, for the meetings must be held at full moon, and the light of that luminary is the only one permitted. Whereas all other degrees in Freemasonry are solar, this degree alone is distinctly lunar in character. How far there is any primitive foundation for this degree it is difficult to say, but, in its present form, it dates probably from the eighteenth century, and is almost certainly Teutonic in origin. The meetings are called chapters, and are presided over by a Knight Commander Lieutenant, who is stated to represent Frederick II of Prussia. The remaining officers are the Knight of Introduction, (2) the Knight of Eloquence, (3) the Knight of Finance, (4) the Knight of Chancery, (5) the Knight of Defence. There are naturally no hangings, and the badge is white satin with a yellow border, with which is worn a black sash from the right shoulder to left hip. The jewel is an equilateral triangle crossed by an arrow.

The traditional history tells us that Peleg was architect of the Tower of Babel, and, as a special mark of God's displeasure, was stricken dumb when the division of tongues fell upon the people at that time.

He wandered across Europe and at length settled in the forests of Prussia, where he built himself a triangular house. Here he lamented his former pride, and passed his days in prayer to the Almighty, who at length forgave him and restored his speech, from which fact the true Noachite is led to believe that God will likewise forgive him his faults.

The special lesson of this degree is humility, and, the more to impress this lesson on the initiate, he is compelled to kiss the pommel of the sword of the Knight Commander. This "kiss of humility" is reminiscent of the so-called "ritual kiss" of the Templars, which also was intended to humble the pride of the novice.

This degree was first announced in Prussia in 1755, but it is possible that some legend of the Tower of Babel was well known at a much earlier date in association with Freemasonry, for there appear to be references not only to Noah and Noachite, which probably relate to the Royal Ark Mariner, but also to the Tower of Babel itself. Phaleg, or Phalec, was, it should be added, an ancestor of Christ, and lived several generations after Noah.

It should be noted that the Order of Mizraim derives its name from the son of Ham, grandson of Noah, who, according to the Hebrew tradition, was the first King of Egypt. The name Osiris is believed by some to have been a title rather than a real name, and had a somewhat similar meaning to "Prince." At a later date in Egyptian history it, of course, meant those who had arisen from the dead.

Twenty-second Degree: Prince of Libanus.—This degree is also known by the name of "Knight of the Axe." It may be regarded as a carpenters' degree. We learn in this degree that the Sidonians cut down the trees for Noah's Ark from the cedars of Mount Lebanon, and at the time of Moses they again supplied cedars from Lebanon for the Ark of the Covenant. We thus see that this degree cleverly suggests a connection between Noah's Ark and the Ark of the Covenant. The legend goes on to state that from the same place came the timbers for the Temple itself in the days of Solomon, and finally from the same mountain, Zerubbabel obtained the wood for the second Temple.

The tradition informs us that the Sidonians formed colleges on Mount Lebanon and there adored the G.A.O.T.U. This reference to the colleges on Lebanon may refer to the Druses, who, as already shown, are very similar to Freemasons. It is possible, therefore, that there is a solid foundation for this degree.

There are two apartments: the first, representing a workshop at Lebanon, with axes, saws, mallets, wedges, and similar carpenters' tools. The Master is called the Most Wise, and his Wardens, Wise Princes. This room is hung with blue and lighted by eleven lights. This assembly is called a "college." Each brother holds an axe.

The second room represents the Council of the Round Table. The chief officer is Grand Patriarch, and the remainder Patriarchs. The room is hung with red, and has a round table in the centre, on which are square, compasses, and other mathematical instruments. Each Patriarch carries a sword.

The collar worn in this degree is celestial blue, lined and bordered with stars. The badge is white, and on it is depicted a round table on which are laid mathematical instruments, plans, etc. The jewel is an axe, crowned, in gold.

Twenty-third Degree: Chief of the Tabernacle.—This degree commemorates the institution of the order of Priesthood in Aaron and his sons Eleazar and Ithamar, and the ceremonies are to a certain extent founded on the instructions given to Moses in Exodus xxix. and xl. In many rites the degree of High Priest is still to be found, and in the Irish ritual of the H.R.A. the High Priest still exists. Even in our M.M. there is a reference to him who had the privilege of entering the Sanctum Sanctorum once in the year. How believes that the ceremony at the installation of the Third Principal of a R.A. Chapter was derived from this ceremony. In the U.S.A. the Order of High Priest is still conferred on the immediate Past First Principal, and somewhat resembles that of a Past Master of a Lodge, and it must be remembered that in America the First Principal is called High Priest.

In the degree under consideration there are three principal officers: e.g. Sovereign Grand Sacrificer and two High Priests. The members are called Levites, and wear a white badge lined with scarlet and bordered with a tricolour ribbon of red, purple, and blue; in the centre is embroidered a six-branched candlestick, while on the flap is a violet-coloured myrtle. The jewel is a thurible, which is suspended from a broad sash of four colours, viz. yellow, purple, blue, and scarlet, which is worn from the left shoulder to the right hip.

The Lodge is hung with white, ornamented with columns of

red and black arranged in pairs at equal distances. The Holy Place is separated from the rest of the room by a railing and curtain.

There is a red altar, on which is the Book of Wisdom and a poniard, while the throne of the Sovereign Grand Sacrificer is elevated on seven steps. There is an altar of burnt sacrifice, and also one of incense, and, in addition, there are two chandeliers of five lights each. There is also an obscure chamber hung with black, which contains an altar and a stool on which are three skulls and also a skeleton, with this inscription, "If you are fearful, go from hence; it is not permitted for men who cannot brave danger without abandoning virtue."

The Grand Sacrificer wears a long red robe over a yellow sleeveless tunic, on his head is a golden mitre, and he wears also a black scarf with silver fringe. The Levites wear white robes with red scarves.

In the prophecy of Zechariah will be found an account of the emblem used in this degree which will well reward a careful study. The most important object which met the eye of the prophet in his vision was "a candlestick all of gold, with a bowl on the top of it, and seven lamps." The image is evidently taken from the candlestick in the Tabernacle, which is the scriptural symbol of the Universal Church.

Twenty-fourth Degree: Prince of the Tabernacle.—This degree relates to the instructions given to Moses by God for the building of the Tabernacle. This was really a sacred tent, and the gold and silver used in its construction was alone worth at least £182,528.

The Lodge is called a "Hierarchy," and its officers are Most Powerful Chief Prince, representing Moses, and three Wardens who represent Aaron, Bezaleel, and Aholiab respectively, and they are placed in the north, south, and west. Two rooms are required for this degree; the first, called the Vestibule, is decorated with the various attributes of Freemasonry, while the second is of circular shape, and hung with tapestry representing a colonnade. On the masonic pavement is depicted a sun, and in the centre a seven-branched candlestick.

The members wear a robe of cloth-of-gold and a short cloak of blue taffeta edged with gold embroidery. On their heads are coronets encircled with stars and surmounted by a luminous triangle. The badge is white lined with scarlet, and bordered with green; the flap is sky-blue. In the centre of the badge a representation of the tabernacle is embroidered.

The twenty-third and twenty-fourth degrees are based on the official duties of the priests, and in this degree Moses represents the law-giver, Aaron the High Priest, Bezaleel and Aholiab the cunning artists under whose direction the Tabernacle was made, while the candidate represents Eleazar, who succeeded Aaron in the High Priesthood. The degree appears to be divided into three sections: in the first the candidate is elevated to the degree of High Priest, and informed that henceforth he is entitled to adore the Most High under the name of Jehovah, which is much more expressive than Adonai, and that so far he has received the masonic science as descended from K. S. and *revived by the Templars.*

In the second section the Royal Art is traced from the Creation through Noah, Abraham, Moses, and Solomon, and other important personages down to Hugo de Payens, the founder of the Templars, and thence to the tragic figure of Jacques de Molay, their last Grand Master.

In the next section the *Grand Word* is revealed to him, and he is told that it was discovered by the Knights Templars while building a church at Jerusalem. The legend states that, when digging under the spot whereon the Holy of Holies had stood in the heart of Mount Moriah, they discovered three stones, on one of which this word was engraved. The Templars, when they had to leave Palestine, carried these relics with them, and used them as the foundation-stones of their first Lodge in Scotland, which event took place on St. Andrew's Day, in commemoration of which event they took the name of Knights of St. Andrew. This secret has ever since been transmitted to their successors, who are thus entitled to the name of High Priests of Jehovah.

This legend appears, from various sources, to be an old one, and this degree is of particular interest in that it connects the Ancient and Accepted Rite with the Masonic Knights Templars.

The fact that "Moses" presides over this body seems a curious anachronism, however, seeing that a large part of the events narrated are supposed to have taken place at a date long subsequent to his death.

It is but fair to add, however, that such anachronisms are often good proofs that a legend or degree is old. Modern fabricators are usually careful to make their legends appear historically probable, whereas old legends grow by accretion in the course of years.

Twenty-fifth Degree: Knight of the Brazen Serpent.—This degree seems to be of long standing, and its theme is based on the events related in Numbers xxi. 6–9.

The ritual states that, in obedience to God's command, Moses placed the brazen serpent upon a *tau* cross, and all who looked towards it were instructed to say "Hatatha" (I have sinned); and, this done, they were immediately healed.

The hangings of the Lodge are red and blue. A transparency depicting the burning bush with the Incommunicable Name in the centre is placed behind the throne. There is only one light, and in the centre of the room is a mount accessible by five steps, upon the summit of which is placed the symbol of the degree. The Lodge is called "The Court of Sinai."

The Most Powerful Grand Master represents "Moses"; the Wardens, who are called Ministers, represent Aaron and Joshua. The Orator is called Pontiff, the Secretary is the Grand Graver, and the candidate is "a Traveller."

The jewel is a serpent entwined round a tau cross (T) standing on a triangle with the inscription יהוה, and it is worn suspended from a red ribbon.

The legend states that this degree was founded in the time of the Crusades by John Ralph, who established it in Palestine as a military and monastic order. He is stated to have given it the name it bears in allusion to the healing and saving virtue of the "brazen serpent" among the Israelites, for it was part of the obligation of the knights to nurse sick travellers and protect them from the infidel.

Serpent Worship is one of the oldest religious systems in the world, and traces of it are to be found in almost every country. In one form it was undoubtedly phallic, and there are sculptures of a somewhat coarse nature to be seen in India, in the temples, which testify undoubtedly to this fact.

In the Temple of Shiva at Madura, in Southern India, there are several striking examples associated with Shiva as the god of birth and rebirth. In this connection, it must be borne in mind that, though Shiva is often depicted in human form, by far the largest number of symbols representing him are phallic carvings. The *tau* cross is also a symbol of the male or creative side of the deity, and is really a conventionalised form of the phallus.

Thus the serpent hung on the *tau* is pre-eminently a sign of the male and creative side of the deity.

The serpent is also a sign of Vishnu the Preserver, and there are numerous statues of Vishnu sleeping while a five-headed cobra shields him from the sun. The serpent has also been identified with the sun in all its phases, but more especially with its preservative side. A similar idea is shown in the statues of Mithra, where the god stands erect on a globe, out of which emerges a serpent, the emblem of life, which, twining round and round the body of Mithra, marked the convolutions of his orb and the cycles of revolving time. When a candidate was initiated into one of the degrees of Mithra a golden serpent was placed in his bosom as an emblem of his regeneration, for, just as the serpent casts off its old skin and comes forth bright and clean, so the initiate emerged frpm this ordeal cleansed and purified. Further, the serpent was by this act considered to typify the sun itself, whose genial warmth is renewed each year when it returns to the vernal signs.

The serpent biting its tail was regarded by some as emblematic of the path of the sun round the world, and also as a symbol of Him who is without beginning or end—which will interest R.C. brethren.

In its aspect of Preserver, it was carried forward into Buddhism, and the Buddha is often depicted sleeping overshadowed by a five-headed cobra, just as Vishnu is found. So sacred is it that at Mintale in Ceylon, on the Great Rock, which for over two thousand years has been used as a Buddhist monastery, travellers may observe a huge five-headed cobra carved in bas-relief on a rock, which forms one side of a great bathing-tank used by the monks.

Even Christianity has brought forward with it the symbol of the preservative side of the serpent, and the brazen serpent is often spoken of as a prototype of Christ upon the cross.

We have considered the serpent as the emblem of Creator and of Preserver, and have referred to its use in Craft Masonry to join the straps of our aprons; but what of the Destroyer?

The Destroyer, among most nations, has become the personification of Evil, and, in these cases, the Serpent Destroyer has taken on a sinister character. The Midgard snake of the Norse, who shall join with Surt and the Sons of the Flame (Chaos) to destroy Valhalla at the last great battle of Ragnarök, is but one example. Apepi, the great snake of the Egyptians, against whom Horus fought, *placing his left foot first on its body*, is another. The evil serpents of the Arunta natives, of the ancient Mexicans, the Chinese Dragon, and a host of other examples occur to the mind.

In India the Destroyer never became the embodiment of Evil. Rather he was the "willing bestower of requests," and he bestowed the greatest blessing of all, Death, on tired humanity, Peace. Moreover, the fact that he also launched the soul once more on its earthly journey robbed Death of much of his terrors. Even the Naga-folk or Snake-people, though they dwelt in the underworld, were not regarded as especially hostile to men as were the Rakshas. Nevertheless, there are evil serpents also in Hindoo mythology (see opposite p. 98).

We could multiply examples of the snake as an emblem of the Creator, Preserver, and Destroyer to any extent. Thus, among the Greeks and Romans, Æsculapius, the healing god, was worshipped under the serpent emblem, and, among the Egyptians, Serapis and Horus are often depicted bearing chalices surrounded with serpents, and this idea was carried forward into Christianity, when St. John is shown holding a cup with a serpent in it. Thus, taking the Hindoo division of the Trinity, we see that the serpent represents all sides of the triangle, and further represents God the Unknown and Unknowable, who lies behind all the gods. This fact is alluded to in the serpent circle of the higher degrees of the Yogi.

Turning for a moment to the Christian division of the deity, we find that God the Father or Creator is represented by the phallic serpent, God the Son by the brazen serpent on the cross, and God the Holy Ghost is regarded by many as depicted under the name of the Shining One, mistranslated "serpent" in the story of Adam and Eve. The serpent as typifying the Wisdom of God and its synchronisation with the dove have already been dealt with earlier, and need not detain us now. In conclusion, mention must be made of the fact that there were serpent goddesses, e.g. at Babylon, and these were probably survivors of the matriarchal era and the reign of the "Great Mother."

Twenty-sixth Degree: The Prince of Mercy.—This degree is

also known as Scotch Trinitarian, and it is a highly philosophical degree with a most impressive ritual.

The assembly is called the "Thrice Heavenly Lodge," and the Chief Prince has the title of Most Excellent, and represents Moses; the S.W., Aaron; and the J.W., Eleazar. The candidate represents Joshua, and the Lodge is hung with green and decorated with nine columns, which are alternately red and white. At each column is a nine-branched candelabum, giving in all eighty-one lights; but these may be reduced to twenty-seven if desirable. The apron is red, bordered with a white fringe and having a blue flap, on which is embroidered the same emblem as constitutes the jewel. This is a gold equilateral triangle, within which is a heart of gold, on which is incribed the Hebrew letter ה, one of the symbols of the tetragrammaton, and it is suspended from a tricolour ribbon of green, white, and red.

This is a Christian degree, despite the Old Testament names of the officers and candidate, and the ritual speaks of the threefold covenant made by God with man. The first is stated to have been made with Abraham by circumcision, the second through Moses, and the third through Jesus Christ.

It is possible to find fault with this definition of the covenants, for there was certainly one with Adam at his creation when he was forbidden to eat the fruit, and a second after his fall, besides such later ones as that with Noah.

Before leaving this degree, we may note that the Hebrew word ברית, *berith*, which is translated "testament," hence Old and New Testament, is more correctly translated as meaning Covenant.

Twenty-seventh Degree: Grand Commander of the Temple.—The body which confers this degree is called a "Court," and the degree itself belongs to the chivalric and military class. The ruler is designated as Most Puissant, the Wardens as Sovereign Grand Commanders, and the ordinary knights as Commanders. The room is hung with red, and has black columns surmounted by torches. On the altar is placed the book of the Evangelists, with a naked sword and a sceptre; there is a lustre of twenty-seven lights on a pedestal.

The members must be placed in a circle, and, if there is no reception, at a round table. The apron is red satin lined and edged with black, with a Teutonic Cross encircled by a wreath of laurel and a key, in black, embroidered on the flap. A red scarf, edged with black, is hung from the right shoulder to the left hip, and bears on it a Teutonic Cross in gold enamel. The jewel is a golden triangle on which is engraved the Ineffable Name of the Most High, in Hebrew, which is suspended from a white collar bound with red and embroidered with four Teutonic Crosses.

As worked on the Continent, this degree is stated to be connected with the Knights Templars, and was probably intended to supply the Templar degree under this rite.

Twenty-eighth Degree: Knight of the Sun.—This is a highly philosophical degree, and a Dutch Mason once told me that it was regularly worked in Holland, and was a most impressive ritual. I have, however, no further personal knowledge on the subject.

It is sometimes called by the following titles: Prince of the Sun, Prince Adept, Key of Masonry, or Chaos Disentangled.

Ragon, who usually speaks contemptuously of the higher degrees, makes a marked exception in favour of this one, declaring it to be of the greatest antiquity, and was really the last degree of perfect initiation.

It teaches the doctrines of natural religion which formed an essential part of the ancient mysteries, and the ceremonies and lectures furnish a history of all the preceding degrees and explain at considerable length the various masonic emblems. If for no other reason than this, it would therefore appear to deserve the most careful study.

The great object of the degree is the inculcation of truth, and there is a fine lecture on the subject.

The two chief officers are Thrice Perfect Father Adam and Brother Truth, and there are seven assistant officers, who are named after the seven angels: Michael, Gabriel, Raphael, Zaphriel, Camael, Azrael, and Zaphiel.

Four rooms are required for the due performance of the ceremony. The first represents a grotto, in the centre of which is a column to which is attached a chain; on one side stands a table having upon it a Bible and a small lamp. The second chamber is hung with black and lighted by three candles in the east, south, and west respectively. Over the entrance to this room is written: "Ye who have not power to subdue passions, flee this sanctuary." The third room is hung with red and lighted by eleven candles.

The fourth and last chamber is decorated in azure blue, and has but one light, which is, however, very powerful as it consists of a large illuminated glass globe, and represents the sun—which is the symbol of God, from whom flow all philosophical principles.

The Master wears a red robe and yellow tunic and holds a sceptre with a golden globe on its top. The badge represents a sun with an eye upon the flap, and a white collar is worn which has on it a chain, and from it is suspended the jewel of the degree, a golden triangle with an eye in the centre.

The historical lecture describes the seven cherubim, whose names are written in the circle of the first heaven, and states that they represent the corporeal pleasures of this life which God gave to man at the Creation; they are: feeling, seeing, hearing, tasting, smelling, tranquillity, and thought.

Reference is made to various missions to earth of members of the angelic host, as, for example, when, in the apocryphal book of Tobit, Raphael tells Tobias that he is one of the seven angels standing before the Lord. Again, St. John (Rev. viii. 2.) saw seven angels standing before the Lord, and this naturally leads on to other mystical sevens, particularly those described in Revelation, such as the seven stars which are the angels of the seven churches. The number seven runs through all Masonry, and is constantly referred to in various degrees. Pythagoras called it the Venerable Number, because it made up the two perfect figures, the triangle and the square. Three has always been regarded among mystics as representing God, and hence the Spiritual, while four, or the square, represents the world and matter generally. So seven represents All that was, is, and shall be, the Almighty.

The basic meaning of the Hebrew word שבע is "sufficiency or completeness," and the number seven was so called because that day God completed the work of creation and rested from its labours.

From this brief summary enough has been written to indicate that this is a most important degree, and it appears to have been worked in England by the Kent Lodge, and was preserved by the Ancients as a most important part of their system.

Twenty-ninth Degree: Knight of St. Andrew.—This degree is

sometimes known as "Patriarch of the Crusades" in allusion to its supposed origin during that period. Another name sometimes employed is "Grand Master of Light."

This is preparatory to the thirtieth degree, and in England a small portion is given to a candidate to qualify him for that degree.

The officers are a Master and two Wardens; the Lodge is illuminated by eighty-one lights arranged on nine groups of nine, and the hangings are red.

The Assembly is called a Grand Lodge, the Master is styled Patriarch, and the other officers Worshipful Masters. They wear scarlet robes with purple scarves from which is suspended the jewel, a triple triangle having in the centre a pair of compasses and beneath it a square reversed, while in the angle is a poniard. The knights wear purple collars, to which is attached their jewel, a St. Andrew's Cross, and they also wear a white sash with gold fringe.

The three chief officers are seated on thrones covered with red cloth fringed wth gold, and behind the Patriarch's throne is a transparency of a luminous triangle, within which are the emblems of this degree.

There is a curious *hierogram* in this degree, , which is explained as follows. The triangle or delta is the mysterious figure of God. G at the top of the triangle refers to the *Grand Cause* of the Masons, S on the left hand the *Submission* to the same order, and U at the right hand to the *Union* that should exist among the brethren, which altogether make but one body, an equal figure in all its parts. The large G in the centre signifies the G.A.O.T.U., who is God.

There is an "inner meaning" for the *hierogram* God, the Grand Superintendent of the Universe. So that, after all, this is only a rather clumsy substitute for the Name we learn in the very first degree in Freemasonry.

It is stated by How that the twenty-ninth was invented by Ramsay, who proposed to substitute it for the ancient craft degrees. Whether this is so or not matters little to-day, but the degree now serves as a passing degree to the thirtieth degree and is to that extent rescued from the oblivion into which many other and finer degrees of the Ancient and Accepted Rite have sunk in England.

Thirtieth Degree: Grand Elected Knight Kadosh.—This degree is also known as Knight of the Black and White Eagle. On the Continent it is strongly Templar in tone, and I believe in France there is still a reference to the fate of Jacques de Molay, and the knights vow vengeance on those responsible for his death; but in England this has been eliminated. In the eighteenth century it was certainly associated with Templary. As this degree is worked in full, the summary given here will be very brief and only given at all to maintain the symmetry of this chapter.

The presiding officer is called Most Illustrious Grand Commander, there are two Lieutenant Grand Commanders, a Grand Chancellor, Grand Marshal, Grand Treasurer, Grand Secretary, and Grand Master of Ceremonies.

When celebrated in ample form, three chambers and an anteroom are required. In France the first room is hung with white, and has neither daïs nor altar; at the end of the room is seen a statue of Wisdom dimly visible by the light of a spirit-lamp placed on a chafing-dish.

In England the room is hung with black, and it is here that the Grand Sacrificator receives the candidate.

The second room, called the "Areopagus," is hung with black, and at the farther end is a table covered with a blue cloth, behind which are the two Lieutenants and a third officer. These three constitute the "Council of the Areopagus." This room is lit by three candles.

The third hall is called the Senate, and hung with red. In the east is the throne, bearing on its canopy the double-headed eagle, crowned, and holding a sword in its claws; hangings of red and black interspersed with red crosses form a pavilion; on either side are two standards. This hall is illuminated with eighty-one lights. It is in this room that the mysterious series of six steps up and six steps down with a top platform is found. The knights wear a four-inch broad black sash suspended from the left shoulder, the point fringed with silver bullion, and on it are embroidered the emblems of the degree, which are: an eagle soaring towards the light holding the Anchor of Hope in his talons; on the extremity, the red flag of England and Wales, bearing three golden lions crossed by the banner of the Supreme Council, and below a red 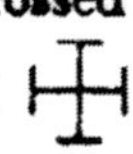 cross. The Breast Jewel is a cross *pattée* in red enamel, the number 30 in gold upon the blue enamel in the centre. A black double spread-eagle, surmounted by a crown and holding a sword in its claws, is to be worn suspended round the neck from a black ribbon one and a half inches wide, with a narrow silver edging.

If a sword is worn, the grip and mounting shall be gilt and scabbard and sword-belt black.

This and the subsequent degrees can only be conferred in the presence of at least three of the Supreme Council, at any rate in England. As a general rule, brethren will have to journey to London and take it at 10, Duke Street, the Headquarters of the Supreme Council; but, of recent years, the Supreme Council have gone down to various important provincial cities from time to time, and so enabled brothers who were unable to come all the way to town to obtain it nearer home.

While many learned brothers think that this is a comparatively modern degree, others, including How, hold that it is extremely old, though no doubt considerably altered in recent times.

Churchward contends that the painting shown in his book, *Signs and Symbols of Primordial Man* (cf. p. 92), which is taken from a vase found at Chama, ancient Mexico, depicts a part of this degree, or at any rate its prototype; but not having taken the degree, I naturally do not know.

The word "Kadosh" first appears in the Bible in Gen. ii. 3: "God blessed the seventh day and *sanctified* it." The strict root meaning of the word appears to be "separated," or consecrated. The Hebrew spelling is קדש, (*kodesh*), and in this degree it is probably derived from the priestly office. For example the plate which was placed on the mitre of the priest had inscribed upon it, "Holiness to the Lord," which in Hebrew was *kodesh-laihovah*. This degree is hardly ever conferred on anyone who has not held the office of M.W.S. and been a Rose Croix Mason for three years.

Enough has been said of the thirtieth degree, and we will now briefly complete the series of degrees conferred by the Supreme Council.

Thirty-first Degree: Grand Inspector Inquisitor Commander.—This is in the main intended to be an administrative degree, the duties of its members being supposed to be the examination and regulation of the subordinate chapters. In practice, however, this work is left to the Supreme Council, or officers specially appointed for that purpose by it.

The numbers of this degree are restricted to 108, and it is conferred as a reward for masonic service.

The meeting is called a Sovereign Tribunal, and the room is hung with white, and there should be eight golden columns, an altar covered with a white cloth, and on the daïs above the presiding officer's throne are the letters J.E. The floor should be covered with a painting, in the centre of which is a cross surrounded by all the attributes of Masonry. In France there is a white apron with a yellow flap embroidered with the attributes of the degree in addition to the rest of the regalia; but in England this is not worn.

In England the clothing, etc., is as follows: A white watered-silk collar, four inches wide, embroidered with the emblems of the order, edged with gold lace, lined with white. On this is worn the jewel, which is a cross, as for the thirtieth degree, but surmounted by a celestial crown and with the number 31 in the centre.

The eagle is similar to that worn in the thirtieth degree, but has the wings and tip of tail gilt. It is to be worn suspended round the neck from a white ribbon one and a half inches wide edged with gold.

The sword has gilt mounts, white scabbard, and black sword-belt.

Thirty-second Degree: Sublime Prince of the Royal Secret.—Until 1786, when Frederick the Great is said to have instituted the thirty-third, this was the summit of the rite. The assembly is called a "Grand Consistory," and should be held in a building of two stories.

The first is called the Chamber of the Guards, and the second is the preparing-room for the candidate. In the third the Consistory itself is held: it is hung with black, and on the hangings are depicted skeletons, tears, and emblems of mortality embroidered in silver. In the east is a throne with similar draperies, raised on seven steps, which is the seat of the President, who is called Thrice Illustrious Commander. The covering, in the French rite, has the letters J.M., in memory of Jacques de Molay.

There is no apron in this degree in England. The collar is black watered-silk four and a half inches wide embroidered with the emblems of the degree, edged with silver lace-lined red watered silk, with a black cross embroidered at the point in gold. The collar jewel is as that worn in the thirty-first degree, but with the number 32. The eagle is similar to that worn in the last degree, but with additional gilding, and is worn suspended round the neck from a red ribbon one and a half inches wide edged with gold. The sword has gilt mountings and a black scabbard and sword-belt. A French apron of this degree can be seen in Grand Lodge Library.

The number admitted to this degree is even more limited, only sixty-three being permitted at any time, "exclusive of members promoted for service in the colonies or residing abroad, or who are no longer subscribing members of a Rose Croix Chapter. This exception is also allowed in the case of the thirty-first degree.

Thirty-third Degree: Sovereign Grand Inspectors-General.—The Lodge is hung with purple, which should display emblems of mortality. In the east is a daïs having in its rear a transparency bearing the sacred name in Hebrew letters. In the centre is a square pedestal covered with crimson, on which are a Bible and a sword.

In the north, How states, there is another pedestal displaying a skeleton which holds a poniard in its right hand and the banner of the order in its left. In the west is a throne raised on three steps before which is a triangular altar covered with crimson. The chamber is illuminated with eleven lights: five in the east, two in the south, three in the west, and one in the north.

The regalia consists of the following: A white watered-silk sash five inches wide edged with gold, and embroidered in the same with the emblems of the degree, viz. a delta surrounded by rays, in centre the number 33 in red. To be worn from left shoulder to right hip. The sash jewel is a similar cross to that worn in the thirty-second degree, but with the number 33, and is to be worn on the right hip at crossing of sash, pendent from a gold rose on a scarlet bow.

The eagle is similar to that worn in the thirty-second degree, but has a silver body and is suspended round the neck from a black oxidised chain.

A plain black velvet cap of the prescribed pattern with the number 33 within a triangle is worn.

Present and Past Inspectors-General of Districts wear the same device imposed on a circle—all of gold or gilt metal.

Inspectors-General, while in charge of Districts, wear the eagle suspended from a silver chain. Mourning is shown by wearing a purple rosette on the breast of the sash.

Members of the Supreme Council, Present and Past, wear the eagle suspended from a golden chain; with a triple cross in red enamel suspended from the blade of the sword in the claws of the eagle, and in front of the cap the eagle charged with the triple cross.

From the members of the thirty-third degree the Supreme Council is constituted. This degree is stated to have been organised by King Frederick in 1786 (but there is little reliable evidence of this) and not more than one Supreme Council can exist in one nation, and it must be composed of nine members, not less than three to form a quorum. There are twenty-eight Inspectors-General, several of whom are stationed abroad, in addition to the nine members of the Supreme Council and the Grand Patron, the Duke of Connaught.

The following is the Supreme Council of the thirty-third degree:

Sovereign Grand Inspectors-General, H.E.

Grand Patron.—Field-Marshal His Royal Highness Arthur, W.P.A. Duke of Connaught and Strathearn, K.G., etc., etc., Thirty-third Degree, Grand Master; P. Prov. G.M. Sussex; P. Dist. G.M. Bombay and P.G.W.; Grand Z. Royal Arch; Grand Master and G.C.T., United Orders of the Temple and Hospital; Grand Master and P. Prov. G.M. Sussex, Mark Master Masons.

Members of Supreme Council

Most Puissant Sovereign Grand Commander.—The Right Honourable the Earl of Donoughmore, K.P., Grand Master of Ireland; P.G.W.; P.G.S.N. Royal Arch; P. Dep. G.M., P.G.W. Mark Master Masons; P.G. Const., G.C.T. United Orders of the Temple and Hospital, Hon. Member S.C., Ireland.

Lieut. Grand Commander.—Edward Nash, P.G.D.; P.G. Std. B. Royal Arch; P.G.O. Mark Master Masons; Great Treasurer; P.G. Std B. United Orders of the Temple and Hospital; P.A.G.D.C. Royal and Select Masters.

Grand Chaplain.—THE VERY REV. JOHN STUDHOLME BROWNRIGG (*Dean of Bocking*), Past Gr. Chap.; Grand J., G. Supt. Bucks, P.A.G.S., Royal Arch; Prov. G.M. Bucks, Mark Master Masons; P.G. Prelate, G.C.T. United Orders of the Temple and Hospital.

Grand Treasurer-General.—JAMES HENRY MATTHEWS, P. Pres. Board of Benevolence, P.D.G.D.C., P.D.G.D. Bengal; P.G.S.N., P.G.D.C. Royal Arch; P.G.O., Mark Master Masons.

Grand Chancellor.—RICHARD LOVELAND LOVELAND, *K.C.*, P.G.W., P. Pres. of the Board of General Purposes, P.G.D.; P.G.S.N., P.A.G.S. Royal Arch; Dep. G.M. Mark Master Masons; Pro Grand Master and Rep. Canada, G.C.T., United Orders of the Temple and Hospital; G.M. Royal and Select Masters; G.M. Allied Degrees; Prov. G.M. Royal Order of Scotland.

Grand Chamberlain.—COLONEL ARTHUR CLIFTON HANSARD, *C.M.G., Late R.A.*, Prov. G.M. Guernsey and Alderney, P.G.D.; G. Supt. Guernsey and Alderney, P.G. Std. Br. Royal Arch; P.G.W. Mark Master Masons; G. Const., P.G. Herald, United Orders of the Temple and Hospital; P.G.P.C. of W. Royal and Select Masters.

Grand Marshal.—EDWARD ARMITAGE, P.G.D., P.Dep. G.D.C., P.Prov. S.G.W. Cumberland and Westmorland: P.A.G.S., P.Dep., G.D.C., P. Prov. G.J. Cambs., P. Dep. G.D.C. Royal Arch; P.G.O. Mark Master Masons; P. Gr.Aide-de-Camp United Orders of the Temple and Hospital; P.G.P.C. of W., P.A.G.D.C. Royal and Select Masters.

Grand Captain-General.—COLONEL SIR ARTHUR HENRY MCMAHON, G.C.M.G., G.C.V.O., K.C.I.E., C.S.I., P.G.W., P.G.D., P.S.G.W. and P.Dist. G.M., Punjab, Mark Master Masons; P.Prov. Prior, Bengal, G.C.T. United Orders of the Temple and Hospital; Dep. Prov. G.M., Royal Order of Scotland.

Grand Secretary-General.—JOHN CHARLES TOWER, P.G.D., P.Dep. G.D.C., P.P.S.G.W. Bucks; P.A.G.S., P.Dep. G.Swd. Br., P.Prov. G.H. Bucks, Royal Arch; P.G.M.O., P.P.S.G.W. Middlesex, Mark Master Masons; P.G. Std. Br., K.C.T. United Orders of the Temple and Hospital; P.G.P.C. of W. Royal and Select Masters.

Honorary Members of Supreme Council

The Earl of Dartrey, Past Sov. Gd. Commander.
Sir Charles Cameron, C.B., Sov. Gd. Commander., S.C. Ireland.
Baron van Ittersum, S.C., Netherlands.
Barton Smith, Sov. Gd. Commander., S.C., N.J., U.S.A.
George Fleming Moore, Sov. Gd. Commander., S.C., S.J., U.S.A.
The Rt. Hon. the Earl of Kintore, G.C.M.G., S.C., Scotland.

A glance at the distinguished masonic names on this list will show how highly valued is this degree, and how influential the Supreme Council. All the degrees from thirty-one to thirty-three inclusive are only conferred as the reward of distinguished masonic service, and are therefore highly valued by their fortunate holders and eagerly desired by those who have not yet achieved them.

Before closing this chapter the attention of my readers should be drawn to the fact that the Ancient and Accepted Rite has two important rivals abroad. These are the Rites of Memphis and Mizraim. The Rite of Memphis, or the Ancient and Primitive Rite, was probably based on the "Rite of Philalethes," which appeared about the year 1778. On this groundwork the Rite of Memphis was organised in 1814 at Montauban in France.

After various vicissitudes, it was carried to New York in 1857, and Illustrious Brother David M'Clellan was made Grand Master General. This body was recognised in 1862 by the parent French body and chartered as a "Sovereign Sanctuary." On June 3rd, 1872, the American Sanctuary granted a Charter for a Sovereign Sanctuary thirty-third degree in and for the United Kingdom of Great Britain and Ireland, and six brothers were installed as officers by Illustrious Brother Harry J. Seymour, thirty-third degree to ninety-sixth degree, in person at Freemasons' Hall, London, on October 8th, 1872. The Grand Master General was Illustrious Brother John Yarkar, thirty-third degree to ninety-sixth degree. This body sanctioned the conferment of the Rite of Mizraim upon members of the Rite of Memphis, the former having no separate governing body in England.

The Rite of Mizraim imposes sixty-three more degrees on the top of the thirty-third degree of the Ancient and Accepted Rite.

I have been unable to trace any genuine survivors of this Sovereign Sanctuary, and probably it disintegrated on the death of Brother Yarkar. The curious will find a summary of the degrees worked in the Rite of Memphis in How's book.

Many are the same as those in the Ancient and Accepted Rite, but the whole rite is strongly tinged with Egyptian lore.

The Rose Croix is the eleventh, and the Kadosh the eighteenth in this series. The twenty-sixth is Patriarch of the Sacred Vedas, and discourses of the ancient and sacred books of the East. The thirtieth degree, or ninetieth degree of Mizraim, deals with the Egyptian mysteries, and when fully worked represents the Great Egyptian Judgment as found in *The Book of the Dead.*

The rite does not restrict its membership to Christians, and in those degrees such as the Rose Croix, which are often regarded in England as purely Christian, it gives a more universal interpretation to the symbols than is done in the English ritual of the Ancient and Accepted Rite. It is only fair to add that both in Latin Europe and in the United States, the Ancient and Accepted Rite is not regarded as essentially Christian.

CHAPTER IV

THE CROSS AND THE VESICA PISCIS

THESE symbols are characteristic of the higher degrees, particularly the Rose Croix and the Royal Order of Scotland.

In the ancient days there were seven lesser and ten greater mysteries. The former are represented in Freemasonry by the craft mark, arch, cryptic, and similar degrees, while the greater mysteries, or mysteries of the cross, are represented by the Rose Croix, the Royal Order, and many of the unworked degrees of the Ancient and Accepted Rite. For example, the Knight of the Brazen Serpent is pre-eminently a cross degree.

On the other hand, there exist a series of "chivalric" degrees which revolve round the cross, but cannot be considered as quite on the same lines as the hermetic degrees, such as the Rose Croix.

These chivalric degrees are the Knight Templar with its pendants of the Mediterranean Pass and the Knights of Malta, the Red Cross of Constantine, and the Knights of the Sepulchre and of St. John. These are avowedly Christian, and claim to derive from the various chivalric orders of the Middle Ages. By far the most important is the Knight Templar, and a special chapter will be devoted to it; but it is evident that the symbolism of these degrees stands in a separate group from that of the hermetic degrees.

But though the cross and the vesica piscis, or rose, are especially associated with the so-called "higher degrees," they are also to be found in craft masonry. This is partly due to the general chaotic state into which the mysteries declined, and probably also to a blending of craft and higher degree work during the eighteenth century, or even earlier.

At the same time a limited reference to the cross, even in the first degree, seems justifiable, for the cross has many aspects and symbolic lessons.

The craft degrees, like the lesser mysteries, teach of the nature of God and the earthly duties incumbent on man. The greater mysteries aim at teaching what happens to a man after death, and in particular the mystery of the cross.

As, however, the cross has a lowlier side, namely its phallic or creative aspect, and as the first degree is the degree of birth, there is good reason for its appearance at the very threshold of Freemasonry. The cross is easily detected, but the mystic rose, or vesica piscis, is disguised, and might be overlooked unless carefully sought; but, before discussing this theme further, one must define the two main types of cross, and this will be done in the next chapter.

There remains one organisation which cannot be ignored in any discussion on the subject of the cross and the rose, and that is the Rosicrucian Society.

The aim of this body is the study of the occult and mystical side of Masonry, of philosophy, the Cabbala and the ancient wisdom. Of recent years there has been a tendency to add archæology to the other subjects studied. This seems a pity, as there are already many masonic bodies who devote much study to the archæological and historical side of Freemasonry, whereas its symbolic and mystical side is catered for very little. But the ritual of this "society" is also based on the rose and cross, and veneration is rendered to Christian Rosencranz, the reputed founder of the mediæval Rosicrucians.

Several parts of the ritual are both interesting and impressive, and show the universal nature of the cross, as well as its particular application on Mount Calvary. The cross of the four cardinal points and the mystic cross of the universe are indicated.

The twelfth degree in the rite of Memphis is somewhat reminiscent of the ritual of their first degree, but whether the Zelator grade is derived from it, or both come from some older source, I am unable to say.

There is also considerable astrological lore, and the astrological use of the cross and circle as symbols of the planets may therefore be of interest. The cross within the circle, ⊕, represents the earth and refers to the mystic crucifixion of the saviours of the world: the cosmic Christ crucified on the cross formed of the four cardinal points is the emblem of Quetzalcoatl, the ancient Mexican god.

The cross above the circle, ♁, represents Mars, and symbolises the passionate nature in unregenerate man. This does not always imply evil, for the Martian type is forceful and often generous, but usually rash and impetuous, and in his heedless forward rush ignores the rights and feelings of others. Therefore the cross above the circle denoted that the animal passions have not yet been brought under control by the spiritual nature depicted by the circle, which, when standing without the cross, and having a point within it, represents the sun, ☉, which is the emblem of God and the Divine Spirit in Man, the point within the circle.

The cross beneath the circle, ♀, stands for Venus, and symbolises the passions subdued and controlled by the Divine Spirit, which is Love. Hence Venus is spoken of as the Planet of Love. In its highest sense this is the divine love which passes all understanding, but it may be diverted and degraded into the lowest form of sexual passion. So that, just as Mars has his good side, so Venus has her bad aspects.

Mercury, the changeable, is represented by this symbol, ☿. We see the half-circle, the symbol of the fickle moon, is above the circle, representing the Divine Spirit. The moon, which takes its light from the sun, was regarded by the astrologers as representing the soul of man, that half material, half spiritual part of us, neither good nor bad, but susceptible to the good or bad influences which surround it. The moon's sign was ☽. The cross beneath the circle shows that the passions have been subdued by the Divine Spirit, but not completely, as with Venus, for the moon symbol shows an instability or at best a variability of character which may lead those astray who are under the influence of Mercury. He was, however, regarded as the giver of many good gifts, among them being adaptability, desire for travel, and good commercial ability.

The sign of Jupiter is the half-circle and the cross, ♃. Those whose planet this is are said to be just men and true, of sound judgment and good understanding generous in word and deed, yet not over-rash in giving, while far from grudging by nature. A happy balance is given to their lives by the benign influence called by the name of Jupiter. Here the cross of the Redeemer has coloured the moon symbol in its benign aspect and the final peace is already at hand.

Saturn is the opposite to Jupiter; his symbol is ♄ the cross above the sign of Luna. He is the Satan, the *Tempter*, or rather Tester. His function is to chastise and tame the unruly passions in the primitive man. To bind those passions in iron bands, whoso has Saturn in the ascendant is likely to have to bear many crosses in his life, to find countless obstacles and many disappointments. His is an unpleasant task, but necessary. The cross of suffering is raised aloft, and the changeful moon takes its colour from it, but gives the cross of suffering a fitful, sudden, and unexpected action. Yet the man who suffers under Saturn's influence will in the end emerge a better man, strengthened by his trials and purged of many faults. Saturn, at his best, produces a cautious and careful nature.

Woe for the man whose planet is Mars with Saturn set square to it or on the angle of the cross! For him life will be hard; yet in time, as the lessons are learnt, the *square* will disappear and a new and benign influence reign in its place.

Saturn at square may spoil almost any good influence. With Venus it changes the divine into the carnal love, but all things which are evil pass in time and only good is eternal. So taught the astrologers, whose system, at its best, was not one of fortune-telling, but of character analysis; nevertheless, from the character of a man they were able to deduce in many cases his probable line of action under different circumstances.

The last two signs are those of the "new planets," unknown to most of the Western astrologers, though the Indians claim to have known of them for ages before they were discovered astronomically. They go further, and claim that there are twelve planets in all, though the others have not yet been seen by man.

These are so far away that at present they do not influence the average man at all, and not till he has risen to far greater heights of spirituality will they be able to do so.

In the same way, Uranus and Neptune were not able to influence most men before the nineteenth century, because they were not sufficiently evolved, spiritually. An exception was Jesus Christ, who, modern astrologers contend, was a typical Neptune man of the most exalted type. Even to-day Neptune and Uranus influence only a few. They are mysterious planets, and their effects little understood. They are said to be most powerful with mystic and psychic people, Neptune affecting the former and Uranus the latter. In the main their influence on ordinary people appears to be unpleasant, to say the least, and their benign side can only come into play, as a rule, with spiritual types.

The symbol of Uranus is ♅, or a cross between two half-circles resting on a circle. We thus see it combines Mars, Jupiter, and Luna, a triple combination which explains the fact that Uranus may take effect on any of the three planes either separately or at once, that is on the spiritual—the psychic or soul plane—and the body, or earth plane.

Its unexpectedness is its most striking characteristic. At its best, it gives a love of the old and of the occult; at its worst, worldly disasters.

Neptune is represented by ♆, which combines the two half-circles and the sign of Mars; but whereas in Uranus the half-circles are touched by the cross at the centre, with Neptune the half-circles are poised on the ends of the arms. As these signs might easily become mistaken for each other if drawn carelessly, in practice they are often drawn in this way: Uranus ♅, thus making an H in memory of Herschell, and Neptune ♆, in reference to the trident of the sea-god. I think this a pity, however, as it destroys much of the meaning of the symbols, and divorces them from the other signs, which are all based on the cross and circle.

In the case of Neptune, the half-moons being raised mark his mystical character, while with Uranus they are placed half-way down to show that the Uranian types are half-way towards the mystical; they are psychic and occult rather than true mystics. The double moons in each case denote the variability of these two planets.

Whatever may be thought of astrology by my readers as a "practical art," I feel sure they will be interested to learn that there is a higher aspect of astrology than that usually portrayed, namely, the analysis of character, while the explanation of the symbols used will no doubt appeal to many who otherwise would have no interest in the subject.

The planets, according to the Hindoo astrologers, are the outward and visible signs of certain great spiritual forces, or, in their language, of gods or angels and attributes of the Deity.

It will be noted that the cross used here is mainly the phallic cross, or cross of *our* passions; but occasionally this blends into the cross of suffering and redemption. These four pages must not be thought to be derived from the Soc. Ros. in Anglia, for they are not, but are the teaching of the astrologers of old.

THE GOD BES, WEARING TEUTONIC CROSS (see p. 239)

CHAPTER V

THE TWO KINDS OF CROSS

THE two main types of cross are (*a*) the tau cross, which represents the old phallic cross of creation, and (*b*) the Latin cross of suffering. But, though the cross has two distinct aspects, they interblend and cannot be separated in every case. Thus Christ was crucified on the cross of *our* passions, but it is the cross of suffering and redemption which is depicted in pictures and sculptures of the event. The two thieves who suffered for their own sins are generally shown fastened on tau crosses usually with their arms bent over them. This is to emphasise the different aspects of the cross. When this has not been done it shows that the artist had lost the old knowledge of symbolism.

I think that too much stress is often laid on the statement that Christ's death was that of the common malefactor, and that crucifixion was just the ordinary form of the death penalty in Palestine at that time. No doubt this is true to some extent, and I can understand why a certain English priest in the fifteenth century set up a gibbet on his altar and hung a figure of Christ from it; but I am glad his bishop censured him, and made him remove it. The priest evidently had lost the symbolic meaning, and was trying to over-emphasise this side of the story. Whether his bishop knew it and therefore censured him, or whether his action was dictated simply by respect for tradition, it is impossible to say; but he was certainly right.

To me, every incident in the story of Jesus Christ is a parable in action, by which I do not mean to imply that Jesus never lived, but that in His life, as in His teaching, he "fulfilled the Scriptures" and taught us by symbols.

Moreover, we may be entitled to regard him as the last Christ who was crucified, but certainly not as the first. To take but one example, among the ancient Mayas there was a similar story, and a manuscript exists which depicts Him crucified on the two poles J and B, joined by a cross-piece, –, making the figure like an H. His hands are tied to the two poles, His feet rest on the cross-piece. As He is crucified on the poles, North and South Poles, or Pole Stars, this means that the picture represents an incident of the stellar cult, and not the solar, as our cross does. He has on His head a crown of thorns, and His heart is pierced by a spear. From the wound gush forth two streams, blood and water. His head is sunk on his left side. And this scene was painted long before our Christ was born. An illustration of this interesting picture will be found in Dr. Churchward's book, with full details. The name of the god depicted was Huitzilopochtli among the Aztecs, and among the Zapotics it was Zipe. He had other names among other races in ancient America. Churchward claims that the hieroglyphs state that his age was thirty-three, and adds that the same age was ascribed to Ptah-Seker-Ausar among the Egyptians, who was their representative of the same divine manifestation.

Now let us turn for a short time to a consideration of the origin of these two crosses, and begin with the oldest, or phallic cross, T.

Originally it was reversed ⊥, and in that form was merely a simplified form of the phallus itself. The phallus is a crude and primitive method of indicating the male of creative function, and hence the Creator of All, just as the vesica pisces, (), is a simplified form of the yoni, which indicated the female, or productive principle in God. As the mother preserves the incipient life and brings it forth as a child, and thereafter suckles it and preserves it till it can stand alone, this symbol has naturally beeome associated with the Preserver, or Saviour. We shall consider this symbol more fully later, and will only add here that the Hindoo form of the Rose and Cross is the more primitive lingam, which is a phallus surrounded by a yoni, thereby typifying the combination of the male and female principle in one, which is God.

Phallic worship, so called, appears to be exceedingly ancient, and probably was the earliest of all; but the phallus was always a symbol of God, and though no doubt there were abuses, yet we are not justified in assuming that they were particularly flagrant in early times any more than they are to-day in India, where the lingam is venerated by millions of perfectly moral people, taking the strictest views we have to-day of what is meant by sexual morality.

In the story of Osiris, it will be remembered that this member was missing when they put together his body, and a wooden substitute was made. Here we have a double symbolism: the phallus and the cross being one, there is a distinct reference to the idea of crucifixion, particularly in the making of a wooden substitute. But, secondly, the risen Osiris, who typified all risen men, had no further need of this member; and so we are taught the lesson that we must destroy the passions which war against the soul. Thus, in this sense, Osiris without that member is the man cleansed of all passions who alone is fit to enter the mansions of bliss.

From this cross probably developed another symbol, the axe. The most primitive people still extant are the Pigmies of Central Africa, whose symbol for the Great Spirit is three sticks crossed thus . The Nilotic negroes have altered this to , a symbol used to-day in certain of the "higher degrees," particularly the Templar group. In its primitive form , it was the ideograph for Amsu, the risen Horus, who corresponds to our Christ.

From the first form it was easy to change it into an axe, the symbol of rule, particularly in the form of the stone axe 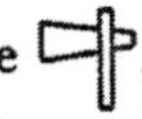, and this developed into the bronze axe, which often took the form of the double-headed axe, thereby retaining the tau shape. In the neolithic axe the haft was socketed, or split and bound, and a part of the stone axe passed through it, retaining thereby the tau shape. Sometimes the stone axe took the form of a hammer, which was the symbol of Jupiter, Indra, and Thor, the kings of the Pantheon. When bronze took the place of stone the axe or hammer had a socket, and the narrow end, passed through the wooden haft, disappeared. The substitution of the double axe restored the ancient symbol. It should be noted that there was a form of the stone war hammer  with a hole through the centre which likewise retained the T form. Sometimes the hammer took on the form of  as with Thor, and if thrown, this form, like a boomerang, returned to the thrower.

The axe, or hammer, is shown in very early times as a symbol of rule and authority among both men and gods. To quote but a few examples, the axe, called *Neter*, was the symbol for God among the ancient Egyptians. It was also the symbol of Indra, who in the heroic age was king of the gods in India.

At Knossos is a temple with a stone chair called by Evans "The House of the Double Axe," because there is an altar of three cubes on which are graven double axes shaped thus . Here we see the primitive pigmy sign  for God developing into the double axe. The arrangement of this building is strongly reminiscent of a modern lodge-room. There is a stone throne for the Worshipful Master, round the sides are stone benches for the columns, and in the centre an altar formed by a treble cube adorned with these ideograms of axes, one on each side of each cube. Probably the god thereby referred to is Zeus, or at least his prototype. Thor of the Norse had as his symbol the axe, and among the Egyptians it was especially associated with Ptah.

Tepoxtecatl, or Quetzalcoatl the Preserver, the so-called pulque god depicted in a Mexican painting in the Biblioteca Nazionale, Florence, bears a neolithic axe. He wears the double crown, having a similar meaning to that worn by the gods in Egypt and their earthly representatives the Pharaohs, while the illustration of him opposite should be studied with care.

Among Greeks and Romans it was also the symbol of authority, the lictors' axes being but one example. Among the Anglo-Saxons it had the same significance, derived no doubt from the axe or hammer of Thor.

The use of the tau cross dates back to the very earliest times, as is shown by a recent discovery in a prehistoric (neolithic) grave in England. Here was found the skeleton of a man, and his wife, who had been slain at his burial and had been laid in the grave with her feet against his side, thus forming a tau cross, T.

Thus we see that the hammer, or gavel, and the tau were originally the same, and this is a natural evolution of symbols, for the tau cross is evolved from the phallus, and that is the symbol of God the Creator, the Father, and by the time man had evolved the axe symbol the patriarchal age had come, and who so suitable to wield authority as the father of the clan, who was the earthly representative of the Heavenly Father ?

STATUE OF THE MEXICAN PRESERVER.

Note exaggerated centre, gavel, apron, and design on cap. Original in the Trocadero, Paris.

(From *Bulletin of Smithsonian Institute, U.S.A.*)

The second cross is the cross of suffering and redemption. It probably had a different origin from the tau, and seems to have been evolved from the two poles B and J crossed so as to divide the heavens into four quarters. When the solar cult was established it became a sign of the utmost importance, but it was certainly known before, the swastika being an early form of it. Enough space has already been devoted to the swastika, so we will pass it by, merely noting that it is to-day a symbol of the sun in its apparent journey round the earth.

On this cross the cosmic Christ is being ever crucified. He is that Paschal Lamb slain before the beginning of the world.

There are many forms of this cross which are pre-Christian. Perhaps the commonest is this form, +, all arms being equal. It is found in large numbers among the archæological remains of Mexico, but is not confined to that country, being indeed traceable all over the world. The Arunta natives have this form, and so have the Santa Cruz Indians in Yucatan to this day, though they are still "pagans." Among numerous savage races in Africa it was found by early explorers long before any missionaries could have brought it, and it was a venerated sign among the Druids. The Huron Red Indians tattooed themselves with a cross or a serpent on the thigh, while the Baratonga tattoo a cross and a square side by side. Egypt, however, has perhaps more variations of the cross than any other country. The so-called Teutonic cross ✠ was a symbol constantly worn by the gods. Bes, the pigmy god, and Nefer-Hetep are both shown in Budge's *The Gods of the Egyptians* wearing this "Christian and Teutonic Cross." The equal-armed cross is constantly found, often with certain characters graven thereon, and, save for the fact that these are in Egyptian instead of Hebrew, it might well be taken for the jewel of the M.W.S. of the eighteenth degree, which in a sense it is, since the characters are Egyptian for a certain holy name. The ankh, ☥, combines the tau and vesica piscis, the male and female emblems. It was the emblem of eternal life, and will be considered fully later. The swastika in many forms, the St. Andrew's cross, X (used also as hieroglyph), and still other varieties are to be found.

We have already pointed out that there exists a pictorial representation of One Crucified in ancient Mexico, but He is hung on the H formed by the two poles J and B; but the ancient people of Central America venerated all forms of the cross, the so-called Latin Cross, †, the ‡, and the ankh ☥ included.

The feature which distinguishes the cross of suffering and redemption from the phallic, or tau cross, is the presence of a fourth arm, or head-piece. The ankh may be regarded as a form of the cross of redemption, as the loop forms a head-piece, but is really constructed from the emblems T and O. It therefore unites both aspects of the cross in one, and was hence the most venerated of all crosses. It must not be forgotten that, among the Hebrews, the tau (T) was regarded as a sacred symbol, and associated with the triangles.

TABLET OF THE CROSS, PALENQUE, CENTRAL AMERICA.

Note cross on regalia of the devotee and C. T. of the priest.

(From *Bulletin of Smithsonian Institute*, *U.S.A.*)

CHAPTER VI

THE CROSSES IN THE CRAFT

Both forms of the cross appear in the craft, but the most important is the tau cross, which we will consider first. The first regular step, what is it? Compare this with the charge (which will be discussed later) made against the Templars, that they trampled on the cross. This action was regarded as anti-Christian, but it was not; the meaning of the act is perfectly clear if it is the T cross, for it implies that our first regular step in F.M. must be to trample underfoot our animal passions. And, moreover, as we begin, so we must continue in each degree, for unless our animal passions are brought under control, we cannot hope to find the c. of the c. It is not the cross of suffering, but the phallic cross, and the lesson a perfectly sound one, and no objection can be taken to it when correctly understood.

But this is not the only place where the tau cross occurs. The gabels, or gavels, are all T crosses and combine in one symbol the hammer, the sign of rule, and the T cross, the symbol of the male or creative side of the Deity; and, lest there should be any mistake, the ⊤ is placed on the apron of the Master of the Lodge, though placed ⊥, so as to give also the symbol of the square, and also to emphasise its phallic meaning. If this is not intended, why not the single square L, which is the form used on other occasions in Lodge? Nor must the significance of who holds the gabel be overlooked. The W.M., S.W., and J.W. wield it, and these are not only the rules in the Lodge, but the representatives of God in His three aspects. Thus, when united, as in R.A., we get the triple tau 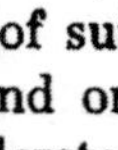 or 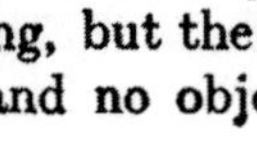

so that even the positions of these officers east, south, and west are indicated in this symbol.

In some foreign jurisdictions the Outer and Inner Guards also use gavels to make the appropriate knocks, though this is not usually the case in England. Personally I consider our system of reserving the gavels for the three chairs better; nevertheless, as both these assistant officers represent the male element, its use is to some extent justified. The Deacons, who represent the mothering and preservative side, never hold the gavels.

The Latin cross, or cross of suffering, is only used in two places in a Craft Lodge, save as a step and there is a reason for its appearance there. These places are the sword of the Tyler, which should be cross-handled, and the S.I. of the I.G.

The first degree is the degree of birth, and reminds us of the suffering of our mother which gave us birth. There is also probably a further reference to the cause of our birth, i.e. the phallic cross, now confounded with the Latin cross.

Then we are reminded of the pain which we, as well as she, felt when we came from the darkness into the light of this world. The proper manner of proceeding in the most important of the craft degrees is a Latin cross—a most significant point.

The Latin cross is, however, more properly part of the ritual of the higher degrees, particularly the Rose Croix, and by Christian derivation in the Templar degrees.

The Mark is really a craft degree also, and we are not surprised to find there the T cross once more. It is disguised under the symbol of the Lewis, or cramp of metal with which pieces of stone were joined together. We are informed that there are many kinds of Lewis, the single one thus, T, the double, H, and the triple, 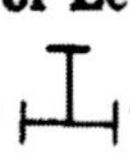. We are further reminded that a Lewis is the son of a mason, and his support in his old age. Bearing in mind the phallic significance of this cross, we see at once that there is a still deeper meaning, and finally the grip, which is likened to a Lewis, reminds us of the T cross of the brazen serpent which saved the Israelites in the desert, and was a prototype of the cross of suffering of our Lord, by which we are saved, while the double H will recall to our memory that in Mexico He is depicted crucified on H.

In the R.A. this sign is described at length, and there is therefore no need to do so here. We should but remember that in its triple form it reminds us of the three-fold nature of the Deity, who is one and yet three, and in the highest sense all Three Persons have the attributes of the other two, so that God the Creator is also the Preserver and the Destroyer, and in India the phallus has, for the reasons already given, become the symbol of Shiva the Destroyer. But, besides the exoteric reason for this, that death to the Hindoo does but usher in a new life, there is an esoteric meaning. For the creative act, being *in time* of necessity, brings with it death, which ends time, and the cross of birth is also the cross of death, which we in the West regard as the Latin cross. Christianity completes the triple T by showing us that because God the Preserver was slain on the cross, we shall be born again to salvation.

The quadruple tau forms the cross of certain higher degrees ; but, as we are now dealing with the craft series, it need not detain us here.

We may, however, note in passing that the tau was a popular masons' mark in mediæval times, and a particularly well cut one is to be seen on one of the pillars in the chapel in the White Tower in the Tower of London. It appears to be contemporary with the column, and, if so, cannot be later than A.D. 1080.

CHAPTER VII

THE VESICA PISCIS

THIS symbol, 0, is nearly always found associated with the cross. It represents the passive, or female principle. Its use is almost universal, and it is found in India and China, often being placed behind the gods or the Buddha. It has already been described as a caste mark, and among the ancient nations it was no less prevalent. In India it is the yoni, which, when associated with the phallus, forms the lingam stone which is a common object of veneration in every Hindoo temple. Groups of these are to be seen, and with them are usually carved stone or brass cobras, these representing the Son (see illustration opposite p. 62). The original Trinity was Father-Creator, Mother-Preserver, and Son-Destroyer. As the Destroyer, or Conqueror of death, Jesus represents the latter, while the serpent is associated with the Holy Ghost, which replaces the Divine Mother. There was a sect of Eastern Christians against whom Mohammed inveighs who regarded the Virgin Mary as the second person of the Trinity, thereby reverting to the ancient Egyptian system.

India now divides the Godhead into three male personalities, and, the Divine Mother having been replaced by Vishnu, who has largely taken her place, the ancient phallic system has become somewhat disorganised. It is still commemorated, however, by these three symbols. We, too, have dethroned the Divine Mother, and made the Son the Preserver, the third person, the Holy Ghost, being a shadowy male being, but distinctly associated with the serpent.

The vesica piscis, however, is always associated with the preservative side of the Deity, and Vishnu is often depicted standing in it. The Buddha, who took the place of Vishnu, is similarly depicted, and in mediæval Europe the saints, and particularly the Virgin, were placed in it likewise.

THE LION INCARNATION OF VISHNU.

Compare this with the story that the Mexican reserver took upon himself the form of a jaguar before he fought with the demon. Vishnu is coming out of a vesica piscis (female) in a pillar (male). Note also the attendant. Vishnu in this incarnation destroyed a certain hostile giant tearing open his centre.

All ecclesiastical seals were placed inside a vesica piscis, because the Church was declared to be the Bride of Christ, and it will be remembered that the bishop at his consecration received a wedding-ring to mark his marriage to the Church. (See illustration of the seal of St. Lawrence.)

Seals of barons, etc., were never placed in this symbol, but usually in a circle.

The 0 became the basis of most mediæval architecture; not only the pointed arch and the rose window were based on it, but often a considerable part of the ground-plan itself. In these cases we find, on careful examination, that it is associated with the cross, thereby showing forth the rose and the cross in architectural form.

In geometry, which is the basis of architecture, the vesica piscis appears in the first proposition of Euclid, and gives birth to the equilateral triangle, the emblem of God Himself.

Thus we can see that this proposition was not only of great practical use to our mediæval brothers, but conveyed to them a tremendous mystical lesson in its simple symbolism. This fact is of special importance to members of the R.A., and also to those who have taken the cryptic degrees, which are in a sense pendants of the R.A., and whose symbol is the reversed equilateral triangle, ▽, which can be formed on the reverse side, thus making the lozenge, which was the form in which a woman was allowed to bear her arms, a point whose full significance will be developed later.

In ancient Egypt the 0 was associated with the T to form the ankh, ☥, or symbol of eternal life. In other words, the earliest form of the Rose Croix and the ☧ of the early Greek Christians had this esoteric significance. As men became more refined, and hesitated to call a spade a spade, there grew up a number of synonyms for this symbol, of which the rose was the most common, and from this new and fanciful meanings were evolved, many pretty and instructive, but tending to obscure the original meaning. Among these is the use of the rose to represent the five wounds of Christ, and sometimes of H. A. B.; red roses to show the colour of the victim's blood, and white his innocence. But, in the main, the rose became associated in Christian times with He who was the Rose of Sharon and the Lily of the Valley. Thus the white lily was substituted for the white rose. In Jacobite times the white rose was associated with another victim, the White Martyr, King Charles, and the white rose became a badge among the Jacobites.

To-day the vesica piscis has been largely submerged by the rose, but it is still used on ecclesiastical seals, and to form the background of pictures of saints in Roman Catholic churches. Modern rose-windows are but feeble copies of mediæval work, and the symbolic meaning is lost by most modern architects.

It may come as a surprise to many of my readers to hear that it is nevertheless present, even in our Craft Lodge, and some may contend that my arguments are far-fetched; but if they will bear in mind that elsewhere the phallic cross is always associated with the vesica piscis, and then how carefully it has been disguised under other forms, and finally consider the arguments I advance, I think they will come to the conclusion that I am right. As a result, they will, I feel sure, acquire a still greater veneration for the square and compasses, which thus represents this most ancient of all symbols.

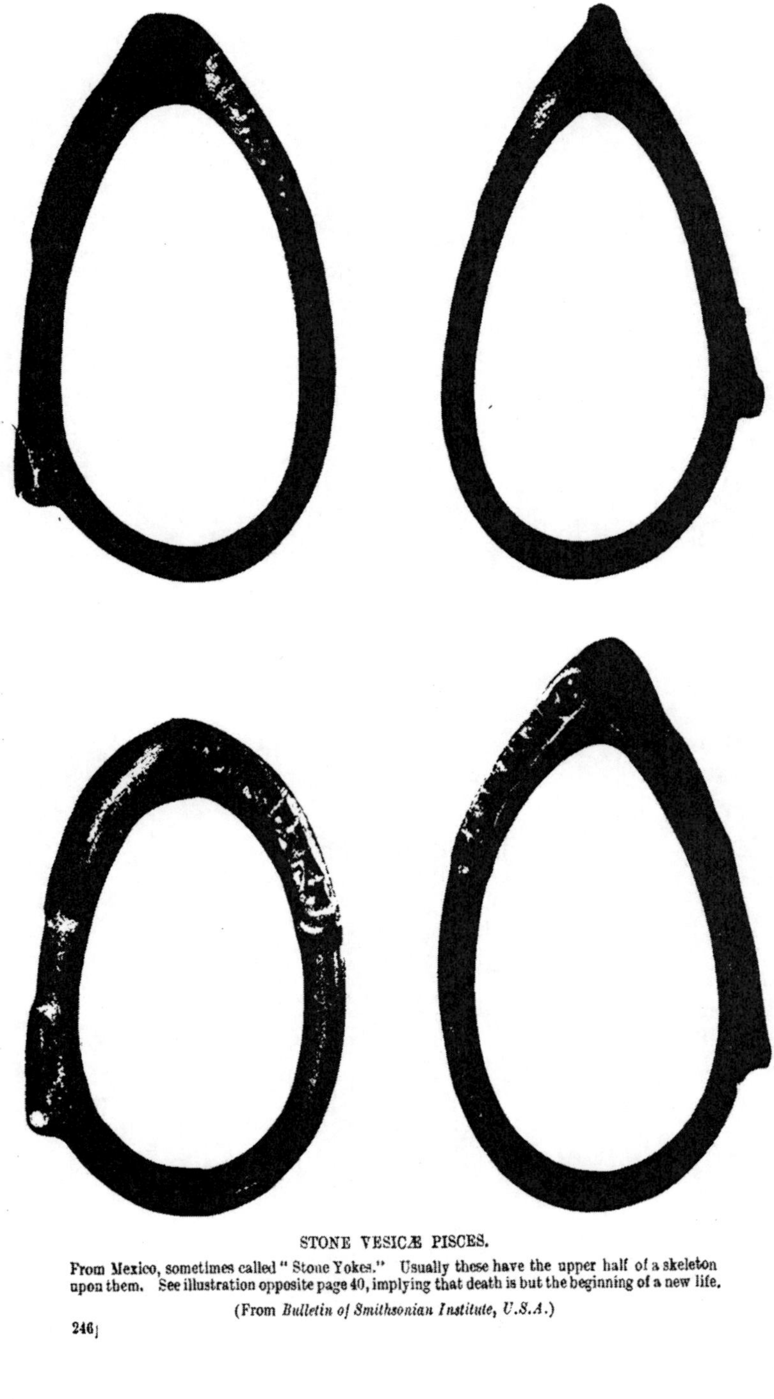

STONE VESICÆ PISCES.

From Mexico, sometimes called "Stone Yokes." Usually these have the upper half of a skeleton upon them. See illustration opposite page 40, implying that death is but the beginning of a new life.

(From *Bulletin of Smithsonian Institute, U.S.A.*)

CHAPTER VIII

THE VESICA PISCIS IN THE CRAFT

ORIGINALLY only straight lines were permitted in the Craft Lodges. The Operatives maintain that round work belonged to those specially trained in arch-work. Be that as it may, the instinct to soften the bluntness of our ritual and to adopt a more restrained attitude in certain matters would account for the tendency to disguise this symbol under a more decorous form. The use of the rose has already been indicated, but in the craft the reverence already devoted to the square and compasses would lead to their being utilised. If we study these three figures we shall see that the evolution was fairly simple.

1 2 3

an was
is was
ozenge
hape?

ERRATUM

Page 247. Symbol No. 2 should appear as 

Ages,
e it is
ys the
fasti-
ngless,

mpass

arranged as above, and by this method the meaning of the  is united with that specially associated with these masonic implements.

Beside it on the p. lies the gavel, or tau, and so the cross and the vesica piscis are brought together in conjunction with the third great light in Masonry, at the very moment when the C. takes his O.

What is the significance of this symbol here? The cross represents the active, or male influence in the Lodge. Before taking *any* action, the Master uses it, but the other symbol is passive and is only active when separated.[1]

The O. is taken on, or rather inside, this emblem. Admitted on the +, ruled by the T, obligated in the 0, the C.'s first lesson is to make the first regular step in F.M. and thereby publicly declare his intention of trampling underfoot those primitive and animal passions which war against the soul.

The 0 is the symbol of the Preserver, and by his O. the candidate is preserved from the fate that would befall a cowan, and promises to preserve the secrets of the degree.

Having been admitted in the first degree on +, the first half of the vesica piscis is presented to his . . . at his O. In the second he is admitted on the s., and it is raised above his head, while it also plays an important part in the O.

In the third he is admitted on the c.'s, and they too are raised over his head, but it plays no part in the O.

Thus he has passed through the vesica piscis in two sections, and that fact has been emphasised twice (or in two sections) at his O.s.

There is an exoteric and an esoteric meaning to these acts, and the esoteric refers, I contend, to the female or passive principle of the Deity, just as the creative or masculine is denoted by the T cross.

This symbol is represented by the double triangle  of a certain higher degree, and by this  the triangle and compasses well known to members of the Royal Order of Scotland. The double triangle  has a further reference in all probability to the two Pole Stars and their mounts.

Thus the C. is reminded that, as he must enter this material world through the vesica piscis, so he must enter the life of initiation by the same road, and only after he has done so can

[1] God the Father, T; God the Son, 0; God the Holy Ghost, V.S.L.

he see the Light. This lesson is repeated each time, even till he finds that this Light is but a glimmering ray as compared with the Light which is from above. This vesica piscis is the female or preservative principle of God, without which we could not exist for a single day, nor without it could we hope to be preserved from the powers of darkness and evil which threaten us upon our spiritual journey.

The double triangle in this form  was used in the ancient mysteries with the same meaning, and must not be confounded with that other double triangle, the symbol of the R.A., ✡, which has been explained at considerable length elsewhere. But symbols shade off into each other, and one often conveys part at least of the meaning of the other.

Thus the cross and vesica piscis are to be found in our Craft Lodges, and it would be strange if they were not, considering how old they are, and how essential a part they played in the ancient primitive initiatory rites of the savages as well as in the ancient mysteries.

This symbol, used often as a hieroglyph, is found all over the world. Ancient Egyptians, Mayas in Central America, and the Druids in Great Britain and Ireland, all had it and associated it with the cross.

But there are two further reminders of this symbol in the craft: firstly the collars of the officers, and secondly, and more significant, the rosettes on our aprons. All full members of the Lodge have these three roses to remind them that their duty is passive, to obey the commands of the W.M., who, to remind us of his masculine function, wears the three taus in place of the three rosettes.

Now these rosettes are worn on all aprons belonging to the craft series save the R.A. Thus, in the Mark and Ark, for example, we find these symbols, and on the W. Mark Master's apron we likewise find the ⊥. In the higher degree, e.g. eighteenth degree, it is naturally missing, being given in a different form.

But why is it lacking in the R.A.? Is it not because in the H.R.A. we are taught the union of the triune nature of the Deity, and His passive and active sides are sufficiently emphasised by the ✡ and the  ?

CHAPTER IX

THE ROSE CROIX AND KINDRED DEGREES

THE preceding chapters must be regarded, in a sense, as introductory to this.

The Cross and the Rose, it has already been shown, are only another name for the cross and the vesica piscis. Sometimes the symbol is depicted thus,  sometimes thus, [illegible] when it is known as the [illegible]. In our more sophisticated days a rose and a Latin cross are the usual form, sometimes the rose being placed at the centre, where the four arms meet, sometimes, as in the star of the Royal Order, five roses are placed on the cross to mark the wounds, sometimes the rose or roses are disposed of in other ways.

Thus the [illegible]g has become united [illegible]c c[illegible]s. This is to signify that Christ was crucified on the cross of our passions, and is still crucified, for each time we sin we do crucify Him afresh.

Various forms of the cross, and particularly of pre-Christian crosses, have already been given; but there are many, some of which were evolved by the heralds in the Middle Ages for the purpose of creating suitable armorial bearings. Thus the quadruple tau  of the knights of St. John and the Holy Sepulchre is an heraldic cross, but it certainly is a pleasing form, and not lacking in appropriateness, for it combines the triple tau of the Jewish religion, and Jehovah worshipped at the Temple on Mount Moriah, with the Christian cross of suffering. It emphasises the fact that Christ was crucified on the cross of our passions.

I have already produced evidence enough to show that the eighteenth degree is not a "modern High Church degree." On the contrary, scenes and parts of the [illegible] in *The Book of the Dead* in Egypt, and show that a similar ceremony took place there ages before the historic [illegible]y. Dr.

1.

2

b *a*

3.

4.

(1) Teaching the candidate a grip.
(2) The God of Death acknowledges the sacrifice Quetzalcoatl is making.
(3) The sacred stone. (*a*) Closed. (*b*) Open, disclosing the sacred name or symbol. See further illustrations.
(4) Teaching candidate two signs.

Quetzalcoatl meets the God of Death, who reminds him whence he came, to which he replies that, though he knows he will descend into the earth and be buried, he will also finally ascend to heaven; which he did, and Maya records relate that after he had passed through the underworld he ascended to heaven and now dwells in that bright morning star (Venus) whose coming heralds the dawn. The characters appear to be in a boat.

FROM MEXICAN CODICES.

(From *Bulletin of Smithsonian Institute, U.S.A.*)

Churchward has adduced abundant evidence and illustrations from original manuscripts also to prove this. In the Egyptian ritual the C., after having been safely conducted through the terrors of the under-world, is led by the mystical ladder to the mansions of bliss, where he is received into the circle of Princes, receives the Word, and partakes with them of food and drink.

He has passed through the Valley of the Shadow amid darkness, difficulties, and dangers, aided by the new and better covenant given by Osiris.[1]

Turning to far-away Mexico, we find a complete record of this degree in picture form. Incident after incident is the same, and the M.W.S. is there. He points to the c. s. which contains the w. He makes the . . . . Previously the C. is shown how to make, not only this sign, but also that of the Benevolent Herdsman.

To this day the Quiché Indians still perform this ceremony, and among the Crow Indians in North America the latter sign, with L.U., is found, and it is answered by a sign showing that the Herdsman came down from the mountains and ultimately returned to them. All over Mexico are to be found representations of these signs given again and again as incidents in a ceremony of initiation.

The sign of the R. Order of Scotland can also be seen, together with a very detailed picture of a ceremony which is evidently a degree beyond the eighteenth, and which Churchward suggests is the prototype of the thirtieth degree.

The Arunta natives have, in their Bora ceremony, a degree which seems to combine our third degree and our eighteenth degree. The candidate passes over a mound shaped to represent a human figure stretched out as if on a cross of this shape, χ. There is no arch of steel, but its place is taken by an arch of boomerangs, and on his journey through this Valley of the Shadow with the symbol of crucified mortality beneath his feet, he is threatened and challenged, gives and receives passwords, and finally emerges into safety, after having been conducted by a dusky R. through darkness and difficulties severe enough to test the courage of any man. These incidents can be seen in the numerous photographs taken of the ceremony by anthropologists, and Churchward adds that they have one of the Rose Croix signs as well. See Appendix.

[1] In the Greek mysteries they had a figure who held a lighted torch in one hand and an extinguished one pointing downwards in the other.

In view of the existence of a ritual of initiation with signs and incidents similar to our R.C. and the fact that the cross was a venerated sign as well as the existence of a story of a god who was crucified, we must, I think, admit that this degree is far earlier than Christianity itself, and cannot possibly have been made up in the eighteenth century. Altered it has been, no doubt, and so have most of our degrees. Even to-day changes are being made, and the tragedy of it is that these changes often rob the degrees of valuable indications of their past history.

Of the rose, the following facts will prove of interest. In ancient days the rose was sacred to Harpocrates, the God of Silence, and in the mysteries the hierophant wore a wreath of roses as emblematic of silence and secrecy. We learn from Apuleius that it was regarded as the flower of Isis, and her priests used it in their ceremonies.

The association with Isis gives us one exoteric interpretation of the rose and the cross, which Ragon uses, namely, that they denote the secret of immortality. We have already shown that, in its esoteric meaning, it is a substitute for the (), but in all the mysteries there was an exoteric meaning which was true as well as the hidden meaning. It was also sacred to Aurora and the sun, and hence the symbol of the Dawn, and, in the natural sequence of thought, the emblem of the Dawn of the Resurrection when conjoined with the cross of redemption. Its full interpretation would thus be: the dawn of eternal life.

When we [illegible] ho[illegible]ave been [illegible]rd into [illegible], even in small things, we shall not be surprised to find the rose transferred to Christ Himself. Indeed, many of the symbols of Christianity were [illegible], though often people do not realise this. Most people know that Christmas is only the old [illegible] of [illegible], held in honour of Balder, who was unwittingly slain by Höder at the instigation of Loki the Norse God of Evil. The weapon that slew him was an [illegible]e, and hence many of the ceremonies popularly associated with it. It may, however, come as a surprise to many to know that the initials on the label placed over every crucifix seen in a Roman Catholic church are far older than the incident to which they are now said to refer. The priest who, on [illegible]y (note the day of the [illegible], or Venus, the Goddess of Love), preaches an eloquent sermon on the letters I.N.R.I., as

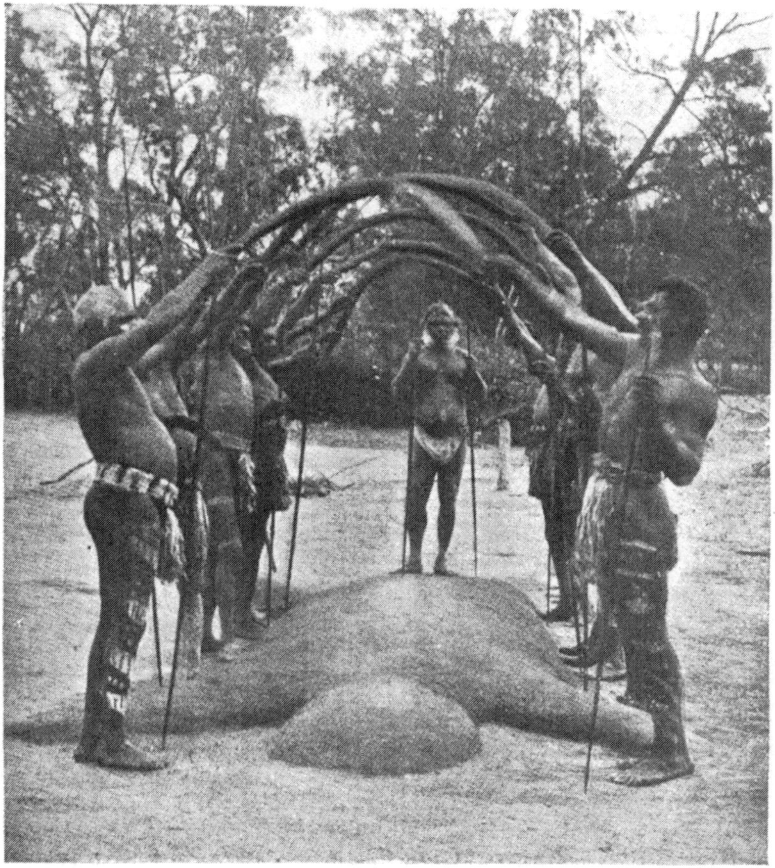

Photo by] [*Kerry & Co.*

AN INITIATION CEREMONY.

The Bora ceremony of the aboriginal tribes of New South Wales is connected with a society whose members are pledged to secrecy. The penalty for any breach of its rules is death.

Photo by] [C. G. Seligmann.

BIRTH CEREMONY.

The Veddas perform certain ceremonies to obtain the protection of their ancestors. Two dancers take part, one of whom should be the woman's father. (Note bush.)

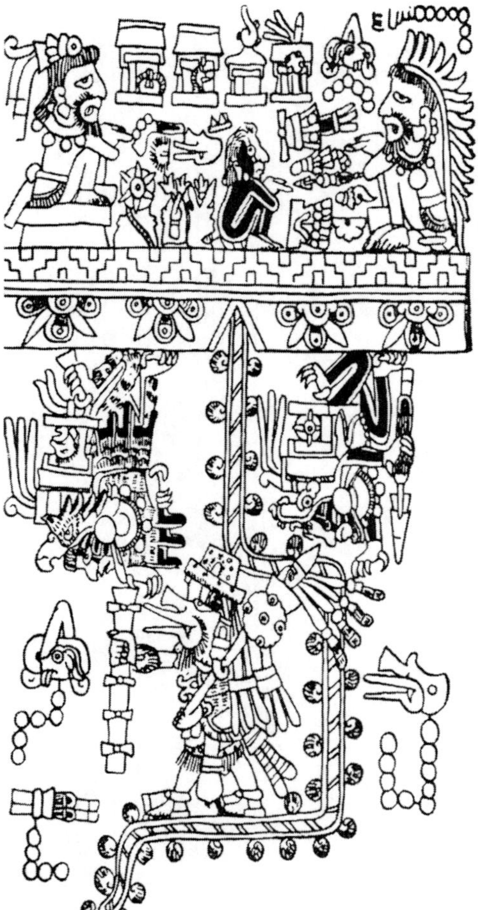

Quetzalcoatl, the Mexican Preserver, descends from the mansions of bliss by a golden ladder of thirty-three steps, corresponding to his age. Two or three steps are covered by the streamers of his staff.

The gods whom he has left are commenting on the great sacrifice he has made.

Compare with figure on the relief of Vishnu sleeping under the protection of the five-headed Cobra of Wisdom.

Quetzalcoatl with the jaguar skin, reminding us of his incarnation as a Jaguar.

Compare with Lion Incarnation of Vishnu. The figure above is his Father in heaven, who acknowledges him to be his son. There appear to have been at least two incarnations of Quetzalcoatl. In the Jaguar one he took upon himself that form to fight a great giant, who wounded him, but he slew the giant; then dying, as he was, he journeyed on towards west and reached the shores of the Great Sea (Pacific). Here he built a funeral pyre and immolated himself, and the winds scattered his ashes to the four cardinal powers of heaven, his spirit meanwhile journeying through the underworld and ascending to heaven. He reigns in that bright morning star whose coming heralds the dawn.

(From *Bulletin of Smithsonian Institute, U.S.A.*)

a rule, has no idea that they were a sacred symbol ages before Pontius Pilate ordered them to be fixed over the head of the Christ. Indeed, it is doubtful if he did place the initials only, as the account in the Gospels gives the words in full, "Jesus of Nazareth, King of the Jews." He may, however, have knowingly placed that inscription there, intending a play on the initials, for these are some of its ancient meanings.

The sages of antiquity used I.N.R.I. to denote "Igne Natura Renovatur Integra" (Entire Nature is renewed by Fire). The ancient Hebrews denoted by these letters the four elements: I = Iammim, Water; N = Nour, fire; R = Rouach, the air; I = Iebeschah, earth.

Later this symbol—for so it is—had other meanings attached to it, for the alchemists used it to denote "Igne nitrum raris invenitur," while the Jesuits gave to it the esoteric meaning, "Justum necare regis impios."

In the hieroglyphic language of Egypt, [illegible], or ☥, m[illegible], and formed part of the character which represented [illegible] = li[illegible] Ra or [illegible], was the sun, or the king thereof, and therefore ☥ ⊙, or Enre = I.N.R.I., and would mean the "Living God of Light." Thus it represented the Eternal Deity, who is life and light, and unites the two great symbols ☥ and ⊙ = External Life, God and Nature. Thus, even in our churches to-day we can see united in these four letters the cross, the rose, and the p. within the c.

We have already shown that a Mexican "Christ" existed, and in the picture which shows Him tied to the [illegible], his age is given as thirty-three.

To return more directly to the R.C. degree, we find in Ceylon, in the ancient ruined city of Anuradhapura, a most interesting relic near one of the ancient dagobas (pagodas).

It consists of a circular slab of dark blue granite, on which are sculptured seven concentric circles. Within each ring is a different sacred emblem. In the innermost are a lion, a horse, a cow, an elephant, and a peculiar long, narrow leaf; and the centre is marked by ∴, which formed the letter S in the ancient Singalese alphabet.

Rossetti gives the following information: "St. Paul, in his Epistle to the Galatians, calls the three apostles who were present on the Mount of Transfiguration *pillars*, and the Paulicians made these three pillars emblematic of the three theological virtues: St. Peter was Faith; St. James, Hope; and St. John, Charity; and in a rite which is supposed to have descended from the Albigenses, three pillars appear with the names of those virtues upon them. The candidate is obliged to travel for thirty-three years (thus they call the thirty-three turns he takes, in allusion to the age of our Lord) to learn the beauties of the new law." He goes on to describe this rite most minutely, and adds: "This new mystery, or new law, is the essence of Dante's *Vita Nuova.* In the *Paradiso* we find this rite described exactly. Before the last vision St. Peter examines him on Faith, St. James on Hope, and St. John on Charity, relating to the three pilgrimages—of the Palmers, or Templars, to St. John of Jerusalem; of the pilgrims, or Albigenses, to St. James in Galicia; and of the Romei, or Ghibellines, to St. Peter's in Rome."

The Rose Croix degree appears to be alluded to in the works of Henry Cornelius Agrippa. He was born in 1486, and his works were printed at Leyden in 1550. He visited England in 1510, and was regarded as a magician by the majority of people at that period.

John Gower, the poet, and friend of Chaucer, is believed to have been a Rosicrucian brother, and his tomb is to be seen in St. Saviour's, Southwark. He is depicted lying at full length on an altar tomb, and round his head is a fillet with roses. In his works references to what appears to be this degree can be traced, and there are also similar references in Chaucer.

The Royal Order of Scotland has two degrees, the Harodim and the Rosy Cross.

The former is the main piece of ritual, the latter being the degree of Knighthood, said to have been conferred by Bruce on those Scottish masons who helped him at the battle of Bannockburn.

The meaning of the word Harodim has been a matter of dispute among masonic students for years, but the most probable interpretation is that it comes from a Hebrew word denoting Overseers.

This degree has several sections, and carries the candidate from the first Temple to the rebuilding of the second, and on into the New Testament. It appears to have been less changed than any other degree I have taken, and to have retained many old and interesting features which have been removed from other masonic rituals. Without disclosing the secrets, I may add that although after the chief-craft degree we should go round

Photo by] [*The Wykeham Studios Ltd.*, 165 Victoria St., S.W. 1.

ROYAL ORDER OF SCOTLAND PROVINCIAL GRAND MASTER (RT. WOR. BRO. H. W. HODGES, F.S.A., SCOT.) SHOWING FULL REGALIA.

A "MALTESE CROSS" FROM THE MEXICAN CODICES.

The veneration of the Holy Tree. Quetzalcoatl at the centre. Note: (*a*) all trees form tau crosses; (*b*) these tau crosses blossom into Latin crosses of suffering bearing the Mexican equivalent of roses. The bird on the top represents the soul; (*c*) each tree is a thorn-tree, but (*d*) throws the thorns as steps upon (*e*) the next one, shows the thorns pointing downwards, while (*f*) the next shows the thorns pointing upwards—that is, the cross is a ladder; (*g*) the small figures adorning the cross-tree also indicate, by the position of their hands, the same idea.

(From *Fejervary Codex*, by permission of the Smithsonian Institute.)

widdershins, or reverse way of the sun, being dead, yet this is the only degree where I have seen this deliberately done.

The reason why, in the R.A., R.C., R.O., etc., we should go the reverse way is that the manes, or ghost, is supposed so to travel, the reverse way, through the underworld, till it returns to the place of Light—God. The search for the lost Word, the lost Holy Grail, and so forth, is a mystical way of describing the search for full knowledge of God—or, if you will, of the heritage of eternal life and fellowship with God lost by the fall of Adam.

The jewel, or the sash of a triangle and compasses, has already been explained, and the jewel on the other sash is a triple interlaced triangle, having within it a circle and a cross, and it is similar to the star of this degree. One meaning of this symbol is—the cross within the circle denoted the mystic Christ crucified in the heavens on that cross which stretches from the centre to the four quarters of the circle of the sky. The triple triangle refers to the triple form of the Trinity in Unity, Father, Mother, Son (Egypt), Creator, Preserver, Destroyer (Indian), God the Father, Jesus the Son, the Holy Ghost, or Wisdom (Christian). This symbol therefore includes the three forms of the Trinity, the point within a circle which denotes the Unknown and Unknowable, and the Christ. It has a further reference to the rose and the cross, and is included in a seven-pointed star, the perfect number. (See illustration facing p. 266.)

This shows the complete star, and it will be noted that there are three circles, five roses on the cross, which refer, according to some, to the five wounds of Christ, and that the three triangles form eighteen or more lesser triangles, and also a nine-sided polygon, while the triple triangle naturally produces a nine-pointed star.

For purposes of comparison, the jewels of the eighteenth degree, of the P.M W.S., and of the Rosicrucian Society are given.

If we study the P.M.W.S. jewel, we shall see that the garter, or double circle, and the Greek cross are the same, but that, in place of the five roses, there are five Hebrew letters which form a certain name. With regard to the Rosicrucian jewel, readers will note that the cross is formed of four ladders, the significance of which is explained in the ritual, and the centre is marked by a pentacle. It, like the cross of the P.M.W.S. and of the Royal Order, is a Greek cross, and all the crosses are red in these jewels.

The background of the Rosicrucian jewel is white enamel, but the most significant feature is that this Order has adopted the lozenge as its form of the vesica piscis instead of the rose, therein bearing out my argument as to the lozenge being one of the stages in the evolution of the (). It will be noted that, despite the name of this society, no rose appears on the jewel, and this is correct, for the rose is represented by the lozenge.

The five-pointed star on the crowns, of course, reminds us of the emblem of G. in the second degree, and of the pentacle, which is strictly the jewel of a Master Mason. Though not worn as a jewel in lodges under the English constitution, it is so used in many foreign jurisdictions. Hence the masonic charms we see exposed for sale, but whose use is rightly, I think, frowned on by many good Masons.

I am not oblivious to the advantages claimed for its use, but cannot help feeling that it parades too openly our connection with F.M. which is a secret society, and not to be exposed to the uninitiated. Moreover, anyone can walk into a jeweller's shop and buy one, and no law exists to punish an impostor who uses such a sign, and its presence is apt to throw a real brother off his guard. (See illustration facing p. 266.)

This symbol is seen worn as a jewel round the neck of ancient Maya chiefs, as well as being found all over the East. It conveys many lessons, including a reference to our five senses, and therefore to "Perfect Man"; in full control of all his faculties, and utilising them only for the good of his fellow-men; hence its presence on the Crown of Glory of the eighteenth degree jewels. Sometimes it is disguised as a five-leafed flower with a dot in the centre, and, as the dot symbolises the p.w.a.c. or God, the Infinite, it would thus convey the meaning that the Perfect Man and God are one in Christ. The Buddha, no doubt, intended to convey a similar lesson when he gave utterance to his famous dictum, "The perfect man is above the gods." This statement of his has been advanced as an argument that his philosophy is a kind of Atheism; but no Buddhist will ever admit the charge. In Burma some of the keenest Masons were Burmans and Buddhists, and they appeared to have no difficulty in taking our oath or making the usual declaration of their belief in God. The Buddhists also use the symbol of the cross within the circle, and in my possession is a Burmese book in red, gold, and black lacquer

PROBABLY A SWASTIKA MADE OF SERPENTS.

Note, however, the position of the gods, particularly their arms, and that one is crucified on a St. Andrew's Cross. The serrated ribbons coming from these beings have long been objects of controversy. The writer suggests that they indicate psychic rods, to which are attached materialisations. They come from the various ossifices of the body, and resemble in appearance the psychic rods produced in the Golingher circle. For further details of the latter see *Journal of Society for Psychical Research.*

(From *Borgian Codex*, by permission of the Smithsonian Institute.)

containing the service for the ordination of a Buddhist monk, and on the cover is the following symbol.

SYMBOL ON A BUDDHIST SERVICE-BOOK.

There are three of these emblems, and on either side of the central one are nats, or Buddhist angels adoring the symbol, their hands folded and raised in prayer.

This symbol should be compared with that used in a R.C. Chapter. There are seven circles, and within the seventh is the cross built up in the peculiar way shown, while the angles have a floral decoration which indicates a rose, not the lotus, the typical Buddhist flower. The fourth circle is much thicker than the others, and no doubt indicates the division between the four = matter, and the three indicating Spirit, though the seven ages of this world are no doubt the main lesson intended.

I need not remind my readers that the pelican is a symbol of the Christ, and hence of His cross.

This symbol should also be compared with the symbol used in the centre of the R.O. star and the P.M.W.S. jewel. Finally, it will be noted that the cross as formed is not only a true Greek cross, but contains in the centre the suwastika 卍, the emblem of death, thereby revealing the fact that the cross within the circle, emblem of life everlasting, springs from death itself.

Though in Burmese Buddhism the phallus itself has practically disappeared, in the neighbouring state of Siam it is still to be seen in the enclosures of the Buddhist pagodas. One particularly large one is to be seen at Bangkok, and is religiously repainted each year, so that it appears unpleasantly natural.

There also exists among the Operative Masons a curious degree called Passed Master, or sixth degree, in which the candidate is stretched on a ×. The centre of this cross is plumbed from the emblem on the roof, which is a G. and the lead must fall directly over the candidate's centre. He is then raised on the cross and carried round the Lodge with further ceremonies. The jewel of a sixth degree Operative is ┌· .

Thus he is *raised* on the centre.

Finally, we cannot ignore the fact that among the Hindoos the cross, besides its phallic significance, is also venerated as the emblem of sacrifice and suffering. The cross-legged figure of Vishnu opposite indicates this point of view and strangely resembles a mediæval effigy of a Templar Knight. The illustration of the returning Vishnu, p. 260, should be studied with care.

CHAPTER X

THE SO-CALLED "YORK RITE" AND THE ALLIED DEGREES

This series is not properly a rite, though in America this title is often used to denote a series of degrees which included the following: Mark, Past Master, Most Excellent, Royal, Select Masters, Royal Arch, Super-excellent Master, Knight Templar, and Knight of Malta.

The *Past Master* is worked as a distinct degree in U.S.A., but the holder of it is *not* entitled to be present at the installation of the Master of a Lodge unless he has been through the Chair of a Craft Lodge. Its purpose is to qualify brethren to take office in the R.A. who otherwise would be precluded. In England we are beginning to feel the need for this degree as our Lodges grow bigger, and the time longer before a brother can work up to the Chair; but, in America, Lodges have grown so huge that many brethren cannot hope to obtain the Chair, Lodges of 400 members and even more being numerous.

It will be remembered that none of the degrees of the so-called "York Rite" are worked on the Continent.

The Mark is well known, and, so far as permissible, I have explained its most important symbolism; but the cryptic degrees deserve more careful study, particularly as in England the separate jewels are seldom worn; and, as the same is true of the clothing, it will be of interest to show what these should be.

The apron of a *Most Excellent Master*, the first of the cryptic degrees, is white, edged with purple, and a collar of purple edged with gold should also be worn. The colour refers to the grief felt for the loss of the third principal H. A. B., whose seat is vacant. No special jewel exists for this degree, which is closely associated with the completion and dedication of the Temple. In the American, though not in the English ritual, there is an interesting ceremony associated with the setting up of the capstone and the keystone of the Arch.

For this degree a candidate must be a Mark Mason, but not necessarily a Royal Arch. In England, however, the four degrees are always worked together, and, as to be a R.A.M. is essential in the case of the other three, it naturally means that only R.A.M. can be admitted to any of the four.

This degree in England being deprived of the most interesting section of the American ritual—the setting up of the capstone—would have but a scanty following if it were not that it is an essential qualification for the *Royal Master*, a most interesting degree.

The badge in this degree should be black, edged with red, and there are three principals who wear robes similar to those worn in the R.A., and represent S. K. of I., H. K. of T., and H. A. B. The candidate is said to be " honoured " with this degree.

The legend of this degree relates in a most dramatic way how the secrets of the R.A. came to be deposited in a certain place. For this reason R.A. Masons should make a point of taking it at the earliest opportunity. Though a comparatively short degree, it is most interesting and instructive.

There is no special jewel.

In the *Select Master* the candidate is said to be " chosen." The jewel is a silver trowel within a triangle of the same metal, and is worn suspended from a black collar edged and lined with red. The apron is white, edged with red and gold, and is of a triangular shape.

This shows the jewel of the cryptic degrees as worn in Scotland, and displays the trowel and triangle of the Select Master. The degree is supposed to be held in an underground vault, or crypt, hence the name of " cryptic degrees " for this series.

The legend of this degree deals with the accidental intrusion of a well-known brother, and is similar to one of the degrees of the Ancient and Accepted Rite. There seems little doubt that it is a genuinely old degree, and was worked quite early at York in the eighteenth century, and probably even earlier. There is a reference to the sword and trowel which reminds us of several other degrees.

This degree is also both dramatic and interesting.

The *Super-excellent Master* brings the story of the first Temple down to the time of its threatened destruction, and so bridges the

VISHNU SLEEPING UNDER THE OVERSHADOWING COBRA OF WISDOM AND ABOUT TO DESCEND TO EARTH. INDRA AND THE COMPANY OF GODS ABOVE COMMENT ON THIS ACT, WHILE HIS ATTENDANTS BELOW SHOULD BE NOTED.

The need for Vishnu is great, for the ogre with the club is about to attack one of Vishnu's attendants, who is drawing his sword, while the other attendants are calling on Him for aid.

gap between the *Most Excellent Master* and the legend of the *R.A.* The symbolic colour is crimson, and a crimson collar edged with gold is worn. The chief officer is Gedaliah. The lesson inculcated is loyalty to Jehovah. There is an interesting piece of symbolism in this degree, the exoteric meaning of which is given in the ritual.

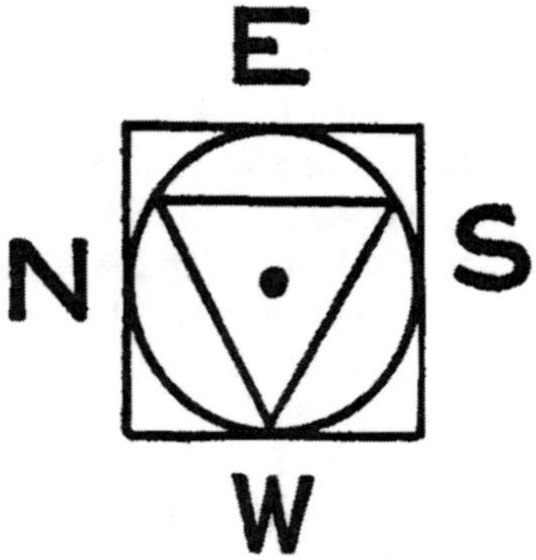

The triangle pointing west is ▽, the symbol of the Preserver, and has been adopted as the jewel of these degrees in England, and it certainly denotes the underlying principle of the series. Thus, despite the loss of the Great Architect, God preserved the work of the Temple, and it was duly completed. In the R. Master we learn how the R.A. secrets came to be preserved. In the next degree we learn how the too-zealous friend of Solomon was preserved from the doom that threatened him, while in the Super-excellent Master we perceive that God preserved a remnant of the people because they preserved their faith in Him.

The ▽ inside the square indicates the descent of the Divine Spirit into matter, while the ○ denotes eternity, and the p. has already been fully explained.

Therefore this symbol means God the Preserver descended from Eternity (Heaven) and entered into matter, or become flesh, and He is one with the All-pervading.

It is, therefore, a most sacred symbol, and the fact that the Ark of the Covenant stands on the c. shows that the New Dispensation arises out of the Old, and the prophetic reference to this fact is further emphasised by the real grip, which should remind us of Him who died on the cross.

Thus this degree has a "prophetic," Messianic, esoteric meaning seldom realised by those who take it.

Although the correct clothing has been given, in practice only the collar of the Super-excellent Master is worn, and even that only by officers. Strictly, a Mark Master's Apron should be worn, but this is seldom done. I cannot help feeling, however, that this is a pity, and the lack of masonic clothing in the columns robs these degrees of some of their true dignity.

The other degrees of this "York Rite" are the Templar and Malta; but these, together with the Red Cross of Constantine and its pendants, the K.'s of St. John and of the Holy Sepulchre, will be discussed in the next chapter. We will, therefore, turn to the collection of degrees now worked under the Allied Council.

These are: *St. Lawrence the Martyr*, the jewel of which is a gridiron, and the ribbon is a broad band of yellow, edged with light blue.

The next degree is that of the *Knight of Constantinople*, and its jewel is a cross surmounted by a crescent moon; it hangs on a dark green ribbon, on which are three small Roman short swords.

The jewel of the *Red Cross of Babylon* hangs on a plain dark green ribbon, and is two crossed swords on a dark green background of enamel set in a seven-pointed star.

That of the *Grand Tyler of King Solomon* is the triangle of the Preserver with the sacred name in gilt on a black background. It hangs from a red ribbon bordered with white, on which is a hand clasping a dagger, and above this a label with three crowns on the top.

The degree of *Secret Monitor* is a cross and a peculiar kind of hackle, and hangs from a black ribbon edged with a black and then a white stripe. Above the jewel is an archer's bow.

The *High Priest* jewel is the triangle of the Creator with the mitre of a bishop, or Jewish High Priest, all in gold, and hangs from a red ribbon.

The ruler of an *Allied Council* is the Master of the Lodge in the St. Lawrence degree, and his jewel depicts the gridiron in a circle.

These are all the degrees at present worked by the Allied Council, though they claim power to work over sixty, most of which are now, however, merely names, even their rituals being unknown. There is also the Templar Priest, which used to be worked at Newcastle, and may still be, for all I know.

A Council of the Allied Degrees must always be opened in the

St. Lawrence degree, and the officers wear a collar of yellow and blue. The Grand Council regalia, however, is green and gold, and is perhaps the prettiest Grand Lodge clothing in Freemasonry.

The St. Lawrence is, as already stated, an operative degree, and has not a great deal of symbolism. The Knight of Constantinople inculcates the useful lesson that all men are equal, and blue blood, unless accompanied by other qualifications, possesses no special merit. The jewel of a cross and crescent appears to be a curious anachronism, as the legend deals with Constantinople in the days of Constantine the Great, and the crescent, the symbol of Islam here, had no place in Constantinople till over a thousand years later.

The next degree, the Red Cross of Babylon, is a most interesting and dramatic degree, and, when properly worked, is most impressive. Those who hold it may be interested to know that, in the United States, the famous argument takes place at the actual banquet, which is spread in a second room. This degree is very similar to a certain degree belonging to the Ancient and Accepted Rite, and parts of the ritual of the Royal Order of Scotland also remind us of it. Unquestionably it is old and deserving of careful study, and in Ireland, I understand, it is connected with the Royal Arch.

Its close association with the R.A. is evident to all who have taken both degrees, and there is an inner meaning as well as the historical one. The crossing of the bridge reminds us of the passage from one quarter of Amenti to another in *The Book of the Dead.* The bridge has played an important part in the eschatology of many religions, Christianity included.

In Caldon Church, Surrey, is a twelfth-century fresco which shows us "The Brig [or bridge] of Dread" which spans the Gulf of Hell.

This curious old north country ballad, or rather dirge, mentions the "Brig o' Dread" which in the picture at Caldon is toothed like a great saw.

A LIKE-WAKE[1] DIRGE

This æ night, this æ night,
Every night and alle;
Fire and salt and candle light,
And Christ receive thy saule.

[1] Like-wake = Litch = corpse-watch.

When thou from hence away art passed,
  Every night and alle;
To Whinny-muir[1] thou comest at last;
  And Christ receive thy saule.

If ever thou gavest hosen and shoon,
  Every night and alle;
Sit thee down and put them on;
  And Christ receive thy saule.

If hosen and shoon thou ne'er gave none,
  Every night and alle;
The whinnes shall prick thee to the bare bone;
  And Christ receive thy saule.

From Whinny-muir when thou mayst pass,
  Every night and alle;
To *Brig o' Dread* thou comest at last;
  And Christ receive thy saule.

* * * * *

(The next two verses are unfortunately lost).

From Brig o' Dread when thou mayst pass,
  Every night and alle;
To Purgatory fire thou comest at last,
  And Christ receive thy saule.

If ever thou gavest meat or drink,
  Every night and alle;
The fire shall never make thee shrink,
  And Christ receive thy saule.

If meat and drink thou never gavest none,
  Every night and alle;
The fire will burn thee to the bare bone;
  And Christ receive thy saule.

This æ night, this æ night,
  Every night and alle;
Fire and salt and candle light,
  And Christ receive thy saule.

Anon. From Scott's *Minstrelsy.*

Unfortunately the old poem is incomplete, and does not tell us what good deeds will save the "traveller" from the sharp teeth of the saw-bridge.

Among the Mohammedans there is a belief in a somewhat

[1] Whinny-muir = a moor covered with furze.

similar bridge—a bar of red-hot iron stretched across a bottomless pit. Over this the soul must pass to attend its final judgment at the throne of Allah. The good works of each "believer" will then assume a substantial form, and interpose themselves between his feet and this Bridge of Dread; but the wicked, having no such protection, will fall headlong into the bottomless pit.[1]

The name Red Cross is difficult to understand, and I have seen no theory to account for it; but the cross is usually associated with Amenti. This degree was worked by the Camp of Baldwyn at Bristol under the name of Knights of the East, Sword and Eagle, while its old title under the Chapter of Clermont was "Knight of the Eagle," and later "Knights of the Sword," and also "Knights of the Red Cross of Palestine." The Cross intended appears to be shaped thus: X. The meaning of the two swords on the jewel is, however, plain to any brother who has taken the degree, while the seven-pointed star will be understood by all, having already been explained in this book.

A green sash should be worn in this degree, and the candidate is actually invested with it. Green is, of course, the colour of the Resurrection, for, just as the spring sun brings forth once more the green shoots of the plants after their apparent death in winter, so shall we rise afresh from our dead bodies.

It is also, of course, regarded as the colour dedicated to Truth, but this is its exoteric meaning.

Some brethren are apt to smile at the use of the word "knight" in the days of Darius, but what is implied, is the elevation of a "mason" to that social position which would entitle him to be a horse-soldier, and not a mere foot-soldier. Thus the Roman Equites may quite correctly be translated "knights." Among the Persians horses were held in the highest esteem, and we are told that the three things which a Persian noble regarded as essential to the training of his son were, that he should learn to shoot, to ride, and *to tell the truth*. Hence the term "knight" is particularly appropriate for members of this degree.

The next degree is "The Grand Tyler of King Solomon," or Mason Elect of Twenty-seven.

[1] The Parsis believe that at 4 a.m. on the third day after death the soul reaches a similar bridge "between heaven and hell." The relatives therefore rise early and pray for it, for if the soul fails to cross the bridge it falls into hell. The Japanese have a similar belief.

Here we are back at the time of the building of the first Temple *before* the Great Tragedy. The principals wear royal robes, the Master crimson bordered with gold, the S.W. a purple one lined with gold, and the J.W. a yellow one. The proper clothing for members of this degree should be, a sash of fiery red with a border of pale grey, to which is attached the jewel, ▽, one side of which is engraved with the letters of the Ineffable Name in the cabalistic order, and on the other the number 27 in the ancient Hebrew characters. Many of the jewels issued by our masonic furnishers are engraved on one side only. The apron is of black satin trimmed with gold; on the centre is a crown and on the flap a hand grasping a sword.

It should be noted that in this degree all members save the three principals are regarded as F.C. This is natural, as the events related are said to have taken place during the lifetime of H. A. B. This degree is somewhat similar to the Select Master, save that the intrusion was entirely accidental and the " date " much earlier.

The most interesting feature of the degree is undoubtedly the Mystic Name, but the degree itself is a very dramatic one.

The Secret Monitor degree is somewhat similar to the first degree of the Secret Monitor worked separately by the Secret Monitor conclaves.

It owes its presence among the Allied Degrees to an unhappy division which took place when the Supreme Conclave of that degree was being formed. This division is now happily healing up, and a compromise has been reached by which brethren who have taken the Secret Monitor under the Council of the Allied Degrees can " affiliate to a Secret Monitor Conclave in precisely the same way as if they had received the degree in another conclave working under the Supreme Council of the Secret Monitor. The jewel worn in the Allied Degrees is, however, entirely different from that of the Secret Monitor, which is shown opposite: whereas the degree conferred by the Allied Council entitles its members to wear the jewel shown opposite, a crown above a curiously shaped hackle with a bow on the ribbon.

The High Priest is, I understand, a most interesting degree, but it can be conferred only on those who have been a Principal in R.A. Chapter. In the U.S.A. a candidate must have been a 1st Principal, but this is not insisted upon in England.

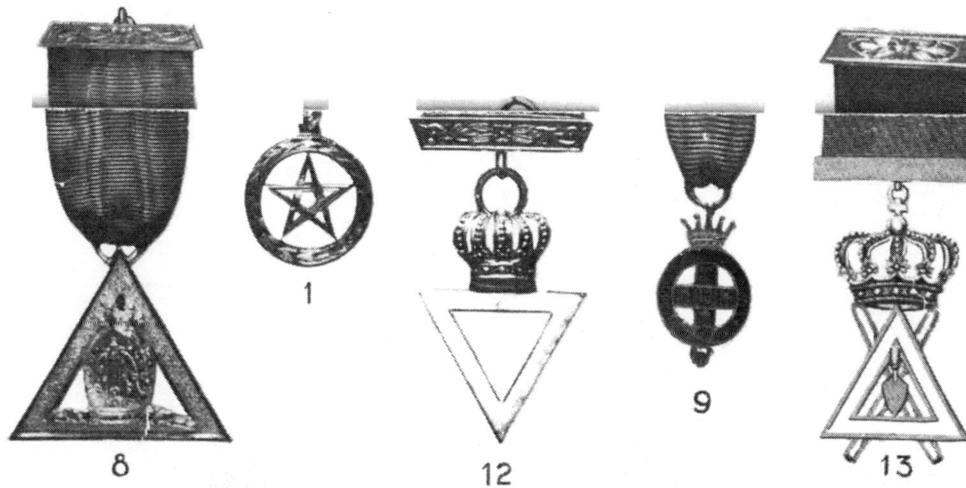

Photographed by kind permission from Originals made by G. Kenning & Son.

JEWELS OF SOME MASONIC DEGREES.

1. The Master Mason Charm.
2. Secret Monitor of the Supreme Council.
3. Secret Monitor of the Allied Degrees.
4. St. Lawrence the Martyr.
5. Knight of Constantinople.
6. Red Cross of Babylon.
7. Grand Tyler of King Solomon.
8. The High Priest.
9. Jewel of the Past M.W.S.
10. The Royal Order of Scotland Star.
11. Cross of the 30.
12. The English Jewel of the Cryptic Degrees.
13. The Scotch Jewel of the Cryptic Degrees.

There appears to be a somewhat similar degree among those of the Ancient and Accepted Rite, and there is little doubt that it is a genuine old degree of considerable interest.

This completes the degrees actually worked under the Cryptic and the Allied Councils, and we will now turn to consider the Templar and other chivalric degrees.

CHAPTER XI

THE KNIGHTS TEMPLARS

In 1118 Hugo de Paganis, or Hugues de Payens, and eight other knights formed themselves into a league to protect the pilgrims who went to the Holy Land. They took their vows before the Bishop of Jerusalem to live as regular canons and fight for Jesus Christ in chastity, obedience, and poverty.

The Order grew at an astounding pace, and within ten years Hugo came again to the Holy Land with [illegible] lineage, mostly ra[illegible]. St. Bernard took them under his patronage, and before his death, in 1157, the Order had spread throughout all Europe, and before the end of the century had become one of the most powerful organisations in Christendom.

There were three distinct classes: the [illegible] who fought, the [illegible] who prayed, both of noble descent, and the [illegible]

Vows could be taken either for life or for a number of years. Poverty was one of their rules, hence their earliest badge was "two knights riding one horse," intended to denote their humility and poverty. But neither of these virtues appertained to them for long. Before many years they were e[illegible] c[illegible] and down the Holy Land, and their [illegible] was becoming proverbial. Baldwin II, King of Jerusalem, gave them a building on Mount Moriah near the former site of King Solomon's Temple, whence they derived their name, and when the city was recovered by the Mohammedans they established their headquarters in their strong "C[illegible]" [illegible], and when driven out of this in 1295 they retired to Cyprus.

The Order first came to England in the reign of Stephen, and set up a Priory at the Old Temple, in Holborn, near what is now Southampton Row, and it was not till 1185 that the knights moved to the Temple in Fleet Street.

Louis VII gave them a site in Paris which became famous in history under the same name. These were their headquarters in England and France, and their chief "recruiting stations," but they soon began to receive endowments of estates in England, Scotland, and France, and at the time of their persecution, they held more than [illegible] large manors. These estates were scattered all over England; in Yorkshire alone, for example, they had t[illegible].

It is but just, however, to say that so long as fighting was going on in Palestine the knights poured out their blood like water, and in many a hard-fought battle proved their devotion to the Cross. At the famous battle of Ascalon they helped to rout Saladin, but the Grand Master and most of the brethren were left dead on the field.

The most peculiar fact about the Order is that there appears to have been a close connection between them and "The Ishmaelites," known among the Christians as "The Assassins," the followers of "The Old Man of the Mountains."

There is, moreover, a tradition that two of the original nine founders of the Order were previously affiliated to this body.

Our readers will remember that at first Assassin did not mean murderer, but a person who took the drug haschish with which these warriors were wont to stimulate themselves before they rushed into battle.

The Assassins were apparently a mystic pantheistic sect, bitterly hostile to the Mohammedans, and equally detested by them, and their first association was probably in the nature of a mutual alliance against the common enemy—Islam.

It is certain, however, that the Assassins had to pay tribute to the Grand Master of the Temple, and in 1249, their chief, "The Old Man of the Mountains," offered to become Christian if released from this obligation (see Bothwell Gosse's *The Knights Templars*).

Twenty years before the knights were driven out, the Assassins were practically annihilated by the Mohammedans; but it is probable that the Druses of Mount Lebanon are their descendants.

Acre fell in the year 1291, when the Grand Master and most of the knights were slain, and the Order gathered together its scattered forces in Cyprus.

Instead, however, of immediately starting a new campaign

against the Infidel, like the Knights of St. John, who carried on a stubborn rearguard fight against Islam for over five hundred years, they did little to fight the Mohammedans, and instead interfered in petty European squabbles.

Thus they appeared to have abandoned their task of defending Christendom, and left themselves open to the attacks of their enemies. Probably the "hiatus" in their crusading activity would have been but temporary had it not been for the intervention of Philip the False.

The blow fell in 1307, and at that date it is stated that they numbered 15,000 active brethren, and the total number affiliated to the Order was close on 40,000.

One of the striking facts about the persecution is that the Templars had hardly a friend in France. Their pride and wealth had alienated the people, while their willingness to admit many "base born" men had aroused the indignation of the nobility, which resented their arrogance the more when it was often coupled with humble origin.

The kings of Europe naturally disliked a cosmopolitan Order which had engrossed some of the finest estates in their kingdoms, and yet owed them no service.

Even the clergy had been alienated by a series of most astonishing privileges granted to them by various Popes. Firstly, the Pope was their bishop, and they were exempt from the authority of the bishop in whose diocese their establishment might be. Therefore he could not excommunicate them or control them in any way. Then Alexander III established a regular priesthood within the Order, and thereby the Templars could confess to their own priests, and so ignore the parochial clergy. In later times confession to the outside clergy was not allowed without special permission. Incidentally this enabled the secrets of the Order to be kept inviolate, and heresy, if it existed, to go on unchecked.

Finally, Innocent III actually released the clergy of the Order from the duty of obedience to the diocesan bishop.

This absolute seclusion naturally gave rise to suspicions, and charges of heresy or worse were freely bruited about.

Nor can we altogether deny that in some matters the Templars appear to have been unorthodox according to the received ideas of the age in which they lived. Thus, it is quite clear from the

THE CROSS-LEGGED VISHNU, THE GREAT SACRIFICE.

Note also the cross within the circle at the right of his head (compare with Mexican picture), likewise the cobra behind his head.

trials that a form of confession and absolution was used which was not the same as that in vogue among the orthodox clergy.

The three important military orders at this date were the Teutonic Knights, the Hospitallers, and the Templars.

The first proceeded to do useful work against the then savage Slavonic tribes on the German frontier. Moreover, they soon concentrated there, and were difficult to seize.

The Hospitallers were not nearly so wealthy as the Templars, were actively engaged in fighting the Turks in the Near East, and, moreover, had a wiser Grand Master.

He, too, received the same summons from Pope Clement V that Jacques de Molay received, but apparently suspected treachery, and made the excuse that he could not come because he was actively engaged in besieging Rhodes.

Philippe le Bel, or Philip the False, as his enemies called him, hated the Templars for many reasons, one being that the Templars had refused to admit him into their Order.

Philip also hated Boniface VIII and demanded an inquiry into his life and actions by the new Pope Clement V, who owed his elevation to the papal throne to the King of France. Philip accused the late Pope of atheism, blasphemy, and immorality, and, to prevent the scandal of a public investigation, Clement would be willing to do much to placate the angry French King.

The Pope was now at Avignon, and practically in the hands of Philip, and at his instigation summoned the Grand Master of the Templars to come to him to discuss a new crusade.

Jacques de Molay came, and on October 13, 1307, was arrested by Philip's orders, together with sixty knights, Philip accusing them of heresy, idolatry, and degrading vices. Sealed orders had previously been sent to all the provincial governors, and on the same day they arrested nearly every member of the Order in France.

The witnesses on whom Philip based his first charges were Roffo de Dei, and Squire de Florian. Both of them had been expelled from the Order for serious crimes, and were, in the nature of things, men on whose word no reliance could be placed.

But Philip relied on something much more effective than these two scoundrels, namely, torture of the most diabolical kind. The Grand Inquisitor was William Imbert, who was aided by the Dominicans, who appear to have detested the Order, and he succeeded, after fiendish tortures, in extracting "confession" from his unfortunate victims.

When the knights were asked, "Do you wish to defend the Order?" all answered, "Even unto death"; and they kept their word, for nearly all were burnt at the stake.

The Pope followed up Philip's action by issuing a Bull in November, 1307, to the various European sovereigns, stating that the heads of the Order had already confessed the truth of the crimes of which they had been accused, and sent instructions to Edward II of England to arrest all the Knights Templars in his kingdom.

The English King at first refused, and told the Pope that the Templars were "faithful to the purity of the Catholic Faith."

But Edward was negotiating for a marriage with Isabella of France, and his future father-in-law exerted such pressure that Edward gave way. The poor man afterwards paid bitterly for his weakness—and his French wife. In obedience to a second papal Bull, he seized their property, but would not arrest or torture them.

This delay was important, as it must have enabled many of the knights to escape into obscurity, warned by what was happening in France, of the fate which threatened them. It would be from these that the Masonic Templar succession would probably derive, if it exists.

In September 1309 the Papal Commission arrived in England, and insisted on the Templars being arrested, and they were taken to London, Lincoln, and York for trial.

But many had escaped, and particularly in the north, where the Sheriff of York was reproved for allowing them "to wander throughout the land."

Scotland, then nominally under English rule, and Ireland were included in the same orders, and the knights from both countries were taken to Dublin for trial. In view of the disturbed state of Scotland at this time, it is unlikely that very many Scottish Templars were captured, and the tradition in the Royal Order of Scotland as well as that of the Templar preceptories may well have a solid foundation.

It is highly probable that these Scottish knights would join the Scottish "rebels" against the English Government, which was persecuting them. Indeed, what else were they to do? They were essentially fighting men. They could not fight against the Infidel, nor could they fight for Edward II; why not fight for his opponent?

Torture was not permitted in England at this time, and, as a result, no confessions were obtained.

In December the King surrendered the accused to the ecclesiastical law, but up to March 1310 nothing had been done. Finally, however, the Pope, after warning Edward II that he was "imperilling himself" by hindering the Inquisition, offered him remission of all sins if the King would give his help. This offer was too tempting to be resisted, and in 1311 Edward permitted torture to be applied. As a result, three of the accused confessed; but the results were, from the papal point of view, very unsatisfactory. At last the prisoners admitted they were "defaimed of heresy," and agreed to do penance. They were accordingly sent for the rest of their lives into various monasteries, but appear to have received quite good pensions, according to the value of money in those days. William de la More, the Master of the Order in England, received two shillings a day, and ordinary members fourpence.

As to their estates, the King gave most of these to his favourites, but some appear to have passed into the hands of the Knights Hospitallers.

In Germany the knights succeeded in convincing the other nobility that they were innocent, and the majority escaped with their lives. No doubt many joined the Teutonic Order, and did good service in Prussia against the Slavs.

In Castile the knights rose in arms and took refuge in the mountains, where they are said to have become anchorites, and such was their holiness that, when they died, their bodies remained uncorrupted, so legend states. (See Bothwell Gosse, to whose book, *The Templars*, I am indebted for much valuable information.)

At Ravenna a Council which held an inquiry decided all were innocent, even those who, for fear of torture, had confessed. But in Florence the torture inflicted induced many to confess the most loathsome crimes.

In Arragon they were acquitted and pensioned, but a new Order was founded in 1317, "L'Order des Chevaliers de Notre Dame de Montesa," and which adopted their rule and clothing with the approval of Pope John XXII. Arragon, involved in constant war with her own Infidels the Moors, could not, indeed, do without them.

In Majorca they were likewise pensioned, and in Portugal, King Dinis met the difficulty in a similar way to Arragon by founding a new Order in 1817, called the " Society [illegible]' which was simply a continuation of the [illegible]. It was formally sanctioned by John XXII in 1818, and into it the Templars migrated, even retaining their original rank. Their castle at Belem, near Lisbon, has on the exterior shields bearing the Templar Cross.

In Bohemia the Templars not only retained their estates, but even bequeathed them to their heirs. In short, only in France were they treated with the grossest injustice and cruelty. In that country no attempt was made to give the knights a fair trial. For example, a Bull, issued by Clement on August 12th pretended to give the results of an examination which was really not held till August 17th, and added that the confessions were spontaneous—an absolute lie..

To show the [illegible] of their p[illegible], and the absolute treachery of the King, I will quote one example. In 1810 Clement called on the Order to defend itself, and show cause why it should not be suppressed. No less than [illegible] knights volunteered to defend the Order, and Philip promised that they should be exempt from danger.

When they appeared before the Papal Commission in Paris they related their sufferings, and one knight showed the Commissioners the small bones of his feet, which had dropped out during the torture by fire.

Having got them in his power, Philip the False broke his word and ordered their prosecution. As some had already confessed under torture, their defence of the Order was treated as a relapse into heresy, and the penalty for that was the stake.

No mercy was shown, and they were burnt in batches, and an awful account of their sufferings exists, particularly of 54 burnt by Philip de Marigni, Archbishop of Sens. We are told that, despite their screams of anguish, not one became an apostate. But many of the others, seeing what awaited them, withdrew their defence, and Aymeric de Villars le Duc, who was hauled before the tribunal on May 15th, three days after he had seen these 54 taken to the stake, told the Commissioners that under torture he would swear anything the Commissioners required, even "that he had slain the Lord Himself" (*Proc.* i. 275).

Some of the tortures used were: splinters of wood were driven into the nails, or into the finger-joints, teeth were wrenched out, heavy weights hung on the most sensitive parts of the body, fire was applied to the soles of the feet, which had been first rubbed with oil—in short, almost every torture associated with the later Spanish Inquisition was applied to these men who, up to 1807, had been regarded as champions of Christianity against the Turks.

Even the dead were not permitted to rest in peace, for Philip ordered the remains of a former Treasurer of the Order, dead nearly a hundred years, to be dug up and burnt.

We will hurry over the rest of the persecution and the confiscation of their property, and close this chapter with the death of Molay. Jacques de Longvy de Molay was of [illegible], and entered the Order in 1265 at Beaune. He proved himself a valiant soldier, and was elected Grand Master in 1298.

After his seizure and fiendish torture he "confessed" and wrote a letter advising other knights to do likewise, as "they were deceived by ancient error." He admitted the denial of Christ, but denied the "permission for the practice of vice."

On November 22nd, 1309, he was brought before the Commission in Paris, and, on being asked if he wished to defend the Order, said that he was there for that sole purpose. On Wednesday, November 26th, he was again brought before the Commission, and they read to him his confession. He was amazed at what it contained, and said he wished to God that the law of the Saracens and Tartars was observed against such evil ones, for they beheaded such calumniators, or caused them to be sawn asunder.

On November 29th he was told that the Order had paid feudal homage to Saladin; this he likewise denied.

After these examinations, he was sent back to prison, and not till 1814 did the final act of the tragedy take place.

The Pope delegated his authority to three cardinals, who condemned de Molay to perpetual imprisonment. As he left the hall with the Master of Normandy, his fellow-sufferer, he cried out before all the people that the Order was innocent of all the charges. This gave [illegible] for which he was waiting, and he condemned him t[illegible].

On March 11th, 1814, they were brought to the little island in the

Seine, between the King's Palace and the Augustine Monastery, and there he made his last speech, which is given in full by Aubert de Vertot d'Aubœuf, and there is a translation of it in Bothwell Gosse's book.

He declared there was no truth in the confession which was wrung from him when the torture of the rack had reduced him to such a state that he did not know what he was doing. It was a lie, and not even to save further torture and death would he confirm it by a second lie; the Order was guiltless of the foul charges.

At the hour of Vespers, Jacques de Molay perished amid the flames, to the last protesting the innocence of the Order, and, dying, he summoned Clement the Pope and Philip of France to meet him before the Throne of God within a year. Philip was gloating over the scene from the wall of his palace garden at the time, but the summons was heard and confirmed by a Greater King. Two months later Clement died of lupus, and, eight months after the death of Molay, Philip died from a fall from his horse.

Nor were these the only two thus summoned by their victims, for another Templar at the stake bade Guillaume Nogaret, one of the Inquisitors, to appear with him in eight days before the Throne of God, and within that time Nogaret died passed to his last judgment.

This, then, is the story of the destruction of the Templars. I could easily have given more terrible details, but enough has been written to show that in France neither justice, truth, nor mercy was shown to the unfortunate victims, and the story is one of the blackest in the black records of Latin Christianity.

CHAPTER XII

WHAT WERE THE BELIEFS OF THE TEMPLARS ?

THE main charges which were finally laid against the Knights Templars were :

1. Denial of Christ and defiling of the cross.
2. Adoration of an idol.
3. A perverted Sacrament performed.
4. Ritual murders.
5. The wearing of a cord of heretical significance.
6. The ritual kiss.
7. Alteration in the ceremony of the Mass and an unorthodox form of absolution.
8. ~~Immorality.~~
9. Treachery to other sections of the Christian forces.

Of these charges, Bothwell Gosse comes to the conclusion that, in a certain sense, the following were true : 1, 5, 6, 7, and, t~~o a limited~~ ex~~tent, 8~~.

Charges 2, 4, and 9 are without foundation, save that 2 probably arose out of veneration for some relic, exaggerated and garbled by ignorant and venomous critics.

Considering these facts, we must bear in mind that they were part of the secret ritual of initiation, overheard by eavesdroppers and misunderstood. The Denial appears to have been part of a dramatic ceremony of initiation, whose meaning was not always fully understood by the candidates. Petrus Picardi, one of the knights, said it was a proof of religious fidelity, and, had he been brave enough to refuse to deny, he would have been deemed worthy to be sent at once to the Holy Land (*Proc.* i. 523).

Gonavilla, Preceptor of Poitou and Aquitaine, stated that this threefold denial was in imitation of St. Peter's thrice repeated denial.

Johannis de Elemosina, who yielded and denied, was told

scornfully by the initiator: "Go, fool, and confess." They repeatedly said the denial was "ore non corde," from the mouth, not the heart.

The spitting at, or spurning of the cross is explainable on the same lines, and here, too, the spitting was "juxta, non supra."

Among the miracle plays of the Middle Ages was one entitled *The Festival of Idiots*, in which the actor who took the part of the unregenerate, or idiot soul, spits on the cross.

There was also a Gnostic "heresy" held, especially by the [illegible], that the cross was an emblem to be loathed, not reverenced, since it was the instrument of death of the Saviour, and these were bitterly persecuted by the orthodox in consequence.

Some of the evidence makes it appear as if the cross was painted or carved on the ground, and in those cases the ceremony resembled a ritual step. The proper manner of advancing from W. to E. in —— is really a Latin cross, as if s . . o . . . . . a . . o . . . . g, though probably many candidates do not realise it, and at the same time he in turn faces N., S., and E.

In this sense we can interpret the spurning of the cross as similar to the three reg. s. in F.M., i.e. trampling on the cross of their passions, which cross (phallic) had caused the death of our Lord. This would, of course, be the esoteric meaning; exoteric, it might well be a trial of the candidate's obedience to the orders of his superiors, i.e. that he *would* do *whatever* he was told, or alternatively of his religious fidelity. We know that both in the denial and in spitting at, or spurning of the cross with the foot, the candidate was threatened by the other knights with drawn swords, just as, in the old Masonic Templar ceremony of the Cup of the Skull, the candidate was threatened if he hesitated to drink.

The Templar Knights brought forth abundant evidence that they "adored" the cross thrice a year, namely, in September, May, and on Good Friday. This act, therefore, could not have been anti-Christian, and must have been symbolic with an inner meaning.

The commonest reason given by the knights when on trial was, "it was the custom of the Order"—an answer which most Masons would also probably give if asked why we did so and so in our ritual.

Charge 2, the adoration of the idol, Bothwell Gosse rejects, but suggests that the name of Bathomet or Baphomet may have been derived from βαφὴ μήτιος, meaning [illegible]. As many of the confessions state that the collect of the Holy Spirit was the principal prayer used at the ceremony of initiation, it may be that the Head was a figure of the Holy Ghost. The Latin Church has always neglected the Third Person of the Trinity, whereas most of the Gnostic sects laid great emphasis on the Holy Wisdom. Some accounts of the Head remind us strongly of the Gnostic symbol for the Manifested Deity—Abraxis, the head of an old, bearded man; but the most probable explanation is that it was a reliquary shaped in the form of a head, and holding probably a skull.

There is little doubt in my mind that the Templars were tinged with Gnosticism, no doubt gathered up while in Palestine. The very shape of their churches is symbolic; but of what? The round, or rather octagon-shaped churches remind us of the veneration for the octagon expressed by the present day operative masons. Their [illegible]  forms an octagon if the points are joined and the circle or the octagon come from the old pre-Christian religions and not from Latin or Greek Christianity. Even the use of the name Temple for their churches may well have had an esoteric meaning quite distinct from the source of their name, Templar, despite the story that it was copied from the church built by the Empress Helena to hold the true cross.

No. 3, the perverted Sacrament, Bothwell Gosse rejects entirely, and also No. 4, the ritual murder.

No. 5 may have been merely the Cistercian Cord of Chastity, for its use was actually laid down in the regulations drawn up by St. Bernard. It was, however, regarded as a sure proof of heresy, when the Inquisitors were persecuting the Cathari, and the Order of the Assassins had a red girdle to which they attached the greatest importance. The Mohammedan dervishes to-day invest the novice with a girdle, and it is possible that it was imported from the East and had an "heretical" meaning, though Bothwell Gosse seems to reject the idea. After all, the monastic use of the girdle was so well known at that time that I cannot help thinking there was more in it than a mere "Cistercian Girdle of Charity"; otherwise, why should the *Chronicle of St. Denis* state that "in their girdles was their Mahommerie (Heresy)," etc.?

(6) The ritual kiss seems undoubtedly established. The chief point about it is, it was usually "in ano." Its object was to inculcate humility. In the Prussian Knight degree we have seen that the candidate had to kiss the pommel of the sword of the principal officer "to show his humility." This is obviously a slight variation of the original idea. In the thirteenth century people were coarser than now, or, at any rate, more primitive, and we may regard this ceremony in the light of the somewhat similar treatment a new boy at school may have to submit to from a bully. There is no reason for imputing anything immoral in this kiss. Nor is there any evidence in support of the charge known as "permission for [unnatural] vice" (No. 8). It is probable that, with regard to ordinary sexual immorality, the Templars were no better nor worse than many of the orthodox clergy of that date; but, in any case, the charge was not pressed.

No substantial evidence of Charge 9, Treachery, was produced, though on occasion the Templars may not have acted with whole-hearted energy in support of their rivals, the Knights of St. John, or of some of the Christian princes in the Holy Land.

This leaves us with Charge 7 to consider. It was that the ceremony of the Mass had been altered, and a peculiar form of absolution used.

As we should expect, the evidence is very conflicting as to the actual alterations; the one outstanding fact is that the form was not strictly orthodox.

That the evidence as to the exact alterations would vary is, I have said, natural. Here there was no question that, if alterations of a substantial kind could be proved, then heresy was established. Every knight would try to reduce the alterations to unimportant points, while every turn of the rack would oblige him to disclose something new. Further, the Mass was celebrated by the priests of the Order, and heresy might vary according to the views of the priests. These would be educated men, with time for meditation and thought. Being free from the restraining influence of the orthodox bishops and clergy, they would be prone to think for themselves, to speculate and to use in their speculations knowledge acquired among the heretical sects of the East. Some, however, would no doubt go further than others, hence genuine differences between different preceptories. The knights were mostly ignorant, ill-educated fighting men. They took on trust what was told them by their own priests, confessed to them only, and had little opportunity of comparing the teaching of their own priests with that of the orthodox clergy outside. Often they could not appreciate the difference between two Latin sentences, though one might be orthodox and the other heretical. Strange to say, the Templar priests do not seem to have been persecuted, at any rate to the same extent as the knights!

On the whole, however, the evidence shows that the Canon of the Mass was left intact, though there are confessions which state that the words "This is My body" were omitted.

The absolution, however, was distinctly unorthodox, and, though here also details vary, one variation is so important that I feel it must be given. Radulphus de Gisisco, a Preceptor, stated that he gave the following absolution in French: "Beau segnurs frères, toutes les choses que vous leyssuz a diere pour la honte de la char ou pour justice de la mayson, tei pardon come je vous fayit je vous en fais de beau cour de bonne volenté: *et Dieu qui pardona la Maria Magdalene ses pêchiez, les vos pardoient*," etc.

Garcerandus de Teus, who was admitted in Catalonia, states that the form of absolution was: "I pray God that He may pardon our sins, as He pardoned St. Mary Magdalen and the thief on the cross."

Now, if this were all, we might think the reference was to Christ's words to the thief on the cross, but Garcerandus goes on to explain what is meant by the thief, and Bothwell Gosse gives the passage in full: "By the thief . . . it means that Jesus, or Christ, who was crucified by the Jews, because he was not God, though *he called himself God* and the king of the Jews, which was an outrage on the true God, who is in heaven. When Jesus . . . had his side pierced with the lance of Longinus he repented that he had called himself God and king of the Jews, and he asked pardon of the true God. Then the true God pardoned him. *It is for this reason* that we apply to the crucified Christ these words: 'As God pardoned the thief who was hung on the cross.'"

Now, if this was the belief generally held by the Order, then there is no question that the Templars were more than heretics, they were not Christians even, in the eyes of the fourteenth-century Church. If these views were held, the spurning of the cross and the denial of Christ were what their enemies said they were—evidence that the Templars were non-Christians, Mohammedans, or what you will; but is this anything more than the personal views of a particular member of the Order? Frankly, I can find no evidence that this view was generally held. Trobati says he was told not to worship a God who was dead (on being shown a crucifix), but that he should put his trust in the idol. This, however, is practically the only evidence in support of this anti-Christian belief.

My own opinion is that the Order did not hold these views, but that their form of absolution was different from the orthodox one, and that laymen as well as priests could absolve in certain cases, and the evidence in support of this largely comes from England, where but little torture was used. There, it will be remembered that the knights, while denying most of the charges, admitted they had been heretical, and agreed to do penance.

We must not overlook one important fact. The Crusades had failed. Christ appeared to have failed to support the defenders of His faith against the Infidel; as a result, many thoughtful minds began to question whether His faith could be the direct Revelation from God that they had been taught it was. They had met men who did not believe it, and these had prevailed; above all, they had met men (*Gnostics*) who interpreted the Christian story in a different way to that of the Western Church, and some of the knights undoubtedly had been led into new lines of thought not compatible with the strict orthodoxy of the day.

Thus, there was the Gnostic tradition that it was not the Christ who was crucified, but one Simon, who bore His cross, by which they understood the passage to mean not that Simon *carried* the cross to Calvary, but was *hung* on it. The Templar (Masonic) tradition of the two Simons may refer to this. In U.S.A. the Skull is sometimes spoken of as "Old Simon." Many of the Gnostics anathematised the cross, some for the reason already given, others because they held a still more extraordinary view. These held that the creator of the world was Lucifer, and that he who hung on the cross was the Messenger of the God [illegible], who came to inflict a hard and impossible code of law on unfortunate men, and Lucifer, to protect men from His oppression, had Him slain. These and other strange, wild doctrines existed in the Near East, and may have affected some of the knights; but we need not pursue this subject further. The average knight was a fairly simple fighting man, and such subtleties would be far beyond him. The phallic significance of the cross he might understand, but not such extreme views.

Before closing this chapter we must just remind our readers of the opening chapter of this book, wherein we showed that the Turkish dervishes have a system of initiation closely resembling our own, and a tradition that we get our ritual from them via the Templars and Richard Cœur-de-Lion. While holding that this does not account for its real origin, I think it is extremely probable that a new infusion of ideas was brought in this way, and that the Templars were thereby brought into close touch with the Comacine Masons of that time.

The appearance of the pointed arch based on the vesica piscis synchronises with the Crusades, and the sudden and rapid way in which its use sprang up all over Western Europe shows that some well-organised body was at work. Other Eastern customs also were adopted in the West; for example, the wimple, which was merely a European form of the Mohammedan veil.

Parts of the secret ritual of Knights Templars may well have been copied from some of t[illegible] of the [illegible]. That the Templars were [illegible]ed with this mysterious body is [illegible], and the latter's probable descendants are the modern Druses, who are known to have at least one masonic sign, besides a somewhat similar system of degrees.

We shall, in the next chapter, consider the various theories which claim that the Templars did not entirely perish, but took refuge in Freemasonry, and are represented in our modern Templar preceptories.

CHAPTER XIII

THE TEMPLAR TRANSMISSION THEORY

IT must be clearly understood that there are at least three possible lines of Templar transmission: English, Scotch, and French. Moreover, all may be independent of each other.

We must remember that the Order was divided into three classes: (1) Knights, (2) Templar Priests, (3) Serving Brothers. This last class was divisible into two classes (*a*) men-at-arms, and (*b*) craftsmen. Many of this class were wealthy and in a position to help their former masters. Neither they nor the priests appear to have been persecuted, the whole fury of Philip being concentrated upon the unfortunate knights. Among these craftsmen were certainly some masons, for the Templars were great builders. One Templar, called Frère Jorge la Maçon, was expelled from the Order for misconduct. Such men would be at this date Comacine Masons, and were not "illiterate workmen," nor were they regarded as such. On the contrary, an existing contract states that John Wood, "Masoun," was allowed "borde for himself as a gentilman and his servant as a yeoman" (*Archælogia*, v., xxiii., p. 381).

The Templars were a self-contained body in every way, having their own priests and their own masons, neither of whom were persecuted. They had also many "concealed estates" up and down Europe, and thousands escaped from their persecutors. One of the simplest methods would be to enter the masonic brotherhood, helped by their former serving men. Fear of a cruel death would quickly humble their pride and convince them of the advisability of doing so.

There are four possible representative bodies:

(1) The knights of the Society of Jesus in Portugal, and the kindred bodies in Spain.

These were undoubtedly descendants of the former Knights Templars, but purged of heresy, if it ever existed in Spain or

Portugal. They have never had any connection with Freemasonry, and have always been exclusively Roman Catholic.

(2) Those knights who are said to have accepted Pierre d'Aumont as the successor of De Molay. This tradition was the basis of the Continental Masonic Rite of the Strict Observance. This rite at one time had a strong following in Germany and Scandinavia, but is now practically extinct.

(3) The French knights who are said to have accepted Jean Marc Larmenius as successor to Molay. These will be considered in detail.

(4) Those knights who acknowledged neither of these knights—mostly English or Scotch. We will consider group (3) first, but it must be clearly understood that even if this body was a genuine Templar survival it would not prove that our Templar degrees were connected with the old Order.

For what follows I am largely indebted to the account of the "Charter of Transmission" by F. J. W. Crowe, in *Ars Quat. Cor.*, vol. xxiv, 1911, pp. 185–98, and for permission to reproduce the photograph of the Charter itself to Brother Songhurst, the learned and indefatigable secretary.

Crowe found and bought it, and presented it to the Grand Priory of the Temple in England, and it now hangs in the Council-room at Mark Masons' Hall, Great Queen Street.

The tradition of the French is that Jacques de Molay, whilst in prison before his martyrdom in 1318, de[illegible] the O[illegible], in spite of its suppression by the Pope, and he therefore assigned his full power and authority to Johannes Marcus Larmenius as his successor. Larmenius, growing old, drew up the *Charta Transmissionis* and transmitted his power toi Theobaldus, and, after this, each succeeding Grand Master appended his acceptance on the original document, down to and including Bernard Raymond in 1804. In an "Inventory of the Charter, Statutes, Relics, and Insignia composing the Sacred Treasury of the Order of the Temple," extracted from the minute of the *procès-verbal*, under date May 18th, 1810, it is thus described :

"1st Piece of Treasure.

"The Charter of Transmission (by J. M. Larmenius) written in two columns and a half on a very large sheet of parchment, ornamented after the style of the time, with designs of Gothic architecture. The letters illuminated in colours of gold and silver. In the first letter, a knight with the costume, armour, and cross of the Order. At the top in the centre is painted a cross in the conventional form. At the end the seal of the knights suspended by strings of parchment. The acceptances of the Grand Masters commence after the middle of the third column, and continue, the third finishing in two rows on either side of the margin."

This quite accurately describes it, as will be seen from the illustrations.

The key of the cypher is as follows:

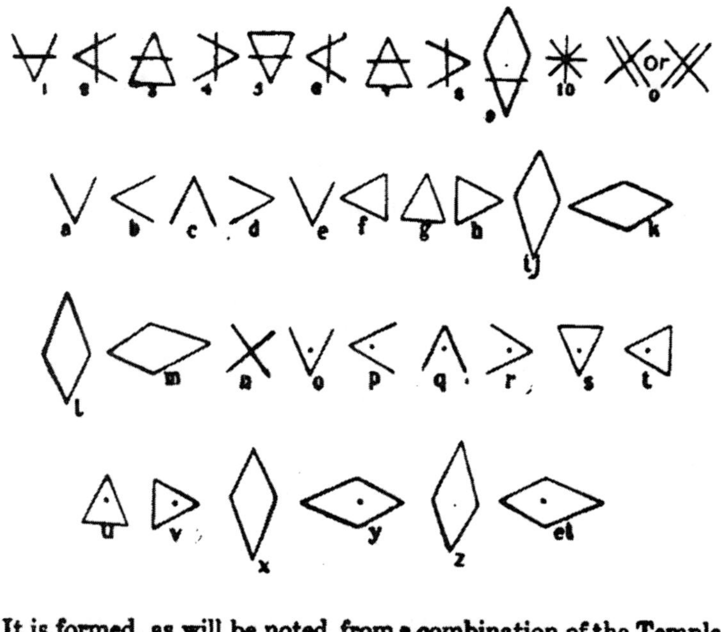

It is formed, as will be noted, from a combination of the Templar and Maltese crosses (see diagram on p. 298) which is actually shown at the head of the central column of the Charter.

Crowe continues:

"I have translated from the cypher as exactly as possible. In cases where there was an obvious slip, such as a dot omitted or a wrong character used, I have inserted the correct one in brackets.

When a letter or word was wanting to make sense, I have done the same."

This is, as far as I can find, the first time an absolutely faithful version of the original document has been given, for Thory, and the Comte le Couteulx de Canteleu seem only to have seen a revised and modernised Latin translation. Burnes saw the original, but did not transcribe it, and accepted the translation. This appears to be what is criticised adversely by Findel (*History of Freemasonry*, 1866, p. 717), and in Gould's *History*, vol. i, p. 498. No one of the above-named mentions that the original Charter is in cypher. They either never saw it, or took for granted the Latin they quote without taking the trouble to translate it for themselves, so as to be sure of its accuracy. Both in Findel and Gould it is said that the Latin is not that of the fourteenth century, and has no abbreviations. Clavel, however, does say that it is a document in cypher, though even he does not give the true Latin. I shall print the version in Thory, as well as my own transcription, in parallel columns, to show the much more ancient character of the latter, whether the original is fabricated or authentic. The " autographs " especially are considerably different, names being added in many cases, and the variations of *Anno Domini*, *Anno Christi*, and other words being entirely ignored. As will be seen, it is *full* of abbreviations, in contradiction of the statement in Gould's *History*. It was, however, quite natural for the writer to suppose that Thory had given a proper version in *Acta Latomorum*.

The Charter runs thus:

MY OWN TRANSCRIPT	THORY'S VERSION
Ego frater Johañes Marcus Larmenius Hierosolymitanus Dei Gratia et Secretiš̃imo Q[v]enerandi sanctiš̃imique Martyris Supremi Templi Militie Mac[g]istri cui honos et c[g]loria Decreto com̃uni Fratrum Consilio ca[o]nfirmato e[s]uperuniuersum Temb[p]li ordina[e]m sum̃o et supremo Magio[s]terio insignitus singulis has decretales literas uisuris salm̃ salm̃ salm̃.	Ego Frater Johannes-Marcus Larmenius, Hierosolymitanus, Dei gratiâ et Secretissimo Venerandi sanctissimique Martyris, Supremi Templi militiæ Magistri (cui honos et gloria) decreto, communi Fratrum consilio confirmato, super universum Templi Ordinem, Summo et Supremo Magisterio insignitus, singulis has decretales litteras visuris, salutem, salutem, salutem.

The above is quoted word for word from Crowe's able article, and he continues to give in parallel columns the two versions, and any reader can see at once that the statements of Findel and Gould are absolutely incorrect. The Latin *is* abbreviated and mediæval in tone throughout, and the correctness of Crowe's version can be proved by anyone who will use a magnifying-glass on the photograph shown opposite, or, better still, study the original at Mark Masons' Hall. I must warn any one who does study the original that some parts come out clearer in the photograph than in the original, despite the reduction in size; at least so it seemed to me when I studied the original Charter.

The signatures also vary considerably both in the style of character and in actual wording both from each other and from Thory's version, as will be seen.

MY OWN TRANSCRIPT	THORY'S VERSION
Ego Johañes Marcus Larmenius dedi die 13 Fe[bruraii] 1324.	Ego Johannes-Marcus Larmenius dedi, die decima tertia februarii, 1324.
Ego Theobaldus supremam magisterim̃ Deo juŝnte aĉeptum habeo ão c̄hti 1324.	Ego Franciscus - Thomas - Theobaldus Alexandrinus, Deo juvante, Supremum Magisterium acceptum habui, 1324.
Ego Arnaldus de Braque suprmum magisterium dea[o]jũante aceptum habeo año dñi 1340.	Ego Arnulphus De Braque, Deo juvante, Supremum Magisterium acceptum habui, 1340.
Ego Johañes de Claromonte sopemũ magisteriũ deo jũante aĉeptũ habeo año dñi 1349 ✠	Ego Joannes Claromontanus, Deo juvante, Supremum Magisterium acceptum habui, 1349.
Ego Bertrãdus Guesclin supremum magisterium deo jũante aĉeptum habeo año c̄hti 1357 ✠	Ego Bertrandus Duguesclin, Deo jubante, Supremum Magisterium acceptum habui, 1357.
Ego fr̃r Johañ arminiace[n]sis supreñ magister˜aĉeptum habeo aõ c˜t˜i 1381.	Ego Johannes Arminiacus, Deo juvante, Supremum Magisterium acceptum habui, 1381.
Ego f[h]uhmilus f˜ bernardus arminiacus supre.num magisterium deo jũante aĉeptum habeo año ch˜ti 1392.	Ego Bernardus Arminiacus, Deo juvante, Supremum Magisterium acceptum habui, 1392.
Ego J˜h˜nes arminiac̃sis supremũ magisteriũ deo jũante aĉeptũ habeo año ch˜ti 1418.	Ego Johannes Arminiacus, Deo juvante, Supremum Magisterium acceptum habui, 1419.
Ego Johañes crouiasencis supremum templi magisterium deo ju˜a˜te aĉeptum habeo a˜o ch˜ti 1451.	Ego Johannes Croyus, Deo juvante, Supremum Magisterium acceptum habui, 1451.
Ego Robertus de Lenoncond Deo-jũante aĉeptum habeo supremum magisterium a˜o dnĩ 1478.	Ego Robertus Lenoncurtius, Deo juvante, Supremum Magisterium acceptum habui, 1478.

THE TEMPLAR CHARTER OF TRANSMISSION.

Now in Mark Masons' Hall. Block kindly lent by the Secretary of the Quatuor Coronate.

Ego Galeas Salazar humil~m militia templi f~tr̃a suprem̃ deo jũante ac̃eptum habeo magisteriũ ão ch~ti 1496.

Ego Philip̃us de chabot deojũante magisterium supremum ac̃eptum habeo anno ch~ti 1516.

Ego gaspardus cesinia salsis de chobanne supremum magisterium deo juante ac̃eptum habeo año d~n~i 1544.

Ego henricus mont moraen [very indistinct] supremum magisterium aceptum habeo anno ch~ti 1574.

Ego Carolus Valesius [name indistinct] supremum magisterium deo jũante ac̃eptum habeo año 1615.

Ego Jac~bus rufelius granceio juãte deo magisterium supremum ac̃eptum habeo anno 1651.

Ego Johañes hẽricus durfortis duracius supremũ deo juante acceptum habeo anno 1681.

Ego philip̃us Aurelianus supremũ magisterii~ deo ju~ante ac̃eptũ habeo año dõi 1705.

Ego ludouicus augustus ba[o]rbonius cenomanensis supremum magisterium acceptum habeo anno 1724.

Ego borbonius condatus [Condæus] supremum magisterium deo juuant acceptum habeo anno domini 1737.

Ego ludouicus franciscus borbonius contenis supremum magisterium deo juuante acceptum habeo anno domini 1741.

Ego de cosse de brissac (lodouicus harcules timoleo) supremum magisterium deo juuante acceptum habeo anno domini 1776.

Ego cladius mateus radix de cheuillon templi senior vicariss magister morbo grarii attectus adstantibus fratribus prospero micaele charpentier de Saintot t[b]ernardo raymondo fabre ta[e]mpli vicarius magistris et Johnne baptiste auguste de coirrchant

Ego Galeatius de Salazar, Deo juvante, Supremum Magisterium acceptum habui, 1497.

Ego Philippus Chabotius, Deo juvante, Supremum Magisterium acceptum habui, 1516.

Ego Gaspardas De Salciaco, Tavannensis, Deo juvante, Supremum Magisterium acceptum habui, 1544.

Ego Henricus De Monte Morenciaco, Deo juvante, Supremum acceptum habui, 1574.

Ego Carolus Valesius, Deo juvante, Supremum Magisterium acceptum habui, 1615.

Ego Jacobus Ruxellius de Granceio, Deo juvante, Supremum Magisterium acceptum habui, 1651.

Ego Jacobus-Henricus De Duro forti, dux de Duras, Deo juvante, Supremum Magisterium acceptum habui, 1681.

Ego Philippus, dux Aurelianensis, Deo juvante, Supremum Magisterium acceptum habui, 1705.

Ego Ludovicus-Augustius Borbonius dux du Maine, Deo juvante, Supremum Magisterium acceptum habui, 1724.

Ego Ludovicus-Henricus Borbonius Condæus, Deo juvante, Supremum Magisterium acceptum habui Supremum Magisterium acceptum habui, 1737.

Ego Ludovicus-Franciscus Borbonius-Conty, Deo juvante, Supremum Magisterium acceptum habui, 1741.

Ego Ludovicus-Henricus-Timoleo de Cossé-Brissac, Deo juvante, Supremum Magisterium acceptum habui, 1776.

Ego Claudius-Mathæus Radix de Chevillon, Templi senior Vicarius Magister, . . . adstantibus Fratribus Prospero-Maria-Petro-Michaele Charpentier de Saintot, Bernardo-Raymundo Fabré, Templi Vicariis Magistris, et Johanne-Baptista-Augusto de supremo precetori litteras decratales a ludouico timoleone de cosse de brissac templi supremo magistro in temporibus infaustis mihi depositas fratri Jacobo Philippo ledru templi seniori uicario magistro mei amicissi et tradidi at istae litterae in tempore opportunis ad perpetuam ordinis nostri memoriam juxta ritum orientalem uigea[n]t die 10 Junii 1804.

Ego bernardus raymundus fabre cardoal albiensis collegarum uicariorum magistroum fratrum commilitonum que uoto annuens suprem magisterium acceptum habeo die quarta nov anno 1804.

Courchant, Supremo Præceptore, hasce litteras decretales a Ludovico-Hercule-Timoleone de Cossé-Brissac, Supremo Magistro, in temporibus infaustis mihi depositas, Fratri Jacobo-Philippo Ledru, Templi seniori Vicario Magistro . . . tradidi, ut istæ litteræ, in tempore opportuno, ad perpetuam Ordinis nostri memoriam, juxta Ritum Orientalem, vigeant: die decima junii, 1804.

Ego Bernardus-Raymundus Fabre, Deo juvante, Supremum Magisterium acceptum habui, die quarta novembris, 1804.

This ends the cypher and Latin portion. The remainder, on front and back of the parchment, being in French, Crowe did not think it necessary to copy out, but gives the following translation of the whole document.

I, Brother John Mark Larmenius, of Jerusalem, by the Grace of God and by the most secret decree of the venerable and most holy Martyr, the Supreme Master of the Knighthood of the Temple (to whom be honour and glory), confirmed by the Common Council of the Brethren, being decorated with the highest and supreme Mastership over the whole Order of the Temple, to all who shall see these Decretal letters, [wish] health, health, health.

Be it known to all both present and future, that, my strength failing on account of extreme age, having taken full account of the perplexity of affairs and the weight of government, to the greater glory of God, and the protection and safety of the Order, the brethren and the Statutes, I the humble Master of the Knighthood of the Temple have determined to entrust the Supreme Mastership into stronger hands.

Therefore, with the help of God, and with the *sole consent of the Supreme Assembly of Knights*, I have conferred and by this decree I do confer for life on the eminent Commander and my dearest Brother Theobald of Alexandria the Supreme Mastership of the Order of the Temple, its authority and privileges, with power according to conditions of time and affairs, of conferring on another brother, having the highest distinction in nobility of origin and attainments and in honourable character, the highest and Supreme Mastership of the Order of the Temple, and the highest authority. Which may tend to preserving the perpetuity of the Mastership, the uninterrupted series of successors, and the integrity of the Statutes. I order, however, that the Mastership may not be transferred without the consent of the General Assembly of the Temple, as often as that Supreme Assembly wills to be gathered together, and, when this takes place, let a successor be chosen at the vote of the knights.

But, in order that the functions of the Supreme Office may not be neglected, let there be now and continually four Vicars of the Supreme Master, holding supreme power, eminence, and authority over the whole Order, saving the right of the Supreme Master; which Vicars should be elected among the Seniors, according to the order of profession. Which Statute is according to the vow (commended to me and the brethren) of the very holy our above-said Venerable and most blessed Master, the Martyr, to whom be honour and glory. Amen.

I, lastly, by the decree of the Supreme Assembly, by Supreme authority committed to me, will, say and order that the Scot-Templars deserters of the Order be blasted by an anathema, and that they and the brethren of St. John of Jerusalem, spoilers of the demesnes of the Knighthood (on whom God have mercy), be outside the circle of the Temple, now and for the future.

I have appointed, therefore, signs unknown, and to be unknown to the false brethren, to be orally delivered to our fellow-knights, and in what manner I have already thought good to deliver them in the Supreme Assembly.

But these signs must only be revealed after due profession and knightly consecration according to the Statutes, rights, and uses of the Order of fellow-knights of the Temple sent by me to the above-said eminent Commander, as I had them delivered into my hands by the Venerable and most holy Master the Martyr (to whom honour and glory). Be it, as I have said, so be it. Amen.

I John Mark Larmenius gave this Feb. 13, 1324.

I Theobald have received the Supreme Mastership, with the help of God, in the year of Christ 1324.

I Arnald de Braque have received the Supreme Mastership with the help of God A.D. 1340.

I John de Clermont have received the Supreme Mastership with the help of God A.D. 1849. ✠

I Bertrand Guesclin &c. in the year of Christ, 1857. ✠

I Brother John of L'Armagnac &c. in the year of Xt. 1881.

I humble Brother Bernard of L'Armagnac &c. in the yr. of Xt. 1892.

I John of L'Armagnac &c. in the yr. of Xt. 1418.

I John Croviacensis [of Croy] &c. in the yr. of Xt. 1451.

I Robert de Lenoncoud &c. A.D. 1478.

I Galeas Salazar a most humble Brother of the Temple &c. in the year of Christ 1496.

I Philip de Chabot . . . A.C. 1516.

I Gaspard Cesinia (?) Salsis de Chobaune &c. A.D. 1544.

I Henry Montmorency (?) . . . A.C. 1574.

I Charles Valasius [de Valois] . . . Anno 1615.

I James Rufelius [de] Grancey . . . Anno 1651.

I John de Durfort of Thônass . . . Anno 1681.

I Philip of Orleans . . . A.D. 1705.

I Louis Auguste Bourbon of Maine . . . Anno 1724.

I Bourbon-Condé . . . A.D. 1737. [There are several places called Condate.]

I Louis Francois Bourbon-Conty . . . A.D. 1741.

I de Cossé-Brissac (Louis Hercules Timoleo) . . . A.D. 1776.

I Cla[u]de Matthew Radix-de-Chevillon, senior Vicar-Master of the Temple, being attacked by severe disease, in the presence of Brothers Prosper Michael Charpentier of Saintot, Bernard Raymond Fabré Vicar-Masters of the Temple, and Jean-Baptiste Auguste de Courchant, Supreme Preceptor, have delivered [these] Decretal letters, deposited with me in unhappy times by Louis Timoleon of Cossé-Brissac, Supreme Master of the Temple, to Brother Jacque Philippe Ledru, Senior Vicar-Master of the Temple of Messines [? Misseniacum], that these letters in a suitable time may thrive to the perpetual memory of our Order according to the Oriental rite. June 10th, 1804.

I Bernard Raymond Fabré Cardoal of Albi, in agreement with the vote of my Colleagues the Vicar-Masters and brethren the Fellow-Knights, have accepted the Supreme Mastership on November 4th, 1804.

We need not give the French portions, however, for the genuineness or otherwise of the document rests on the earlier sections before 1804.

Findel rejects the Charter on grounds which, to my mind, are worthless. He says (1) the Latin is not of the fourteenth century; (2) that no Grand Master could nominate his successor; (3) the deed is unnecessary; (4) the institution of four Vicars-General was unnecessary; (5) the anathema against the Scotch Freemasons means that it is eighteenth-century work and aimed at the higher masonic degrees. (6) The signature of Chevillon "leads to the same conclusion, for this deed was without any doubt prepared under the rule of his predecessor, Cossé-Brissac (1776–92); it must have been delivered over to Chevillon in the hottest fury of the Revolution of 1792, when everything like aristocracy, and these Templars into the bargain, were suffering persecution. For, if this document, and all the signatures accompanying it, were genuine, France, since the fourteenth century, would have seen many *tempora infausta,* which would have afforded those Grand Masters, as well as Chevillon, at the period of the Revolution, the opportunity of adding any remark they chose to their signatures; which was not the case, for each signature is the counterpart of the other, Chevillon's alone excepted, that and Brissac's being the only genuine ones, and the very deviation of the former from the counterfeit signatures proving it to be a genuine one."

He continues: "The manner in which the names of these Parisian Templar Masters succeed each other is incorrect, and, as evidence of their being a fabrication, the Grand Master Everard de Bar, instead of being mentioned as entering on his office in 1149, is said to have done so in 1152; Philip of Naples, instead of in 1116, in 1169"; and he continues to quote the names of Grand Masters *prior* to the suppression of the Order, and who therefore naturally do not appear at all in the "Charter of Transmission," as will be seen by glancing at the transliteration of the original.

He then proceeds to point out other discrepancies, as he thinks them, for example: "Bertrand du Guesclin, 1357–81, Constable of France, certainly did not sign his name, for it is a well-known historical fact that he could neither read nor write."

Not one of these arguments is worth the paper it is printed on, and may be refuted in detail.

No 1. The Latin *is* abbreviated and might easily be fourteenth-century. Sir George Warner, Keeper of the MSS. of the British

Museum, and one of the greatest experts on the subject, carefully examined the *original*, which Findel had not done. Sir George considered the Latin *was* similar to fourteenth-century, but the illumination was later—probably fifteenth-century.

The whole truth of the matter is that Findel based his arguments on Thory's version, and never saw the original at all, or, if he did, never troubled to decipher it himself.

No. 2. Larmenius expressly says: " . . . and with the sole consent of the Supreme Assembly of Knights I have conferred," etc.

No. 3. In view of the disorganised state of the Order, such a charter *would be* valuable as proving to any brother that the holder was entitled to be regarded as Grand Master. Whereas, in former days, there could be no doubt as to who was elected, now that concealment was necessary such a document would be most useful.

No. 4. Owing to the scattered nature of the Order and the danger that the Master might be discovered and slain by their persecutors, four Vicars would be a very reasonable plan. In short, changed circumstances would naturally necessitate, and justify, new methods.

No. 5 is a pure assumption, and the worst kind of *a priori* argument. Not one tittle of evidence is produced. On the contrary, this point can be used just as strongly to support the genuineness of the document, and these Scottish knights would then be those who were the men who helped Bruce and joined Scotch Freemasonry, either as hinted at in the Royal Order, or according to the Masonic Templar traditions of that country.

No. 6. Findel produces no evidence at all. His argument that all previous signatures are the same is untrue. In a cypher like this, it is not casy to have a very distinctive handwriting, yet the signatures are by no means precisely the same, and when we come to compare the actual wording of the "acceptances" in the original we find they vary so naturally and completely that it is hard to believe that any forger would have been clever enough to do it, and even make the mistakes that do occur. His reference to Chevillon is almost ludicrous. I have an old family Bible running back into the beginning of the eighteenth century, in which my ancestors have inserted, in turn, the birth, marriage, and death of the members of the family. These entries are short and terse. M. marries N., has a son G., who marries H., and so forth, with dates. But in the third quarter of the nineteenth century one old lady suddenly filled two valuable pages with a verbose account of the funeral of her husband and a recital of his virtues. Findel would, therefore, I presume adduce this as evidence that all the previous entries must be forgeries, for there must have been other funerals and no doubt other and earlier husbands had some good deeds also to their credit. After all, the Revolution was a worse hour of trial for the nobility than any previous event in French history, and no doubt Chevillon was garrulous.

Briefly, Findel's arguments are valueless, and so are Gould's, because they did not have a true version of the text, and relied on Thory's.

Clavel's theory, which places the date of the forgery as 1705, is given in full by Crowe; but, as Clavel gives no evidence to support his theory, it is of little value. He did know it was in cypher, but apparently did not know the real Latin. His theory has no substantial basis, for he produces no evidence, documentary, or otherwise, for his story, and the appearance of the Latin, and indeed of the whole Charter, is against so late a date as 1705. Any Mason who is prepared to accept it must also accept the view that Scotch Templary existed in 1705.

My own feeling is that the document is genuine, though I hesitate to fly in the face of the accepted theory that it is a forgery. Though I was a history scholar of my college, I should hesitate to declare the document genuine solely on my own authority, though I venture to think that it looks quite as genuine as many fourteenth and fifteenth century MSS. whose authenticity is unquestioned. The view of Sir George Warner seems to me, however, to outweigh those of our masonic students who declare it is a forgery. I suggest that they are influenced by the characteristic fault of many masonic students who are so nervous of declaring that anything connected with Freemasonry is older than the eighteenth century, that they prefer to declare any evidence on the other side as forged or based on imagination.

This attitude, however, has had its day, and the new masonic generation will, I think, no longer be content to fix their eyes on the eighteenth century only.

But, if genuine, this document does not prove necessarily that our Templar degrees come from the Ancient Order. It might, however, explain certain Templar traditions, and Templar influence in Masonry, but mainly on the Continent, though, no doubt, Continental Masonry might have influenced English, and particularly Scotch Freemasonry.

So far as I can trace them, the descendants of the Paris Templars have become extinct, though when that happened I cannot say. This body was apparently still in existence up to about 1850, and was not masonic.

Between 1804 and that date it seems to have fallen into rather undesirable hands, and its final extinction is, I think, proved by the fact that Brother Crowe was able to purchase its greatest treasure, and that not as "The Charter" but as a "Knight Templar Certificate"!

With regard to the doctrines taught by the Paris Templars between 1804 and 1850, I need only say that they appear to have been a kind of vague Pantheism.

Before closing, I would, however, stress the point that the tale told in the Charter is a perfectly reasonable one. If the remnants of the knights in France wished to carry on the Order as a secret and mystical society, the method therein said to have been adopted was probably the best possible.

The cross has been cited as evidence of the late date of the Charter on the grounds that it is the cross of the Knights Hospitaller combined with that of the Temple, but is this correct? The cross now called Templar is , and is the one adopted by the English Templars, but Crowe seems to regard this cross ✠ as Templar. In common parlance, however, this is the Maltese Cross, or Cross of the Hospitallers, and can be seen on the stamps of Queen Victoria used in Malta. Have we any evidence that the cross now called the Cross of the Hospitallers  was adopted by them before the suppression of the Templars?

My reason for asking this query is that, in the Paris MS. of the Rules and Regulations, three letters of the cypher alphabet occur, namely, c, g, v.

Bothwell Gosse ascribes this MS. to 1250–1300, and says, "On the first two pages there are inscriptions in fourteenth-century writing, 'Memento finis' and 'Betracht die end' on the first page, and on the second several inscriptions, and three letters of the Templars' cypher alphabet, viz. c, g, v.

The Paris copy is incomplete, but, if added to the Dijon MS., which is 1150–1200, it makes a complete document.

The Dijon MS. is in ancient Northern French, and the MS. is mentioned in the inventory of Voulaine-lez-Temple, which was an important and wealthy priory.

The third MS. of the Rules and Regulations of the Order, and the most complete, is the Roman MS. from the Corsini Library, and appears to be 1250–1300. It is interesting to note that the masonic sign .·. occurs in this MS.

Returning to the ✠, I would like to point out that the apron shown to me by an Irish brother as the apron of St. John of Malta had this cross upon it. In G. Lodge Library there is an old Masonic Templar Apron with an ordinary Latin cross upon it.

Frater Ladislas de Malcrovich of Budapesth, to whom we shall again refer later, thought that the cross pattée ✠ came into use towards the latter part of Templar history, and that earlier a plain cross had been used.

Henriquez, in 1630, calls the eight-pointed cross (or Conventional Cross) ✵, the cross of the Templars. Hollar, about 1650, painted a picture of a knight with the cross ✠. Now, if the cypher letters in the Paris MS. are contemporary, they prove that the eight-pointed cross *was* used by the Templars, since the cypher is based on the cross. This cross forms an octagon when the points are joined, and so we get the key to cypher and octagon church at one stroke.

If the round churches of the Templars are examined it will be found that the space inside the columns forms an octagon, and this can be seen still more clearly in the Temple in London.

The X here used as a cypher for N marks the centre, and is the cross of initiation in many mysteries. This is the cross X of the operative sixth degree, also of the Bora ceremony among the Australian blacks. Also, to pass through this octagon, one would have to trample on the cross. As has been already pointed out, the proper manner of advancing from W. to E. in the — degree is to make a cross, and at the c. are the emblems of M. Now, some of the Operative Lodges still perform the ceremony of passing through the octagon, and, to do so, must trample on the cross, and since, in the *Confessions*, we find the expression "passait par-dessus" the cross, we see that this ritual act is a ritual step, and one still in use in our L.·.

Now, the real point under consideration is, was the eight-

∧ = C.
Δ = G.
▷ = V.

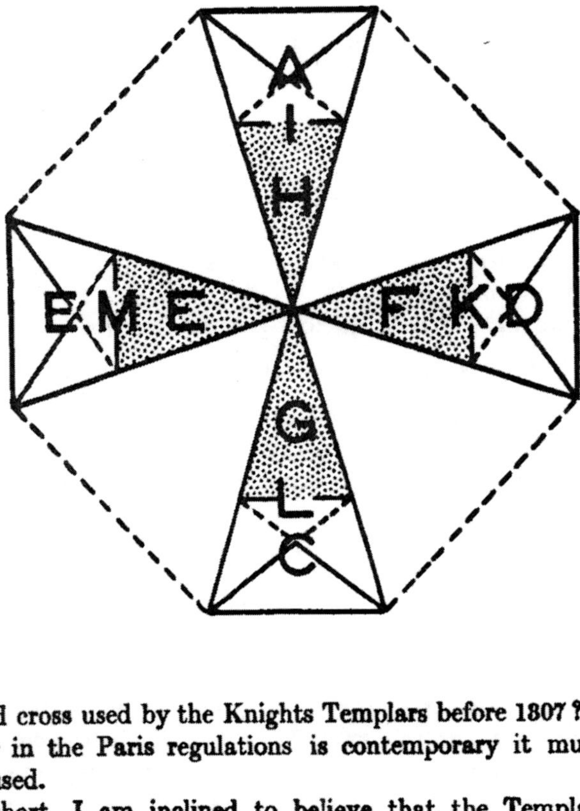

pointed cross used by the Knights Templars before 1307? If the cypher in the Paris regulations is contemporary it must have been used.

In short, I am inclined to believe that the Templars used several types of cross, and that it was the colour, red on white, and not the shape, which showed a Templar. The simpler shapes would be used, as a rule, on clothing or architectural details, while the more ornate would be found in manuscripts, seals and so forth; but, up to their suppression, there was not one sole and peculiar

Templar cross. The Knights of St. John had a white cross on a black ground, and the forms of the eight-pointed cross and also the cross pattée, I think, only became peculiarly associated with the Hospitallers after the suppression of the Templars. Things were much more fluid in the early Middle Ages, and the disappearance of the only other formidable rivals to the title of Knights of the Cross left the Hospitallers in undisputed possession of these crosses.

The symbolic meaning of the cross has been considered at some length already, but it ought to be mentioned that, in its cosmic sense, it symbolises the points of the compass and the limitations of matter within the infinity of spirit. This was one of the senses in which it was venerated in ancient Central America. It will be noticed, also, that the cross pattée is formed of four equal triangles, and the eight-pointed cross of sixteen triangles, or the square of four, the symbol of matter made out of triangles, the symbol of spirit.

The English and Scottish Knights

Let us now turn to consider the English and Scottish knights.

On the tombs of old Knights Templars are found many symbols associated to-day with Freemasonry, and similar emblems are likewise to be met with graven on the walls of their buildings. One of the most usual is the double triangle ✡, and Clavel says that in the seventeenth century, in Germany, the grave of a Templar who had died before the destruction of the Order was opened, and in it was found a stone graven with masonic emblems, including square, compasses, the pentalpha, a celestial globe, and various pointed stars.

Moreover, many of the phrases used by the knights, when being tried, are practically masonic phrases.

Now, what happened to the knights who survived? Out of 15,000 knights, only 800 are mentioned by name as having been slain or imprisoned, and, though many names may never have been recorded, the most liberal allowance leaves many thousands who escaped altogether.

Thus the Preceptor of Lorraine, on hearing the result of the

French Commission, released all those under him, and told them to *shave their beards* and abandon their robes. The Templars, be it remembered, were peculiar, in that, at a time when most knights shaved, they wore beards, and this point is worth remembering, as often it will enable the effigy of a Knight Templar to be distinguished from that of a lay knight.

The Preceptor of Auvergne happened to be in England when Molay was arrested, and took care to remain there. In England, Scotland, and Ireland there were no executions, nor, with two or three slight exceptions, were there any in Germany or Tuscany.

In all the higher degrees, or degrees of the cross, there appear to be two influences, hermetic and mystical on the one hand, and Templar on the other, and, to account for the latter, two lines of transmission have been suggested: (1) *The Aboriginal Scottish Legend* associated with Bruce and "Mother Kilwinning." (2) *The Emigrant French Legend*, associated with the Highlands and Aberdeen.

Considering (1) first, we find the following facts. David I introduced the Templars into Scotland before 1153, and they obtained an estate called Temple on South Esk, and by the fourteenth century their possessions were to be found all over Scotland.

At the time of suppression, [illegible] was endeav[illegible] Scotland against Edward II, and when the I[illegible] at Holyrood in 1309, only two Templars appeared, the others having joined Bruce's army, which was at that very time advancing against the English.

The *General Regulations of Royal Arch Masonry in Scotland* considers that it was these wars which saved the Templars in Scotland. The Duke of Antin, in his speech in Paris in 1714, says that the nobles who agreed to support Bruce were admitted Freemasons in Kilwinning when James, Lord Steward of Scotland, was made Grand Master; but whether he had any *evidence* in support of the statement I cannot say.

On St. John the Baptist's Day, 1314, Bruce routed [illegible] and, according to the Royal Order of Scotland, conferred the rank of Knights of the Rosy Cross on those "[illegible]" who had so valiantly helped him. If the "Charter of Transmissions" is genuine, the anathema of Larmenius in 1324 is explicable by the fact that the Masons were really Templars who had based the ceremonies of this new Order on the old reception ceremony of the Templars without authority from himself, the rightful successor of Jacques de Molay.

The dates of the two incidents make this story the more plausible. What happened to these old Templar knights after the fighting ended? No doubt they received estates, some, the old Templar property confirmed to them personally, others would receive lands taken from the supporters of Edward II. These, no doubt, would marry and pass them on to their descendants, but the secret ritual, changing as time went on in many of its details, would be kept on as secret ceremony among their descendants and friends.

This legend connecting Kilwinning and Templary is persistent, and crops up all over Europe, and in many different degrees.

The estates which were not *concealed* Templar lands mainly passed to the Knights of St. John, and about this some interesting points in connection with the cross are worth mentioning. The Templar houses in Leith and Edinburgh were surmounted by a cross, and the tenants were subject to the Knights and only able to answer in their courts. The Hospitallers seem to have used the same cross, and to this day, Keith says, there are crosses upon several buildings in these cities "which formerly belonged to them and are as yet subject to the jurisdiction of those who acquired them at the Reformation."

Many knights took refuge in the Order of St. John; in some cases they were ordered to do so, but, strange to say, these lands still retained the name of Terræ Templariæ, despite edicts to the contrary (*Statistical History:* "Account of Hospitallers"). Why? Bothwell Gosse adds that "many estates were not held in common." At the Reformation some of the Hospitallers turned Protestant and received the lands of the Order as private property from the King, but others remained staunch, and elected David Seaton as their Head. Deuchar states that, as early as 1590, *Templars* had incorporated themselves in Freemasonry. If there is any substantial proof of this, the matter would be settled definitely. Many monasteries in Scotland survived up to 1588, for the Reformation took longer there than in England, owing to the weakness of the royal authority and the strength of local barons in certain districts.

The Lodge at Stirling *is stated* to have had a chapter of "Cross-legged Masons," or Templars, as early as 1590, and worked various higher degrees also, including Rose Croix, Royal Arch, and Knight

Templar up to 1736. In the metrical description of Perth by Henry Adamson, M.A., 1638, *The Muses, Threnodie*, we find the following lines :

> "For we are Brethren of the Rosie Cross,
> We have the Masons' word and second sight."

This shows (1) That there were Speculative Masons in Perth in 1638, for Adamson was an M.A.

(2) That not merely Masonry, but Rose Croix, was known and worked at that date.

(3) That they had a secret and mystic word, [illegible] occult powers.

Up to 1799 Mother Kilwinning worked Templary, for, according to Murray Lyon, the minutes show that in that year they granted a charter to the Irish Kilwinning Lodge to work R.A. and K.T.

In 1813, however, they had ceased to practise these higher degrees, and even denied that they ever had, the reason being apparently that the Grand Lodge of Scotland had in 1800 threatened that any Lodge which worked these higher degrees would lose its charter. Had this happened the members of Mother Kilwinning might have found themselves liable to prosecution under the Secret Society Act of 1799, for the exception therein made in favour of Freemasonry might not have been considered to cover them once their own Grand Lodge had struck them off the list. In any case, they preferred to lose their higher degrees rather than their craft.

This might account for their repudiation of Templary in 1813 after granting a charter for it to another Lodge in 1799. The same attack on the higher degrees was beginning in Scotland which we have already seen took place in England after the Act of Union, 1813, despite the clause in the Constitution which expressly permits Lodges which already did so to work the chivalric degrees. This repudiation, however, in no way invalidates the proof that they formerly worked these degrees. Again, in 1671, the Earl of Cassilis was Deacon, which may here mean Master, of Kilwinning. The Lodge of Aberdeen is believed to date from 1541, though, owing to a fire, the records go back no further than 1670, and, even at that date, more than half the members were non-operatives, among whom were earls, ministers, doctors, lawyers, etc.

The peculiar thing about this Aberdeen Lodge was that it met in the open, in remote fields—as a Templar encampment this was natural, though not for an Operative Lodge, and there are other accounts of Lodges or bodies of Masons in Scotland who met in the open.

Later we know it worked the higher degrees, and so did the Renfrew Lodge. Now Kilwinning, Stirling, Aberdeen, Perth, and Renfrew were all either in or near the position of ancient Templar Preceptories.

In England we find that Bristol, Bath, and York all have old Masonic Templar Preceptories, and were the sites of mediæval Templar Preceptories.

All three are remote from the central Government in London, and therefore members of the Order were less likely to be thoroughly dispersed.

The *French Emigrant Legend* states that Pierre d'Aumont, Grand Master (*sic*) of Auvergne, accompanied by five knights and two commanders, fled to Mull disguised as Operative Masons, and, agreeing to continue the Order, chose d'Aumont as Grand Master, assumed the name of Freemasons, and adopted many of their symbols. In 1361 they moved to Aberdeen, and thence Freemasonry spread throughout Europe. This legend is the basis of the Rite of Strict Observance.

We need not, however, consider it in detail, as, at the most, if true, these men could but have strengthened the hand of the local Templars, and might have been the reason why Larmenius's attention was directed to them. He would be more angry with French knights who forsook their compatriots than with Scottish Templars who had at a difficult time struck out on their own.

In England, fewer legends and facts about the intervening period, between 1307 and 1750, are known than in Scotland, but one point must not be overlooked. All the legends and theories relate to the knights, but what of the Templar priests? It is highly probable that such men would endeavour to keep alive some at least of the Templar secret mysteries, and it would be even easier for them than for the knights to associate with operative Freemasons. A church is being altered, and the Vicar, and perhaps a few old clerical friends, take a perfectly natural interest in the work. From this to talking about the inner meaning of the symbols employed would be a short step. The priests would appreciate the esoteric meaning of the masonic symbolism in a way which would surprise the Masons, used only to the narrow orthodoxy of the ordinary clergy. Further talks would naturally lead to a closer union and understanding, and the priests would see a chance of saving the old loved ritual and mysticism from being entirely lost, and, once started, such a movement would grow. Our wandering Lodge, now in possession of the secrets and signs, would test other priests, and so more Templars would be discovered, and naturally more incorporated into the Society of Freemasons.

The Middle Ages abounded not only in mysticism but in all kinds of heretical societies, which only survived at all because of the greatest secrecy. Thus there would quite early grow up Lodges of Masons who had some of the Templar rites and signs while others had not.

Now, what parts of our present ritual can be derived from the ancient knights? Many things have been adopted in comparatively recent times, and are due to our greater historical knowledge. Thus our mantles, sword-belts, and tunics are similar to those worn in the Middle Ages, but they are of fairly recent importation. In the eighteenth century aprons and sashes were worn. The cross of the Order appears to have been changed several times. The flags are the old ones, but when were they revived? They may have come down through the ages, of course, but, as they were never secret, anyone who wished to revive the Order of the Temple would revive them also.

The black and white banner[1] has, however, an esoteric meaning which may interest my brother knights. A study of stellar symbolism shows that it has a cosmic significance, light and darkness, day and night, and suggests the range of the solar system, which, according to mediæval belief, was bounded on its outmost limit by the "sphere" of Saturn, to whom was assigned the colour *black*, while its inner was the "sphere" of the moon, whose colour was white. Thus it signifies the linking of Heaven and Earth, the unifying of Man and the Universe. The significance of the cross in its cosmic sense—the material within the

[1] Every knight had to have a black and white coverlet, which indicates this design, and had an esoteric significance, otherwise why should it be carefully laid down in the Regulation?

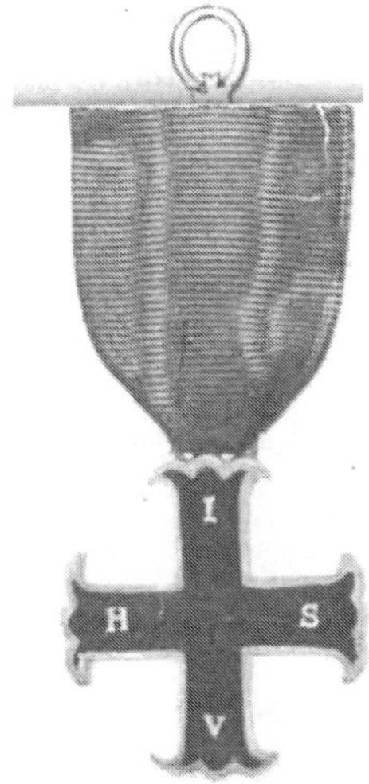

5

6

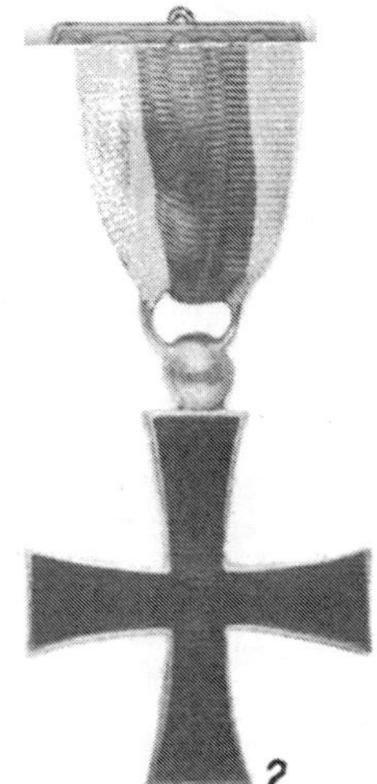

2

Photographed by kind permission from Originals made by G. Kenning & Son.

JEWELS OF CHIVALRIC DEGREES.

1. The Star of a Knight Templar.
2. The Knights of Templar Cross.
3. The St. John of Malta Cross.
4. Past Preceptor Cross.
5. Cross of Red Cross of Constantine.
6. Cross of K.H.S.
7. Scotch Knights Templar Cross.
8. P. Preceptor and Prior Jewel.
9. Jewel of the Rosicrucian Society.

spiritual—has already been indicated, and a red cross on a white field was their other banner.

The seal used at first was two knights riding one horse. Its exoteric meaning was that the knights were so poor that they could afford only one horse between two. This also indicated their humility.

In *Procès*, vol. ii, p. 195, appears a story which suggests there may have been another and less innocent meaning. It runs as follows.

Of old, two Templars were riding one horse to battle, and the one in front commended himself to Christ, whereas the knight behind commended himself " to he who best could help." As a result, the first knight was wounded, while the other escaped uninjured. The latter was a demon, and told his human companion that, if the knights would believe in the powers of evil, the Order would flourish. Hence came disbelief into the Order.

It is, however, probable that this story is an invention of their enemies. The badge may, however, have a reference to other "twin riders" who really represent the duality of the human soul; in short, to the stellar personalities, Castor and Pollux. Later this emblem was changed into the Winged Horse, the symbol of illumination. This emblem can still be seen in the City Temple. There are a number of old Templar seals still in existence, and Bothwell Gosse says that some have inscriptions *in the Templar script*.

The Agnus Dei was another emblem. This was at one time a symbol of Mithra—the ram and the sword, or cross. Its later adoption by the Christians is, however, sufficient to account for its presence in an avowedly Christian Order.

CHAPTER XIV

ARE THERE ANY TRACES OF THE OLD TEMPLAR CEREMONIES IN THE MASONIC TEMPLAR RITUAL?

IN dealing with this subject it becomes necessary to speak with caution lest the uninitiated should penetrate our mysteries.

Obviously certain parts of our regalia and ritual could have been made up from the facts commonly known about the Templars; for example, our seal, our banners, etc. These, therefore, we need discuss no further.

On the other hand, a clever archæologist might have reconstructed the old ceremony from the Regulations and the Confessions; but, instead, we find a somewhat purged ritual full of curious anachronisms and old and modern ideas.

The division into three sections would correspond with the three stages in a knight's career: novice, esquire, knight.

The ritual kiss "in ano" has vanished, though a very similar act appears in Prussian Knight of the Ancient and Accepted Rite. The Meditation may well be old, but the Anathema is, perhaps, the most striking act in the earlier part. It is in a peculiarly unpleasant form, and, before the ritual was amended in recent times, it went so far in some rituals as to call on the former owner of the s. to haunt the breaker of his oath. It does not sound eighteenth-century work, but is much more in the nature of mediæval necromancy. I must warn my readers that our English ritual has been revised at least five times in modern times, and many valuable details eliminated. Alas, the pity of it!

Again, the cup to all those valiant . . . was once drunk from a cup formed of a s., and any who hesitated to drink were threatened with the swords of the surrounding knights. This, I understand, is still done in U.S.A. Now whose s. was this? Some say it was Simon the traitor. Who was this traitor? Does it refer to that other Simon, who bore the cross of our Lord, and, if so, is there any reference to the Gnostic heresy that it was that Simon the Jew, and not Christ, who actually died on the cross?

For the third time the s. appears—on the altar with its accompanying emblems of mortality. Why? To remind us of Calvary is the exoteric meaning, but here we come to an old mediæval Templar legend which is related in some of the reports of the trial.

A great lady of Maraclea was loved by a Templar, a Lord of *Sidon*; but she died in her youth, and on the night of her burial this wicked lover crept to the grave, dug up her body, and violated it. Then a voice from the void bade him return in nine months' time, for he would find a son. He obeyed the injunction, and at the appointed time opened the grave again and found *a head on the leg bones* of the skeleton (skull and cross-bones). The same voice bade him "guard it well, for it would be the giver of all good things," and so he carried it away with him. It became his protecting genius, and he was able to defeat his enemies by merely showing them the magic head. In due course it passed into the possession of the Order.

In reference to this tale, we must remember the charges against the Templars of worshipping a head. Many knights admitted that there was such a head, and some added that they thought it was a skull.

A head or skull *was* found by the Papal Commissioners in Paris. There are other versions of this legend of the magic skull, or head. What do they mean?

Evidently they refer to some initiation ceremony narrated by an ignorant eavesdropper, and garbled and made more horrible by ignorant and vulgar minds.

In the Egyptian mystery legend of Osiris we are told that, on discovering the dead body of the murdered Osiris, Isis threw herself upon the corpse and had intercourse with it, and from this came the birth of Horus, the avenger of Osiris. To prevent a repetition of this, Set tore the body of Osiris into many pieces and scattered them throughout Egypt.

This Templar ceremony would be the mystic marriage, old symbol of the attainment of a divine union. Here we get death and the tomb, and after the tomb a birth or rebirth. The body, female, dies; but the spirit, male, rejuvenates it, and a new life begins; above all a skull and cross-bones, the age-old emblems in all the mysteries of the world, emblems of death, and, since death does but lead to a new birth, the emblems also of life.

Perhaps, then, we have here in our modern ritual the last relics of the old ceremony, now shorn of most of its interest. Is the name Simon a corruption of this Lord of Sidon?

Then, too, we get legends that the Templars are the guardians of the Holy Grail, and keep it in a lonely chapel on a mountain surrounded by a huge forest.

The ordinary sign has a double significance, and really refers to the penalty, and, if you analyse it, it is a strange penalty. The scorching rays refer, I think, to the fire which shall not be quenched, just as the E.A.p. implies that the soul shall have neither peace nor rest until the Judgment Day, for the b. is b. in soil which can never be consecrated, and that other part of the p.—between earth and heaven—like those unfortunate spirits who, in some mediæval legends, are stated to wander in the void, unable to enter Hell or Heaven. Finally, De Malcrovich, in *Ars Quatuor Coronatorum*, tells a most interesting story of Hungary. There was in his native town an old hall which had at one time belonged to the Templars and was still called by their name. As a boy, the peasants told him a strange story of a ghost of a Templar who used to appear in this hall from time to time, and had been seen by some of them, and the ghost always *appeared in a peculiar position.* This "position" they described to him minutely. What was his surprise, years afterwards, when he was made a Templar here, to find that the position taken up by the ghost was the same as that taught to him by the Preceptor *as the grand sign* of the Order.

Now, what are the possible explanations of this legend, bearing in mind that English Templary does not exist in Hungary? There are only two, and you may choose which suits your feelings best.

(1) That there was a ghost who did appear as stated. In that case we see that the old Templars used our Masonic Templar sign, and attached great importance to it.

(2) That the tradition of the Templars had lingered on in the neighbourhood, and dim remembrances of the ritual, and in particular this sign, had remained in possession of the peasants ever since the Templars passed away.

In either case the result is the same, that this sign is derived from old mediæval Templary. Moreover, such a sign would be regarded as "heresy," if not blasphemy, by the Inquisitors, and proof in support of the charge of mocking the cross. Its esoteric meaning among the knights would be that all men suffered as He did, the eternal c. of the human race. Rank heresy in the eyes of the Papacy. And, by its suffering, humanity shall in time attain to perfection, and not by a vicarious sacrifice. A most damnable heresy in the eyes of the papal curia.

The mediæval knights were deprived of everything save their underclothing, and in some cases of everything, for Walsingham, in his *Life of Edward II*, says: "Adduxerunt illum ad locum privatum et totaliter denudanerunt." In the reception of Hugo de Buris, he "removed all the clothes he was wearing, except his underclothing," etc., while Geraldus de Pasagio said he "took off the coloured clothes he was wearing behind the altar except his shirt, breeches, socks, and boots . . . and put on a garment of camels' hair" (*Proc.*, i, pp. 205 and 214). Johannis de Turno and William de Raynbur also bear witness to the same procedure.

The Preceptor later on invested the candidate with the robe of the Order, and the *birretum*. Probably it was after the investment with the regalia that the secret ceremonies took place.

During the ceremony, which took place usually at cock-crow (dawn), and with two candles burning, the Temple was closely guarded by two guards with drawn swords at the door, and a third on the roof outside. It will be remembered that the Temples are round buildings, and from the top of the roof a sentry could see all round the outside and effectively prevent eavesdroppers. It is possible that our name Tyler is derived from this Templar sentry.

Throughout not only the ceremony of admittance, but also during his whole life, the number three played a significant part. Thus we find a *threefold* vow of Chastity, Obedience, and Poverty, while the Ritual Kiss and the Symbolic Denial were also *threefold*. As a knight, he was allowed to keep *three* horses, and vowed not to fly before three enemies. *Three* times a week he was allowed to eat meat, and also had to give alms. Again, *thrice* a week Mass was said, and *thrice* a year they met for the Adoration of the Cross.

Now, if we cast back our minds to our present ritual, we shall perceive a similar reverence for the number *three* and detect numerous other small points which resemble the original mediæval ceremony, so far as we can reconstruct it.

No doubt after the suppression many of the obviously heretical practices were abandoned; but were they all? Bread, water, and wine; one of the charges against the Templars was that they altered the form of the Mass, Ruppe Talhato stating that it was customary to omit the words "Hoc est enim corpus meum." Bzonius and a Templar Priest also say the same, though, on the other hand, many knights denied this charge, which, if true, was of itself sufficient to prove them heretics.

To all those valiant knights—in the Continental Templar degrees of the A. and A. Rite—Jacques de Molay and the other martyrs were commemorated in the Cup of Vengeance. I wonder whether it has been cut out of our ritual in recent times.

In our ritual there occurs a certain word which also occurs in the ritual of the R.O. of Scotland. Why? There does not seem any particular reason for it. Yet, what if the tradition of the R.O. is correct and the degrees it contains were reorganised by Bruce and Templars admitted? The old Templars wore beards, and this was a peculiar feature in a time when all European lay knights avoided them. Perhaps they copied the custom from the natives of the Near East, who, we know, when distressed, pluck out their own beards, and, when angry with another man, tear out handfuls of his beard.

After travelling in the East, many crusaders brought back Eastern customs. The wimple was one, and there were—others.

In England the Order is now known as the United Order of the Temple and the Hospitallers. So far as the present ritual of the St. John degree is concerned, I am doubtful whether any of it comes from the real knights. That body existed intact up to the last years of the eighteenth century, and in fact as a more or less honorary body still exists at Rome. One of its last Grand Masters was a Hapsburg, and membership is strictly confined to Roman Catholics of noble lineage.

The Order was always, so far as we can find, strictly orthodox, and its history covers some of the most romantic pages in the book of valiant deeds. From 1300 to nearly 1800 they waged a stubborn rearguard action against the Infidel. Year after year, with varying success but unvarying gallantry, they fought against the onward rushing tide of Turkish conquest. When Rhodes fell, after one of the most stirring sieges in history, they retired to Malta, which was granted to them by Charles V in the opening years of the sixteenth century.

Among the list of officers in our priories appears one whose name puzzles most of the modern knights; it is "The Turcopolier." He was the leader of the Turcopoles, who were a Eurasian class who sprang up in the Near East owing to the presence of European merchants who contracted relations with Asiatic women. Sometimes it was the other way, and everyone knows the legend of Gilbert and the Saracen princess who followed him to London, and whose son was Thomas à Becket, the fierce, martyred Archbishop. Modern historians are sceptical of the pretty legend, but of the ordinary Turcopoles there is no doubt.

The Hospitallers were much perturbed at the probable fate of these half-caste children, and undertook the care of all unwanted boys. These they brought up as Christians, and turned into men-at-arms and light cavalry. They were distinguished from the true knights of the Order by wearing turbans instead of helmets; of course, not being of noble descent, they could not become knights.

Over them was placed an officer called the Turcopolier, and this office was apparently always conferred upon an Englishman. It is interesting to see that thus early in our history Englishmen showed their aptitude for leading Eastern soldiers trained in Western methods.

There was another interesting group of Englishmen in the East during the Crusades (Saxons, perhaps, would more accurately describe them) and these constituted the Varangian Guard of the Byzantine Emperors; and well they fought for their foreign lord. When the Fourth Crusade was diverted from its original task of destroying the Turks to that of destroying the Christian Empire of Byzantium the Varangian Guard fought bravely to the end.

The Turcopoles under their English officer fought valiantly on many a bloody field, and during the siege of Rhodes excelled themselves.

After the retreat to Malta, the knights reorganised themselves and fought the Infidel upon the high seas. Then came the tremendous struggle for Malta, when for three long years the knights held the Turks at bay. It has always filled me with the deepest regret, as I have read the account of the siege, that, in that hour of need, no English knights were present to take their stand beside those of other nations. For, between the fall of Rhodes and the siege of Malta had come the Reformation, and Henry VIII had dissolved the Order.

It may not be known to everyone that the crypt and chancel of their great Priory Church of St. John at Jerusalem, Clerkenwell, is still standing, and a narrow alley close by it is still known by the name of "Jerusalem." The gate is no doubt known to many, as it is just on the left as one approaches Farringdon Street from Clerkenwell. No serious charges were made against the Order, and the Prior received a most generous pension for those days. "But," says Stowe, "he never touched one penny of it, for gold, though the best of all medicines, is unable to mend a broken heart. He died the day after he received the news that the Order was suppressed."

So there were no English knights at the siege of Malta; nevertheless when, by the battle of Lepanto, Don Juan defeated the Turkish fleet and relieved the knights, Queen Elizabeth ordered solemn Te Deum to be sung in old St. Paul's for the victory of Christendom over the Infidel.

But the knights were not content to sit down in idleness. Instead they struck out a new line and took upon themselves the policing of the Mediterranean. Their galleys carried on a never-ending war against the Algerian Corsairs, who plundered the shipping of the sea and even raided the southern coasts of Europe. In the nineteenth century, when the knights had passed away, the French were compelled to attack and conquer Algiers to put an end to these depredations.

So, all through the seventeenth and eighteenth centuries, the knights continued their crusade against the Infidel, adopting new methods and adapting themselves to the changing circumstances of the centuries.

But there came a day when Napoleon's ships appeared before the walls of Valetta, but no longer was the Grand Master made of the same stern metal as his predecessors. The island could have stood a long siege, and the British fleet was hastening to the rescue, but he surrendered. The British came and drove out the French, and sat themselves down in the seats of the Knights of St. John. Henceforth their work was done, and the policing of the seas passed into British hands. Still their descendants hung on—at Rome, shorn alike of work and glory; but the pages of history know them no more.

A revival of the knights took place in England about 1825, and to-day King George is head of the Order. The knights meet in the crypt of St. John at Jerusalem, Clerkenwell, and still busy themselves in the work of helping those who are wounded or injured. The Red Cross is an offshoot of the Order, and still works in close conjunction. Theirs were the first ambulances placed on the streets of London, and during the war a dozen great motor-ambulances might be seen any day near the priory gate of St. John at Jerusalem.

But this body has no connection with the masonic body of the Knights of Malta.

Of our ritual we may say that the most interesting part is the drawing on the octagonal table, and, while some parts of the ceremony may be based on traditions of the Order, etc., it seems as if the degree itself is late eighteenth-century work. The Hospitallers appear to have been orthodox all through their history, and no secret initiation ceremony would be necessary. The official ritual of the old knights still appertains to the Order in Rome, and I gather the ceremony of the Order at St. John's, Clerkenwell, closely follows the ancient ritual and does not resemble ours.

The Templars were different—they had a secret ceremony, and, if they carried it on inside the Order of St. John after their suppression, or independently as Masons, it might well survive after the dissolution of the Hospitallers because it had an esoteric and symbolic meaning which theirs had not.

CHAPTER XV

THE OTHER CHIVALRIC DEGREES IN FREEMASONRY

There still remain a number of chivalric degrees. In reality these are three, and a chair degree, but, for all practical purposes, they now constitute one Order with three sections in the ceremony.

These are "Knights of the Red Cross of Constantine, of St. John, and of the Holy Sepulchre."

The ceremonies are based on various mediæval legends of the cross, including the cross which Constantine the Great saw in the sky, and which led him to adopt Christianity, the legend of the discovery of the True Cross, and so forth.

On looking at the regalia, my readers will notice several interesting points. Thus, the jewel of the Knight of St. John, etc., is placed within the lozenge, which, as already stated, is the same as the vesica piscis. It therefore corresponds exactly with the linga of the Hindoos. The Commander of St. John wears a jewel formed of four taus, with four equal-armed crosses between the taus, thus making nine crosses. This reminds us of the nine months of the legend of the Templar and the skull, and it includes the phallic cross of creation and the + of suffering, which brings forth the new life. These equal-armed crosses are similar to the cross of the Red Cross of Constantine. The Knights of St. John and Holy Sepulchre wear this jewel.

It has the fourfold phallic cross of matter within the circle of eternity, which forms the heart of the fourfold tau cross within the lozenge, or vesica piscis.

These crosses should be compared with that shown on the sash of the thirtieth degree. The eagle of St. John is, of course, also representative of one of the four cardinal points, and the eagle has always been regarded as the emblem of the spirit ascending towards God.

The ritual, particularly of the second and third sections, is most impressive, and, while I cannot say, as yet, whether any parts are genuinely old, they are certainly most interesting. The usual belief among brothers is that this degree was imported from Malta about forty years ago by Brother R. W. Little. As a matter of fact, he did a great deal to revive it when it had almost perished; but, as far back as 1780 we find that Major Charles Shereff and others were working it, though whether they derived their material from Malta and the knights there I cannot say. William White, Grand Secretary from 1780, and other prominent Masons were members, and in 1796 Lord Rancliffe was Grand Master of these degrees, as well as of the Knights Templars. He was succeeded by Judge Walter Rodwell Wright in 1804, and after him H.R.H. the Duke of Sussex was installed Grand Master for life. Sussex did his best to destroy these, as he did all the Christian degrees. Probably this was his real object in taking the supreme office in most of them, as they had been safeguarded by the clause in the Act of Union expressly permitting those Lodges which had the power to do so to continue to work the chivalric degrees. He was nearly, though not quite, successful, and when the degrees were revived no doubt much of the ritual had to be obtained from U.S.A., though probably Malta, where it still lingered, provided much valuable information.

In America these degrees appear to be worked under a body called "The Thrice Illustrious Council of the Cross," which body seems also to control a somewhat similar degree not worked in England. This is entitled, "Knights of the Christian Mark and Guardians of the Temple," and is quite an interesting little piece of ritual.

My readers should also study the sashes of these degrees. That of the Grand Imperial Council has four fleur-de-lis in place of the crosses of the Commander. The fleurs-de-lis has a long history behind it, but we will merely consider its Christian significance here. It is the emblem of the Blessed Virgin, and reminds us that the Cross of Calvary on which Christ expiated our sins caused by our passions would not have been possible but for her motherhood, and therefore symbolises the cross and the vesica piscis.

The radiated triangle within two squares 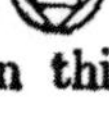 reminds us of the divine spark within man, who is placed in this material world, which is itself set in the limitless spaces of eternity here depicted by the circle. In the case of the knights and commanders who are not members of the Grand Imperial Council it will be noticed that one of the squares is replaced by a parallelogram.

The type of cross used in this degree—the quadruple tau—has long been associated with Jerusalem of the Crusades, and in particular it symbolically refers, not only to Mount Calvary, but even more to the Sepulchre itself, for that Body which suffered on the cross of our passions is represented by the four taus—animal matter—but it was raised to life again on the third day. And so the tomb is the womb of the new life, the triangle of the Divine Spirit revivifies the square of matter and expands it into the circle of the infinite.

With regard to the cross which Constantine saw in the heavens, I have seen the sun towards evening make a huge red cross across the sky; but this was in an eastern land—Burma. And behind the cross which fell upon the slight clouds which seemed to gather around the sun in the west, the sky itself turned green like turquoise, blue as sapphire, purple as amethyst, like the sash of the knight of this degree; and, as the sun sank down into the west, it seemed as if a purple curtain came down fold by fold, and the purple turned to black of an almost velvety texture, and the stars rushed out, while the crescent moon swam into view, the emblem of Islam; while, black and solemn, now stood the great Buddhist Shwe Dagoon Pagoda, its golden sheath no longer reflecting the glory of a tropic sun. The voice of the grass-hoppers failed, and the stillness of a tropic night fell on the world, broken only by the lapping of the waters of the lake.

And the cross in the sky is the symbol of the Cosmic Christ, who is ever crucified afresh; it is the symbol of Humanity, which suffers that by suffering it may rise out of matter into the circle of eternity. It is the cross of the four cardinal points, the Maya cross, and it is, as aforesaid, the cross within the circle, matter within eternity. So, "in this sign thou shalt conquer" means more than merely the historic incident. By suffering matter triumphs and becomes illumined with the light which comes from the sun, emblem of the Supreme Being, and, as the cross descends from the sun, and, spreading out in all directions, covers the whole earth, so in that sign shall each man conquer, raising himself by that ladder of light which is within him and without him; one with God, whence it came, yet one with man in whom it dwells. "He was that light, and the light shone in the darkness, and the *darkness* comprehended it not. . . . But as many as believed on Him, power gave He them to become the sons of God, even such as call on His holy name." Therefore Lux = Light and the cross is synonymous with light, for the cross is not only made of light, but is light. *Crux* is but *lux*, with ☧ substituted for L. The square gives place to the X, and all is light. From the point within the circle it radiates till it touches the circumference, and, refusing even to be bounded by the circle of heaven, it stretches out N., E., S., W., beyond the limits of the limitless, till the T, seal of salvation, is placed on the forehead of every human being.

Thus we will close this part of the book. We began with the cross in the Entered Apprentice, and we end with the cross of the Knights of St. John. We took our oath on the vesica piscis, we have seen the Rose of Sharon rise from the womb of the Holy Sepulchre, and the Mystic Rose of the Sun change into the cross of Constantine.

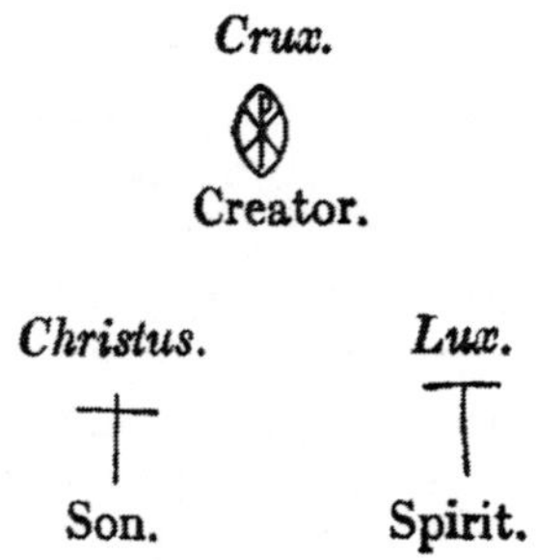

END OF PART II

PART III

CHAPTER I

ICONOCLASM IN FREEMASONRY

THE old system of the mysteries consisted of seven lesser and ten greater mysteries, but these have been shattered to pieces, so that only the fragments remain. Yet the fact that surprises us is that these fragments do exist, rather than that they have been broken into pieces. Freemasonry, in short, consists of these fragments. Some parts have been lost altogether, while in others the same fragment has been repeated several times. But Masonry, as we now call it, stretches back beyond even the mysteries, and still retains, in many cases, traces of its origin—the primitive rites of our prehistoric ancestors. These rites, the origin not merely of the mysteries, but of all the religious systems of the world, exist at any rate in part to-day. Worn down, developed, or distorted as the case may be, they still show their common origin with ours by their signs, grips, and tokens, as well as by their use of many of our most cherished symbols. Study carefully the illustration opposite p. 142, showing the four Buddhas and the Buddha who is to be arranged in a cross. If you are a Scottish craft mason you will recognise one sign. If you have taken our various higher degrees you will recognise others. The sign in the left-hand corner is that of the vesica piscis, and is the pair to the cross sign of the figure in the centre. This Buddha at the centre is the Buddha to be, and his use of the cross is most significant. The sign of — is known in Easter Island and New Guinea, in the West Indies and in Mexico, and throughout Africa and Asia by men who never entered a Lodge. Royal Arch, Rose Croix, Royal Order of Scotland, Entered Apprentice Fellow Craft, Master Mason, we find their signs, even parts of their ritual, all over the world among the most primitive peoples.

In Egypt we can trace practically the whole of our system, and likewise in Mexico, including the so-called "Christian degrees." We have traced our signs via the Dionysian Artificers, the Roman Collegia, and the Comacines down to the Freemasons of mediæval Europe, whence our own speculatives derive.

When came the really shattering blow? I consider it took place in the eighteenth and early nineteenth centuries. The protests of the Ancients were well founded: the Moderns *had* altered the ancient ritual, and, what is more, they are still doing so to-day.

The Act of Union brought many blessings, but it brought serious evils also. The Moderns had to give way on many points, and in consequence the Ancients also had to make concessions, and in many cases these meant that the higher degrees were left to their fate. But the compromise was not carried out in the spirit as well as in the letter, for Sussex used the spirit of conciliation to obtain control of those chivalric degrees whose existence the Ancients thought they had successfully safeguarded. Having done so, he appears to have used all his influence in a most unscrupulous endeavour to smother them, and even altered the Royal Arch, a degree he had acknowledged as forming an integral part of Freemasonry. In short, Sussex seems to be the chief person responsible for shattering the whole system. He appears to have been a bigoted Deist, and anything that savoured of Christianity was anathema to him. In his policy he was no doubt helped by two factors:

(1) The attitude of the Moderns, or at any rate that group of them who insisted on the clause: "Freemasonry consists of three degrees, and three degrees only, including the R.A."

(2) The spirit, far too prevalent even to-day, which says because a man is in a high social position he should therefore have high rank in the craft, and, if he has high position in the craft, whatever he does must be supported.

That the higher degrees survived at all is a wonder, and shows that they had a real intrinsic value. This spirit of contempt for them is still far from dead, though it is dying; but I have met many old Masons who speak with a sneer of the higher degrees, and boast that *they* have never taken them. Incidentally the mere fact that they have never taken them disqualifies them from giving any opinion on their value.

The higher degrees struggled on despite the opposition of

the powers that were, and, though some undoubtedly perished altogether and others passed into abeyance, the most valuable as a rule survived and reorganised themselves as best they could. Various supreme bodies were set up, often with little regard for historic tradition, and with ill-defined jurisdiction. By degrees compacts and alliances were formed. Different bodies retained one set of degrees, and gave up jurisdiction over others. As an example of what is meant, the Rose Croix and Templar degrees were closely associated in the eighteenth century, and the Baldwyn Chapter at Bristol, a Time Immemorial chapter, still insists on the connection between them, and during the ceremony a visiting Rose Croix Mason who is not a Templar is requested to retire from the chapter for a few minutes. This was not an isolated case; in the eighteenth century, on the contrary, we find that in England and Scotland Templary and Rose Croix nearly always go together, and what are practically our Templar rites form part of the Ancient and Accepted Rite on the Continent to this day; and rightly, for the Templar ritual is a ritual of the cross of the greater mysteries.

Again, the Baldwyn Royal Arch chapter still has the ceremony of passing the veils, which is now known in Scotland as the Excellent Master, and which also existed in England, but has now vanished, and must not be confounded with that of Most Excellent Master, given in the cryptic degrees.

But the damage begun in the opening years of the nineteenth century has not ended yet.

One learned brother obtained quite a reputation for rewriting rituals. No doubt he meant well, but he and those like him have robbed us of invaluable details, because they did not know what they meant. Indeed, to this school of thought, if a piece of ritual is not obvious in its meaning, it must be rewritten, and henceforth the brethren are deprived of the possibility of studying it and discovering what it *does* mean. The Templar ritual has been revised five times in the last few years! I have given an example of tampering with our F.C. degree, which is now spreading in London—I mean by the substitution of "accepted" for "permitted," thus preventing an earnest student from seeing the important meaning underlying the use of this word, and its analogy with the Yogi system, wherein a brother is not *permitted* to extend his researches into the hidden mysteries of

THE "SACRED TREE."

On each side of it stands a winged figure, wearing the two-horned cap and holding a chaplet in the left hand, performing an act of worship (?). Adoration of "The Tree" in ancient Babylonia. Compare with similar scene depicted in the Mexican cross patée. The garlands or necklets are probably representative of the female principle, as "The Tree" is of the male, and resemble those used in the worship of Priapaus in ancient Rome. It will be noticed that the Tree has fifteen bunches of leaves, seven leaves to a bunch. From the palace of Ashur-nasir-pal at Calah (Nimrud). Now in the British Museum.

(Reproduced by the permission of the Trustees of the British Museum.)

nature and occult science until he has proved that he is thoroughly acquainted with the ordinary moral code. Recently a newly initiated member of the Royal Order told me he wished *they* would rewrite the ritual in modern English.

But it is not only in the matter of ritual that the iconoclast of the nineteenth century has been at work. In our social entertainment after labour the same spirit is also noticeable, particularly in London. The provinces still keep up many of the old customs, but the tendency is, I am afraid, to copy London. Why? In many ways the provincial Lodges have a better masonic spirit than the London Lodges.

By this I mean that there is more of the spirit of real brotherhood and of good fellowship than in London. There are many reasons for this, no doubt. They usually meet more often; ten or twelves times a year is quite usual in the provinces, whereas six regular meetings are a fair average for a London Lodge. This fact militates against brothers getting to know each other, a task already more difficult in a huge city like London than it is even in a large provincial city like Leeds or Sheffield.

One of the pleasantest recollections I have in Freemasonry was when I visited two Lodges at Leeds. The spirit was *right*, and one of the things that made one feel perfectly at home was the old masonic songs. Frankly, do we not all get rather tired of the after-dinner speeches, consisting often of insincere compliments, and, even when sincere, long and trite? Instead of trying to add to our masonic knowledge, they usually consist of saying how well Brother Brown did the ceremony to-night, and everyone knows what a shining example in Freemasonry such and such a grand officer is.

Or, if music is given, often the musicians are hired for the occasion. Worst of all, some lady is led in, sings an ordinary sentimental ditty, and is whisked out again till the next toast has been drunk, when she is led in once more. Or perhaps it is the latest music-hall song by some hired "low comedian."

How often do you hear the old, jolly mason songs in London? Why, even the Entered Apprentice's song is hardly ever sung, and some brothers are so *affected* as to find fault with its "banal sentiment and poor poetry." I think the Entered Apprentice's song is excellent. It *is* what it pretends to be—a song to be sung by men who are not professional singers, but who can pick up a chorus, and roar it out in unison. It is eighteenth-century in versification and music, and admirably suitable in every way. And the sentiment, too, is sound and healthy. But there are many other fine old songs, such as "The Lads with their Aprons on." If wanted, a good healthy programme could still be constructed to include the E.A. song, "The Lads with their Aprons on," "Here's to his Health in a Song," together with old eighteenth-century songs, carols, and such like.

I give a few examples, and we can afford to be catholic; "John Peel"; "Come, Landlord, fill the Flowing Bowl"; "Simon the Cellarer"; "Here's a Health unto His Majesty"; "Macpherson swore a Feud"; "The Leather Bottel"; "The Vicar of Bray"; "The Harp that Once"; "Down among the Dead Men let him lie"; "Oft in the Stilly Night"; "Hearts of Oak"; "Tom Bowling"; "Wi' a Hundred Pipers an' a,' an' a'." Then, if we want ladies' songs, we have "Here's to the Maiden of Bashful Fifteen"; "The Girl I left behind Me"; "Drink to Me only with Thine Eyes"; "O Mistress Mine."

And for days of mourning such songs occur as: "The Flowers of the Forest"; "Though Dark are our Sorrows"; while, of course, we can conclude with "For he's a Jolly Good Fellow" and "Auld Lang Syne."

There is no difficulty in getting these songs; most are in *Gaudeamus*, and the masonic songs, together with many others, can be got from any masonic publisher.

These are the kind of songs which you will not hear at the music-hall, but are just the kind suitable for gatherings of "good fellows." Then, how often does one see the old firing-glasses, which at one time were used in every Lodge? My mother Lodge, Isaac Newton, Cambridge, still uses them, I am glad to say, and I introduced them at the foundation of the Industries Lodge, No. 4100; but the number of Lodges which do use them is comparatively few. Examples can be seen in Grand Lodge Library, and, for the benefit of a few who may not know their exact use, I will add that they begin the masonic fire p.l.r. crash, then the fire continues with the hands, as at present. The significance of p.l.r. is, of course, that it refers to the penalty of an E.A., implying that we will guard our secrets at the board as carefully as in Lodge.

The firing glass should also be used for masonic applause, and in connection therewith I recollect an interesting little incident at my mother Lodge. Some inexperienced new brethren, after a song had been particularly well sung, hammered several times on the table, and the W.M. rose and said, "Let me remind the brethren that masonic applause is one stroke, and one stroke only, of the firing-glass, and for this reason: every brother will do his best, we know, and no one can do more; and therefore applause should be the same for everyone." This is sound masonic etiquette.

One of the most severe losses inflicted on Freemasonry by the disappearance of the firing-glass is that to-day one seldom hears that interesting old toast denominated "The Secretary's Toast." Despite its name, it is not in honour of that hardworking official, but of our mother Lodge, and so called because the Secretary should know the number of the mother Lodge of every member, and is therefore the person who, as a rule, starts the toast instead of the W.M.

The complete ritual varies, but the following is probably the best form:

Secretary whispers right and left, "As the tide ebbs form a cable-tow for the Secretary's toast; pass it on." As the sentence reaches each brother in turn he links hands, as in "Auld Lang Syne," and when the other sides of chain meet at the Master's chair he returns in the same way the following message:

W.M. (whispers): "As the tide flows, what is the Secretary's toast?"

To which the Secretary sends back the whispered reply:

Secretary: "A mother of Masons."

W.M. (whispers back round the chains): "How old is she?"

Secretary, aloud: "Proclaim it aloud, my mother is 859."

The chain breaks as each brother in turn raises his glass and cries aloud the number of his mother Lodge; but this time the message runs from the left of the Secretary back to his right in turn, not double, and at the same time as when the messages were whispered.

When it returns to the Secretary he rises and says:

"Be upstanding; the gavel is in my hands. Brethren, charge your glasses for a bumper. By command of the Worshipful Master I give you the Secretary's Toast to a mother of Masons—my mother Lodge."

Omnes: "My mother Lodge."

Then comes the fire.

Starting from the left of the Secretary, each brother strikes one in turn. This is repeated three times round. Then follows the roll fire, three times round also, in unison. This is given by crashing in unison, and then grinding the edge of the glass on the table, pausing, and doing it again twice more.

Finally the Secretary says, "P. l. r." thrice, "Altogether," and the glasses descend in one tremendous crash.

Usually the hand-fire is omitted, though sometimes it is given as well, after the crash, "On the top of the Tide."

This piece of ritual needs a little practice at first, but, once the custom has been established, new brothers pick it up very easily, and the whole ceremony is most impressive. My mother Lodge used to have this toast from time to time, though in a slightly different form. Usually it started from the W.M., who whispered to his right only.

If the Secretary gives it he should be seated at the head of the middle table when they are arranged in an E ——.

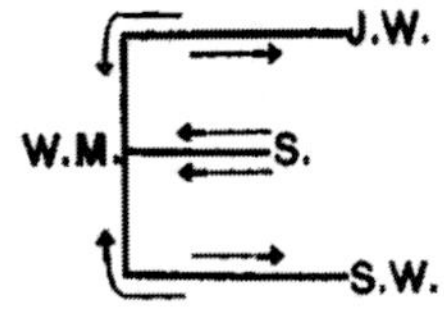

Our mother Lodge should have a special place in the heart of every Mason, and this is a most appropriate way of giving verbal expression to this feeling.

Another pretty custom in use in few Lodges is copied from a ceremony at the R.A. Dinner.

W.M.: "Brother Senior Warden, what are the three Grand Principles on which our Order is founded?"

S.W.: "Brotherly Love, Relief, and Truth."

W.M.: "I will ask you to define them."

The ceremony then proceeds on the lines of the questions and answers in the Sixth Section of the First Lecture and ends with:

W.M.: "Let us drink to the three Grand Principles on which our Order is founded."

These and many other customs might well be revived. Otherwise, what is left to distinguish our dinners from being simply an excuse for a guzzle?

Good dinners are all very well in their way, but a masonic dinner should be *sui generis*, and at present the tendency seems more and more to make them just like any ordinary dinner.

I am not one who wishes to abolish the dinner, far from it. I believe that without it we should never get to know each other at all, but it ought to be more than an ordinary dinner, and it is just these masonic customs which achieve that object. If the tendency which is appearing in London continues there will soon be nothing to distinguish a masonic dinner from any other.

And when on this subject I ask, Is it essential always to drink champagne at 30*s.* a bottle? Once a year, at the Installation, such extravagance may be justifiable, but not every time, nor is it really essential to have wine at all. Good beer, cider, and whisky will form a " wine list " which most men will find quite to their taste. I have as keen an appreciation of good wine as most men. My college was Trinity Hall, Cambridge, a college famous in these matters; but I think the time has come to call a halt in the increasing cost of masonic dinners: 25*s.* is quite a common visitors' dinner fee in London now, and, in view of the wines supplied, I doubt if the Treasurer makes on the transaction; but obviously such a charge reduces the number of visitors a brother can afford to invite in the year. Masonic hospitality is one of our greatest virtues, and it would be a thousand pities if anything was allowed to check it. Moreover, the Lodge visited often derives real benefit from the facts a visiting brother can communicate, while he on his part may well pick up some useful points from the Lodges he visits.

Some Lodges, I am glad to say, are showing a tendency to reduce their expenditure on wine, and in some cases even to spend the money so saved on masonic charity—a most admirable course, and I am sure their dinner tastes all the better for this act of self-sacrifice.

Another little point is the waiters. Waiters, we know, expect tips, but the system which allows a waiter to pass round a plate at the dinner is thoroughly bad. I consider the tips should be paid in a lump sum to the head waiter for distribution among the rest, and this sum charged to the expenses of the dinner. A much more worthy recipient of these tips would be the charity box, but visiting brothers should not be *allowed* to contribute. Lodge charity should be derived from its own members only.

Similarly, the habit of allowing Tylers to put out a plate in the cloak-room is all wrong. They should be paid a sufficient sum for their services, and tipping absolutely forbidden. The habit is vexatious to members, and, worse still, humiliating to the Tyler. He is, be it remembered, a brother, and should always be addressed as such: he is *not* a hired waiter.

Both these points are rigidly enforced in the Industries Lodge, and everyone is delighted with the result.

A little way back we spoke of the Lectures. These are practically never given in open Lodge, and yet they contain most valuable information. If, instead of rushing candidates through the three degrees in as many meetings, they had to attend Lodge and hear these Lectures, and were not allowed to take the next step till they were able to answer questions on at least a part of them, instead of being merely crammed with a few questions, they would be more understanding Masons ever afterwards. There is a mass of interesting legend and real information in these Lectures, and they are genuine old matter; yet I venture to think that not one Mason in a thousand has ever read them.

If we are told that in that case we could not make all the men Masons who desired to enter our Order, I would reply: (1) The number of initiates might be reduced with advantage. (2) More Lodges could be founded which would have genuine work to do, and this would be advantageous in many ways, for it would enable energetic brothers to work their way into office within a reasonable time after their initiation—a thing often impossible now. This is what leads to so many men dropping out of active Freemasonry. They see they have no chance of reaching even the humblest office for fifteen or twenty years, and they grow tired of seeing a repetition of the same ceremonies over and over again, with no effort to explain their meaning. Why, even many of our Grand Officers can give no reasonable explanation of our rites and ceremonies, and so how can we expect it of lesser folk? If you reply that there are Lodges of research, I would answer: (*a*) many men cannot afford time to belong to several Lodges; (*b*) that often these Lodges consist of a small coterie, who are interested only in the historical aspects of Freemasonry, "the dry-as-dust school," as many humble members of the craft call them, though unjustly, I think.

But as to the real meaning of the ceremony it is seldom one hears anything. Why step off ——? Because the Preserver, Horus in Egypt, Krishna in India, did so on the great serpent of evil in the conflict with that monster described in the legends and allegories of those two countries. We, too, must trample underfoot the powers of evil (see illustration of Krishna, facing p. 98) if we would progress towards light. This and a hundred questions occur to the newly made brother, but no one tells him—no one, as a rule, can do so. Everyone may not be able to travel round the world, or spend the time studying anthropological books which will throw light on the meaning of our mysteries; but everyone can study the Lectures, and gain at least the exoteric meaning of some of our ritual.

But, though all these points are worthy of consideration, they will not restore the unity of the old system broken in the eighteenth and nineteenth centuries. Is there no way of doing so?

Some, of course, might say they did not want this unity restored, but most, I think, would answer that while theoretically it was desirable, in practice it was quite impossible, Firstly, they would point out that the Act of Union prevented the craft having anything to do with the higher degrees, and of course it would be impossible even to contemplate the higher degrees having control of the craft. Further, they would point out that even in America, where there was no conflict between ancients and moderns, there are several distinct governing bodies. Finally, they would add that, even to obtain a further amalgamation of the present ruling bodies would be next to impossible, for, to speak plainly, it would mean fewer grand officers. If A and B were amalgamated there would be fewer officers in future for the aspiring Mason.

With regard to the last point, I think its weakness lies in the fact that, to a large extent, the same individuals hold grand office in the different high degrees—sovereign bodies and the amalgamated body would be larger than either of the separate units, though doubtless not so large as both added together. The other two arguments are, however, strong ones, and the first is indeed a complete answer, I fear, since most Masons regard the Act of Union as a treaty which cannot be altered or abrogated. Whether this is so may be disputed academically, but practically such a change would be impossible.

There is, however, a method which, while safeguarding the rights of all sovereign bodies now existent, would give us a large measure of practical unity, and at the same time lead to a more thorough study and appreciation of all our degrees. This method will be considered in the latter part of this book.

RELIEF AT BÔROBUDÛR.

Note the Prince on the throne.

(From *Indian Sculpture and Painting*, by E. B. Havell.)

CHAPTER II

BRIEF SUMMARY OF EVIDENCE AS TO THE ANTIQUITY OF OUR SIGNS

ABUNDANT evidence has been given throughout this book that certain signs, grips, and symbols are known and used with the same essential meaning all over the world, and at all periods of the history of man on earth.

For convenience of reference we will summarise the essential points according to their geographical distribution by continents.

ASIA

China.—1. See Chinese painting.

2. The symbolic use of the cross is shown in the Chinese painting reproduced at p. 142 with the future Buddha (Preserver) at the centre of the cross, the idea corresponding with the sixth degree ritual of the cross of the Operatives in England.

3. Use of masonic phrases in the ancient Chinese classics.

4. An ancient religious system, now apparently extinct, which taught its doctrines by the use of masonic symbols, the allegory of *a temple built in a desert,* and had an organisation similar in almost every way to a masonic Lodge.

5. The existence of a perfect network of secret societies with pass-words, grips, and rituals, of which, however, little is known, and further investigation is urgently required.

6. Seal on " chop " with pillar sign with same meaning. Also similarity of shape of chop to mark jewel.

Malaya.—1. See Drum.

2. Secret societies and strange initiatory rites are also known to exist.

3. The presence of Mohammedanism almost certainly means that similar signs to those in use in Turkey among the dervishes

would be found by a careful investigator; but more information is required.

India.—1. Illustrations from India and Java.

2. Crossing the legs of Vishnu.

3. Y[illegible] explains much of our craft and arch ritual.

4. Use of all of our symbols, and their true meaning only intelligible after studying their Hindoo meaning: ⊙, ✡, ▽, etc.

5. The Hindoo conception of the Deity, and particularly of the Trinity, the same as that taught in our Lodges. Attributes of three principal officers the same as that of Brahma, Vishnu, Shiva.

6. Details of our ritual, such as l. ft. f., etc., explained by our knowledge of Hindoo legends.

7. Stories showing that Hindoos recognise the potency of our R.A. and M.M. signs, and will admit those who know them into their *sanctum sanctorum.*

Ceylon.—R.A. sign and bush possessed with a spirit, ceremony.

Near East.—1. Among the dervishes there exists a complete system of initiation to all intents and purposes the same as our own craft degrees. Practically all our signs and grips are known and used by them, so far as the craft is concerned, and this fact I have seen with my own eyes. The Arabs also have one which they use when they want help.

2. In addition they have a rite similar to our R.A., and also use a grip known to M.M.M.

3. They use many of our symbols with the same meaning as ourselves, e.g. ✡.

4. They have a tradition that our Masonry is derived from them via Saladin, King Richard I, *and the Templars.*

5. They have higher degrees, but I have been unable to obtain any information concerning them.

6. These ceremonies include highly metaphysical and mystical explanations.

7. These dervish rites seem to appear in every country where Islam flourishes.

8. The [illegible] claim to be descendants of the [illegible] b[illegible]ers.

9. They also have a system of initiation similar to our

ANUBIS WEIGHING THE HEART OF THE SCRIBE ANI IN THE GREAT SCALES AGAINST THE FEATHER SYMBOLICAL OF THE LAW.

The ibis-headed Thoth is noting the result, and reporting the same to the great gods. Behind him stands the monster Amemit, which devoured souls that were condemned in the Great Judgment. Notice the twelve judges seated on squares, and compare these symbolic seats with the ordinary Egyptian chairs shown in the illustrations of the frescoes from Thebes.

(Reproduced by permission of the Trustees of the British Museum.)

own, venerate similar symbols, and have at least one known to us.

Ancient Assyria.—F.C. signs and others, also symbols used—e.g. 

Africa

In savage Africa we find:

1. See illustration of circumcision in British East Africa.

2. See second illustration after operation has been completed.

3. The natives of Portuguese East Africa have the lion grip, eagle's claw, and G. D.

4. The West African Hausas use lion grip plus sign of F. thrice.

5. S. of G. D. used and recognised throughout all West Africa.

6. Secret societies in West Africa with initiatory rites and secret signs of recognition. More information required.

7. Initiatory rites which include blindfolding (and usually circumcision) among tribes in East, South, and West Africa.

8. Use of an "apron" of leaves in Central African initiatory rites.

9. The Senussi in North Africa have our various signs, probably derived from dervish rites.

10. Modern Egyptians have major points, lion grip and other signs also probably derived from dervish rite.

11. The Nilotic negroes use p.s. of E.A. as the binding form of an oath.

Ancient Egypt.—We find the following signs used under appropriate circumstances.

1. (1) F.C. (2) R.C. (3) 5 major point. (4) lion grips, etc. See also illustrations.

2. Their whole system of the mysteries throws a flood of light on our work. E.g., l. ft. f. Certain penalties, such as that Apepi, the great serpent of evil, was cut in half, and the body burnt to ashes on the centre, and these ashes scattered to the four cardinal points, the Rose Croix rite, admission to the Circle of Princes.

3. The ceremonies of the cross, its various shapes, reverence for the cross and the vesica piscis.

4. Lariat Bandage, etc., plucking out h.

5. The use of the hammer or axe as the symbol of rule and of the Godhead.

6. Use of all our masonic tools in a symbolic sense, as shown by their arrangement under an obelisk.

7. The gods seated on squares.

8. The legend of Osiris, and in particular certain details.

9. Veneration for similar symbols.

10. Craft tradition connecting Egypt and Freemasonry, and possible line of connection via the Egyptian workmen who assisted at the building of the Temple.

11. The original J. and B.

Europe

1. The Dionysian Artificers, with their secret rites, enter Greece.

2. The Roman *collegia:* (*a*) Masonic temple at Pompeii. (*b*) Use of masonic emblems on tombs. (*c*) Two pillars. (*d*) ✡. (*e*) "Tracing-board" with masonic emblems. (*f*) See fresco.

3. The rite of Mithra. The lion grip, etc. Their systems lead to the same conclusion as the R.A.

4. The Comacine Masons. Use of secret signs. J. and B. Masons' marks, ✡, etc.

5. See Byzantine Ivory

6. Mediæval examples of our signs. In Italy and at Peterborough. Numerous other examples. Legend of third degree carved in a certain cathedral, etc.

America

Ancient Central America gives us abundant evidence.

1. See Mexican illustrations.

2. Similar ceremony to R.C.

3. Veneration for cross and various kinds thereof, also of vesica piscis.

4. Various other symbols, venerated: axe, square and pentacle, etc.

5. A still higher degree ceremony.

6. Emblems of mortality associated with a significant sign, ×, vesica piscis.

In Ancient West Indies.—Pictograph and a charm.

A MEXICAN GOD COMMENTING ON THE SACRIFICE MADE BY THE PRESERVER.

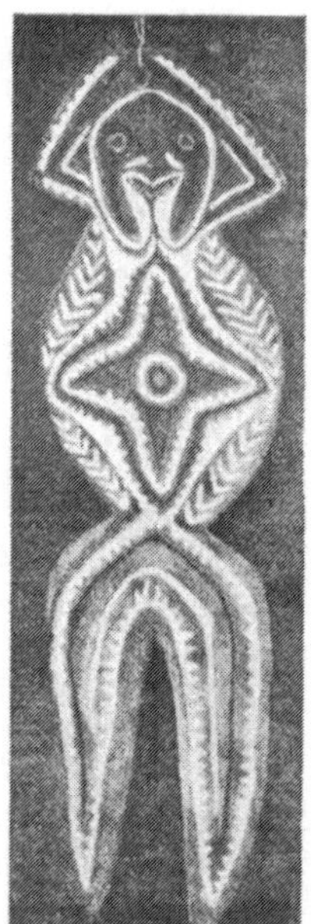

NEW GUINEA GODS.

(From *Man.*)

Ancient Peru.—See a sepulchral vase at 27, Great Queen Street.

Modern Indian Signs.—Similar to those known in craft and higher degrees.

Australasia

1. *Easter Island.*—See illustration.
2. *New Guinea.*—See tipperu used in their third degree of initiation.
3. *Australian rites.*—Bora ceremony, similar to a craft degree and a higher degree. S. of R.C.; also of R.A.; significance of fire and burning bush; their J. and B.; use of veil.

Thus we see that certain signs and symbols, grips and tokens, are found in every continent, and, with the exception of Europe, they are employed by men who cannot in our modern sense be called Freemasons.

Perhaps I ought to make it clear that the s. of G. D. alluded to is that used in Scotland. I have been unable to find our English version, though it may of course exist. Personally I have no doubt that the Scottish is the original sign.

Next, I would repeat that I do not call a New Guinea native a Freemason because he uses a certain masonic sign. What I contend is:

That these signs were part of the original initiatory rites of the savages, and these rites were the basis from which have developed the mysteries and the modern religious systems of the world.

I contend that Freemasonry has developed from a branch of those mysteries, which became the peculiar property of the men who built the temples of the gods. In early days these rites were secret to men, but open to *all men* of the tribe when they reached a certain age.

As definite religious systems developed these signs continued, but became attached to the gods and initiates. Their secret meaning was restricted by the priests to those permitted to enter those mysteries, although the gods continued to be sculptured in significant positions. This is still the case in India.

In various countries different developments took place, but the more evolved nations tended to make these signs more and more secret things, not to be divulged to the ignorant.

When they passed into operative masonic keeping they gained a practical utility as proofs of membership, and gradually their use on sculptured figures ceased.

But our whole system of Freemasonry becomes intelligible if we apply the wisdom of such countries as Egypt, Mexico, and modern India to their elucidation, because there the teaching was, or is, intact.

Freemasonry's peculiar glory consists in the fact that it has kept up the old system, and moreover has done so in such a way that, while the permanent and essential foundations remain, the details of doctrinal extravagance which inevitably breed schism and controversy are not developed.

Hence, though we can find the seeds from which have developed practically every dogma in the world, they are so small in Freemasonry that no man need take offence, and consequently Hindoo, Mohammedan, Buddhist, and Christian can all meet on the level and part on the square in Lodge.

Now, if this is so, the first question which arises is, How can we best study Freemasonry and test this thesis?

The answer to this leads on to the noble ideal of a Grand Lodge of the world, which I shall propound in the next chapter, so we will deal with it in the one subsequent.

ANCIENT INITIATORY CEREMONY DEPICTED ON A VASE, FROM CHAMA, MEXICO.
(By permission of the Smithsonian Institute, U.S.A.)

CHAPTER III

THE GRAND IDEAL

WHEN we consider that our grips, signs, and ritual are practically the same in every country where Speculative Freemasonry exists, it seems strange that the masonic world has neither definite head nor centre. People are talking glibly of a League of Nations, and all the time a real League of Nations exists, a spiritual union, stronger than religious or national prejudice. Cannot this real League be made articulate? I contend it can, and in our own lifetime if we desire to bring it about. Already a peculiarly close link binds together the Grand Lodges of England, Scotland, and Ireland with the sister Grand Lodges which have developed from them in various portions of our far flung-Empire. Again in the U.S.A. there already exists a Supreme Grand Lodge of which the Grand Lodges of the various States form a part.

Here, then, we have a living prototype for the Grand Lodge of the World and in our sister British Lodges we have the material for building this finer and still greater Grand Lodge.

It is seldom realised that, out of the 3,500,000 Masons who range under the banners of the Order nearly 3,250,000 are English-speaking. If the Grand Lodges of the Empire could form a perpetual league or federation with those of the U.S.A. other Grand Lodges would either come in at once, or, if they refused, could be ignored. The Grand Orient of France, which has obtained so much notoriety on the Continent, is really a small affair, with hardly 30,000 members, and I doubt if Continental Masonry, despite its supposed "influence," numbers, all told, 250,000 men.

Already the common bond of Freemasonry has had the profoundest influence again and again on Anglo-American relations, *and always for good.* When, a few years before the war, feeling was running high and foolish people in both countries were threatening war, the Grand Lodges of the States sent a message to the Grand Lodge of England: "We, who represent nearly 3,000,000 Masons in the States, declare to you, our English brothers, that there shall not be war between England and America. Our statesmen and yours must find a way of composing our differences." And it was done.

The united influence for good, and, above all, for peace which the Masons of the world could exert is enormous. No Chauvinistic Government could resist it, and Masonry, tried and tested, is a far stronger and safer implement with which to attain that object than a paper league of nations.

But how to begin? Surely the first step has already been made by the alliance entered into quite recently between the three Grand Lodges of the British Isles. The next step is to extend that alliance to every Grand Lodge within the British Empire. Next, to go a step further, and form a supreme Grand Lodge of the British Empire; and who so suitable to be its first Grand Master as Edward, Prince of Wales, he who has already visited almost every corner of our far-flung Empire? And if by that date—for time must elapse before we are able to carry through such a change—if, I say, it should be that the G.A.O.T.U. has summoned him to ascend the throne, though God grant it may not be for many years, has he not a Mason brother?

Then cannot the Supreme Grand Lodge of the Empire, whose seat, I trust, will be in the New Temple we are raising in memory of those who died that the world might be free, enter into a perpetual alliance with the Supreme Grand Lodge of America, and these two elder brothers with all other Grand Lodges whose principles are sound and who acknowledge the G.A.O.T.U.?

And when this has been achieved then the time will be ripe for the formation of the Supreme Grand Lodge of the world, whose Grand Master could be elected for a term of years, so that in rotation all its constituent members should have their turn in filling a post compared with which even that of the Popes will fall into insignificance.

Then will this Grand Lodge, by its *influence* rather than by mixing in politics, be able to prevent entirely the folly of an appeal to arms, while its constituent members alone will deal with the domestic masonic affairs of each nation.

So gradually, and step by step, can we build up a Masonic

Temple to the glory of God and the good of humanity. A temple not of stone, but of living men, a pale reflection of that spiritual Grand Lodge above where the World's Great Architect rules and reigns supreme.

Is it not worth striving for, and working for, such an ideal? Under her banner shall all religions and races meet on the level, and, guided by the united wisdom of the best men in Freemasonry and inspired by our age-old principles, we shall be indeed a fit vehicle for the work of the Most High.

And this ideal can be achieved step by step. The next step is so easy, and after that is accomplished the next—a Supreme Grand Lodge of the Empire—will be no more difficult. What is required is education among our members, the constant repetition of the ideal. Slowly but surely it will grow till the idea is accepted by everyone. No doubt, then, those who originated the idea will find that others have taken it to their hearts and gained the credit; but what does that matter? So long as the ideal bears fruit what matters personal aggrandisement?

Freemasonry is, I contend, the mightiest force in the world. All that is best in religion and nationality is united with all that is best in internationalism. Far removed from the petty struggles of the politician, with its history stretching back into the dim dawn of man, it stands calm and serene. To it the passions of a day and the jealousies of nations are but as the quarrels of naughty children, to be smiled at with the pitying smile with which the angels regard our faults. Let us set our ideals high, but strive to attain them by practical methods. That should be our aim.

Masonry has not survived the fall of mighty empires and the corroding hand of Time to remain, in the midst of this world agony, merely a pleasant social club and a place where men may congregate to eat good dinners. The signs of the times point to the coming of great changes, and from little things great ones grow. In Tanganyika the seeds are being planted of a new development in Freemasonry, for in that former German colony a body of Freemasons are establishing a colony which shall be a great co-operative society restricted to Freemasons and governed by them. The Lodge as a governing body—that is what this means, and, if it is a success, we may expect many others. In America the Lodges manage all manner of activities for their members, from country outings to cemeteries, and from these seeds will grow that insight into the administration of world affairs which will enable the rulers of Freemasonry to use their influence with foresight and intelligence.

Every one of us can play a humble part, and we must lay the foundations truly and well; we must spread the grand ideal throughout the Lodges of the land, and cement together the fabric of our Order by bringing together our various degrees. Above all, we must keep burning the lamp of spiritual truth, which has ever burnt within our Lodges throughout the long-drawn ages, and to achieve this we must restore to the " columns " the meaning of our ritual, and this work can all be started by the " First Steps " I propose in the next chapter.

CHAPTER IV

THE FIRST STEPS

WHAT is required is to create a body of enthusiastic missionaries, who, as they visit various Lodges up and down the country, will spread a knowledge of the meaning of our wonderful ritual and inculcate the grand ideal of Masonic Union.

The visitor has usually an unrivalled opportunity of doing this, for there is always a Visitors' Toast, and in his reply, after the opening compliments, he can proceed to give an indication of the meaning of some piece of the ritual which has just been given in Lodge; such information is always received with the keenest appreciation. In my masonic career good fortune has carried me into many places, so that I have "borne fraternal greetings to the Lodges East and West," and the hunger for some suggestion as to the *meaning* of our ritual was almost pathetic. As I travelled more, and studied more, I felt that I dared to explain more of our ritual, and my suggestions, often merely a few sentences in reply to the toast of my health, were received with delight. I was pressed to come again and tell them more, but Fate seldom permitted this. Yet the experience thus gained convinced me that our ordinary members of the craft were only too anxious to learn and follow up suggestions, if only someone would give them a little help. It is of them that I am thinking, those kindly brethren who extended a right good masonic greeting to a strange brother, whether it was in the cosmopolitan Lodge Victoria in Burma, or the ancient Lodges of Leeds—dumb and inarticulate brothers often, who never hoped for Grand Lodge honours, but quietly did their duty in maintaining the grand fundamental principles of our Order. If the grand ideals I have indicated are ever to come to fruition their aid must be enlisted, and they will give it gladly, of that I am sure, if the leaders will come forth.

We must create these leaders—missionaries if you like—who

will restore the true meaning to our ritual and help to rediscover the lost word, the ancient wisdom, which lie hidden in the vault within each Lodge. And these are the practical steps which I suggest.

First, a Lodge must be founded, to be followed by others in due course. This Lodge will be a full working Lodge, with power to initiate, but it will only exercise the right to a very limited extent. It will be essentially a Lodge of Research, but, instead of regarding Masonry from the point of view of the Authentic School, it will adopt the anthropological attitude. Its special function will be to study and collect information about the ancient mysteries and the primitive initiatory rites of savage races. It will do so from the strictly masonic point of view, but will nevertheless take a broad outlook, recognising that, as the savage rites decay, parts may become lost, but, by comparing the system in vogue in one district with that employed in another, we may be able to explain those rites, and perceive the basis of some of our masonic degrees.

The Lodge will collect and co-ordinate facts collected from every source. It will place them on permanent record in its library, and make that library one dealing with *man*, not with the dead bones of history.

It will endeavour to collect anthropological curios and articles which seem to throw light on our ceremonies or on similar systems, either living or dead. This will be its main function, and, to carry out its work, it will start by gathering together a group of men interested in these ideals. When the Lodge has reached a reasonable size it will follow the example of the Quatuor Coronati, and form an Outer Circle, to which every Master Mason in good standing will be eligible, while the Inner Circle will become a body, election to which will be only granted as vacancies occur, and for which brethren will have to qualify by papers read or good research work done.

Initiation into this Lodge will be restricted to explorers and anthropologists, men of outstanding literary merit, and so forth, who have already proved their ability. All members of the Outer Circle would be free to attend the meeting, receive the printed transactions, and dine with the Inner Circle, but would not vote or be eligible for office.

Vacancies in the Inner Circle would mainly, however, be filled from members of the Outer Circle.

This Lodge would be formed, like any other Lodge, by petition to Grand Lodge, and would, I feel sure, be welcomed by that broad-minded body. Some of its members might disbelieve in the anthropological method, but they are far too wide-minded to place any obstacle in the way of research.

This Lodge would be careful to allot part of its time to the study of the symbolism and meaning of our ritual, and one point would be that the Lectures should be worked and discussed.

Thus we should gradually spread the results of our researches through the ranks of our Outer Circle, which would be open to members of any Grand Lodge in union with our own, and thus we should in time have correspondents the world over, whose reports on native customs would be placed on permanent record.

Our Outer Circle would constitute missionaries to their own Lodges, and if, after a time, some in a particular locality desired to form a similar body, the mother Lodge would not only help them to start, but would be prepared to federate with them on the lines of the Federation of Temperance Lodges in London. One advantage of this would be that books and exhibits would be loaned from the mother Lodge to its daughters.

Thus we should start an ever-widening circle of Lodges of Anthropological Research. I attach considerable importance to retaining the right to "make Masons." This for many reasons. We do not want the Lodge to pass too much into the hands of those past middle life; they are apt to get into a rut. Moreover, we particularly want to attract travellers and students of anthropology, who can speak from personal experience. Such men would be invaluable. The Lodge would, of course, be scrupulously obedient to Grand Lodge.

Once the Craft Lodge is going well, the Inner Circle would form itself into a new body, consisting of Mark Masons, and petition Mark Grand Lodge for permission to found a Mark Lodge of Anthropological Research on precisely the same lines, but under the rule of Mark Grand Lodge.

They would consist of precisely the same men as the original Lodge, and would thus be inspired with the same ideals, and in this way unity between the craft and mark would be established strictly within the constitution. This "unity of individuality," if so one may call it, would become increasingly valuable, and by degrees one would establish a proper sequence in taking these higher degrees,

The Outer Circle would be eligible for the Outer Circle here also, but Masons not members of the Outer Circle of the craft would not. Advancement into the Mark Lodge would be restricted to members of the Craft Lodge not yet Mark Masons, and possibly this would include members of the Outer Circle, at any rate, until the number fixed as the maximum was reached. Members of the Outer Circles would often be asked to read papers before the whole body.

When the Mark Lodge is well established the same process would be repeated to form a Royal Arch Chapter, members of which must be members of the Mark Lodge. This established on precisely similar lines, we should petition for a chapter of the Cryptic degrees. Thus we should round off the early pre-Messianic period in our legendary lore. After this we should follow with a council of allied degrees, which would be well worth while, as it would direct attention to the interesting Red Cross of Babylon and the High Priest. Then we should approach the Supreme Council for permission to found a Rose Croix Chapter. This would throw open to our study all the intermediate degrees, the fourth to seventeenth degrees inclusive. Already well grounded in the Cryptic and Allied degrees, particularly the Red Cross of Babylon, we should be the better qualified to study the meaning of these interesting intermediates and unworked degrees. We should not, of course, expect the Supreme Council Thirty-third Degree to give us power to work these degrees; there is no need to do so, and, if we wish to see them worked, we have only to attend the festival of King Edward VII Rose Croix Chapter of Instruction; but we should aim at studying their meaning, and how far there existed any similar rites among the savages, or in the ancient mysteries.

Next, we should obtain a charter to form a chapter of Harodim of the Royal Order of Scotland, with power to make candidates Harods; but not Rosy Cross, for that degree can only be given in a Provincial Grand Lodge of the Royal Order. This, however, would in no way interfere with our members obtaining that degree, for we should attend Provincial Grand Lodge to receive it. Then would come Templar and Malta, to be followed in due course by Red Cross of Constantine and St. John and the Holy Sepulchre.

When this was achieved we should have reunited all the essential fragments of Masonry into a united whole below the thirtieth degrees. It might be that, if the Supreme Council approved of our labours, they would grant us permission to form a study circle of those of us who held the thirtieth degree without, of course, power to work it. If so this would free us to study the whole of the intermediate degrees, nineteenth to twenty-ninth degrees inclusive, and, as there is reason to suppose that a degree similar to the thirtieth degree existed among the Mexicans, and that certain facts relating to it are traceable elsewhere, this study circle would be invaluable.

But, leaving that aside for the moment, see what we should gain by this process.

There are practically no Lodges of Research above the third degree, and reference to the high degrees must therefore be closely veiled.

The whole advantage of a Lodge of Research over a magazine by itself is, that you can speak more freely in "open Lodge." But, when you come to the higher degrees, unless they were thus tied together you would be unable to speak of any degree except the one in which you open, except, of course, craft. By this system the brethren would be able to show the connection between craft mark R.A., Red Cross of Babylon, Rose Croix, Royal Order, and so forth, with no fear that some brother was not a member of all. In the case of the Mark and Arch this is particularly important, as, though in Scotland a man must be Mark before he can take the Arch, this is not so in England. Again, the Royal Arch in Ireland has certain points in it which are similar to those in the Royal Order of Scotland; and again, one of the intermediate degrees is very similar to the Red Cross of Babylon, while the similarity to and difference between certain degrees in the Cryptic and Allied and the intermediate degrees would provoke subjects of discussion.

Moreover, these various degrees do throw light on each other; and the native rites often show the intermingling of signs and pieces of ritual which in our ritual are found in distinct degrees. Take, for example, the Dervish rite. We find craft details, mark grip, R.A. manner of advancing, clothing the novice in Templar style, and also his proclamation.

Any brother who visited any other Lodge, chapter, or council would thus be in a position to give interesting information on that particular degree. He would interest brethren in the whole movement, and above all bring home to them in a striking way the essential unity of *all* the degrees in Freemasonry. From this to speaking about the grand ideal, a formal alliance of all the English-speaking Lodges, would be a simple step, and, where that object was achieved at last, the Grand Lodge of the world would consist of men who did understand both the real antiquity of the Order and what it really meant. To them it would not be merely an interesting survival of bygone days, but a living spiritual force, strong for good, guided by wisdom and understanding.

Some may object to this system on the ground that it would be impossible to get men to form the higher degree bodies if it was restricted to one group, and in any case would delay the formation of a valuable research body, like that for the Rose Croix, until less interesting degrees were started. My answer is:

(1) In practice one finds that the higher degrees are made up of very largely the same men, once the Mark and Arch are passed.

(2) That the fact that members of the Outer Circle would be eligible till the chapter was going strong, and possibly in the case of these higher degrees always, would give us as wide a choice as would be required.

(3) That the essential idea of the scheme is to produce a spiritual unity, and to obtain this we must be prepared, if necessary, to wait.

Some may cavil at the order I have suggested, but this is the natural and proper order, the only possible variation being the position of the chivalric degrees; but it seems to me that they continue the story of the Rose Croix in a sense. They are the practical application of the principles thus taught; and, after all, the Crusades came after Christ.

The Royal Order, as it were, gathers up all the preceding degrees, including Rose Croix and the Red Cross of Babylon, and makes a fitting termination to the Hermetic series and the mysteries of Amenti, which is what it really depicts in a Biblical form. Practically all the incidents—guarders, tower, bridge, journey, etc.—can be found in their Egyptian form in *The Book of the Dead*. Indeed, this degree shows the most complete form of the mysteries which has survived.

Other degrees could, of course, be worked into the scheme, but the most important omitted is the Rosicrucian Society. This, owing to its complicated system of grades, presents certain practical difficulties; but, if desirable, in due course, it could no doubt be managed.

And what are the methods of research we should apply, as

distinct from those of the Authentic School? We should not ignore their methods—far from it—but our main system would be based on those which have been so successfully employed in recent years by the student of comparative religion, of folklore, and of anthropology generally.

As a concrete suggestion I would advocate a careful examination of the Dervish rites. Something has already been done, but, in view of the number of Masons who, owing to the war, have travelled in the Near East, and the certainty that this area is likely for many years to attract Europeans, I feel certain that much valuable information could be obtained.

India is another source of knowledge far too little comprehended, and in every part of the world there are Masons who, once they had grasped the essential things to look for, would be able to send us important evidence. It is the multiplicity of little streams which form the mighty ocean, and the system I dream of will be the sea of knowledge into which all this information would flow.

And, after labour, could we not restore the old masonic customs, which make a real masonic banquet one of the pleasantest incidents in our daily life? We might well become in these points also a centre of information on the old customs of the Order, which are not "frills," as some people pretend, but essential parts of that system which aims at peace upon earth, good-will *among* men.

CHAPTER V

THE ANCIENT WISDOM AND MODERN MASONRY

In the pages that have gone before we have seen that Freemasonry is the survivor of the ancient mysteries—nay, we may go further, and call it the guardian of the mysteries.

I have not endeavoured to show that it is descended directly from the Egyptian and Maya mysteries; rather, I contend that it comes via the Dionysian Artificers, the actual builders of the Temple, who were no doubt influenced by Egyptian and other mysteries; but the main basis on which the system was built up was the primitive initiatory rites, which with them, as with the Egyptians and Mayas, developed into a mystery.

Freemasonry, if this thesis is correct, is so old as to justify the claim it makes that it has survived the wreck of mighty empires and the corroding hand of Time. In short, we find in our ritual the foundation of all the religious systems of the world, and it is therefore natural that we can receive into our Lodges men of every kind of religious belief. Even our so-called Christian degrees have taken on a Christian colour merely because, in the main, we are Christians, and not because they are in essence Christian. By which I mean to imply that similar rites are found among non-Christian races, although these also inculcate very similar teaching. Only one type of man is barred from our Lodges, and that is the avowed atheist, for, since Freemasonry consists of the essentials of religion, though untrammelled by dogma, he who denies any kind of God cannot be a part of the brotherhood. It is significant that the outstanding example of a Grand Lodge, the Grand Orient of Paris, which does not insist on this ancient landmark, is also the outstanding example of political Freemasonry, a thing in itself also contrary to the ancient landmarks. This is only natural, for, if you destroy the foundation on which Freemasonry exists, the search for the lost word—comprehension of God—you must create some other purpose, or it will perish.

Freemasonry, to me, is the most wonderful thing in the world. In it there is a spiritual vitality which has enabled it to survive its worst enemies—those within, who have wrought more evil than those without, the Order. Despite ignorance, despite deliberate attempts to destroy some of her most glorious treasures, she yet survives, and, waxing in strength and beauty, spreads her branches over the whole earth. North, east, south, and west, we find the Lodges, and, where they are, there men gather to seek for that which was lost. Within her portals anger and discord cease, and peace and harmony reign. Amid the battle-fields of France her influence was felt, often the only hand which checked the brutality of foemen drunk with the cruelty of war. Where the "ancient gods look down" on strangers from a northern land, Lodges arise where these foreign rulers mingle on terms of equality with the men they have come to rule and lead along the path of progress.

And every day there stand at her gates crowds who clamour to be admitted into her mysteries till men grow weary at the work.

But, as she grows in strength and beauty, it needs must be that she must recognise greater responsibilities and readjust her organisation to meet them. But the Grand Lodge of the World would be but the revival of the ancient Comacine Guild, and, as of old throughout Europe the brethren responded instantly to the inspiration sent out from the centre (as when they adopted the pointed arch), so to-morrow the brethren throughout the world will respond to the inspiration of this central body.

Meanwhile, our task must be to restore the lost meaning to our ritual, and collect evidence of our signs and symbols still surviving among the primitive races. For this, time is all too short; the old ceremonies are fading away, and soon the world will know them no more. A modern type of education which they can ill understand is producing a mass of half-educated natives, who are too ignorant to understand the true meaning of these old customs, and too educated to accept and venerate them because they are old.

Before all have perished it is for us to collect the details which will enable us to perceive our common ancestry and the better to interpret our own rites.

The old order changes. Nay, the very foundations of our

modern civilisation are shaken, and fragments of the vast edifice crumble before our eyes. What if the Temple again be overthrown, the earth be darkened, and the blazing star be extinguished, while once more the cubic stone gushes forth blood and water, yea, even the word itself be lost, and the brethren left to wander disconsolate over the face of the earth?

The plain man, who never studied the ancient wisdom, and laughs at the message of the stars, can see the writing on the wall; but those who are grounded in the ancient wisdom and the cosmic lore know full well that this *is* the age of Mars, the Destroyer. In days of old the Christ came when the point of the vernal equinox was in the new sign Pisces, and that sign ushered in the new dispensation and our modern world.

To-day Pisces is falling from his high estate, and a new sign draws nigh. It is Aquarius, the sign of the perfected man. Under his rule we may look to see a great awakening of the spiritual in man, an uplifting of man towards the Godhead in place of the descent of the Godhead into man. This means a new dispensation, a new type of religious outlook, but above all the passing of the gross materialism which disfigured the nineteenth century. We are moving towards a better, a more spiritual world, but before us lie darkness, difficulties, and danger, it may even be the Valley of the Shadow of Death, for Mars still has his work to do ere the moon shines forth and proclaims the time of change, and is succeeded by the sun in all his glory, and the reign of the new era is established. Mars, the Destroyer; for twelve years now he has wrought at his work, and twenty years, by the ancient astrological laws, lie before him. If they speak truth, whom will he slay and whom spare?

> Who then shall survive, O Fafnir,
> The tale of the battle to tell?

One thing I know will survive, as it has previously survived the wreck, not merely of mighty empires, but of civilisations themselves—Freemasonry. As individuals we shall not all live to see that day, but some will, and meanwhile to work lest the night come upon us when no man can work.

In the new age which is passing through the long-drawn travail of its birth, Freemasonry will be there, as of old, to lay the broad foundations on which the new religion will be built. Errors and false dogmas will pass away, and among them perhaps some which appear to our poor blinded eyes the most essential, but the Real Truth will always remain—for truth is eternal—and the bases of truth are within our Order. Out of them shall rise a new and better covenant once more, and still will Freemasonry remain to be as the Ark of Refuge when once more the waters of destruction threaten the earth long ages hence.

But ever the path is upward, after every change, and He who is changeless watches over us and knows.

Thus, looking forward, we stand on the threshold of strange times, and belike the hearts of some may fail when they look into the blackness of night, and strive to pierce its gloom. But, as once in their masonic career, they saw a faint light in the east, though it but served to illumine an ——, so now they will also see *that* light, and remember that it changed into that bright Morning Star whose light brings salvation to the earth. In every race and every creed we find a prophecy of a coming Salvator, not necessarily the return of one who has gone before, though sometimes this is so:

THE PRESERVER

Whether they call Him the Madi,
Where the Crescent swings in the sky,
Or speak of the Christ returned to earth
From His throne in the azure sky.
Whether they hail Him by Buddha's name
Or Kalki, of Vishnu sprung,
They tell us a truth for all the same
And by every mystic sung.

For ever the Lord of Salvation
His task must fashion anew.
As the sun in his heat and glory
Sucks up the mist and dew,
And returning them to earth,
Renews the verdant plain,
So the Lord of Death and Birth
Returns to us again.

J. W.

This then was, is, and shall be the task of Freemasonry, to keep alive the hidden wisdom, the hoarded wealth from of old, and to bind together with bands of fraternal love all humanity, to serve as an Ark of Refuge, and also as the Ark of the Covenant, within which is hidden the mystic stone on which is inscribed the lost word.

The waters of ignorance have swept over the Ark many times, and the turgid waves of materialism have torn away the carven woodwork which one time adorned it, but the Ark is built as an equilateral triangle,[1] and neither the tyranny of the waves nor the soft, persuasive patter of the rain can make the stout planks open. She has ridden through many storms, for the form in which she is built is invulnerable, and, though fresh storms threaten her, yet those within remember that presently the rainbow will appear in the sky, and the sun of peace will shine forth in renewed splendour.

MASONIC SIGNS

From Yucatan to Java's strand
We have followed thy trail o'er sea and land.
When Pharaoh lived he knew this sign,
Brother of mine, brother of mine.

Where Vishnu sits enthroned on high
I noted Hanuman passing by,
And as He passed He made this sign,
Brother of mine, brother of mine.

In far Canton a Buddha stood,
A gilded image of carven wood,
And, strange to say, he made this sign,
Perfect Prince and Brother of mine.

Where Tigris flows—one blazing day—
Two Arabs appeared, as I passed that way,
And as they met they made this sign,
Companions all, brothers of mine.

---

[1] In Scandinavia, some years ago, a model of the Ark of Noah was made in conformity with the account in the Bible. I saw a photograph thereof, and it was an equilateral triangle in section, and the experimenters, after testing it in stormy weather on the open sea, declared it proved to be absolutely invulnerable.

Amid the bush by Zanzibar
Tribesmen were gathering from afar,
And one, I swear, did make this sign,
Royal Order of Brethren mine.

. . . . . .

In the Ocean of Peace I came to a land
Where silence broods on an empty strand,
Where ancient gods of carven stone
Gaze o'er the waters, still and lone,
And, search as I might, I could but find
Fragments of wood which bring to mind
Ancient writings of bygone days. . . .
Whilst on the hieroglyphs I gaze
I find that they also knew the sign,
Brothers now dead, yet brothers of mine!

J. W.

CONCLUSION

Terminat hora diem; terminat auctor opus

APPENDIX

THE BORA CEREMONY

R.C. MASONS will be interested to have further details of the Bora Ceremony of the Arunta natives of Australia.

The ground for the ceremony is carefully prepared in the bush, and in the most usual form consists of *three* parts. The first is a large circular space cleared of shrubs, etc., and surrounded by a low embankment. The second is a prepared pathway four or five hundred yards long, leading from the large circle through the bush to a smaller circle also surrounded by an embankment. No women may enter the path to the second circle under pain of death.

Along the path are various drawings; some are scratched on the ground, while others are made in the shape of low mounds or bas-reliefs of sand. The trees along this path are also decorated with carvings of animals and geometrical patterns. At the entrance to the smaller circle there is a mound figure of a man (see illustration, p. 354) stretched out in the form of a X. On either side of this figure, the Arunta form an arch of boomerangs, as shown in the picture, and the candidate is conducted by a dusky R. through this valley of the shadow over the body. As he goes, he is threatened by those who form the arch, pass-words are demanded and given, and he passes safely into the Circle of Princes. The figure of the crucified man represents Baiame, the God of Initiation, who presides over these ceremonies. If they are carefully done, he is pleased; if carelessly performed, he is angry.

The course of the ceremony is somewhat as follows. The candidates assemble in the first lodge circle (the large one), and the old women are permitted to be present, but as soon as the candidate sets out on his travels they are excluded. On his journey the various drawings are explained to him, and magic tricks and pantomimes are performed, some descriptive of the drawings, while others appear to be intended to test his nerve. All the time the weird noise of the bull-roarer is heard, sometimes near at hand, sometimes far off. At one point in the ceremony a veil is thrown over the head of each candidate (usually a piece of blanket, or skin). The candidates are told that the noise (of the bull-roarer) is the voice of the gods, and they are naturally terrified. A front tooth is knocked out as a sacrifice to the malignant powers, who, it is believed, will be satisfied with this offering and not damage the boy's remaining teeth. These ceremonies often take days to perform, and the boys live with their conductors in little huts in the bush and do not return to the village. Absolute obedience to their conductors is essential, and insubordination means instant death.

For some time after the Bora, often for several months, the boys continue to live with their conductors in the bush and are instructed in the laws and customs of their tribes. During this period they must not see any women nor be seen by them.

For complete initiation, the candidate must attend many Boras, and the final ceremony, or Engura, is often not reached till the candidate has become an old man. As he works through the different " degrees " various prohibitions are removed, e.g. he is permitted to eat certain kinds of favourite food, such as emu, which have heretofore been forbidden him.

When he has been admitted into the Circle of Chiefs (in the smaller circle) he is shown a bull-roarer, and told that it is with this that the weird noises have been made, and not by the evil spirits. He is also warned that this fact must never be made known to any woman or uninitiated man, and that the same secrecy must be maintained with regard to all the ceremonies under the penalty of death.

Now the points to notice are: (1) The three "rooms" required for the due performance of the ceremony. (2) That the candidate travels in search of the lost—knowledge. (3) That he has, at the end of this journey, to pass through the Valley of the Shadow of Death amid darkness and difficulties (his head is usually covered by a veil), and he is then admitted into the Circle of the Chiefs (fully initiated men) in the Mansions of Bliss (the smaller circle).

I have omitted many of these trials, but it should be noted that the candidate is usually circumcised, and has various painful mutilations performed upon him generally, with the idea of safeguarding the whole body from the malignant spirits at cost of sacrificing a small part of it. Churchward says that they use one of the R.C. signs in these ceremonies.

The ceremony, in short, not only trains the candidate to be a worthy member of society, but teaches him that he must some day die, but that death does not end all, and that after death he will travel through dangers and difficulties in the underworld till he ultimately reaches the happy hunting-grounds and partakes of the food of the gods, e.g. emu flesh, heretofore withheld from him, and eaten only by the fully initiated.

The Engura ceremony comes much later than the ordinary Bora ceremony, and takes many weeks to carry through: it has apparently a rudimentary similarity to the R.A. Its most striking characteristic is the "Burning Bush," which is first shown to the candidates, and when the fire has died down they have to lie on green branches which have been flung on the embers. Here they must remain for hours without speaking or moving, with *legs crossed* (see photograph p. 351).

The heat and smoke are stifling, and, although the green boughs prevent them from being actually burnt severely, the ceremony must entail considerable endurance. As they return to the camp after this final ceremony, they make a certain sign as if shading their eyes (a photograph of this sign can be seen in *Northern Tribes of Australia*, by Spencer and Gillen).

The secret ceremonies are now finished, but this sign is the signal for the women of the camp to make two large fires and then cover them with green boughs. The candidates must each go to one of these fires and kneel down in the middle of the thickest smoke, and one of the women then presses him down by holding his shoulders.

This final and public ceremony is probably intended to proclaim to everyone that he is now a full member of the tribe, and also to prove his courage and endurance. After this they retire into the bush away from camp, or "lodge ground," to meditate on what they have experienced.

One small point is of particular interest: a man hides in a bush shelter and speaks or sings from it to a crowd of natives, who advance towards it waving branches which are afterwards set on fire.

Among the natives of New Guinea the bull-roarer which is given to the candidate after he has taken their third "degree" has a most interesting painting upon it, and the same figure is shown on the belt used when dancing, which can be worn only by third degree men (see illustrations). Similar figures are shown from other parts of the world, e.g. the Malay Peninsula, the West Indies, and ancient Mexico, and this same sign is used in the initiatory rites of tribes in East Africa. Also in this case, after the "sacrifice" has been made, the candidate makes the other sign shown. With these people a similar "circumcision" takes place in the case of the girls, but they do not make these signs. Has this no significance?

Many of these initiation ceremonies are dying out, and, even when still carried on, are performed more and more carelessly. The natives seldom pretend to know their real meaning, being content to say, "It is our custom."

THE FIRE CEREMONY—WARRAMUNGA TRIBE.

The men are dancing in front of a bough shelter in which other men are seated singing. The objects they are carrying are torches that are set on fire and used in a later part of the ceremony. (Note bush.)

(From *The Northern Tribes of Central Australia*, by kind permission of Messrs. Macmillan & Co.)

THE FIRE CEREMONY—ARUNTA TRIBE.

The young men who are being initiated have to lie down on a fire covered with green boughs. Although the heat and smoke are stifling, none of them is allowed to get up till the older men give the order to do so.

(From *The Northern Tribes of Central Australia*, by permission of Messrs. Macmillan & Co.)

FIRE CEREMONIES—ARUNTA TRIBE.

During the final stage of the initiation of the young men, the youths who are being initiated have burning grass and sticks thrown over them by the women, and then must lie down as here shown for some time without speaking. (Note crossed legs.)

(From *The Northern Tribes of Central Australia*, by permission of Messrs. Macmillan & Co.)

BIBLIOGRAPHY

No attempts have been made to give an exhaustive bibliography. Such a work would fill three or four volumes on Masonry alone, and if anthropological and folklore books which throw light on the customs of primitive races in connection with Freemasonry were included, the bibliography would have to be extended to a library.

With a view, however, of giving some helpful guidance to students, a short bibliography is attached hereto containing the most essential books, in particular those which have been consulted by the Author. Further, to facilitate research, they have been grouped under the Libraries where they can most conveniently be found. In general, brethren will find a great many at the Masonic Library at Freemasons' Hall, Great Queen Street, W.C., and at the very fine Library of the Quatuor Coronati, 27, Great Queen Street, is almost every book connected with Masonry; and the Rosicrucian Library, which is now also housed in 27, Great Queen Street, contains many books dealing with religious systems and occult matters. In the Quatuor Coronati Library will be found a German three-volume bibliography of Freemasonry, which gives not only books, but even articles, up to the year 1918; and further reference should be made to the British Museum, the Royal Geographical Society's Library, the Royal Asiatic Society's, the Anthropological Society's, etc.

BOOKS IN THE ROSICRUCIAN LIBRARY

Waite, A. E.: "The real History of the Rosicrucians." 8vo. London, 1887.

"The Fame and Confession of the Fraternity of R.C., commonly of the Rosie Cross," translated from the original German by Eugenius Philalethes. 12mo. London, 1652.

Westcott, Wm. Wynn: "The Rosicrucians, their History and Aims." 8vo. London, N.D.

Sadler, Henry: "Thomas Dunckerley, his Life, Labours, and Letters." 8vo. London, 1891.

Pancoast, S. M. D.: "The Kabbala; or, The True Source of Light." 8vo. Philadelphia, 1877.

"The Book of Enoch." Translated by Richard Laurence. 8vo. London, 1882, K. Paul.

Murray, Aynsley, Mrs.: "The Symbolism of the East and West." 4to. London, 1900.

How, Jeremiah: "The Freemason's Manual." 8vo. London, 1881 S. and M.

Mead, G. R. S.: "Fragments of a Faith Forgotten." The Gnostics. 8vo. London, 1900, Theosophical Publishing Co.

Calmet's "Dictionary of the Holy Bible." Edited by Charles Taylor. London, 1852 (Bohn) G. Bell & Sons.

Petrie, W. M. Flinders: "Religion and Life in Ancient Egypt." 8vo. London, 1898.

Anon: "Franc Masonnerie Templière, Origines de la." Bruxelles, 1904.

James, Hugh: "On Solar Symbolism in Masonry." A Lecture. 1904 (typed).

Hopkins, Edward Washburn: "Religions of India." Boston, 1902.

"Religious Systems of the World." A Collection of Addresses. London, 1904, Sonnenschein (Geo. Allen & Unwin).

Stevens, Albert C.: "A Cyclopædia of Fraternities." New York, 1899.

Wilkinson, Sir Gardner: "The Manners and Customs of the Ancient Egyptians." Vols. I–V. London, John Murray.

Gould, Robert Freke: "A Concise History of Freemasonry." London, 1903, Gale and Polden.

Hurd, William: "A View of all Religions." Large fol. (contains a Chapter on Soc. Rosæ Crucis).

Oldham, C. F.: "The Sun and the Serpent." London, 1905.

Underhill, John: "Description of the Grand Priory of St. John's, Clerkenwell," with plates by William Monck. Large fol.

Jacolliot, Louis: "Occult Science in India." Roy. 8vo. New York, 1884.

"Soc. Ros., Metropolitan College Reports." 8vo. London, 1892 and onwards.

Paton, C. J.: "Freemasonry: its Symbolism, Religious Nature, and Law of Perfection." Roy. 8vo. Reeves, London, 1873.

Wigston, W. F. G.: "Francis Bacon and Phantom Captain Shakspeare." Kegan Paul, 1891.

Wigston, W. F. G.: "Bacon, Shakespeare and the Rosicrucians." Redway, London, 1858. Kegan Paul.

Garrison, J. F.: "The Tetragrammaton" (pamphlet). A contribution to the History of the Lost Word.. Manchester N.H., S. C. Gould, 1906.

Philpott, J. H.: "The Sacred Tree, or the Trees in Religion and Myth." London, Macmillan, 1897.

Gunn, B. B.: "The Instruction of Ptah-Hotep and the Instruction of Kegemni." The oldest books in the world, translated from the Egyptian (Wisdom of the East Series). London, Murray, 1906.

Gatliff, Hamilton: "Eleusis: her Mysteries, Ruins and Museum." Translated from the French of Demetrius Philoes (Director of Excavations, 1882–94). London, S. Appleton, 1906.

Wancke, G. W.: "An Enquiry respecting the Derivation and Legitimacy of the Constantinean Orders of Knighthood. Chicago, 1908.

"I.N.R.I.": No. 1 Nottingham, April-May, 1906 } All published.
"I.N.R.I.": No. 2 Nottingham, May-June, 1906. }

Robertson, J. M.: "Christ and Krishna." 8vo. London, Bonner, 1878.

"The Rosicrucian" (Quarterly). Vol. I, No. 1, January 1907. M. Gould, Manchester N.H.

Deane, Rev. J. Bathurst, M.A., F.S.A.: "The Worship of the Serpent." London, Remingtons, 1838.

"ARS QUATUOR CORONATORUM" AND GRAND LODGE LIBRARIES

Abbott: "History of Lion and Lamb Lodge."
"Ancient Charges, The."
Anderson: "Book of Constitutions."
Armitage: "Short Masonic History." 2 vols.
Arnold: "History and Philosophy of Freemasonry."
"Ars Quatuor Coronatorum" (Publications.)
Ashmole: "Diary."
Bothwell-Gosse: "The Templars."
Calvert: "The Grand Lodge of England." Jenkins.
Calvert: "Grand Stewards and Red Apron Lodges."
Carr: "The Swastika."
Condor: "Hole Craft and Fellowship of Masonry."
Crowe: "Things a Freemason Ought to Know."
"Encyclopædia Britannica" (article) Freemasonry. Office.
Fergusson: "History of Architecture." Murray.
Findel: "History of Masonry." Asher.
Finlayson: "Symbols of Freemasonry."
Fort: "Early History and Antiquities of Masonry."
Gould: "Atholl Lodges."
Gould: "Essays on Freemasonry."

Gould: "History of Masonry." 4 vols.
Gould: "Military Lodges." Gale and Polden.
Hammond, William: "Masonic Emblems and Jewels."
Hastings: "Encyclopædia of Religion" (article) Freemasonry.
Hawkins: "Concise Cyclopædia of Freemasonry."
Holland: "Freemasonry and the Great Pyramid."
Hughan: "History of the English Rite."
Hughan: "Masonic Sketches and Reprints."
Hughan and Stillson: "History of Masonry and Concordant Orders."
Hutchinson: "The Spirit of Freemasonry."
Lawrence: "Practical Masonic Lectures."
Lawrence: "Sidelights on Freemasonry."
Leicester Lodge of Research: Translations.
MacBride: "Speculative Masonry."
Machey: "Encyclopædia of Freemasonry." New York.
Machey: "Symbolism of Masonry."
Manchester Lodge of Research: "Transactions."
Morris: "Lights and Shadows of Masonry."
Morris: "The Poetry of Masonry."
Newton, Joseph Fort: "The Builders."
Oliver: "Masonic Antiquities."
Oliver: "Masonic Sermons."
Oliver: "Revelations of the Square."
Oliver: "Theocratic Philosophy of Masonry." Spencer, 1856.
Patton: "Freemasonry, its Symbolism." Reeves.
Pike: "Morals and Dogma."
Pound: "The Philosophy of Masonry."
Preston: "Illustrations of Freemasonry." Spencer, 1861.
Ravenscroft: "The Comacines." Published by Elliott Stock, London.
St. Andrew's Lodge: "Centennial Memorial."
Scott Leader: "The Cathedral Builders." Low.
Sibley: "The Story of Freemasonry."
Smith: "English Guilds."
Steinbrenner: "History of Masonry."
Stevens: "Symbolical Teaching, or Masonry and its Message."
Tyler: Oaths, their Origin, Nature, and History.
Vibert: "Freemasonry before the Grand Lodges.
Waite: "Secret Tradition in Masonry." Robinson.
Waite: "Studies in Mysticism." Hodder and Stoughton.
Watts: "The Word in the Pattern." Mowbray.
Yarkar: "Arcane Schools."
Yarkar: "Recapitulation of all Masonry."
Yarkar: "The Guild Charges."

BRITISH MUSEUM: ROYAL GEOGRAPHICAL AND OTHER LIBRARIES

Apuleius: "Metamorphoses."
Aynsley: "Symbolism, East and West."
Bacon: "New Atlantis."
Bayley: "Lost Language of Symbolism."
Boutelle: "The Man of Mount Moriah."
Breasted: "Religion and Thought in Egypt."
Bromwell: "Restorations of Masonic Geometry."
Budge: "The Gods of Egypt."
Capart: "Primitive Art."
Cheetham, C.: "Mysteries, Pagan and Christian."
Churchward: "Signs and Symbols of Primordial Man.
Churchward: "The Arcana of Freemasonry."
Cumont: "Mysteries of Mithra."
Da Costa: "Dionysian Artificers."
Darrah: "The Masters' Assistant."
De Clifford: "Egypt the Cradle of Masonry."
Dill: "Roman Life."
Evans and Gilbert: "The Tribes of the North-West Territory" (Australia).
Evans, Sir Arthur: "Tree and Pillar Cult."
Giles: "Freemasonry in China."
Gopinatha Rao, J. A.: "Elements of Hindoo Iconography." Published by Law Printing House, Madras.
Gorringe: "Egyptian Obelisks."
Gotch, J. A.: "Architecture of the Renaissance."
Haige: "Symbolism."
Hallam, H: "The Middle Ages." Refers to the Statute of Labourers and the Freemasons.
Harrison: "Ancient Art and Ritual."
Hartland: "Ritual and Belief."
"Jewish Encyclopedia."
Josephus, Flavius: the Works of.
Legge: "Chinese Classics."
Leo, Allan: "Astrology for All."
Lethabby: "Architecture."
Lewis: "Scotch Masons' Marks, etc." British Archæological Association, 1888.
Lundy: "Monumental Christianity."
"Man," and other publications of the R. Anthropological Society.
Marshall: "Nature, a book of Symbols."

Maspero : "Dawn of Civilisation."
Mead : "A Ritual of Mithra."
Mead : "Quests, new and old."
Moehler : "Symbolism."
Moret : "Kings and Gods of Egypt."
Mozart : "The Magic Flute."
Pick : "The Cabala."
Plotte, Dr. : "Natural History of Staffordshire, 1086." Has an account of Freemasonry.
Plutarch : "De Iside et Osoride."
Reade : "The Veil of Isis."
Robinson : See art. on the Arch in Brewster's *Edinburgh Encyclopedia*.
Rogers, T. : "History of Agriculture and Prices in England."
Schure : "Hermes and Plato."
Schure : "Pythagoras."
Smithsonian Institute : "Bulletins and Reports."
Steiner : "The Way of Initiation."
Strabo : Lib. XIV *et seq*.
Underhill : "Mysticism."
Webster : "Primitive Secret Societies."
Wright : "Indian Masonry."

INDEX